W. J. ECCLES

CANADA UNDER LOUIS XIV 1663-1701

The Canadian Centenary Series

McClelland and Stewart

To E. R. Adair

© 1964 McClelland and Stewart Limited
Reprinted, 1968
Reprinted in paperback, 1978

0-7710-3046-0

The Canadian Publishers
McClelland and Stewart Limited
25 Hollinger Road, Toronto

THE
CANADIAN
CENTENARY
SERIES

A History of Canada

W. L. Morton, EXECUTIVE EDITOR

D. G. Creighton, ADVISORY EDITOR

VOLUMES STARRED ARE PUBLISHED

CONTENTS

Canada under Louis XIV

MAPS AND ILLUSTRATIONS

New France, based on a contemporary map drawn for the
Mohawk Campaign, 1666
43

The French Empire in the West, 1663-1701
107

Acadia in the Seventeenth Century
195

FACING PAGE 100

Bust of Louis XIV, 1665, by Giovanni Lorenzo Bernini
Jolliet map of North America, 1678
New France, 1678
Jean-Baptiste Colbert; Jean Talon
Alexandre de Prouville, Sieur de Tracy; Daniel de Rémy, Sieur de Courcelle
Quebec, *circa* 1670
Fort St Louis, residence of the governors of New France
Jesuit map of the West, 1682

FACING PAGE 164

Quebec under attack by the New England forces, 1690
Monseigneur François de Montmorency-Laval; Pierre Boucher
Jacques Réné de Brisay, Marquis de Denonville; Monseigneur Jean-Baptiste
de la Croix de Chevrières de Saint-Vallier
Section from map of New France by Jean-Baptiste Louis Franquelin
Page of an abstract of a dispatch from Canada
Acadia, 1702
North America, 1701
Quebec, 1699

FOREWORD

The Canadian Centenary Series

Half a century has elapsed since *Canada and Its Provinces*, the first large-scale co-operative history of Canada, was published. During that time, new historical materials have been made available in archives and libraries; new research has been carried out, and its results published; new interpretations have been advanced and tested. In these same years Canada itself has greatly grown and changed. These facts, together with the centenary of Confederation, justify the publication of a new co-operative history of Canada.

The form chosen for this enterprise was that of a series of volumes. The series was planned by the editors, but each volume will be designed and executed by a single author. The general theme of the work is the development of those regional communities which have for the past century made up the Canadian nation; and the series will be composed of a number of volumes sufficiently large to permit an adequate treatment of all the phases of the theme in the light of modern knowledge.

The Centenary History, then, was planned as a series to have a certain common character and to follow a common method but to be written by individual authors, specialists in their fields. As a whole it will be a work of specialized knowledge, the great advantage of scholarly co-operation, and at the same time each volume will have the unity and distinctive character of individual authorship. It was agreed that a general narrative treatment was necessary and that each author should deal in a balanced way with economic, political and social history. The result, it is hoped, will be an interpretive, varied, and comprehensive account, at once useful to the student and interesting to the general reader.

The difficulties of organizing and executing such a series are apparent: the overlapping of separate narratives, the risk of omissions, the imposition of divisions which are relevant to some themes but not to others. Not so apparent, but quite as troublesome, are the problems of scale, perspective, and scope, problems which perplex the writer of a one-volume history and are magnified in a series. It is by deliberate choice that certain parts of the history are told twice, in different volumes from different points of view, in the belief that the benefits gained outweigh the unavoidable disadvantages.

The editors are glad to introduce *Canada under Louis* XIV, by Professor W. J. Eccles, as the third volume to be published in the Series. The years it covers, those from 1663 to 1701, are among the most eventful but least systematically understood in the history of New France. The formation and nature of the original institutions of New France, as they took shape in the heat and pressure of those years, have rarely been rigorously studied, or described with professional skill. Neither has the transformation of the small mission and fur-trading outpost into a claim to continental empire been explained in terms at once scholarly and exciting. The volume will, we hope, become the interpretation for its generation of the formative period of French Canada.

W. L. MORTON,
Executive Editor.
D. G. CREIGHTON,
Advisory Editor.

PREFACE

Canada under Louis XIV

This book is an attempt to discuss the more important aspects of Canada's history, within the framework of a narrative account, during the period 1663-1701. The year 1663 was chosen because in that year the administration of the colony was taken out of the hands of the Company of New France and placed directly under the control of the King and his ministers. The year 1701 was chosen as a terminal date, rather than 1715 when Louis XIV died, because in 1701, on the eve of the War of the Spanish Succession, French policy in North America was changed radically. Thus the period 1663-1701 has a certain unity. During these years Acadia was regained and held for France. In the north, in Hudson Bay, the French held their own, while in the west they established posts throughout the Great Lakes basin and down the Mississippi valley to the Gulf of Mexico. In 1663 the French held only the shoreline of the St Lawrence from Tadoussac to Montreal; at the end of the century they held half the continent in fee.

These things were accomplished because Louis XIV poured capital, manpower, military force, and administrative talent into the colony with a lavish hand. It was during this period, too, that the institutions of New France were firmly established. These institutions, the basic values, and concepts of society upon which they rested, were to endure until the conquest in 1760. Even then, some of these values and attitudes toward life were not completely destroyed, they were too deep-rooted; they subsequently merged with, or changed in reaction to, the alien values and attitudes of the English conquerors. Yet something of their essence always persisted, to perplex at times Canadians of other than French descent. Although this period deserves to be studied for its intrinsic interest and should not have to justify itself before the bar of utilitarianism, it may well be that an understanding of it will aid in comprehending the values and aspirations of present-day French Canada.

In my use of reference notes I have not cited documents or other sources for every statement of fact, as one would do in a scholarly monograph. At the same time, to have dispensed with references entirely would likely have left doubts on some points in the minds of fellow toilers in the historical vineyard. I have, therefore, cited documents or other sources only when I was utilizing source material not used, or used very rarely, by other scholars; or where my interpretation of events is not in accord with earlier studies. Wherever a question dealt with has been treated in detail in a reputable scholarly work, using the same sources that I have used, then I have cited the monograph rather than given the same documentary sources *in extenso*. In other words, I have sought to give the scholar the reassurance he has a right to expect without annoying the general reader with an ostentatious display of erudition. Explanatory notes, giving necessary information that could not be worked into the text without destroying the cohesion of the narrative are given at the foot of the page. One or two such, giving information of interest only to scholars, have, however, been placed with the reference notes at the back of the book.

In the preparation of this work many people and institutions have been of great assistance in many ways. Much of the material used in this book was garnered in France for an earlier work. This was made possible only by a French government scholarship. Grants in aid of research from the Canada Council and the Ewart Foundation Fund of the University of Manitoba enabled me to spend my summers at the various archives in Ottawa, Quebec, Boston, and Albany. The staff research fund of the University of Alberta provided the means to have the manuscript typed. The archivists at all these places were invariably most helpful; this work could not have been done without the assistance they afforded me. Mr S. V. Ozere, Assistant Deputy Minister of Fisheries, Ottawa, and Mr C. M. Cross, Chief of the Tidal and Current Survey, Canadian Hydrographic Services, Ottawa, provided me with much detailed information on certain technical points. For assistance in finding suitable illustrations I am indebted to M. Gérard Morisset of the Musée Provinciale, Quebec.

To the editors of the series, Professors W. L. Morton and D. G. Creighton, who read and criticized the manuscript I owe a debt of gratitude. Theirs was no easy task. I am also indebted to Professor Marcel Trudel for his appraisal of the manuscript. Colonel C. P. Stacey kindly read one chapter dealing with military matters and his sage comments were of great benefit. The critical and editorial abilities of Miss Claire Pratt, editor for the publishers, made my task much easier. Their comments and criticism greatly improved the quality of this work, saving it from innumerable flaws and errors of omission and commission; for this I express my sincere thanks.

W. J. ECCLES

CHAPTER 1

France and New France, 1663

In the second half of the seventeenth century, European civilization entered a new phase in its development. The flames of the long, cruel wars of religion had almost burned themselves out; only the embers still flickered and gave off heat. Henceforth wars were to be fought, not for the control of men's souls, but for the product of their energies and the bounty of the lands they occupied. In this pursuit of gain, men from the nations bordering on the Atlantic were seizing as much as they could hold of the North American continent, and at the same time they still hopefully sought an easy water route through the land mass to the Pacific and the riches of the Orient beyond. At mid century they had no clear idea of the extent of North America, and men who claimed to have discovered such a route found ready listeners at the Courts of Europe; occasionally they even found financial backing.

By 1660, of all the countries in Europe, France was in the best position to avail herself of the latent opportunities in North America. The Thirty Years' War had left her enemies enfeebled, drained of their blood and treasure. Spain had been forced, by the Treaty of the Pyrenees, to cede Roussillon and Cerdagne to France, thus establishing a secure frontier along the crest of the mountain range. The Austrian Hapsburgs were still menaced by the Turks who occupied the Balkans and most of Hungary to within two days' march of Vienna. Germany, which had been fought over by all the armies in western Europe, was devastated, fragmented into over three hundred separate states. England had just thrown off the irksome rule of the Puritans; the Stuart monarchy had been restored, but the country was still deeply divided and Charles II was fully occupied with the internal affairs of his kingdom. Italy, like Germany, was merely a geographic expression, and the newly independent Dutch Netherlands wanted only to be left alone to expand their rich overseas trade and to enjoy their high standard of living.

France, by comparison, had emerged from the holocaust of the recent wars with her territory enlarged and her armies growing in strength; no single state, or even a coalition of states, could now successfully challenge her dominant position. Internally, the power of the French monarchy was at last secure. The old feudal nobility and the newer nobility of the *Parlement* had risen in a disorganized revolt against the centralized power of the Crown, recently established by Cardinal Richelieu, and had finally been subdued by Richelieu's successor, Cardinal Mazarin. With the crushing of this Fronde the feudal nobility were to be converted into an ornamental courtier caste and an élite cannon fodder for the royal armies. The *Parlement* of Paris had had hopes of achieving power equal to that of Parliament in England – which it resembled in little more than name – but the attempt had failed and it was now completely cowed. Thus, with the feudal and legal lords reduced almost to subservience, the monarchy was at last master in the kingdom, but its power was still exercised, not by the monarch but by the Cardinal-Minister, Mazarin.

When, on March 9, 1661, Mazarin died, everyone wondered who would succeed him. The twenty-two-year-old King, Louis XIV, did not leave them long in doubt. A few hours after Mazarin had breathed his last Louis ordered the Secretaries of State to sign nothing without his sanction and the Chancellor to place the royal seal on nothing without his permission. When the president of the assembly of the clergy, then in session, asked to whom they should go to learn the wishes of the government and to regulate their affairs, Louis succinctly replied: "To me, Monsieur the Archbishop." Thus Louis XIV made his dramatic entry as ruler of the kingdom of France.

*This turn of events was to affect profoundly the future development, not only of France, but of the whole of Europe. More than that, it was to be a determining factor in the history of North America. During the preceding quarter-century the French monarchy, enmeshed in wars and turmoil in Europe, had hardly been aware that Frenchmen had claimed title to vast areas in the New World and had founded colonies in Acadia on the North Atlantic seaboard and in New France, a thousand miles inland along the banks of the St Lawrence River. Now, when stock was taken of these possessions, their condition was found to leave much to be desired. Acadia had been in the hands of the English since 1654 when a New England expedition, commissioned by Cromwell, had seized the French posts around the shores of the Bay of Fundy, from Pentagôuet to Port Royal. In 1662 William Temple of Boston obtained from Charles II a commission as Governor of Nova Scotia and Acadia. He, however, made no attempt to settle these lands, being content merely to exploit the fur trade at the old French posts, and the original French settlers were allowed to remain on their lands undisturbed.

In Canada, too, the situation was far from good. New France, during these years, had like Old France been torn by dissension within and was under constant assault from without. The development of the colony had been entrusted to a private company, the Company of New France, which had blithely agreed to fulfil obligations that were beyond its resources in return for control of the colony's trade. The main concern of this company was, naturally enough, profits for the shareholders, and these profits could most easily be realized in the fur trade, which required relatively little capital or manpower. Thus, the company's obligations to bring out large numbers of settlers had not been fulfilled, and many of those who had been brought out had returned to France at the first opportunity.

Those who had remained had had to withstand the almost continual assaults of the Iroquois confederacy which, for fifty years, had been striving to drive the French out of the St Lawrence valley. Occupying the lands south of the St Lawrence River and Lake Ontario between Lake Champlain and Niagara, they obtained firearms and other supplies from the Dutch traders at Fort Orange – later to be named Albany – in exchange for furs. Since Champlain's time the French had obtained their furs from the Algonquins and Hurons north of the Great Lakes. These tribes were the traditional foes of the Iroquois, and the French commercial alliance had led, inevitably, to a military alliance against the Iroquois, who were quick to strike back. Although relatively few in numbers, numbering only some 2,300 fighting men, the five nations* of the Iroquois were the most feared of all the eastern forest tribes and until almost the end of the century they remained the strongest military force in North America. Their main military attributes were great stealth, endurance, cunning, and cruelty. They never attacked unless they could be sure of an easy victory; they always preferred to strike from ambush and, when they struck, men, women, and children alike were cut down in insensate fury.

This was the foe that the early settlers in New France had to face. When they went to till their fields they could never be sure the Iroquois would not be lurking in wait. In 1663 Pierre Boucher, Governor of Trois Rivières, stated:

> The Iroquois ... hem us in so close they prevent us availing ourselves of the country's resources; one cannot go hunting or fishing without fear of being killed or captured by those knaves : nor can one cultivate the land, still less harvest the grain, except in continual risk; for they wait in ambush on all sides. ... A wife is always uneasy lest her husband, who left in the morning for his work, should be taken or killed and that never will she see him again. This is why the majority of the habitants are poor, the Iroquois frequently

* The five nations of the Iroquois confederacy were the Mohawks, Oneidas, Onondagas, Cayugas, and Senecas.

killing the cattle, sometimes preventing the harvest, and burning or pillaging the homes whenever they have the opportunity.

And some years later an Iroquois chief boasted, "We plyed the French home in the warr with them, that they were not able to goe over a door to pisse."

The funds for the administration of the colony were derived from the fur trade; some years this was reduced to a trickle by the Iroquois ambushes on the trade routes; thus the colony frequently teetered on the edge of bankruptcy. To make matters worse, it was very difficult to get competent administrators to act as governors in the colony, and those appointed quickly became disheartened, for theirs was indeed a thankless task. Conflicts arose between the governors and the leading men in the colony on procedural and administrative matters and between the governors and the clergy on questions of policy. The lay clergy, with their strong-willed bishop François de Laval at their head, were filled with religious zeal and determined to keep the colony as free as possible of what they regarded as sin. Unfortunately, their definition of sin and that of the lay community were not always in accord. The powerful Jesuit order, long established in New France, also held strong views on colonial policy. To it New France was a bastion of the faith and a base to carry on their missionary work among the Indian tribes. Anything that hindered this work they opposed most vigorously. Moreover, the task of the clergy was their life work; they expected to remain in the colony permanently, whereas the governors expected to remain only a few years. Thus, the clergy tended to believe that their role was the more important one and that their views should prevail. The governors, however, who were almost invariably men of military experience, accustomed to being obeyed, would not tolerate opposition to their views. Inevitably, others in the colony took sides, factions formed, until eventually the governor resigned in disgust or was recalled.

This, then, was the condition of the French possessions in North America in 1661 when Louis XIV took the government of the kingdom into his own hands; Acadia was in the hands of the English, New France enfeebled, and seemingly growing weaker. With the English colonies to the south steadily developing firmer roots, there was reason to fear that before long New France would go the way of Acadia. French colonial enterprise in North America appeared to have failed dismally.

Yet, forty years later, the French were dominant in North America; the interior of the continent from Hudson Bay to the Gulf of Mexico was under their control. They had regained Acadia, the Iroquois had been humbled, all the attempts of the English to conquer New France and recapture Acadia had been repulsed, and the English colonies now expressed grave fears for the security of their own frontiers. A new colony, Louisiana, had been founded at the mouth of the Mississippi, and a chain of French forts in the basin of the Great Lakes and down the Mississippi valley threatened to hem the English in between the Alleghany Mountains and the Atlantic. Nor was this all, for with this unleashing of great human energy, and out of the terrible strife and suffering it engendered, emerged a new nation. Much that was accomplished during these four decades was eventually to be destroyed, but a distinct Canadian identity was to survive.

CHAPTER 2

Royal Intervention

In May 1663 Canada was taken out of the hands of the Company of New France and made a royal province, governed directly by the Crown just as were the other provinces of France. The man who then took charge of Canada's destinies was Jean-Baptiste Colbert. At that time he held only the post of *intendant de finance* but he was soon to become a minister, member of the great council of state and, under the King, the most powerful man in France. Virtually everything in the kingdom not under the jurisdiction of the ministers of war and foreign affairs was to be in his charge: finance, industry, commerce, arts, letters and science, royal buildings, the navy and the colonies – all were under his direction and all very quickly felt the impact of his ideas and driving energy.

Colbert was forty-four years old in 1663. The son of a draper at Reims, he had had some experience in commerce and banking, then, in 1639, entered the Ministry of War under Michel Le Tellier. Subsequently transferred to the service of the Cardinal-Minister Mazarin, it was he who restored Mazarin's immense private fortune, depleted by the Fronde, at the same time acquiring for himself a fortune and the title of Marquis de Seignelay. A cold, forbidding person, named "Monsieur du Nord" by the courtiers, his only pleasure was hard work. Always methodical, before making a decision he gathered all the information possible on the subject, compiled a complete dossier, then, after turning it over in his mind until every aspect of the problem was clear, he would make his decision and prepare a succinct précis for future reference.

From the moment he entered the royal service he sought power for himself. In the achievement of his ambitions one man stood in his way, Nicolas Fouquet, the *surintendant de finance*. Fouquet was the wealthiest man in France; in fact, the royal exchequer was virtually his personal exchequer, and he intended to gather into his own hands the power that Mazarin had enjoyed but that Louis XIV had decided no one but himself should have.

At Mazarin's death, however, Louis was not yet sufficiently sure of his own power to dismiss Fouquet, fearing that Fouquet might resist such a move and bring on another Fronde with invasion by foreign armies in its train, for which fear there were good grounds. Instead, with Colbert as his accomplice, he began conspiring against his own minister. For six months Colbert and Louis worked to encompass Fouquet's downfall; then, on September 5, 1661, the trap was suddenly sprung and he was arrested. Up until the moment of his arrest he had never suspected that Louis's seeming high regard for him was not sincere. He later remarked bitterly: "Good faith and decency were not conspicuous in the whole affair." But Louis XIV wrote that although many were disturbed by the event, "they see that it is best to attach themselves to me." For Louis, this was justification enough. It was, however, another six months before a sufficiently strong case was made to bring Fouquet before the courts. The trial itself lasted from March 1662 until his conviction and sentence to life imprisonment in December 1664. And until Fouquet was finally removed from the scene Colbert's own position was anything but secure. This did not prevent him making plans for the reorganization of the French economy, but it did prevent him devoting all his energies to the task; and it is against this background that events in Canada down to 1665 have to be examined.

What Colbert ultimately aimed to do was to bring order out of the chaos wrought by the years of war and internal disorder, then to make France the leading power in the world by restoring the country's economic strength. Surveying the European scene, he became convinced that wealth, expressed in hard cash, was power. He noted that the great wealth of the tiny republic of Venice had made it a power to be reckoned with; he saw how the one-time humble house of Hapsburg had risen to control a great empire through the wealth of its Styrian silver mines, and later, the bullion of the Americas; and how the swampy lands at the mouth of the Rhine had developed into a rich and powerful state, able to assert its independence and gain control of much of Europe's foreign trade. Like most thinking men of his age he believed that there was only a limited amount of money available in Europe; this amount being augmented from time to time by bullion from the Americas. He also believed that the amount of commerce that could be transacted was fixed, as long as the population remained stable and the people's consumption of goods did not vary. Thus, France could only hope to increase its wealth either by finding new sources of commerce, which was uncertain, or by taking away the commerce of other nations. He estimated that some 20,000 ships carried the commerce of Europe: 16,000 of these ships were owned by the Dutch; 3,000 to 4,000 by the English; some 200 by the French. France could, then, increase its trade only at the expense of the English or Dutch. To Colbert that was axiomatic. Trade and commerce were, therefore, merely war fought with economic weapons, and he intended to wage that war by keeping as much as possible of the nation's bullion within its borders and attracting as much as possible from other states. This he proposed to do by making France economically self-sufficient, by exporting any surplus, and thus producing a favourable balance of foreign trade. To achieve this aim he intended to utilize to the full all the resources of the kingdom, including its overseas possessions. He had particularly noted the great wealth that the Dutch and the English were deriving from their colonies and overseas trading-posts, and also in trade with the French colonies.* He was determined to emulate them, and Acadia and New France figured prominently in his, as yet, vaguely conceived plans.

It was while Colbert was busily gathering information and turning these schemes over in his mind, and only a few weeks after the arrest of Fouquet, that Pierre Boucher, the Governor of Trois Rivières in New France, arrived at the Court to plead for aid for the hard-pressed settlers. He had been sent by the newly appointed Governor of the colony, the Baron d'Avaugour, who had been quick to see the latent possibilities in New France and equally quick to see that substantial assistance would have to be sent from France to end the constant harrying attacks of the Iroquois. Louis XIV and Colbert gave Boucher a sympathetic hearing. Boucher impressed on them the need to furnish aid swiftly and the benefits that could accrue to both France and New France were its vast resources to be properly exploited. All of this was completely in accord with Colbert's own thinking but, at that juncture of events, with Fouquet and his supporters still to be disposed of and the chaotic legacy of Mazarin's administration still to be cleared away, all that Louis XIV could do was to promise to send a regiment of regular troops in the near future to quell the Iroquois. In the meantime he authorized the sending of one hundred soldiers and two hundred indentured labourers to Quebec with Boucher when he returned the following year.

Commanding the soldiers when they sailed in 1662 was the Sieur Dumont with explicit instructions from Colbert to make a detailed report on conditions in the colony. En route, Dumont called at Newfoundland,

---

* According to one document, dated 1742, the trade with Canada prior to 1663 had been taken over by foreign merchants, mainly Dutch, who bought the bulk of the beaver pelts cheaply in the colony, then sold them at much higher prices to the French hat-makers guild. No other evidence to support this contention has so far been discovered. It may, however, not be without significance that in 1685 Denonville, Governor of New France, complained that the only charts of the St Lawrence available were unreliable Dutch ones.[1]

took possession of Plaisance in the name of the King, and left a priest with twenty soldiers to establish more securely French claims to this important fishing-station. Unfortunately, the voyage lasted four months, and the ships' captains had provisions for only two. Some forty of the colonists and soldiers died at sea and the survivors were in such a sad physical state that it strained the resources of the colony to restore them to health. This slight aid did, however, put heart into the colonists since there was the promise of more substantial forces to follow.

Meanwhile, in New France Governor d'Avaugour had come into conflict over questions of policy with the Bishop, the Jesuits, the Messieurs de St Sulpice, the Governor of Montreal, and some of the colony's leading merchants. His authoritarian and rather extravagant actions had thrown the colony into an uproar. Letters of complaint from all parties were sent to persons of consequence in France. D'Avaugour, a proud soldier, scorned to defend himself against these charges but he did send his secretary to the Court to plead for strong military forces to be sent to aid the colony. Bishop Laval and Father Raguenau of the Jesuits also crossed to France to plead for aid and to ask the King to take steps to restore order within the colony.

Colbert had not had time to work out in detail, as he would have liked, his plans for French overseas possessions, nor to recruit the trained administrators needed to put the plans into effect, yet Bishop Laval made it abundantly clear that immediate action was imperative in New France. One thing was very obvious: the colony could hardly hope to survive, let alone prosper, if left under the control of the nearly moribund Company of New France. Colbert therefore gave the company fair warning that New France was to revert to the Crown and, on February 24, 1663, the directors agreed to turn over all the assets of the company and accept whatever compensation the King might care to make. Later they were to protest bitterly, but to no avail, that the compensation they had received was quite inadequate.

In the official letter of reunion of New France to the Crown, signed and sealed in May, Colbert, writing for the King, made his own views plain. He wrote:

> Since it has pleased God to give peace to our kingdom, we have had nothing more persistently in mind than the restoration of commerce, as being the source and principle of prosperity which we are determined, by all means, to procure for our people. And since the principal and greater part of commerce consists of trade with overseas colonies, before thinking of establishing any new colonies we believe it to be necessary to maintain, protect, and augment those already established. This has motivated us to discover exactly what is the state of New France, which the late King . . . gave over to a company composed of one hundred persons, by the treaty of 1628.

But instead of finding that this colony was populated as it should have been, considering the long time that it has been in the possession of our subjects, we have learned with regret that not only is the number of inhabitants very small, but that they were continually in danger of being driven out by the Iroquois, which makes it necessary to take action. Considering that this Company of a hundred men was nearly defunct owing to the withdrawal of most of the members, and that the few who remained were not capable of sustaining the country and sending the forces and men necessary both to people and to defend it, we have decided to withdraw it from the hands of the members of the same Company.[2]

This decision made, it now remained for the Crown to take steps to establish a new administration and to furnish the succour that the Company of New France had failed to provide. This was clearly going to take time – it took all of two years in fact – but some measures had to be taken immediately; a new administrative body had to be established to replace the old Council at Quebec. This was quickly done, in April, by a royal edict establishing a Sovereign Council composed of the governor of the colony, representing the King, the bishop, or the senior ecclesiastic in the colony, five councillors to be chosen by the governor and bishop and who were to serve for a term of one year or longer as the governor and bishop thought fit, and an attorney general. In addition, the governor and bishop were to appoint a clerk to keep the records of the Council. The duties of this Sovereign Council were to register and promulgate the laws of the kingdom, to hear criminal and civil cases in first instance and appeals from the lower courts according to the form and practice of the *Parlement de Paris*. It was also empowered to establish lower courts of first instance at Quebec, Montreal, and Trois Rivières. In addition, it had certain legislative powers, but the King reserved the right to change, amplify, or annul any laws or ordinances of the Sovereign Council. By this means Canada became a royal province of France, and Louis XIV was King of New France in the same way that he was King of Normandie, Anjou, or any other French province. The government of Canada now resided, not at Quebec, but wherever Louis XIV and Colbert happened to be.

To establish a new administrative system in New France was one thing; to find competent administrators was something else again. Colbert had his hands full finding competent men for the various departments in his charge in France, let alone persuading men of this calibre to expose themselves to the dangers and hardships of life in far-off Canada. When he took charge of economic and financial affairs in the kingdom, the calibre of the officials in the Department of Marine appears to have been very low indeed. Their reports were meagre in content and badly written, the product of ill-informed, untidy minds. By the end of the decade, however, a marked change had taken place: the reports and memoranda of the department were now always succinct and well written, giving clear evidence that the authors knew what they were about. It appears to have taken Colbert only four or five years to reorganize the department, weed out the incompetents, and replace them by men of exceptional ability. This in itself was no small achievement.

In 1662, however, all this was yet to be done and, with the ultimate outcome of Fouquet's trial still uncertain, Colbert had much with which to occupy himself. Consequently, when it had been decided that the swiftest way to end the faction fights and civil turmoil in New France would be to replace d'Avaugour, Colbert and Louis XIV delegated to Bishop Laval the task of finding a suitable candidate to serve as governor in the new Royal province. And since he knew, better than any other appointed official, the conditions and circumstances in the colony, they allowed him to retain the equal authority in the Sovereign Council that he had had on the Council established by the Company of New France. This was indicative, not so much of the power and influence of Laval and the clergy at the Court, as of Colbert's and Louis's preoccupation with more pressing problems in France.

Laval's choice for governor fell on Augustin de Saffray, Chevalier de Mésy, Town-Major of Caen in Normandie. Laval had spent some time at a religious house in Caen and had there formed a high opinion of Mésy, who gave every appearance of piety and lack of worldly ambition. Mésy, however, was reluctant to accept the appointment, pleading that he could not because he had heavy personal debts which he had to discharge. It was only after Louis XIV paid these debts for him and personally pressed him to accept the post that he agreed to go for a three-year term.

In the French provinces the most important of the royal officials was the intendant of justice, administration, and finance. It was the intendants who really ran the provinces, the governors being reduced to mere figureheads. They were the principal agents of royal absolutism and they had to be both honest and efficient; were they to prove wanting in these essential qualities they were quickly dismissed. Men of the calibre needed for such important posts were, however, scarce in the 1660's. Louis Robert, Sieur de Fortel, a relative of Colbert, was commissioned as intendant of New France, but he apparently thought better of it and, despite Colbert's best efforts, no one could be found to replace him. The best that Colbert was able to do was to send Louis Gaudais, Sieur du Pont, to Quebec with the Bishop and new Governor to investigate conditions in the colony and return in the autumn to report. Colbert gave Gaudais extremely detailed instructions, requiring information on every conceivable thing, the geography and climate of the colony, the fertility of the soil, the amount of land cleared and the amount available to be cleared, descriptions of the towns and the settlements, the population and its mode of living. The forest and mineral resources had to be assessed, and how best to wean the colonists from the fur trade into agriculture, fishing, mining, lumbering, and ship-building. Gaudais had also to observe how the Sovereign Council functioned, whether good men were selected to serve on it, and whether the colonists had confidence in its ability to render justice and administer the affairs of the colony equitably.

In addition to these all-embracing instructions, which clearly reflect Colbert's desire to base his policies on the fullest possible knowledge, Gaudais was given a separate set of secret instructions which are equally revealing.[3] In them he was charged to inquire into the past conduct of d'Avaugour, the opinion held of him by Laval, the Jesuits, the leading residents of the colony, the people generally, and the motives they had for their expressed opinions. He was further instructed to inquire into the conduct of the Bishop in both spiritual and temporal affairs, but to do so with such prudence and discretion that Laval would never suspect that he was being investigated. Similarly, he had to report on the activities of the Jesuits and to observe carefully whether or not Mésy performed the functions of governor properly and to the satisfaction of the people.

On September 15, 1663, the King's ships with Laval, Mésy, and Gaudais arrived at Quebec. With them were one hundred and fifty-nine indentured labourers and settlers who had survived the three months' voyage; sixty others had died at sea. The retiring Governor, d'Avaugour, had already left for France when they arrived. On September 18, the Sovereign Council was established and the colony declared to be a royal province of France; a province whose full extent no one really knew.

The settled areas were scattered here and there along the banks of the great river, a few shallow indentations in the virgin forest. On the north shore, from Cap Tourmente, some twenty miles below Quebec, to Cap Rouge seven miles above it, the land was cleared, fields running straight back from the river with the farmhouses on the bank above. Farther up the river there were some seigneuries with settlers well established, but much of the land was still covered by virgin hardwood forest. Quebec, the administrative centre of the province and the head of navigation for ships from Europe, had as fine a site as could be imagined. On the great promontory dominating the river were the governor's residence and fortress, the Château St Louis, and the religious houses; the cathedral, the Jesuit college, the Ursulines convent, and the Hôtel Dieu. There were also a few private homes belonging to the wealthier residents. At the foot of the cliffs, along the edge of the St Lawrence and the St Charles rivers, the latter flanking the northern side of the promontory, were more homes and merchants' warehouses. Most of the houses were built of wood, or wood and plaster, but some were of stone with the steep pitched roofs found on the houses and châteaux of northern France. All told, some eight hundred people resided at Quebec.

Upstream was another cluster of farms at Cap de la Madeleine, and farther on was the small town of Trois Rivières. From this settlement to Montreal the Iroquois lurked constantly; here no one ever felt safe, and most of the rich soil lay uncultivated. Montreal, begun as a missionary settlement, had quickly become the centre of the fur trade, but fewer than five hundred persons were settled on the island. Most of them remained clustered close to the fort, for to venture even a few hundred paces from the shelter of its walls was to risk falling into an ambush.

This, then, was the state of the province when the King's newly appointed Governor and *commissaire* arrived. In the three days that elapsed between their arrival and the establishment of the Sovereign Council they certainly did not have sufficient time to form an opinion of the merits of the councillors; thus it must have been Bishop Laval who selected Louis Rouer sieur de Villeray, Jean Juchereau sieur de la Ferté, Denis Joseph Ruette d'Auteuil sieur de Monceaux, Charles Legardeur sieur de Tilly, Mathieu Damours sieur de Chaufour, along with Jean Bourdon sieur de St Jean et de St François as Attorney General, and Jean Baptiste Peuvret sieur de Mesnu as Clerk and Secretary. These were men who had played leading roles in the direction of the colony's affairs under the company's rule and on this account had been accused of having served their own interests rather than those of the colony or the company. How much truth there was in these accusations it is difficult to say, as the evidence is scanty and unreliable; but if their previous conduct can be judged by the manner in which they later performed their duties on the Sovereign Council, then the charges deserve little credence. One thing is certain, however: they were all men who had sided with Bishop Laval in the earlier disputes with Governor d'Avaugour and had suffered for it. They could, therefore, be relied on to support the Bishop in the future. With Mésy and Laval on such excellent terms there seemed to be little likelihood of a division occurring, but this tranquil state of affairs was to endure less than a year, when the dissension and quarrelling, endemic in French administrative circles, was to begin again.*

* It was not only in Canada that the officials squabbled viciously. In the West Indies, too, the intendants and governors fought with each other, and Colbert frequently had to threaten to terminate the careers of intendants who were

Although the advent of royal government did not effect any immediate sweeping changes in the colony, it did make a considerable difference to the twenty-five hundred colonists. Most notably, it gave them confidence in the future by promising them eventual surcease from the constant Iroquois attacks. At this time the Iroquois were being hard pressed by their foes, the Algonquins, Mohicans, and Andastes; in addition they had suffered heavy losses from the ravages of smallpox. When they learned from some of their French captives that reinforcements had arrived from France and that more were soon to come, their attacks slackened and their chiefs began sounding out the Jesuit missionaries on the possibility of a peace settlement. The Jesuits' *Relation* for 1663 reported: "Our enemies, being this year engaged elsewhere, have suffered us to till our fields in safety, and to enjoy a sort of foretaste of the quiet which our incomparable Monarch is about to secure for us. . . . Montreal alone has been stained with the blood of Frenchmen, Iroquois, and Hurons."

In the general administration of the colony and in the dispensing of justice the people could not have remarked any radical changes, since none were made. The Sovereign Council took over where the preceding Council had left off. At Trois Rivières and Montreal, Pierre Boucher and Paul de Chomedy, Sieur de Maisonneuve, remained as local governors, but were now granted royal commissions. Royal courts of law, having a judge, an attorney general, a clerk, and a bailiff, were established at these two centres. One of the first edicts issued by the Sovereign Council, on September 28, forbade anyone to trade liquor, directly or indirectly, with the Indians on pain of heavy fines or banishment. The brandy traffic had been an extremely contentious issue for a long time. The clergy were vigorously opposed to its sale to the Indians because they drank only to become intoxicated, believing that liquor transported them into the strange world of their primitive gods and that they themselves became akin to the gods when drunk. But, lacking the inhibitions that restrain Europeans, too many of them went berserk and committed heinous crimes while intoxicated and afterwards disclaimed all responsibility for their actions.[5] So eager were many of them to obtain liquor that they would trade all of their furs for a jug or two of brandy. For the more unscrupulous of the French traders this offered an excellent opportunity to make very great profits. In 1660 Bishop Laval had declared that anyone selling liquor to the Indians would be excommunicated. The civil governors, however, always jealous of their rights, claimed that the clergy were hereby usurping powers that belonged to the civil authorities, and some merchants and fur-traders were quick to agree with them. This had resulted, in the past, in violent disputes

insubordinate to the governors and to plead with the governors of the different islands to at least tolerate the other officials' existence in their part of the world.[4]

between the clerical and lay authorities. The edict of the Sovereign Council promulgated under Mésy, banning the sale of liquor to the Indians, effectively ended this dispute for the time being and was a good beginning for the new régime.

Before the year was out Bishop Laval had founded his seminary at Quebec, approval for which had been granted by Louis XIV when Laval was in France. It was now hoped that within a few years the colony would be able to provide at least some of its own clergy. The maintenance of parish priests was, however, to prove a contentious issue. To maintain them, tithes were required and Laval decreed a rate of one-thirteenth of the produce of the land. The Canadian *habitants*, however, objected strenuously to this, declaring the rate to be much more than they could afford. After a lengthy and rather acrimonious dispute, the Sovereign Council in 1667 reduced the tithe to one twenty-sixth of the produce of the land, to be paid in threshed grain. New land concessions were exempt for five years. The *habitants* interpreted the edict to mean one twenty-sixth of the wheat grown, not one twenty-sixth of all the land's produce, payed in wheat, and subsequent attempts on the part of the clergy to alter this interpretation met with no success whatsoever.

The administrative costs of the colony, that is, the salaries of the officials, the pay of the garrison soldiers, and grants to the religious orders had, in the past, been paid by leasing the monopoly on the purchase of beaver pelts from the *habitants* for fifty thousand *livres*. D'Avaugour had, without consulting the local council, leased this monopoly for two years, along with a monopoly of the fur trade at Tadoussac and the right to sell liquor to the Indians, to a group of seventeen of the more substantial colonists, three of whom, Juchereau de la Ferté, Le Gardeur de Tilly, and Jean Bourdon, were members of the Sovereign Council. Owing to the depressed state of the fur trade, caused by a drop in the price of beaver pelts in France and the interruption in the supply coming to the colony's traders from the west as a result of Iroquois attacks on the Algonquin middlemen, the holders of the lease found themselves unable to meet their obligations. Mésy declared their lease null and void on the grounds that the sale of liquor to the Indians was contrary to the King's edicts and that d'Avaugour had exceeded his authority. He ordered the lease-holders to account for the sums they had received, and then had the lease put up for auction. The bidding at this auction was quite spirited; on the third day the customary three candles were lit consecutively, and before the third had guttered out, Aubert de la Chesnaye topped Jean Bourdon's final bid and obtained the lease for a three-year term for 46,500 *livres*.

The following year the 10 per cent tax levied on all goods entering the colony to pay off the debts of the *Communauté des Habitants*, which had been founded in 1645 to pay the administrative costs of the colony in return for the monopoly on the beaver trade, was reduced to a 10 per cent tax on wines, spirits, and tobacco. This afforded some relief to the *habitants* who had found themselves caught between low prices for their beaver pelts and rising prices for goods imported from France. This 10 per cent tax and the deduction of 25 per cent of the value of the beaver pelts they sold to La Chesnaye – this last being known as the *quart* – were the only taxes the people in Canada paid and, compared to their counterparts in France who were taxed almost out of existence, they had little to complain about. If, however, they were spared heavy taxation, they had to pay dearly for all goods imported from France. To protect consumers against over-charging by the merchants, Mésy and the council fixed the prices at which imported goods could be sold, allowing a 65 per cent mark-up over the prices paid for similar goods in France and, on liquor, 100 per cent. At the same time ocean freight rates were fixed at eighty *livres** the ton. That these regulations were not to be disregarded was made plain when several merchants were heavily fined for charging more than the tariff allowed.

To encourage the *habitants* to clear more land and grow more grain in the face of a large wheat surplus, in 1664 the Sovereign Council purchased a thousand bushels, at the generous price of five *livres* the bushel, to be stored for the use of the regular troops expected from France the following year. The wages of indentured labourers were also fixed by law at sixty to ninety *livres* a year for a three-year term, after which they were free to obtain land of their own. Thus, during the first year of Mésy's administration, some worthwhile legislation was enacted. But before that year was out trouble had arisen between the Governor and the Bishop.

Mésy, although he represented the King in the colony and had supreme authority, had in fact less real power than had the Bishop. Mésy had been appointed for only a three-year term and could be recalled by the King at any time. The Bishop, on the other hand, was there permanently and in addition to his seat on the Council had the power and prestige of his clerical rank. Moreover, Bishop Laval was a very strong-willed man who regarded any opposition to his wishes as essentially wicked. The clergy had clearly expected Mésy to remain subservient to Bishop Laval, deferring to him in all things, but this Mésy soon showed he was not prepared to be.

During the winter Mésy appears to have become convinced that the Bishop, supported by some members of the Council, was seeking to under-

* To estimate accurately the value of the *livre* in present-day currency is extremely difficult. At this time the *livre Tournois* was valued at one shilling six pence sterling; the Canadian *livre* was at a discount of 25 per cent. The closest approximation that one could give would be that the Canadian *livre* was worth roughly $1.50 to $2.00 in today's (1963) currency. There were 20 *sols* in the *livre* and 12 *deniers* in the *sol*.

mine his authority. According to the Royal edict establishing the Sovereign Council, the governor represented the person of the King; Mésy therefore decided to take steps to assert his prerogatives. On February 13 he sent the major of his garrison to inform the Bishop of his intention to exclude Villeray, Auteuil, and Bourdon from the Council on the grounds that they had formed a cabal and behaved in a manner contrary to the interests of the King and the people. He also declared that replacements for those now excluded would be chosen by a public assembly. Laval, as was to be expected, refused to entertain this innovation, or to sanction the dismissal of the two Council members and the Attorney General. Tilly, La Ferté, and Damours, however, supported Mésy and signed an ordinance suspending Laval's adherents.

Without an attorney general justice could not be dispensed, and the *habitants* of the district who had litigation before the court protested vigorously. Mésy therefore asked the Bishop to agree to the appointment of a deputy attorney general. Laval refused but declared he would not openly oppose the Governor in any action he took on his own authority. On March 10 the rump Council duly appointed Louis-Théandre Chartier de Lotbinière to the vacant attorney general's post, and the work of the Council proceeded. Subsequently, a reconciliation of the disputing factions was effected. Lotbinière gracefully retired, and Bourdon was reinstated.

In July, however, trouble again erupted, this time over the election of a syndic for Quebec. The previous November the offices of mayor and alderman had been abolished by the Council, and it was then decided that the old office of syndic should be reinstituted to represent the interests of the people before the Council. Not until the following August 2 was an election held and Claude Charron, a merchant of Quebec, elected *in absentia* by twenty-three local residents.

Meanwhile, a year having nearly passed since the establishment of the Sovereign Council, Mésy repeatedly requested Laval to agree to the replacement of some of its members and the confirmation in office of certain of the others. The Bishop, knowing which members Mésy wished to exclude, refused to accede to this legitimate request. On August 25 Mésy sent Laval a courteously worded note asking that they should co-operate in good faith to appoint a new Council as ordered in the Royal edict of April 1663.[6] He proposed that he should draw up a list of twelve men suitable to hold office and that the Bishop should select any four; or, the Bishop could name twelve candidates and allow the Governor to choose four of them. Under the circumstances, this was a fair proposal. Laval, however, in a terse note, informed Mésy that he had received word from the Minister of Marine that Seigneur de Tracy, recently appointed Lieutenant-General over all French possessions in America with the powers of a viceroy, would arrive at Quebec in the spring; therefore they should await his arrival before making any changes in the membership of the Council.[7] This meant that Mésy would have to face further opposition in the Council for the best part of a year. Unfortunately, the terms in the Royal edict establishing the Sovereign Council gave no guidance for an impasse such as this.[8]

Then, on September 19, after some of the citizens had protested the election of Charron as syndic on the grounds that too few people had voted in the election and that he was more likely to favour the interests of the merchants than those of the consumers, Charron was persuaded to resign and a new election was called. This assembly was also poorly attended, and no election was held. Mésy was convinced that his old foes, the clergy and their adherents in the Council, were responsible for this state of affairs. He therefore sent notes to a large number of townspeople to attend a meeting without stating its purpose. When they assembled he and Damours held the election, and Jean Lemire was duly elected syndic. However, La Ferté, Auteuil, and the Bishop's deputy, the Sieur de Charny, protested this election at the next meeting of the Sovereign Council and refused to allow Lemire to be installed. Mésy regarded this as chicanery, and being, as he stated, unaccustomed to such ways he decided to deal with the situation as would a cavalier defending the King's interests. On his own authority he dismissed from the Council Villeray, who had previously sailed for France, Auteuil, La Ferté, and Bourdon; Tilly and Damours he retained. As replacements he appointed Denys de la Trinité, Louis Peronne de Mazé, and Denis-Jacques de Cailhaut de la Tesserie, with Lotbinière once again to serve as Attorney General, and Michel Fillion as Clerk. Jean Bourdon, however, unlike the others, refused to accept his dismissal, declaring the Governor's action to be illegal, which, strictly speaking, it of course was. A violent argument ensued, and Mésy lost control of himself. He attacked Bourdon, striking him first with his cane, then with the flat of his sword, pursued him out of the chamber and wounded him in the hand. Bishop Laval immediately protested Mésy's reconstitution of the Council, declaring it to be contrary to the King's edict, and the following Sunday he made his views known to the public in a statement read from the pulpit by one of his priests. Mésy, lacking a pulpit, retaliated by posting notices about the town defending his own actions and attacking the Bishop, whereupon he was refused confession and absolution by the clergy. He promptly threatened to refuse to authorize the payment of the semi-annual grant of funds to the clergy.

What the people of the colony thought of this fracas is not known but it certainly could not have enhanced their respect for either the secular or religious authorities. But through it all Mésy's reconstituted Sovereign Council continued to function, meting out justice, carrying on the normal processes of the administration, and showing a proper sense of responsibility. Then, early in March 1665, Mésy fell seriously ill. When he expressed a desire to be reconciled with the clergy, all their earlier rancour was forgotten. Before Mésy expired, during the night of May 5-6, the Bishop said mass for him every day, and in his will the Governor made bequests to the poor, to charitable organizations, to the church, and to five residents of Quebec, one of them being Villeray.

Shortly before his death Mésy commissioned Le Neuf de La Poterie to succeed him as his deputy, but when the acting Attorney General presented the commission to the Sovereign Council this body refused to register it, maintaining that the Governor had had no power to appoint his successor; only the King could do this. In France, meanwhile, numerous complaints against Mésy's conduct had reached the Court, to which Bourdon and Villeray had also gone. Their account of events convinced the minister that Mésy's conduct could not be condoned. Unaware that the Governor was dead, Colbert ordered that the charges against him be investigated, and if substantiated he was to be placed under arrest and sent back to France to stand trial.

It is unfortunate that Mésy's own papers have not survived; were they available to counterbalance the charges levelled at him in the writings of the clergy which have been preserved, he might appear in a better light. At least it can be said that his had been no easy position, sharing power with Bishop Laval. He acted with violence on occasion, it is true; but he did so, not without some provocation. Although the clash of personalities played no small part in the conflict, strongly held differences of opinion on what should be done for the better administration of the colony were also involved. Certainly the main reason why things reached such an impasse was the ill-conceived phrasing of the edict establishing the Sovereign Council. The governor and the bishop were expected to work in unison, sharing authority. But when they disagreed over an issue or a policy their authority could not be exercised effectively. All too easily this could, and did, lead to chaos. At all events, these conflicts should not be allowed to obscure the fact that during Mésy's brief term as governor, royal government was established in the colony, justice was dispensed equitably, and some useful legislation was enacted.[9]

Mésy's régime had been, in fact, little more than a caretaker government to tide the colony over while Colbert completed his ambitious plans for colonial development. The detailed reports that he had already received on conditions in all the French colonies had made it plain that radical measures were urgently needed. Trade with the West Indies was largely in the hands of the Dutch, and the administration of some of the islands had become so corrupt that the planters were abandoning their estates. Colbert immediately decided to send, as an emergency measure, "a man of ability and of authority" with adequate forces to visit all the French possessions in America, restore order, establish a sound administration, and enable the residents to conduct their commercial affairs in freedom and security.

The man he chose for this task was Alexander Prouville, Seigneur de Tracy. Sixty years of age, Tracy had served as *Commissaire Général* with the French army in Germany during the Thirty Years' War, and during the Fronde he had remained staunchly loyal to the Crown – that is, to Mazarin. Promoted Lieutenant-General in 1651, he had maintained an army in the field when funds were lacking and all was chaos, holding the vital Garonne valley against the Frondeurs and their Spanish allies. He was a man of exceptional integrity, a very conscientious administrator held in great respect by all, not least by Colbert. His commission, dated November 19, 1663, appointed him "Lieutenant-General in all the lands of our obedience situated in North and South America and in the islands of America." He was, in fact, a viceroy, given supreme command of all French forces in America on land and sea, and also, supreme judicial power. His task was to administer an oath of allegiance to all French officials and subjects, "to establish the power of the King" and "to make all the people obedient unto him." On February 26, 1664, he set sail from France for the West Indies, to establish a new régime in the islands and then proceed to Quebec to perform the same task there.

While Tracy was engaged in this preliminary but vital task, in France Colbert was bringing his carefully worked out plans for colonial development to fruition. He had made a close study of the activities and methods of the great Dutch and English trading companies, which were reaping large profits for their shareholders. He decided to emulate them in an attempt to do in a few short years what the Dutch and English had taken over a century to do, not to mention also drastic social, religious, and political upheavals. Ignoring, or unaware, of the fact that the commercial systems of these powers were unsuited to the French social and economic framework, he set about establishing a French commercial company to exploit the resources of the French colonies and compete with the powerful Dutch and English companies. In May 1664 the letters patent creating the *Compagnie de l'Occident* were issued.[10] All property rights in the French possessions in North and South America, and also the west coast of Africa, were vested in the company. It now became the suzerain *grand seigneur* in Canada, Acadia, and Newfoundland, empowered to grant lands in fief, to build forts, levy troops, appoint all officials, administer justice, legislate, declare war on the King's enemies, and make treaties in the King's name. A monopoly of all trade with the colonies was granted for forty years, with the exception of the Newfoundland fisheries, where a monopoly would have been inimical to the training of the maximum number of sailors as well as being impossible to maintain. What was perhaps even more significant, the government offered subsidies to encourage trade with and among the colonies.

A scheme as ambitious as this required vast amounts of capital, and Colbert intended that it should be provided by private citizens, both French and foreign, rather than by the Crown. Foreigners who subscribed twenty thousand *livres* acquired the rights of French nationals for as long as that credit remained on the company's books, and after twenty years these rights of nationality became irrevocable. The main inducement to subscribe was, of course, the hope of profits, but very few men with money, either French or foreign, saw any such hope. Colbert's cousin, Colbert de Terron, the intendant at the Atlantic naval base Rochefort, held out little hope for the company's success. In February 1664 he informed Colbert that he would comply with the Minister's instructions and try to induce the merchants of La Rochelle to invest in it, but he was not sanguine as to the results because, as he put it, "our merchants lack the necessary vigour to engage in a business they know little about, moreover they can be cured only with great difficulty of the fear they have for the Dutch."[11] Colbert de Terron was himself willing to invest only ten thousand *livres* in the company, and he clearly did this with considerable reluctance. In the end, the Crown had to provide nearly 60 per cent of the capital raised, and nearly all the remainder was provided by the farmers of the revenue,* tax collectors, officials, and other persons who were dependent on Colbert and who therefore had to do his bidding. When, in 1669, a dividend was declared to attract new subscribers it had to be paid out of the royal exchequer. Thus, the *Compagnie de l'Occident* was really a Crown corporation created by Colbert, maintained out of the royal treasury, and governed and directed by Colbert.[12]

So ended the first two years of royal government in Canada. It did not appear on the surface that much had been accomplished; respect for the new administration had certainly not been engendered by the squabbles at Quebec; the Iroquois were still inflicting casualties on the settlers at Montreal, and the economic foundations of the colony remained very

* Under the old régime in France, the right to collect the indirect taxes for specified periods, or "bails," was leased (that is, "farmed") for fixed sums to syndicates of financiers, known as "tax farmers."

shaky. It was in France rather than in Canada that changes had occurred which very soon would alter the entire aspect of the colony. During these past two years Colbert and the subordinate officials, whom he was forging into an exceptionally efficient administrative organization, had been busily gathering information, learning from past mistakes, selecting personnel, and making plans for the economic expansion of the French colonial empire.

At the same time Louis XIV had successfully completed a series of heavy-handed diplomatic manœuvres to make plain to all the unchallengeable dominance of France. The King of Spain, ruler of the greatest empire the world had seen, had been obliged to allow that the French ambassadors took precedence over those of Spain in all the Courts of Europe, and Charles II of England was forced to agree that French ships, meeting those of England in "the narrow seas," need not dip their ensigns in salute first. The only person left in Europe with prestige to rival that of Louis was the Pope. On Louis's orders the French ambassador at Rome forced a quarrel with the Papal guards, incited violence against his retinue, and then withdrew from the city for the security of his person. As soon as Louis was informed of these events he dismissed the Papal nuncio from his Court, pretended to be outraged by the threat to his ambassador's safety, and in November 1663 ordered an army to march on the Italian frontier. In February the Pope gave way and accepted Louis's demands for an apology and reparations. The French army was then recalled, and Colbert was thus able to write to Bishop Laval at Quebec: "The Italian affair being fortunately settled to the satisfaction of the King, His Majesty has decided to send a good regiment of infantry to Canada at the end of this year or in February to crush the Iroquois."[13]

With these external and internal issues satisfactorily settled Louis XIV and Colbert were able to devote more attention to the colonial empire, and in Canada the results were quickly to be felt.

CHAPTER 3

The Institutional Framework

The decision to recall Mésy having been made, Daniel de Rémy, Sieur de Courcelle, a soldier noted for his bravery if not his prudence was appointed to succeed him. Since his chief task was to crush the Iroquois, he seemed well qualified for the post. It proved, however, a more difficult task to find a suitable man for the post of intendant. On February 8, 1664, Colbert de Terron, Intendant at Rochefort, wrote to Colbert informing him that since regular troops were to be sent to Canada "an intendant capable of taking charge of everything concerning justice, administration and finance must be sent, I hold this appointment to be as necessary for the colony as the troops themselves." Colbert was in complete agreement but he had little success in finding the right man. In November 1664 he wrote: "I despair of being able to find an intendant who has the proper qualities for this post, those who would acquit themselves worthily lack the mettle to risk the long voyage, and those who would undertake it lack the intelligence, integrity and ability needed to be of some use there."[1] By the following February, however, a man with the requisite qualities was found who was willing to go to Canada for a two-year term. His name was Jean Talon.

This man, who was to have such an impact on the colony, was about forty years of age when he came to Canada. Educated by the Jesuits, he had served Mazarin loyally and very efficiently throughout the Fronde as intendant with the French army on the Flanders frontier. As a reward for his services during these violent times he was appointed, in 1655, intendant of Hainaut. That Colbert was able to get men of the calibre of Tracy, Courcelle, and Talon to agree to serve in the wilds of North America, even for short terms, is an indication that a radical improvement had been effected in the French administration. Before Talon sailed to take up his new post he had meetings with Jesuit missionaries who had served in Canada, and also with Bourdon and Villeray then in Paris, and was well briefed by them on conditions in the colony. Colbert provided him with

very detailed written instructions covering every aspect of his responsibilities, and he also received a curt summons to appear at the Court immediately, as Louis XIV wished to discuss certain matters with him
privately. Thus, there could have been no doubt in his mind what was
expected of him in his new post, nor that both Colbert and the King attached great importance to it.

By November 1664 Le Tellier, the Minister of War, had issued orders
for the munitions, supplies, and transport of one thousand officers and men
of the Carignan-Salières regiment to Canada to quell the Iroquois. The
officers were informed that they would remain in Canada only for one
campaign and could expect to be back in France within eighteen months.
Considering that of the 117 officers who accompanied the regiment some
fifty were fifty years of age or more, thirty-odd over sixty, and five over
seventy, this was an important consideration for many of them.[2] While en
route to La Rochelle the men rioted on two occasions but, having in mind
their ultimate destination, Le Tellier ruled that they should not be
punished.[3]

At La Rochelle Talon was already hard at work superintending the load-
ing of supplies and the embarcation of the troops. When he called the roll
he was surprised to discover, not that half the men had deserted as was
usually the case, but that the eight companies were more than seventy men
over strength with more men presenting themselves every day, hopeful of
a free passage to Quebec. Talon promptly gave orders that all who were
physically fit should be enrolled. The *Compagnie de l'Occident* was sending
four hundred workmen to Canada in the convoy with the troops, and
Talon found more than the stipulated number on the ships. In addition,
a dozen young women appeared and asked to be given passage. Since they
all looked healthy and strong enough, Talon decided to take them along
lest a refusal should discourage others from emigrating in the future.
Before he knew it he was short of shipping space, but nothing daunted
he located a Swedish frigate in Nantes and contracted with its Dutch owner
to bring the freight that would otherwise have had to be left behind. The
news that the King had great plans for Canada had spread far and wide,
attracting the adventurous from all sides.

On June 30, 1665, Tracy arrived at Quebec with the four companies of
regular troops that had accompanied him to the West Indies. A few days
before, four companies of the Carignan-Salières regiment had arrived, and
the remainder landed late in August. Prior to Tracy's arrival, carpenters
and masons had been working overtime on renovations to the Château
St Louis, making it fit for one of his eminence. Fortunately for them his

ship was delayed in the Gulf for a month by contrary winds, and they were able to complete the work the day prior to his arrival. The delay was not so fortunate for Tracy, however; he had been taken ill and when his ship finally docked he was "so weak and reduced by fever that nothing but his courage sufficed to sustain him."[4] The people of Quebec had planned a great reception, but Tracy had to decline all honours. Nothing, however, could have prevented the citizens of the town cheering themselves hoarse, or the clamour of the church bells, as Tracy, barely able to walk, slowly made his way up the steep hill to the church where the Bishop and the clergy waited to escort him to the place of honour to hear the *Te Deum* chanted. To the people of New France, and particularly those at Quebec, these must have been exciting times. Throughout July and August ships kept arriving with more troops and supplies. On one of the ships were some horses which greatly impressed the Indians. They were astonished by the tractability of these "French moose."

Although it was too late in the season to undertake a campaign that year, Tracy wasted no time. On July 23 the first four companies of the troops to arrive, commanded by the Sieur de Chambly and accompanied by a number of *habitants* under the Sieur de Repentigny, were sent to build a fort on the Richelieu River. Their arrival at Trois Rivières relieved the people there of all fear of the Iroquois who had recently slain some settlers near the town and taken others prisoner. Before the end of November two more forts had been built along the Richelieu to bar this main route used by the Iroquois in their incursions against the colony. The forts were also intended to serve as advance bases to open the way to attack the Iroquois villages and to forestall any attempts contemplated by the English or Dutch to occupy the area. In addition, a party of troops was sent to explore the entrance to Lake Champlain. Even these hardened campaigners were impressed by the savage beauty of the land: the blue waters of the vast lake stretching far off in the distance, reflecting along the shore the verdant green of the tall pines and the brilliant scarlet and gold of the autumn foliage on the adjacent hills.

In mid September Tracy's labours were lightened considerably with the arrival of Talon and Courcelle. The new Governor, "breathing nothing but war," immediately concerned himself with the troops and the fortifications, and Talon was kept busy organizing convoys of food supplies for the garrisons of the forts, arranging for their winter quarters, and gathering all the information he could at first hand on conditions in the colony. It must have seemed to the people of New France that this new official was everywhere at once, visiting every seigneury, asking innumerable questions and causing the seigneurs who had not been too energetic in getting their lands cleared and settled to become active.

The clergy were not idle, either. The nuns at the Hôtel Dieu had 130 seriously ill soldiers to care for and, given no rest day or night, they worked themselves nearly to death. The facilities of the hospital were quite inadequate to care for this many sick. Mattresses had to be placed in the parish church, and when this building was filled Talon had to commandeer nearby buildings to shelter the remainder. When it was discovered that there were several Huguenots among the officers and men, every effort was made to convert them. Before September was out, twenty had been persuaded to adopt the Roman faith, to the great satisfaction, and relief, of both the clergy and the officials. Since the days of Richelieu Huguenots had been barred from settling in the colony, and the clergy and the civil authorities were very nervous on this score. Owing to the proximity of the Protestant English colonies, the French feared that in the event of war the Huguenots would ally themselves with their co-religionists.[5] They could remember all too clearly the events in France of only a few years back, when the Huguenots had fought against the Crown in alliance with the English, and also with Catholic Spain on occasion. The English were in much greater strength than the French in North America, and only the previous year they had captured New Amsterdam from the Dutch and renamed it New York; hence this danger seemed very real. Moreover, the presence of a sizable body of Huguenots practising their religion in New France would have been the source of bitter disputes that could only have disrupted, weakened, and perhaps wrecked the colony. In the seventeenth century, religious tolerance was not regarded as a virtue but as a source of grave weakness.

In New France the authorities had enough trouble as it was, keeping the peace between rival factions of the Roman clergy. Between the Jesuits and the Sulpicians no love was lost and the latter let slip no opportunity to criticize covertly the work and methods of the Jesuit missionaries.[6] In the face of these attacks the Jesuits, being much better disciplined than the Sulpicians,[7] maintained a cold silence which was in itself infuriating. Colbert, however, was extremely suspicious of the Jesuits. He had informed both Tracy and Talon that they had caused much trouble in the past by encroaching in the sphere of the civil authorities. He instructed Tracy and the Intendant to prevent this occurring in the future; the Jesuits were to be kept firmly in their place. Shortly after his arrival in the colony Talon reported that if this had been their habit in the past, they had certainly changed their ways and he did not anticipate any trouble on this score in the future.[8] For their part the Jesuits were well impressed by Talon and by his plans for the development of the colony. Unfortunately, this mutual esteem was soon to be dispelled.

There can be no doubt that, under the old régime the clergy had exercised considerable authority and even greater influence in the colony's affairs. This was, to some extent, due to the character of Bishop Laval. An exceptionally strong-willed and exceedingly devout man, François Montmorency de Laval was willing to make any sacrifice for the advancement of the faith, and to oppose anything that seemed detrimental to it, with the utmost vigour. In his character there was no discernible trace of humour, and for him compromise was virtually impossible. Since he was always convinced of his own rectitude, any who opposed his views he tended to regard as opposing the faith, and when their views prevailed he was able to ascribe this only to God's punishment for the colony's sins.

With the appointment of an intendant in the colony, the Bishop's influence and authority in civil matters was greatly diminished, and he soon found this official exercising powers that previously had devolved on him. Although the Bishop retained his seat on the Sovereign Council, in 1665 he was deprived of the right to appoint, jointly with the governor, the members of the Council. This right was to be restored briefly in 1674, only to be removed again the following year. With this prerogative gone the Bishop's influence in the Council waned, and he attended its meetings less frequently. In fact, clerical authority in civil affairs ended, because there was no longer any need for it. The intendant now fulfilled the function the clergy had sought to discharge, and the clerics accepted this change with good grace because they were, on the whole, well-enough satisfied with the civil administration established by the intendants. In any event, they knew only too well that it would do no good to protest.

That the secular officials were now firmly in control was made apparent from the moment that Tracy, Courcelle, and Talon set foot in the colony. As soon as they arrived they convened the existing Sovereign Council, but only to have their commissions and the letters patent of the *Compagnie de l'Occident* officially registered. They had been empowered to reconstitute this body, reinstating or replacing the incumbent councillors as they saw fit. They decided, however, to wait until they had had sufficient opportunity to judge the characters, merits, and talents of those considered suitable for posts on the Council. In the meantime, Jean Talon dealt with the backlog of civil cases himself as he was empowered to do by his commission. Not until early in December 1666 was the Sovereign Council reconstituted with Villeray, Gorribon, Tilly, Damours, and Tesserie appointed as councillors in that order of seniority; Bourdon was reappointed Attorney General, and Peuvret de Mesnu, Clerk and Secretary. The agent of the *Compagnie de l'Occident*, Barrois, was also given a seat on the Council. It is worthy of note that Villeray, Tilly, Damours, Bourdon, and Peuvret had been members of the original Council, all but Damours and Tilly having been dismissed by Mésy, while Tesserie had been a member of Mésy's unconstitutional council. Gorribon, who had been a member of the Judicial Tribunal of Marennes in France, was a newcomer to the colony.

With the re-establishment of the Sovereign Council, and with an intendant of justice, administration, and finance in the colony, the governmental framework of New France had at last achieved the form that it was to retain, with some significant modifications, down to the end of the French régime. Under this system all power and authority stemmed from the King who ruled by divine right, a principle that was generally accepted and certainly not challenged during Louis XIV's reign. Yet to say that Louis XIV was an absolute monarch could be misleading. He was not absolute in the sense that the latter-day dictators have made themselves absolute; in fact, he seemed to be far more an absolute ruler than he actually was, and this is the measure of his skill as a politician; he had a very acute sense of the limits to which he could go and he never exceeded them; thus there appeared to be no opposition and he appeared to be absolute. But far more frequently than was generally known Louis was unable to take action, or was obliged to make unpalatable decisions to avoid bringing latent opposition into the open. Moreover, absolute rule by the monarch was impossible because it was quite beyond the powers of one man. Although Louis was a prodigious worker, which at first caused considerable wonder and amusement at the Court, he could not concern himself with everything that the government was required to do.

The chief aim of Colbert and Louis XIV was to create a highly centralized efficient administration, with all important policy decisions made by the ministers, with Louis's concurrence. To the vast majority of the French people this did not appear as tyranny but as a long overdue reform, bringing order and freedom from oppression by local tyrants out of the recent chaos. Colbert made it plain that he wanted the people of France, and New France, to enjoy the maximum personal liberty to go about their work, always provided that their work suited his long-range plans to increase the wealth of the kingdom.[9]

In New France, owing to the difficulty of communications with the central government when the colony was cut off from all contact with Europe for six or seven months in the year, and dispatches could not normally be answered within a twelvemonth, some degree of discretion had to be permitted the local officials. Yet they were still little more than administrators. All major policy matters, and many seemingly trivial ones, had to be referred to the Minister; he depended to a very large degree on the advice of the men on the spot before making a decision, and they had to keep him informed in the greatest detail of local conditions and all that occurred. Once he had found efficient administrators for his departments, he read few of these dispatches himself. Since they frequently ran to fifty and more folio pages this is not to be wondered at; but he did read the abstracts made of them by his *commis*, who left a wide margin for his terse comments and decisions. On the basis of these comments the *commis* then drafted the Minister's reply in the language and style of Colbert himself. Under Colbert this system worked very well but it required a minister who had both wide knowledge and a great capacity for work.

Louis XIV also sent a lengthy dispatch to the governor and intendant in each of the colonies every year. These dispatches, however, merely repeated in more general terms the instructions to the Minister and they were, in fact, actually drafted by the Minister, then written in Louis XIV's customary style by one of his four private secretaries. His signature was then appended by the first secretary *qui avait la plume*, that is, the authority to forge Louis's signature on the massive pile of correspondence that went out over his name. This is not to say that Louis was not informed of all that went on; he was, and by Colbert, but he preferred to be informed orally in a few sentences; he did not like having to read any but the most important state papers dealing with foreign policy and war. And considering the vast amount of work to be attended to, the masses of dispatches, letters, and memoirs that flowed in from all corners of the kingdom, Louis could never have dealt with even a fraction of it. To a large degree, Louis XIV, and the kingdom, were dependent on the ministers, they dependent on their *commis*, who in turn had to rely on the provincial officials. Thus, when New France had a good governor and intendant, the people had relatively good government; when they did not, some among them were always quick to inform the Minister and he was equally quick to investigate complaints. An intendant or a governor, who failed to heed the Minister's warnings to mend his ways could not expect to retain his post for long.

In New France itself the Governor General held the senior post. Almost without exception he was a noble and a soldier. He represented the King, and his orders could be questioned but not challenged by the subordinate officials. He could veto any decision made by the intendant, or the Sovereign Council and the junior officials, but he could do so only in extreme cases and he had to justify his action to the Minister. Colbert sent repeated orders to the governors that they were not to interfere with the work of the officers of justice unless they were convinced that these officials were abusing their authority. Thus, apart from military affairs and diplomatic relations with the Indian nations, the governor's only real functions were to hold a watching brief over colonial affairs to ensure that the other officials discharged their duties honestly and efficiently and report them to the Minister when they did not; and to serve as a figurehead, a living symbol of the King's authority.

The intendant was undoubtedly the most important official in New France. Receiving a salary of twelve thousand *livres* a year, as much as the governor who, however, received an additional twelve thousand a year for expenses, the intendant was responsible for the civil administration of the colony, for ensuring that the people received swift and impartial justice, and for the colony's finances. In France the office of intendant had begun as a military appointment, in which men would be appointed to the armies campaigning in foreign lands to care for civil matters in the occupied areas and to serve the army in a non-combatant capacity. This had proved to be so successful an innovation that intendants had eventually been appointed in the French provinces to strengthen the royal power in areas threatened by the turbulent nobility. Under Richelieu, the powers previously enjoyed by the provincial governors had been whittled away and given to the intendants. The men appointed to these posts were always skilled administrators, well educated, and usually with a sound legal training. Invariably, they were recruited from among the *noblesse de robe*,* usually after they had proven themselves in more junior posts. They were essentially career men, whose prospects for promotion in the royal service depended on the manner in which they performed their duties rather than on influential connections at the court.

When the intendant travelled about the colony, he was accompanied by two archers, and in religious processions he walked at the head, beside the governor. In the cathedral at Quebec and in the parish church of Montreal a place of honour was always reserved for him. In these ways were the people constantly reminded of the high dignity of his office. In fact, his activities affected them continually. He was responsible for the maintenance of law and order, and for ensuring that the people obtained swift justice before the courts. He was held responsible in no small measure for the development of the colony's economy and was continually urging the *habitants* to clear more land, raise more cattle, and experiment with new crops such as hemp or flax. He was, in fact, as the King's servant, to act virtually *in loco parentis* to the King's subjects in the colony. The instructions given to Jean Talon in 1665 made this very clear:

The King, considering all his Canadian subjects from the highest to the

---

* The *noblesse de robe* (nobility of the robe) was the order of nobility to which entrance was gained by the acquisition of certain high offices, the title going with the office. The long robe of the legal profession was the distinguishing mark of many of these offices, hence the name, distinguishing the members of the *noblesse de robe* from the descendants of the feudal aristocracy, known as the *noblesse d'épée* (nobility of the sword).

lowest as though they were virtually his own children, and wishing to fulfil the obligation he is in to extend to them the benefits and the felicity of his rule, as much as to those who reside in France, the Sieur Talon will study above all things how to assist them in every way and to encourage them in their trade and commerce, which alone can create abundance in the country and cause the families to prosper.[10]

And, in the instructions given to the intendants who succeeded Talon, this major premise of Louis XIV's reign was spelled out in more detail. Jean Bochart de Champigny, in 1686, was instructed:

His Majesty wishes him to know that his entire conduct must lead to two principal ends; the one to ensure that the French inhabitants established in that country enjoy complete tranquillity among themselves, and are maintained in the just possession of all that belongs to them, and the other to conserve the said inhabitants and to increase their numbers by all means possible. . . .

His Majesty wishes him to visit once a year all the habitations that are situated between the Gulf and the Island of Montreal, to inform himself of all that goes on, pay heed to all the inhabitants' complaints and their needs, and attend to them as much as he possibly can, and so arrange it that they live together in peace, that they aid each other in their necessities and that they be not diverted from their work.[11]

In New France the intendant also had a great many military duties to discharge. In fact, when the colony was at war these were among the most important of his functions; the success or failure of military operations were to no small extent dependent on how efficiently he discharged these responsibilities. He was responsible for paying, feeding, and clothing the troops, keeping them supplied with arms and munitions, arranging for their billets – there were no barracks in the colony – and, when necessary, for their hospitalization. He also had to allocate materials and labour for work on the colony's fortifications, as well as transport and supplies during campaigns. It was, however, the governor who decided what use to make of the available men and material. In all such matters the governor was expected to confer with the intendant; once a decision to undertake military measures had been reached by the governor, the intendant provided the necessary supplies and labour; then kept the governor informed as to their cost.[12]

There was, unavoidably, some overlapping of the powers of the governor and intendant, and in the early years of royal government this resulted in considerable friction. This was the fault, not so much of the system, but of the parties involved, and these conflicts did result in the powers of the governor, the intendant, and the officers of justice being more clearly defined by the King. The authority of the intendant was thereby considerably enhanced at the expense of the governor. The latter official, however, still represented the King, his was the supreme authority, and subordinate officials were not allowed to defy, or even to be too critical of him lest it establish a dangerous precedent that might conceivably lead to defiance of the monarch himself. Louis XIV and his ministers could recall all too clearly the events of the Fronde and the recent shocking developments in England where opposition to the King had led to civil war, regicide, and the establishment of that most detestable of all things, a republic. It was, therefore, never the intention that the intendant would serve as a check on the governor, or the governor on the intendant. The system of checks and balances was quite foreign to the thinking of Louis XIV and Colbert; in fact, they would never have tolerated such a notion for a moment.

In the Sovereign Council the intendant quickly became the dominant figure. Although occupying the third place in rank in the Council, after the governor and bishop, it was the intendant who came to preside over the meetings. Considering the manner in which the Council deliberated and reached its decisions, this was of considerable importance. When a case was heard, the attorney general first gave his statement and opinion on the facts of the case, the presiding officer then "asked for the opinions, collected the voices and delivered the judgements." This meant that each councillor in turn, beginning with the most junior, declared his views and gave his verdict; when all had been heard, the presiding officer then rendered a decision in accordance with what he took to be the general or majority opinion. No motions were made and no votes taken, which meant in effect that the verdicts of the Sovereign Council were those of the presiding officer acting on the advice of the other members. Since in the early days of the Council its members had had no legal training, except that which they might have culled for themselves from books on jurisprudence – Villeray being the only one of the early Council who troubled to do this[13] – and had no other basis for their judgement than their own common sense and a knowledge of the people and conditions in the colony, such a system had much to recommend it.

Appeals from the verdicts of the Sovereign Council could, in theory, be taken to the *Conseil des Parties* in France. Although it was very expensive, many persons in the colony began to avail themselves of this recourse. Eventually Colbert, who had to make a decision for the King on all such cases after receiving the deliberations of this supreme court of appeal, became quite incensed. Declaring irately that a governor and an intendant had been sent by the King, and a Sovereign Council established, to deal with such matters in the colony where the circumstances were known rather than in Paris where they were not, in 1677 he sent all the cases then pending back to the Sovereign Council in Quebec.[14] Thus, in effect, the Sovereign Council became the supreme court of appeal for Canada.

In petty civil cases, those where amounts of 100 *livres* or less were involved, the intendant was empowered to deal with them alone and appeals against his judgements could be taken to the Sovereign Council. Since they were dealt with by the intendant very swiftly and there were no fees, this system was a great boon to the *habitants* and also to the merchants. In other civil cases the intendant could offer to arbitrate or serve as *juge consul*, but he could not oblige litigants to have their cases brought before him rather than before the courts. In August 1667 Talon and de Tracy, in an attempt to facilitate the work of the courts, had an edict passed by the Council whereby Talon could examine all the litigation and cases pending, then decide by which body each one should be handled: the Sovereign Council, the Prévôté Court, or by himself alone. Courcelle, however, registered his objection to this *ordonnance* on two occasions, declaring that it was contrary to the authority vested in the governor of the colony and harmful to the public weal. This objection presaged further conflicts between the Governor and the Intendant which eventually had to be settled by Louis XIV himself.

One peculiarity of the legal system of New France was the absence of lawyers in the colony, but when account is taken of the venality of the legal profession in France at this time, the colony was fortunate to be spared them. In 1682, when the Intendant Jacques de Meulles first arrived in the colony, he remarked, "Never was anything so fittingly done as to ensure that there would be no lawyers or attorneys here."[15] The drawing up of contracts and work of that sort was performed by notaries; by the end of the century there was enough of this to warrant four notaries at Quebec, three at Montreal, and one at Trois Rivières.[16]

To prevent possible abuses a committee of the Sovereign Council drew up a tariff of fees which could be charged by the officers of justice – judges, procureurs, notaries, clerks, and bailiffs. After study and amendment by the King in council the list was promulgated in 1678. The most noteworthy features of this tariff were its comprehensiveness and the moderateness of the fees. The highest was 8 *livres* a day that a judge could charge when he was required to travel into the countryside on a civil case. For interrogating a witness he could charge only 1 *livre* 4 *sols*, and royal notaries could charge the same amount for searching a title. In criminal cases the fees were of the same order. It is small wonder then that the Canadians were notoriously litigious; they could afford to be.[17]

The great influx of soldiers, settlers, and indentured labourers after 1665 led, inevitably, to an increase in the incidence of crime, particularly crimes of violence. According to the charter of the *Compagnie de l'Occident*, the law code of the colony was to be the *Coutume de Paris*. This legal system differed considerably from that employed in Canada today. It differed also from that employed in England in the seventeenth century, but in some significant respects the French system compares favourably with that of England until near the end of the century. There was, for example, no imprisonment for debt in New France, nor could a farmer's cattle or farm implements be seized for debt. Unlike in England, human rights were more important than property rights.

When a crime was committed in New France the judge of a lower court or the Attorney General of the Sovereign Council questioned all who might have knowledge of the crime and ordered the arrest of the likeliest suspect. The prisoner was then interrogated under oath by the judge or Attorney General, without his being informed of the charges against him. This was known as the *question ordinaire*. If the prisoner proved recalcitrant under questioning he could be subjected to torture, the *question extraordinaire*, inflicted by the *maître des hautes oeuvres*. Once adequate evidence had been obtained the accused was brought to trial and he now, for the first time, was able to confront the witnesses who had given evidence against him in sworn statements, which they would be loath to change or qualify under the accused's questioning lest they be later charged with perjury. In England at this time, too, it should be noted an accused was not allowed legal counsel before or during a trial since the burden of proof rested with the prosecution;[18] moreover, the death penalty could be invoked for the theft of property worth more than a shilling.[19]

If the accused were found guilty the judge, or judges, then meted out punishment that fitted not only the crime but the circumstances of the crime. Thus the death penalty might be imposed for one murder, a lengthy sentence to the galleys for another. All severe sentences by a lower court in the colony – death, corporal punishment, the galleys, or banishment from the colony – had to be appealed to the Sovereign Council. Sometimes this court of appeal ordered a new trial and very frequently reduced the sentence to one much less severe.[20]

When an accused was found guilty, as was usually the case, punishment followed swiftly and was harsh. Prisons were regarded as places to keep persons awaiting trial or sentence, not as houses of correction where criminals were lodged in idleness at the Crown's expense. Thus, monetary fines, sentence to the galleys, torture – ranging from being placed in the stocks and subjected to public ridicule, to being branded with a red-hot iron or broken on the wheel – or death, were the penalties for crime. Men convicted of crimes such as murder or rape usually heard their sentence in the morning and suffered it in the afternoon; rarely were they kept waiting as long as three days before the sentence was carried out. Those convicted of such crimes were marched from the prison through the streets of the town, barefooted and clad only in their shirt, with a rope about their necks and carrying a lighted torch, to the steps of the parish church where they knelt to beg forgiveness of God and the King. From there they were led to the public square where they were hanged from the gibbet. Once dead, their heads and right hands were severed and nailed to a post in plain view to serve as a deterrent to others. Frequently the sentence called for the severing of the right hand before being hanged, but this was usually commuted by the court as an act of clemency. Harsh though such punishments may seem, they were in keeping with the temper of the age and were intended to serve as a deterrent.

Although on the increase, criminal cases occupied comparatively little of the Sovereign Council's time. Royal edicts had to be registered and enforced but the Council could, and several times did, send a remonstrance to the King which resulted in a royal amendment to the original edict. But the Council's main occupation was dealing with civil litigation and administrative regulations for the colony: the regulation of weights, measures, currency; of market days and urban traffic; building regulations in the towns; the fixing of fair prices of foodstuffs in times of shortage, and of consumer goods to prevent profiteering. In fact, all the regulations needed for a well-ordered society were enacted by the intendant either alone or with the Sovereign Council. Over the years, however, the intendants referred less and less of this administrative legislation to the Council, which thus became mainly a court of law.

Prior to the establishment of Royal government the people of Quebec, Montreal, and Trois Rivières had elected syndics to represent their interests in the Council at Quebec. The office was retained, with interruptions and modifications after 1663, but subsequently was quietly suppressed on the instructions of Colbert. In 1673 he informed Frontenac: "It will be necessary when the colony is stronger than it is at present, quietly to abolish the syndic who presents requests in the name of all the *habitants*, it being a good thing that each man speak for himself and that no one speaks for all."[21]

It would be an error to claim that the demise of this office was the death of representative government, for the syndics had never had any legislative authority. They had merely made the wishes of the people known to the Council at Quebec on occasion. With an intendant in the colony, one of whose duties was to listen to any complaints the people might have and to take action when it seemed warranted, the need for a syndic disappeared. This might seem a retrograde step to persons of the present day and age, but to the Canadians of the seventeenth century it was merely a natural development in the trend toward a more efficient form of administration. When, however, major issues came up which affected all the people in the colony, or of a certain area, assemblies were held to solicit the views of the people before administrative action was taken. The Brandy Parliament of 1678 was one such. The King ordered that an assembly of twenty leading residents of the colony, engaged in the fur trade, be convened to give their views on whether or not the sale of liquor to the Indians should be subject to restrictions. Upon the basis of their expressed opinions the King issued an edict which, despite the strong opposition of the Governor and of Colbert himself, did impose restrictions.[22] Again, in 1695, Frontenac and Champigny held an assembly of the leading citizens of Quebec to discover their views on regulating the price of meat during a time of chronic shortage. The Intendant was opposed to the fixing of prices on principle, but the assembly disagreed with him and the price of meat was duly regulated.[23] In all, seventeen such assemblies were held between 1672 and 1700.[24] In 1702, however, when the Governor and Intendant called a meeting of all the citizens of Quebec to solicit their views on a proposal to eliminate the *quart* on beaver, so few people bothered to attend that the assembly was deferred until the following year.[25]

There was one rather intriguing suggestion for the establishment of representative government in New France, a Canadian Estates General in fact, put forward by the Intendant Jean Bochart de Champigny in 1700. The manner in which he discusses this scheme is rather mysterious. His remarks on the subject are contained in a dispatch to the Minister dated October 15, 1700:

If you adopt some resolution, Monseigneur, to make this colony a *pays d'états*, the assembly could be composed of the Governor-General who would preside over it, the Bishop and the Intendant, the last having a deliberative voice with the other two; he would be responsible for the gathering of the voices and for writing up what transpires. The other members would be two deputies from the clergy, two from the Sovereign Council, a judge of the Quebec Prévôté, the judge of Trois Rivières and the one of the Montreal, two seigneurs from the parishes of each of the local governments who would be deputed by the gentlemen and seigneurs, three merchants of Quebec deputed by the city, one of Trois Rivières and two of Montreal. In this assembly the affairs of the province would be decided by the plurality of votes and it would see to the levying of the tax that the province would be required to furnish. There, Monseigneur, are my views, in accord with the slight knowledge that I have of what the practice is in the *pays d'états*. If you desire further explanations, please take the trouble, Monseigneur, to have some *memoires* sent me in order that I may indicate to you my thoughts on their contents.[26]

Unfortunately, it is impossible to divine what stimulated Champigny to write this rather enigmatic proposal, and no matter what he had in mind, nothing ever came of it.

One new office did emerge shortly after royal government was instituted, and that was the office of captain of militia. In 1669 Courcelle was ordered by Louis XIV to establish militia companies throughout the colony, comprising all the able-bodied men, and to see to it that they were trained in the use of arms. In each district in the colony a captain was appointed to command the local militia unit and, although he received no pay, his position did carry a great deal of prestige. Chosen from among the *habitants*, these *capitaines de milice* by the very nature of their office were the most respected men in their communities, the men to whom the *habitants* naturally turned for leadership. In many instances they were more respected than the seigneurs and their function was, if anything, of greater importance, for in addition to their military duties they had civil functions to perform; they acted as the intendant's agents in the rural districts, communicating his orders to the *habitants* and seeing to it that they were carried out. In fact, when the intendant ordered a *corvée* for work on roads or bridges, the *capitaines de milice* were in charge, and the seigneurs, who had to do their share of the work, did so under the militia captains' orders. Just how these officers were appointed is not known, but of necessity they had to be men acceptable to those serving under them, and to this extent they might be claimed to have supplied a vestige of representative government. In any event, their importance should not be minimized for they performed in New France much the same function as the justices of the peace in seventeenth-century England; but unlike the English justices of the peace the Canadian *capitaines de milice* were of the common people, hence they did much to integrate the administration with the general mass of society. This also ensured that the seigneurs as a group or class could not become too powerful and oppress the *habitants* or pose a threat in any way to the royal authority. Within a few years of the establishment of the *capitaines de milice*, they had become a vital cog in the administrative machinery; in fact, it is difficult to see how the colony could have been governed effectively without them.

The system of government and administration established in both France and New France by Louis XIV and Colbert was patently authoritarian and paternalistic. Yet it could not be said that it was arbitrarily imposed on the people; the system developed naturally out of French society and its historical circumstances. At this period the great mass of the people had no desire for self-government; were quite incapable of it even if they had been able to conceive of it. What they wanted was sound and equitable government: and this Louis XIV and his ministers tried, with remarkable success, to give them. The main reason for this success is, oddly enough, the reason why a later age vigorously condemned it,[27] that it was so paternalistic. Yet this paternalism was really nothing more than a manifestation of the sense of responsibility that the King had, and was expected to have, for the well-being of his subjects. Certainly, in 1665 the people of New France had good cause to believe that, with the establishment of this authoritarian, paternalistic régime, their future was much brighter.

CHAPTER 4

Military and Economic Foundations

Before Colbert's ambitious plans for Canada could be implemented, one major obstacle had to be removed: the constant harrying attacks by the Iroquois. With the arrival of the Carignan-Salières regiment the means was at hand to cope with the problem. At this time the Iroquois were being weakened by the ravages of smallpox and in addition they were being hard pressed by their foes, the Mohicans and Andastes. Upon hearing that a large number of troops had arrived at Quebec, their chiefs were quick to make overtures for peace. They sent a delegation of six Onondagas and an Oneida captain, including the great chiefs Garakontié and Hotreouati, to discuss a peace settlement with Tracy. The French put little trust in their declarations; too many times in the past had the Iroquois been guilty of rank treachery to allow any faith to be placed in what they now had to say. Tracy therefore gave them little satisfaction, but he was rather perturbed to discover that they already knew he was planning a campaign against the Mohawks. Preparations for this campaign went on apace, however, and it was decided to try to take the enemy unawares by launching the attack early in January 1666. This was, to say the least, rather rash. To march with an army of some six hundred troops, all but seventy or eighty just recently arrived from Europe, through the wilderness in the depths of winter into the heart of the enemy country, even though the Mohawks numbered only three to four hundred fighting men, was to invite disaster.

Nevertheless, on January 9 the little army left Quebec, commanded by the Governor, Courcelle. By the time it had reached Trois Rivières several of the men were suffering severely from the intense cold. At Fort St Louis some of the troops, whose limbs were badly frozen, were replaced by members of the garrisons of the forts along the Richelieu. Here they were also joined by seventy *habitants* from Montreal. Courcelle expected a party of Algonquins to join his forces to guide him to the Mohawk villages, but when they had not appeared by the 29th he set off without them. The snow in the forest was four feet deep and the men had to march on snowshoes, a skill which they had had no opportunity to master. Moreover, each man, including the officers and even Courcelle himself, had to carry his supplies and weapons on his back. At night, more dead than alive, they had to bed down in the snow, wondering if they would ever see the settlements of New France again, and many of them past caring. To make matters worse, the lack of guides caused the army to follow innumerable false trails. Hardly knowing which way they were heading they eventually, on February 15, found themselves close to the Dutch settlement of Schenectady. Unaware that they were three days' march from the enemy villages, when they encountered a Mohawk hunting-party which fled precipitately at their approach, Courcelle sent a detachment of sixty men in pursuit. When the fleeing Mohawks led his men into an ambush, he got his first taste of Indian-style warfare. An officer and ten men were killed and several others wounded, while the Mohawks lost only three of their warriors.

As soon as word of the presence of the French was received at Albany, three of the leading inhabitants went to demand of Courcelle why he had marched so large a force into the dominions of his Britannic Majesty without informing the Governor of the province of his intentions. Neither Courcelle nor the authorities at Albany were aware that England and France were then at war and had been for the past fortnight. Courcelle, in fact, was surprised to learn that the English had gained title to the province from the Dutch, and he ruefully commented with unwitting prescience "that the King of England did grasp at all America." He assured the Albany authorities, however, that he had no intention of molesting the English King's subjects or of attempting to conquer his territory; instead he requested permission to purchase provisions for his troops and asked that his wounded might be cared for in Albany, it being plain that they could not survive the march back to Canada. When the emissaries offered himself and his troops all the accommodation that Schenectady afforded, Courcelle declined with thanks, knowing full well that if his men once got near a chimney corner it would be very difficult to make them continue to march. Seven of the wounded were taken to Albany where they were cared for by the Dutch, who also provided the army with food supplies and were well paid for it.

While these negotiations were going on it had continued to rain heavily, and it was feared that the ice on the lakes and rivers might open if the thaw continued; therefore, on Sunday night, February 21, the army broke camp and began the return march. At Lake Champlain the food cached for the return journey was found to have been despoiled. With Mohawk war parties pursuing them the men struggled back as best they could, the fit carrying those unable to walk. It was not until March 8 that Courcelle and his bedraggled little army reached Fort St Louis. More than sixty men, weakened by hunger, had dropped in their tracks during the march and frozen to death. An English official at Albany later commented: "surely soe bould and hardy an attempt (circumstances considered) hath not hapned in any age."[1]

Although only very slight damage had been inflicted on the Mohawks, the mere fact that the French had been able to march an army into their country during the winter had a profound effect, more particularly when the Iroquois learned from the prisoners they had taken that another campaign was intended the following summer. By then, however, more than punitive expeditions by the French against the aborigines was at issue; in fact, European and North American power politics had become extremely involved, in some ways inhibiting the spreading of hostilities among the Europeans in North America, in others presaging the momentous conflicts to come.

In Europe, England and the Dutch Netherlands had been at war since March 1665. Louis XIV, who was bound by a mutual defence treaty to aid the Dutch, tried to negotiate a settlement, failed, then remained neutral until the Duke of York gained a naval victory over the Dutch fleet at Lowestoft. Fearing that this would give England a preponderance of naval power just when France was beginning to establish her own navy, Louis finally honoured his treaty obligations to the Dutch and declared war on England in January 1666; but France still took no active military measures against England. As soon, however, as navigation to Canada opened, instructions were sent to Tracy to examine whether it would be best to refrain from hostilities with the English colonies, or to attack them. If it appeared that they could be easily conquered, he was empowered to do so; if neutrality seemed the more prudent course, he was to follow it but not to undertake any negotiations to this end, only to entertain any proposals for neutrality they might make; for to open such negotiations would lower the prestige of the French crown. Although he gave Tracy a free hand in this vital matter, Louis XIV made it clear that the conquest of the northern English colonies would be preferable to the maintenance of the status quo.[2]

In Canada, meanwhile, prior to the receipt of these instructions, Tracy and Courcelle had organized another campaign against the Iroquois. Two war parties of two hundred men each were formed, and were ready to march when word was received from Albany that the Iroquois desired peace. At this Courcelle informed the authorities at Albany that the French expedition had been recalled and that the Iroquois embassy would be given safe conduct. After the Iroquois chiefs had arrived, and while peace terms were being discussed, a war party killed seven French, including four officers, who had gone hunting. Tracy regarded this as rank treachery, taxed the Albany authorities with being a partner to it, and declared the peace negotiations to be at an end. On July 24 two hundred French troops and ninety allied Indians, commanded by the Sieur de Sorel, were sent to attack the Iroquois. When they were some fifty miles from the Mohawk villages an Iroquois embassy met them; they were on their way to Quebec to make amends for the breach of the truce and had with them some French prisoners whom they were returning as a display of their good faith. The expedition then turned back and the peace negotiations were resumed at Quebec.

While these negotiations were underway the first ships of the year reached Quebec with the dispatches from the Court. When it was learned that France, allied with the United Provinces, was at war with England, the entire military situation appeared in a new light. Talon was firmly of the opinion that no peace treaty should be negotiated with the Iroquois until after they had been crushed in a full-scale campaign. He pointed out that twelve hundred regular troops, munitions, and supplies had been sent from France at great expense for this express purpose; moreover, past events had shown all too clearly that no trust could be placed in any assurance the Iroquois might give or treaty they might sign. No better time than the present, he argued, would be found for a campaign, since the Mohawks, relying on the recent peace negotiations, would not be on their guard, and once the Mohawks were crushed the way would be open to attack Albany. There was also good cause to hope that the Dutch residents of New York would welcome the French as liberators from English rule, and this would remove the danger of an English assault on Canada.[3] These arguments were more than adequate to convince Tracy and Courcelle. Talon immediately set to work organizing transport and supplies. By September 14 one thousand regular troops and four hundred *habitants* were mobilized, ready for the campaign.

In the English colonies, too, there was some debate as to what action to take now that England and France were at war. Early in July Governor Richard Nicolls of New York had received premature reports that seven hundred French troops were marching towards Albany. He immediately appealed to the authorities in New England to join their forces with his, destroy this French army, and then go on to conquer Canada; but he received no satisfaction whatever, owing to the involved alliances of these colonies with the neighbouring Indian tribes. New York derived considerable commercial benefits from the trade in furs with the Iroquois, and hence had no desire to see them crushed by the French. New England, however,

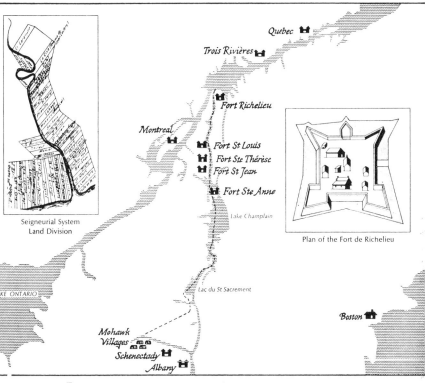

Seigneurial System
Land Division

Plan of the Fort de Richelieu

1 : *From a contemporary map for Tracy's campaign, 1666.*

and more particularly Connecticut, had to maintain good relations with the Mohicans on their borders, and this nation was the ancient and bitter foe of the Iroquois; thus the authorities in New England had no desire to aid the Mohawks, and they had a hard time persuading the Mohicans not to join with the French in the campaign against their old foes. It was also argued that the terrain between New England and New France was "an uninhabited mountaineous wilderness" where roamed a "multitude of barbarous heathen that may be feared to be treacherous." It was also claimed that it was too late in the season, and New England therefore excused itself from making any move to aid New York against the French.[4] This was not to be the last occasion when disunity in the English colonies would render Canada immune from attack.

On September 28 the French forces, led by Tracy and Courcelle, accompanied by one hundred Hurons and Algonquins, set out from Fort Ste Anne

on Lake Champlain in a fleet of light boats and canoes. When they dis-
embarked at the foot of the lake and began their long march through the
forest, ablaze with autumn colour, they were quickly discovered by an
Iroquois scouting party. Thus, when the army reached the first of the
Mohawk villages, they found it deserted. Quickly pressing on they found
the others likewise abandoned. At the most remote village, fortified by a
triple palisade twenty feet high, it appeared that the Mohawks had intended
to make a stand but they too had fled as the army approached. The only
humans found were some old men and women, too decrepit to flee, and
the mutilated bodies of two or three Mohicans, recently burned over a slow
fire. The four villages, containing over one hundred longhouses, and the
surrounding cornfields were then put to the torch, destroying the entire
food supply of the Mohawk nation. It was anticipated that as many would
die of starvation as would have been killed by French arms, had the enemy
stood and fought, and that those who survived would now be willing to
accept, and keep, such conditions for peace as the French might impose.

Before beginning the long march home Tracy marshalled his forces in
full battle array before the main village of Andaraque. A cross was planted,
and a post bearing the arms of Louis XIV. The cry Vive la roi rang out three
times through the forest; then Jean Baptiste de Bois, Sieur de Cocreaumont
et de St Morice, one time commander of the King's artillery in the army of
Italy, acting as deputy of the Intendant, claimed possession of the Mohawk
lands in the name of the King by right of conquest. By November 5 Tracy
was back at Quebec with the army, having lost only nine or ten men who
were drowned on Lake Champlain during a storm. The campaign had
proven to be little more than an arduous route march, but it had served
its purpose. The following July the Iroquois accepted Tracy's terms which
required the Five Nations to live at peace, not only with the French, but
with their Huron and Algonquin allies. It was clear to the authorities in
New France, however, that the Iroquois, still the greatest single military
force in North America, would remain at peace with the French only as
long as they had the Mohicans and Andastes to contend with. The French
now held the balance of power, but it was a precarious balance, and they
could only keep the Iroquois at peace by keeping them "in a state of fear."

The war in Europe had also ended. By the terms of the Treaty of Breda,
1667, Charles II returned Dunkirk and Acadia to France in exchange for
the islands of Antigua, Montserrat, and St Christopher in the West Indies.
It proved singularly difficult, however, to make William Temple, the English
Governor of Nova Scotia, comply with the treaty terms. He refused to
evacuate the province, claiming that the French had not handed over the

island of St Christopher, and that he had not received his promised indem-
nity of £16,200 from Charles II. After several protests from the French
ambassador, Charles II finally obliged Temple to submit and in July 1670
he, very reluctantly, handed the province over.[5] He was, however, very
much aware of the potential worth of the province's resources, so much
so in fact that in 1671, when Talon's deputy, the Sieur Patoulet, made a tour
of inspection of Acadia for Colbert, Temple approached him to solicit
his aid in obtaining French naturalization papers and title to his properties
at Port Royal.[6] Nothing, however, appears to have come of this.

The Chevalier de Grandfontaine was now appointed Governor of Acadia,
subordinate to the Governor at Quebec and at a salary one-tenth the
latter's emoluments. With fifty-odd regular troops, a lieutenant, and an
ensign, he was required to maintain French authority over some half-dozen
forts and settlements along the Atlantic and Bay of Fundy shores, and over
the wilderness of the interior from the Kennebec River to the St Lawrence
on the north and the Atlantic on the east, including Cape Breton. All
British subjects resident in these territories were to be allowed to remain
and retain all their property, upon taking an oath of allegiance to the King
of France. Those who preferred to remain British subjects were to be granted
one year to remove or dispose of their property.[7] Friendly relations were
to be maintained with Boston in order that supplies required by the province could be obtained there without difficulty, and to this end Grandfontaine was instructed to allow the New England fishermen to fish in
Acadian waters on the same terms as they had allowed the French before
the restitution.[8] Grandfontaine's main tasks, he was informed, were to
strengthen the province's defences, prepare a detailed report on the numbers
and condition of the inhabitants and, most important of all, discover the
best communication route to Quebec.[9] The following year thirty young
men and thirty girls were sent from France to augment the province's
meagre population of 389.[10]

When compared to the effort then being made to develop New France,
the aid afforded to Acadia appears pitifully inadequate. Colbert and Louis
XIV seem to have been content to regain title to the province, and then to
allow it to remain fallow, perhaps to wait until the plans for New France
had been implemented, perhaps because they were too preoccupied to
devote much attention to it. Whatever the reason, Acadia serves as a start-
ling contrast to New France; the one receiving negligible assistance from
the Crown and almost withering on the vine, the other receiving a vast
amount of aid over a short period and in consequence expanding by leaps
and bounds.

By August 1667, when the Seigneur de Tracy returned to France, his mission completed, and honoured and respected by all, much had already been accomplished in the Canadian colony. The Jesuit author of the *Relation* for 1666-67 put it very well when he wrote:

> Since the King has had the kindness to extend his protection over this country, by sending hither the *Régiment de Carignan-Salières*, we have witnessed a notable change in the appearance of Canada. We can assert that it is no longer the forbidding and frost-bound land which was formerly painted in so unfavourable colours, but a veritable New France – not only in the salubrity of its climate and fertility of its soil, but in the other conveniences of life, which are being revealed more and more every day.
>
> The Iroquois used to keep us so closely confined that we did not even dare till the lands that were under the cannon of the forts, much less go to a distance to ascertain the points of excellence of a soil which hardly differs at all from that of France.
>
> But now, since the fear of His Majesty's arms has filled these barbarians with alarm, and compelled them to seek our friendship, instead of constantly molesting us with bloody wars, as they used to, we are, during the calm, bringing to light the possibilities of this country's wealth, and the extent of its probable resources in the future.

With the security of the colony assured, Colbert was now able to put his plans for its economic development into effect. His first intention was to bring New France to the point where it could stand on its own feet without depending on military or economic support from the mother country. It had first of all to be made self-sufficient in the essentials: food, shelter, and clothing. In the detailed instructions given him before he left France, Talon was informed: "He will note that one of the greatest needs of Canada is to establish manufactures and to attract craftsmen to produce the things of daily use, for to date it has been necessary to transport to that country the cloth to clothe the people and even shoes that they might have something on their feet."

To make the colony self-supporting was the foundation for all Colbert's plans for the colony, but it was only the foundation. Colbert wanted the colony to provide a market for French manufactured goods, and to pay for these imports it had to export something of value. In the past, the colony's only export had been furs, but in recent years the price of beaver pelts on the European market had declined considerably. Moreover, this market was at the mercy of the vagaries of fashion; a narrower brim on men's beaver hats reduced the amount required, and the use of other materials such as rabbit fur played havoc with the beaver market. Thus, Colbert was very eager to have the colony's economy based on fishing, lumbering, mining, manufacturing, and trade with the West Indies. The Gulf of St Lawrence abounded in fish, whales, porpoises, and seals; there were limitless forests of oak, pine, and fir suitable for ship-building and timber; some deposits of coal had been located at Cape Breton and rumours of other mineral deposits were constant. The West Indies offered a sizable market for cheap foodstuffs to feed the plantation slaves, and for barrel staves to ship sugar and molasses.

Before these economic possibilities could be developed, however, three things were needed: capital, skilled labour, and enterprising men with managerial ability. The colony lacked all three, but Colbert and Talon made a prodigious effort to overcome the deficiency. The Minister sent as large a supply of labour as he could, but it was by no means easy to find skilled tradesmen who were willing to risk the voyage to Canada, and Colbert himself was partly to blame for this. Under his stimulus the French economy was developing rapidly; new industries were being founded, and old ones expanded. Thus in France there was a grave shortage of skilled workers. When Colbert did induce experienced tradesmen to emigrate to Canada he was merely robbing Peter to pay Paul. Moreover, he had to offer these men contracts for two or three years, stipulating considerably higher wages than were paid in France and guaranteeing that they could return to France when their contract expired. The amazing thing is, considering the shortage of labour in France resulting from the rapid expansion of both the economy and the armed forces, that Colbert sent as many able-bodied men and women to Canada as he did. Moreover, it cost the Crown 100 *livres* for each emigrant sent to Canada. Of this sum, however, thirty *livres* were reclaimed from their employers in the colony.[11]

Each year now Colbert sent to the colony up to five hundred men and one hundred and fifty girls of marriageable age. He gave firm instructions that those sent were to be physically fit and of good moral character, "for it is important," he commented, "in the establishment of a country to sow good seed."[12] Some young ladies of quality were also sent to become wives of the officers who had decided to remain in Canada. Several of the officers had not been in the colony long before they capitulated to the daughters of resident families, and were led to the altar. When the regiment was recalled to France in 1668 more than four hundred of the men chose to remain. Each man received a discharge grant of 100 *livres* or 50 *livres* and a year's rations; the sergeants received 150 *livres* or 100 *livres* and rations for a year. This, most likely, was more money than they had ever had at one time and must have been a strong inducement to remain in the colony. The following year, in emulation of the Roman colonizing schemes, six army captains came to Canada, each with a company of fifty men, and a total of twenty-four junior officers, with the express intention of settling on the land. The captains had no trouble recruiting men in France; in fact, they were thirty-three men over strength when they sailed.

Talon had hostels built to house the girls sent out by the King, but the aim was to get the girls married as quickly as possible. To encourage this, after the arrival of the immigrant ships, bachelors in the colony were forbidden to go hunting or fishing or to engage in the fur trade until all the King's girls were married. To encourage early marriages men marrying at twenty or younger, and girls at sixteen or less, received a wedding present of twenty *livres* from the King; parents whose sons were not married by the time they were twenty, and daughters by sixteen, had to be able to give good reasons or be liable to a fine. At the same time a system of "baby-bonuses" was inaugurated; parents with ten living legitimate children, none of whom had entered the clergy, received a pension of three hundred *livres* a year, and with twelve children, four hundred *livres* a year. Under this stimulus the population increased very rapidly; in 1666 it had grown to 5,870, and ten years later there were nearly 10,000 people in the colony. Cattle, sheep, horses, and goats were also sent out by the King as well as being imported by individuals. They throve exceedingly well; by 1668 there were 3,400 head of cattle in the colony, and Talon was able to inform Colbert that there was no need to send more livestock, that the colony was raising all it could support.

By this time almost all the land on both sides of the St Lawrence from below Quebec to Montreal was cleared and settled, and more was being cleared along the Richelieu.[13] The St Lawrence was, of course, the main thoroughfare of the colony, in summer by canoe or small boat, in winter by sleigh along the ice, and every settler wanted access to the river. Thus the land concessions had to be granted with river frontage, and as the population increased the concessions became narrow strips running far back from the river, with the farm house near the shore, until eventually houses were dotted at close intervals making the shores of the St Lawrence look rather like a sprawling village street. Attempts were made to have settlements established with compact villages, the *habitants'* houses clustered around the church, mill, and manor house, with the fields radiating out on all sides. Colbert wanted the land settled in this fashion because it would afford greater protection to the settlers in the event of attacks by the Iroquois, and also allow the authorities to keep a closer check on the activities of the *habitants*; but the attempts to inaugurate this system foundered. The *habitants* insisted on having river frontage; in fact, they really needed it, and in addition they did not take kindly to being herded together in villages.

The title to all land in the colony rested with the *Compagnie de l'Occident* until 1674, when it reverted to the Crown. There can be no doubt that this seigneurial system of land tenure had much to recommend it. It was based on ancient French legal principles and customs but modified considerably to suit conditions in the colony. It was, in fact, more a land settlement than a land-tenure system, for its main purpose was to get the land settled on an equitable basis. The Company, or the Crown, granted concessions of land to private individuals, referred to as seigneurs, who in return had to settle a certain number of *habitants* on their concession or seigneury. The seigneurs and the *habitants* had rights and obligations to each other which were precisely stated, and it was one of the main functions of the intendant to see to it that both the seigneurs and the *habitants* fulfilled their obligations. The seigneur, upon receiving a seigneury, had to perform the *acte de foi et hommage*, that is, bend the knee to the intendant and declare himself to be the King's vassal; this meant that he undertook to discharge all the obligations imposed on him as a seigneur. When required, he had to give a detailed account of his seigneury, the names of his *censitaires*, the dues he received from them, and the amount of land under cultivation. To prevent speculation in land, since it was granted not to enable the grantee to make a quick profit but to get it settled and cultivated, the *droit de quint*, one-fifth of the value of the concession, had to be paid to the Crown when a seigneury changed hands, except when it was inherited in line direct. After 1665 the concessions granted were not overly large; the Crown preferred to see a goodly number of modest-sized seigneuries rather than to have vast areas of the colony held by a few individuals who might someday become too powerful for comfort. In 1667 Talon refused to grant the Sieur de Sorel, an officer in the Carignan-Salières regiment, the 50,000 *arpents** that he requested; and this was only one of several such demands.[14]

The average size of the concessions granted by the seigneurs to their *censitaires* appears to have been about three *arpents* of river frontage and thirty *arpents* in depth, but as the population increased and since river frontage was limited these strips tended to become even narrower. The seigneurs usually retained for themselves only as much of their concession as they could work with the labour available, and labour was always in short supply. On each seigneury there was also a tract of common land for the pasturing of cattle which made improvement by selective breeding virtually impossible.

In addition to his obligations to the Crown the seigneur had obligations to his *censitaires*. He had to maintain a manor house on his seigneury, and when not in residence he had to leave someone responsible in charge. He was obliged to build a mill to grind the *habitants*' grain. This was an

---

* The *arpent* equalled approximately one and a half acres.

onerous and expensive undertaking, but if a seigneur failed to provide a mill within a reasonable time the intendant could force him to do so, or even have the mill built and make the seigneur pay the cost. If, however, a *censitaire* offered to build a mill the intendant would allow it. Since wheat bread was the staple of the people's diet – average consumption being two loaves of six to seven pounds a person a week – a mill was vital, and the fee for the grinding of wheat was fixed at one-fortieth of the flour ground. The seigneur also had to pay his share of the cost of the parish church and presbytery; if the church was built of stone, and when the supply of clergy permitted, he was given the advowson. Perhaps most significant of all, when a royal *corvée* was called – usually to work on roads and bridges – he had to do his share of the work along with his *censitaires*, under the orders of the local *capitaine de milice*.

The most important of the seigneur's obligations was to grant land to settlers: this was the main purpose of the system. The seigneur was obliged to have settlers on his concession and, when a *habitant* requested land, the seigneur could not refuse without justifying his refusal to the intendant. This, however, rarely happened, for a seigneur who failed to get settlers on his seigneury could have it taken away from him, and this did happen from time to time.* Thus, far from having *habitants* seeking land, the seigneurs were very anxious to get *habitants* to accept land on their concessions and they had to treat them well to keep them.

To compensate for these quite onerous obligations, the seigneur enjoyed certain specified prerogatives and privileges. Social status was all important, but in this period it was gauged on a scale quite different from that of today. The seigneur was clearly a member of an élite social class which was distinguished by the civil and ecclesiastical privileges accorded it. Since social life revolved around the church, most of the honours the seigneur received were of an ecclesiastical nature. He had a special pew in the parish church, in front of and to the right of the altar, with more leg room than the other pews. The parish priest always offered up prayers for the seigneur and his family; the seigneur had precedence in the church ritual, receiving the wafer at communion, the candles, and the incense before anyone else; he walked directly behind the priest in processions and he had the privilege of being buried in the church, beneath his pew. Here too, the intendant saw to it that he received the honours due him, and that he did not demand more. On May 1 the maypole was traditionally planted in front of the

---

* One of the first edicts registered by the Sovereign Council was an *arrêt* of the *Conseil d'Etat* dated March 21, 1663, declaring that all persons who had been granted land would have their concessions revoked if the land were not cleared within six months.

manor house; then the *censitaires* paid their *cens* to the seigneur, but on this he did not get rich since they consisted of only one or two *sols* per *arpent* of frontage, thus the average *cens* amounted to about fifty cents a year and was in fact merely a token payment. The planting of the maypole always called for a great celebration and more likely than not, the seigneur would be out of pocket.

The other dues accruing to the seigneur were hardly more remunerative. The *rentes* to be paid by the *censitaires* were stipulated in the title to the concession and could not be changed. They were usually about a *livre* for each *arpent* of frontage, that is, about three *livres* a year for each *censitaire*. Anyone purchasing a *censitaire's* land had to pay *lods et ventes*, amounting to one-twelfth of its value, to the seigneur. If a *censitaire* sold his land at too low a price, the seigneur could, within forty days, buy it in at that price. This was really only a device to curb speculation in land. The seigneurs could impose *corvées* on their *censitaires*, that is, oblige them to work on their seigneur's land for nothing, but this was no great imposition since the *corvée* days were strictly limited to three or four a year at most. Moreover, any *censitaire* could excuse himself from his seigneur's *corvée* by paying him two *livres* a day. The seigneur was entitled to a percentage of the fish caught by the *censitaire*; four barrels of eels a year, one-tenth of all porpoises caught, and one-twentieth of all other fish. Finally, if a *censitaire* failed to build a house, live on his concession and clear and cultivate it, the seigneur could appeal to the intendant who would quickly revoke the *censitaire's* title, whereat the land reverted to the seigneur's demesne.[15]

As a means of settling land this seigneurial system had a great deal to recommend it. Everything was carefully regulated; everyone, *censitaires* and seigneurs, knew exactly what his duties and his rights were, and the intendant was always there to ensure that all parties discharged their responsibilities and received their rights. The settlers were not pitched into the wilderness to fend for themselves; upon receiving free title to some 180 acres they became part of a well-organized social unit with a seigneur and, eventually, a parish priest and a *capitaine de milice* to provide counsel, guidance, and leadership. In more tangible things, there was a manor house, a church, and a mill on each seigneury to cater to their needs. For all this the *censitaires* paid the equivalent of approximately one hundred dollars a year in present-day money values. The *habitant* was thus well off; it was the seigneur who, in the seventeenth century, had a very hard time to make ends meet, and it is not to be wondered at if the Intendant Jacques Duchesneau remarked that, with few exceptions, it was difficult to tell the seigneur and his *censitaires* apart. A few years later the Intendant Champigny commented that the *habitants* "who really laboured on their land were well off, or at least lived very comfortably, having their fields, a goodly number of cattle and good fishing close to their homes."[16]

The great influx of troops, indentured labourers – many with their families – skilled tradesmen and the materials of their trades, not to mention cattle and livestock of all kinds, represented a considerable capital investment. Louis XIV meant what he said when, in 1665, he informed Talon, "His Majesty will contribute by opening his coffers, being well persuaded that he could not put a goodly sum of money to better use."[17] In all, the Crown during these first years of royal government was investing over 200,000 *livres* a year in the colony, over and above 36,000 a year for the fixed costs of the administration – the salaries of the officials and grants to the clergy. Colbert expected that eventually the colony would be able to provide its own capital for economic development, but in the meantime the pump had to be primed. Some of this capital went in direct subsidies to new industries. In 1671, for example, the Crown granted 40,000 *livres* to help establish the ship-building and lumber industries; 10,000 *livres* for preliminary work on some iron-ore deposits; and 600 *livres* to begin the manufacture of tar.*

In New France then, as in old France, economic development and expansion came about, not under the stimulus of private enterprise, but under the stimulus of the Crown; that is, of Colbert and his agent in Canada, the intendant. Jean Talon was an excellent example of the type of man now being attracted into the government service. In a later age and different country he would undoubtedly have become a captain of industry, and to a remarkable extent this is what he was in New France. Immediately after his arrival there, he had begun investigating the economic possibilities, discovering what the soil would grow, surveying the forests, and sending men out to search for minerals. In fact, on his way up the river to Quebec he had gone ashore at several points to collect rock samples and later had them examined for traces of minerals. He had been amazed by the fertility of the soil and the excellence of the timber. He found that a bushel of seed wheat brought a return of fifteen, twenty, and even thirty bushels. He estimated that within fifteen years the colony could supply the West Indies with all the fish, grain, and timber they could require, and he quickly set about to achieve this aim. Large quantities of foodstuffs were needed for the troops, but once the Iroquois had been subdued the Carignan-Salières

---

* Talon drew up a budget for the colony of 46,500 *livres*, this being the sum fixed by the auction of the beaver trade under Mésy. The *Compagnie de l'Occident* claimed this was too much and Colbert agreed, reducing the fixed charges to 36,000 *livres*.[18]

regiment was disbanded. This fact, combined with the great increase in the extent of cleared land, resulted in sizable surpluses of grain and peas, and the only external market was the West Indies. Colbert was continually urging Talon and the officials in the islands to establish a three-way trade in foodstuffs, timber, and barrel staves to the islands in exchange for sugar and molasses to be exported to France, which would in turn be exchanged for manufactured goods to be brought back to Canada. At Talon's suggestion Colbert removed the import duty on sugar when brought to France by Canadian ships in the hopes that this would stimulate the trade.

Colbert was also eager to see thriving ship-building industries developed in both Canada and France. Canada, he hoped, would produce the materials to build her own ships and also supply the shipyards of France, thus removing the need to import ship masts and timber from the Baltic countries. Ships also needed hemp for rope and caulking, flax for canvas sails, and vast quantities of tar. Talon began distributing flax and hemp seeds to the *habitants*, and when he found that they were growing only enough hemp for their own needs he sequestered all the rope in the colony and allowed the *habitants* to purchase supplies only upon agreeing to raise more hemp.

Colbert was particularly anxious to have *flûtes*, long, narrow ships with hatches in the stern to allow ship masts and lengthy balks of timber to be loaded easily, built in Canada as well as warships for the navy. In 1669 he gave orders that the construction of two *flûtes* of three hundred tons each be undertaken in Canada, and within three or four years he wanted four warships of six to seven hundred tons built in the colony. Skilled ships' carpenters, tarmakers, blacksmiths, foundry workers, and the necessary supplies, were sent out by Colbert de Terron. They began by building a barque of 120 tons, followed by a larger one, and by 1672 a 46-gun warship was under construction at Quebec. To encourage others in the colony Talon went into partnership with a Quebec merchant and shipped cargoes of dried cod fish, salted salmon, eels, peas, oil, barrel staves, and planks to the West Indies.

Unfortunately, the problems that had to be surmounted before these infant industries could flourish proved to be great. The cost of manufacturing ships, owing to the necessity to import skilled labour at high wages, the lack of iron in the colony, as well as the fact that new industries always require heavy capital outlays, was much greater than in France. Patoulet, Talon's one-time deputy, and later *commissaire de marine* at Rochefort, declared that one day Canada would be able to produce an abundance of tar, but that currently it cost far more than Dutch tar. He also stated that ships cost much more to build in Canada than in France and he recommended that their construction in the colony for the navy be halted until such time as iron could be forged there and the supply of Canadian hemp was adequate to rig them.[19] His superior, Colbert de Terron, had earlier questioned the wisdom of importing Canadian timber, since only three or four French ships were available to transport it, whereas the Dutch had hundreds of ships in the Baltic timber trade and could provide timber for much less than it cost to bring it from Canada. Moreover, four ships of Canadian timber a year was only a tiny fraction of the amount consumed annually in France; hence it hardly seemed worth the trouble.[20]

Both the nascent Canadian ship-building industry and overseas trade suffered a severe setback when two of Talon's ships were lost at sea, a loss of some 36,000 *livres*. Indeed maritime trade from Quebec to the West Indies had to overcome severe handicaps; ships could sail only in the summer months, which is the hurricane season in southern waters; they had to run the gauntlet of English privateers in wartime and pirates all the time and, in addition, they had to face the competition of the New England mariners who could sell much the same goods as New France produced at lower cost, and all year round. Moreover, Colbert's attempts to have the *Compagnie de l'Occident* supply the French islands with negro slaves were unsuccessful, and the French planters had to depend on English and Dutch slavers to supply them with labour. This opened the door to the English and Dutch to provide all other goods and ruined any prospects there might have been of Canada's retaining the market. Despite these handicaps, however, at least one Quebec merchant, la Chesnaye, continued to send ships to the West Indies, and there may well have been others.

The failure to retain the West Indies market in the face of Dutch and English competition sounded the death knell of the *Compagnie de l'Occident*. It had failed conspicuously to attract private capital and in New France it had been vigorously attacked by the colony's merchants, by the *habitants*, and by Talon. They all claimed that the Company overcharged for the goods it shipped to the colony, too often did not provide the right type of merchandise, demanded payment in cash or furs, and refused to extend credit. They all demanded freedom of trade for the colony. Finally, in December 1674, Colbert admitted defeat, and in that month the Company's books were closed. Its rights and privileges now reverted to the Crown and trade with the colonies was made open to all.[21] This meant, in effect, that a small group of merchants in the colony handled the retail trade and obtained their supplies from the wholesale merchants of La Rochelle.

The one industry in New France which seemed to offer the greatest promise was fishing, and Colbert gave it every possible aid. Subsidies were provided for the necessary equipment, and Canadian cod paid the same duties on entering France as did that brought in by the fishermen of Normandie. Here again, however, the Canadian fishermen had to overcome handicaps, the chief of which was the lack of salt in the colony. Fishermen from

France could take catches of fish on the Grand Banks and sell it in France for considerably less than could the Canadian fishermen. Meanwhile, New England seamen grew wealthy, fishing in Acadian waters and along the Gaspé coast. Talon made a valiant effort to establish a whale and porpoise fishery to produce oil for the soap industry. Although it had an encouraging beginning, it was found that the Canadians could not compete with the Basque fishermen who had been engaged in this work for generations. Thus, despite large expenditures of energy and capital, the Canadian fishing industry did not progress much beyond the supplying of the colony's needs.

One enterprise that did make a promising beginning was the brewery built by Talon at Quebec. Beer had been brewed in the colony for home consumption for some time but it had not been brewed commercially before. It was hoped that this would reduce the amount of strong spirits being consumed, which was blamed for much of the lawlessness in the colony; reduce the adverse balance of trade and the drain on the colony's slender supplies of specie by reducing the amount of wine and brandy imported; and also provide a market for the colony's surplus grain. This last, it was hoped, would help to maintain grain prices and so encourage the *habitants* to clear and cultivate more land. Colbert fully approved of the project and he gave orders that the edict of the Sovereign Council at Quebec, limiting the annual imports of wine and spirits to 8,000 barrels of wine and 4,000 barrels of brandy, be strictly enforced.

That Colbert encouraged an enterprise in Canada which would reduce the market for the products of French vineyards, particularly since he was striving to dispose of a surplus of wine and brandy on foreign markets by all means possible, indicates how eager he was that Canada should be self-supporting and its trade with the mother country kept in balance. For this reason he also encouraged the manufacture of some consumer goods in the colony and had master craftsmen sent from France to teach the colonists their trades. By 1668 shoes and hats were being made and a tannery was planned; some linen was being woven, and it was expected that the great increase in the number of sheep would lead to the production of wool. It was not long before the *habitants* were able to clothe themselves with cloth spun from the wool of their own sheep, with linen from the flax they raised themselves, and in shoes made of locally tanned leather. The towns-people, however, would not wear these rough fabrics and insisted on the latest styles imported from France.

There can be little doubt that the colony would not have witnessed such an extensive or diversified economic expansion without the drive and executive ability of Talon. In addition, he also provided some of the capital which was utilized for this industrial expansion. Upon discovering, shortly after his arrival in the colony, that there was a great shortage of consumer goods, he sold part of the goods he had brought for his own use at a sizable profit. When Colbert learned of this he warned Talon that the intendant's task was to make the colony flourish, not to seize opportunities to enrich himself in private commercing at the colony's expense.[22] Talon, however, paid no attention to this injunction. He was entitled to import goods for his own use on the King's ships free of duty and freight charges. He stretched this privilege to the limit, building a large warehouse in Lower Town at Quebec to store his goods and employing several men to handle the business for him. In 1669, for example, he ordered sent from La Rochelle for his own account, among other things, 104 barrels of Bordeaux wine, 96 barrels of Charente wine and 220 barrels of brandy.[23] It is hardly likely that he would consume all of this in his own household; if he did, then it would explain the poor state of his health. Before long the colony's merchants began to complain that the intendant was putting them out of business by underselling them; this he was easily able to do since they had to pay heavy freight rates and a 10 per cent duty on wines and spirits.[24] Talon also became very active in the fur trade and must have made considerable profits. What percentage of these profits he devoted to industrial development is not known, but certainly there would have been less economic activity in the colony without his investment of capital.

In 1672 two events occurred which caused a marked slow-down of the colony's development: Jean Talon returned to France, and no intendant was appointed to replace him until 1675; and in April 1672 France, allied with England, declared war on the Dutch republic. From this point on, Colbert was able to devote less attention, and less capital funds, to the colonies. In fact, in 1669, when giving orders for one hundred and fifty to two hundred girls to be sent to Canada the following year, he had stated that the colony should now be able to stand on its own feet. During the seven-year period 1665-1672 the economic development of the colony had made tremendous advances under the stimulus of these royal officials: Colbert, Colbert de Terron, and Jean Talon. Over a million *livres* had been provided by the Crown to establish new industries and develop trade and commerce. That the degree of success achieved was perhaps not as great as Colbert had hoped for can be attributed to two main factors; Colbert was striving to make the colonial economy run before it had learned to walk, and the ethos of French society was not particularly well suited to the achieving of his aims. Capital he had been able to provide from the royal coffers, labour he could provide by a subsidized emigration policy – this item alone had cost the Crown over 50,000 *livres* a year[25] – but the entrepreneurial skills that were equally vital could not so easily be conjured into existence. The men of proven ability and enterprise in the colony were nearly all retail merchants, fur traders, or both; or else, like Pierre Boucher, they had entered the ranks of officialdom.

In France itself commerce and industry had little appeal to men with talent and ambition. The framework of society was mainly the cause of this. In France the aristocracy was a highly privileged class, and its members were barred from engaging in commerce or industry. What was more to the point, they showed exceedingly little inclination to engage in these pursuits. Moreover, in France unlike in England, all the children of the nobility enjoyed its attendant status and privileges. For those not born into the ranks of the aristocracy the only legitimate way to gain entry was to purchase, or somehow obtain, a post in the administration which carried with it noble status. There were a great number of such posts, but the purchase price was always very high. This was really a form of indirect taxation which denied capital to private enterprise. Nor was money alone sufficient to obtain them; a high degree of talent and ability was also required. Those who had succeeded in obtaining these posts had come to form the new noble class, the *noblesse de robe*. Although the old feudal nobility looked down on these new men of wealth and proven ability, the members of this *noblesse de robe* accepted the values of the older aristocracy and sought to emulate them in their mode of living. Their aim was to be discriminating enough to distinguish the better things in life, acquire the means to enjoy them, and let everyone see that they were being enjoyed. Even more important, however, were the intangibles: personal reputation, honour, the esteem of a man's peers and above all of the King, summed up in the untranslatable phrase, *la gloire*.

This dominance of the aristocratic ethos resulted in the bourgeois values of thrift, industry, and prudence, prevalent in England and the Netherlands, being held if not in contempt then certainly in low repute. Rather than plough profits, however made, into commerce or industry in order to amass more capital to invest, the ambitious Frenchman invested his money in government bonds and land; sought to purchase a post in the administration; and then to obtain commissions in the army for his sons, where they would mingle with the feudal nobility. Thus, with the Crown monopolizing the nation's supply of brains, ability, and capital, any expansion of the national economy, at home or in the colonies, had to be implemented by the Crown. Under Colbert this expansion took place with great rapidity, and he accomplished in twenty years what the English and Dutch had taken over a century to do under private auspices. It would be worse than futile to debate the merits of the two differing systems. The social system of France, hence of New France, dictated the need for state direction and paternalism, if there was to be any expansion and betterment of conditions for the people in Canada. Suffice it to say that state direction and paternalism in New France did not stifle initiative, rather the reverse, for without them the colony could not have survived, and what it became was due very largely to the efforts of the Crown officials.

Although there was no *noblesse d'épée* to speak of in New France in the seventeenth century and those who did receive titles of nobility were exempted from the edicts forbidding members of their estate to engage in trade, yet the ethos of the feudal nobility still prevailed. The man who made his money as a merchant, usually in the fur trade, became a seigneur, perhaps a member of the Sovereign Council, and his sons obtained commissions in the colonial regular troops, or perhaps in the navy or the army in France. It is this which distinguishes New France from the English and Dutch colonies in North America. Although it was one of the basic causes of the colony's economic weakness, it was its greatest asset in other, and perhaps more important, respects. The military virtues were extolled and social life in New France was much more agreeable than in the colonies to the south.[26] Thus, to state that New France lagged far behind the English colonies in economic development, although true, is really to state only a half-truth, for the aims of the two societies were quite different.

CHAPTER 5

Colbert's Compact Colony Policy

Ironically, the factor that did most to undermine Colbert's plans for the economic development of New France was the colony's main source of economic vitality, the fur trade. The implementation of his plans for the diversification of the Canadian economy required that the available resources of capital, ability, and labour be concentrated within the settled areas of the colony. He saw clearly that the fur trade, unless strictly controlled, would cripple these other, and to him more vital, economic activities.

Unfortunately for Colbert's hopes, all the things that Canada could produce at this time could be obtained at far less cost elsewhere; except furs. In Europe there was a ready market for furs of all kinds and, in particular, for beaver fur. In the seventeenth century male fashions decreed that wide-brimmed felt hats, costing twenty to thirty *livres*, should be worn by all gentlemen. The ideal material for the manufacture of these hats was the soft under-fur of the beaver, because the strands of this fur had tiny barbs which caused them to cling tenaciously when matted into felt. The Canadian beaver, owing to the cold northern climate, grew a heavier fur than did the European beaver – by then virtually extinct – or the beaver trapped in more southerly parts of the North American continent. By the same token, the Indians of the north used beaver robes to a much greater extent for protection against the cold than did the Indians to the south, and it was beaver pelts that had been worn or slept in, hence known as *castor gras* or greasy beaver, that commanded the highest prices on the European market. The grease and sweat on the Indians' bodies and the smoke in their lodges made the pelts supple and loosened the long guard hairs which then were easily removed, leaving only the soft under-fur needed for the finer quality of felt. The Canadian Shield with its vast expanse of lakes, rivers, streams, and swamps, bordered by poplar, birch, and willow, the food of the beaver, was an ideal breeding-ground. Moreover, beaver-constructed dams and houses, hence were much easier to locate and trap than most animals.

Other furs – otter, mink, weasel, marten, fox – were much in demand for the luxury trade, and sizable quantities were used for trimming the robes of clerics and senior officials. Until the turn of the century, however, beaver dominated the market; after that date these "luxury" furs, known as *menus pelleteries*, took an increasingly larger share of the market. Beaver, surplus to the requirements of the French domestic market, was exported to Holland whence much of it was transhipped to Russia.[1] For moose hides, too, there was a large market, leather being in far more demand than it is today. The army needed large quantities, and so did the civilian saddlery trade.

In addition to an assured market the Canadian fur trade enjoyed other marked advantages over all other economic activities. Little capital was needed, merely a supply of trade goods: guns, ammunition, knives, hatchets, pots and kettles, blankets, trinkets such as mirrors and glass beads, gaudy clothing and, last but far from least, brandy. Nor was there any need for skilled labour; the Indians trapped the animals and their squaws dressed the furs. The Indians also transported the furs to Montreal, in the early years of the fur trade at least; thus the Canadians merely served as middlemen and transhipped the furs to France, making considerable profits in the process. By comparison, such activities as fishing, lumbering, ship-building, and the manufacture of consumer goods required vast outlays of capital, labour, and mental effort, with little prospect of sizable profit for several years. Even agriculture appeared uninviting when compared with the attractions of the fur trade. The lands in the St Lawrence valley were covered with hardwood forests, mainly oak. Before a crop could be planted the trees had to be felled, trimmed, and somehow removed; then came the hardest task of all, pulling out the stumps. To clear an *arpent*, by dint of back-breaking labour, was all that one man could hope to accomplish in one year.

Perhaps the most important factor of all in determining Canada's concentration on the fur trade, despite Colbert's plans and edicts, was the great river system providing easy access into the interior of the continent. From Montreal it was possible to travel by canoe to the Rocky Mountains, to Hudson Bay, or the Gulf of Mexico by way of the St Lawrence, the Ottawa, the Great Lakes, the Mississippi, and their tributary rivers and lakes. The English and Dutch to the south, on the other hand, were hemmed in by the Alleghany Mountains. Their only gateway through this mountain barrier was the Hudson and Mohawk river system, and the five nations of the Iroquois confederacy effectively barred their access to the interior by that route.

Not only were these river routes accessible to the French, and to no other European colonies, but the best means to travel along the rivers was also available to the French and to no other Europeans. This mode of transport was, of course, the birchbark canoe. Light in weight, hence easily transported over portages, these canoes were surprisingly durable and could be manufactured or repaired from materials readily available in the forest; cedar slats for the frame, birchbark for the outer shell, root sinews or rawhide for the seams and joints, spruce gum for caulking. The only tools really needed were an axe and a knife. These canoes, usually fifteen to twenty feet long, could be paddled from dawn to dusk by two or three men, carrying a cargo of some 2,500 pounds. Two weeks was considered to be reasonably good time to travel from Michilimackinac, at the junction of Lakes Michigan and Huron, to Montreal, even when Iroquois war parties had to be avoided.

The Canadians had a decided advantage over the English and Dutch fur-traders, for the birch tree of a girth providing bark suitable for the manufacture of canoes grew in abundance only in the areas dominated by the French.[2] The Iroquois to the south had to obtain their supplies of birchbark from the lands north of the Great Lakes and in time of war they frequently had to make do with clumsy and less durable elmbark canoes. Another factor was the food supply. The fur-trading areas of the Great Lakes basin abounded in fish and game; in addition, in the St Lawrence valley, the area south of the Canadian shield and on the western prairies south of the present United States – Canadian border, maize or Indian corn grew in abundance. This was a highly nutritive form of food, and the corn kernels, in their hard shell, were almost indestructible, or at least could be stored for long periods of time. Without this source of food, travel, whether for trade or exploration, in the North American west, would have been a much more difficult undertaking than it actually was.

Prior to the quelling of the Iroquois menace by Tracy and Courcelle in 1666, few Canadians had ventured into the west, the colony had had to rely on the Ottawa tribes to bring the furs to Montreal, running the gauntlet of Iroquois ambush along the Ottawa River, or travelling far to the north to descend the St Maurice River to Trois Rivières, as they did in 1665. After the Iroquois had been forced to come to terms with the French in 1666, the volume of fur coming into the colony began to increase rapidly. In 1666 furs worth 100,000 *livres* were exported to La Rochelle, and the following year 550,000 *livres* worth of fur were exported to France. This great increase in supply had the usual effect on the market price; in 1666 it declined from eleven *livres* the pound to eight or nine *livres*, and the

Compagnie de l'Occident warned that either these prices would have to be lowered or it would have to raise the price of the goods it sold in the colony by 30 per cent. By 1670 the prices paid in the colony had to be lowered to six *livres* the pound for greasy beaver and three *livres* for dry beaver, this last being beaver pelts that had not been worn by the Indians. At the same time the price of moose hides was fixed at one *livre* the pound. These prices, however, did not represent the value received by the Canadians for their beaver and moose hides. In 1666 the *Compagnie de l'Occident* was granted the right to impose a tax of 25 per cent on the value of beaver and 10 per cent on moose hides exported from the colony.

Despite the decline of prices, or perhaps because of it, the fur trade continued to expand. Every year, now, some four to six hundred western Indians, some of whom had never before had dealings with Europeans, came down to Montreal with canoe loads of furs they had obtained from tribes to the south, tribes that lacked canoes and had to depend on the Ottawas to act as middlemen. When they arrived at Montreal a great fair was held on the common between the town and the river, and the *habitants* from all parts of the colony voyaged upriver to trade with them. For the people of Montreal this was the most important event of the year. It was not long before merchants from France began coming out with cargoes of merchandise and setting up stalls on the common.

These fairs must have presented a spectacle unique in the seventeenth century. Here were the black soutaned priests of St Sulpice; seigneurs of the island, allocating the sites for the stalls; *habitants* in their rough clothing; sailors and merchants of La Rochelle; merchants of Montreal, Trois Rivières, and Quebec; royal officials, from the governor general down to the guards of the local governor there to maintain order; housewives, ladies, children, and the inevitable *flâneurs* strolling about to see the sights; all rubbing shoulders on the fairground, in the streets of the town, and likely in the taverns, with the bronzed, fur-clad warriors of the northwestern lakes and forests. The one group a product of the age of Louis XIV, the most civilized epoch since the age of Pericles, the other barely emerging from the stone age.

The governor and the intendant usually attended these fairs and before the trading began, a general assembly was held: the governor, seated, surrounded by the other officials and clerical dignitaries, the Indians squatting in their fur robes, puffing stolidly on their pipes, the colonists standing about watching or striving to restrain their children who wished to engage in rough and tumble with the Indian boys. The Indians, with their love of ceremonial and oratory, listened to the interminable speeches of their chiefs and grunted in approval when the dangers and ardours of their journey were dwelt on in detail, or the hope expressed that the prices of trade goods would be lower and the quality higher than in other years. As each chief ended his oration, he presented a bale of choice furs to the governor "to open his ears" to their requests. When they eventually finished, the governor replied, through an interpreter, always speaking like a father to his children, dwelling on the power and the glory of his King across the sea, impressing on them how fortunate they were to have dealings with the French, pleading with them to hearken to the words of the missionaries in their villages and to remain at peace, one tribe with another. This done, he distributed his presents to the chiefs; plumed hats, gay-coloured coats, muskets, powder and ammunition, dresses and trinkets for their squaws, toys for their children. Then came the great feast, usually held in the courtyard of the Hôtel Dieu. All day, huge cauldrons had been bubbling over the fire, containing a flavoursome *ragout* of corn, chunks of bear meat, moose, beaver, and several fat dogs and cats which had previously been seared over hot coals to remove their fur; plums and raisins were added later for flavouring. When this had been consumed, the Indians wiped their greasy hands on their fur robes and gave loud belches out of politeness to show their appreciation of the feast. Then the trading could begin.

These affairs afforded the Canadian settlers an opportunity to make a quick profit, and the bills of exchange they received for the furs they had obtained in trade with the Indians enabled them to settle their accounts with the local merchants, and likely with the tavern keepers.

Colbert, however, entertained serious doubts of the wisdom of allowing the Canadians to engage in the fur trade at all. He feared that it might distract them from their principal task of clearing the land, and a few years later, when the fur trade suffered a temporary decline, he informed Talon that such things were to be expected periodically and that if Canada "found itself deprived of this trade, the settlers would be obliged to engage in fishing, prospecting and manufacturing, which would yield them far greater benefits." To keep the settlers concentrated in the central colony and engaged in these more worthwhile pursuits, Colbert insisted that they must be prevented at all costs from going to the distant Indian villages to obtain furs; instead, the Indians had to be encouraged to bring their furs down to the colony. This was the keystone of his policies for New France, and edict after edict was issued forbidding the Canadians to leave the confines of the colony to engage in the fur trade.

Talon, however, had different ideas. He had been in the colony only a few weeks when he advised Colbert that there was nothing to prevent the French expanding south as far as Florida, or even Mexico. Colbert, with his feet more firmly on the ground, was quick to inform Talon that it would be far better to concentrate French activities within an area which they could hope to hold securely, than to grasp too great an expanse in the interior and one day be forced to abandon part of it with a consequent loss of prestige for France.[3] Talon and Courcelle next proposed building and garrisoning forts on the shores of Lake Ontario with a sailing galley to cruise on the lake. Such establishments, Talon argued, would keep the Iroquois in submission and divert to Montreal the furs that the Iroquois trapped on the lands claimed by the French Crown on the north side of the lake. He estimated the value of these furs to be over a million *livres* and this, he maintained, would pay the costs of the colony. Colbert was not at all enthusiastic about this scheme; he declined to provide the hundred regular troops needed to man the forts and the galley, or the 15,000 *livres* to build them. He told Talon to discuss the project with Courcelle and, if the Governor approved of the plan, then something might be done. At this particular time, however, relations between Talon and Courcelle were very strained, and hence nothing more was said.

Meanwhile, Talon had begun exploiting the western fur trade by the expedient of exploration parties. Following his return to Canada in 1670, after a two-year absence in France, he began sending parties to discover new routes to the north, west, and south. He informed Colbert that he thus hoped to discover river routes to Mexico and to the southern ocean "which separates this continent from China." They were also to search for copper mines and other mineral deposits and, of course, claim all the lands they traversed for France. Father Albanel, S.J., and the Sieur de St Simon were sent north to Hudson Bay to persuade the Indians of the region to trade their furs with the French, and at the same time to discover if ships could winter in the Bay and establish a supply base which could then be used to discover the northwest passage linking the northern and southern oceans. Father Albanel and the Sieur de St Simon subsequently sent back letters with ominous news. The northern Indians had informed them that five English ships had wintered in the Bay and there obtained a vast amount of beaver pelts.[4]

From the west, reports had been received of a great river below Green Bay on the west side of Lake Michigan, and it was assumed that it had to empty into either the "Sea of Florida or that of California." Other reports also told of a western sea some two hundred leagues beyond the missionary post of St Esprit at Chagouamigon near the western end of Lake Superior. Talon now sent out the Sieur de St Lusson in command of a party with orders to go as far as food supplies would allow to discover if a route existed to the western ocean, and also to try to locate the copper mines reputed to exist somewhere in the west. Accompanied by Nicholas Perrot, St Lusson left Montreal in October 1670 and went as far as Green Bay and then returned to Sault Ste Marie where, on 14 June 1671, they and four Jesuit missionaries held a council meeting with representatives from fourteen of the western Indian tribes. They claimed possession in the name of Louis XIV of all the lands inhabited by these tribes. To the southwest Réné-Robert Cavelier, Sieur de la Salle, who had made a previous trip to Lake Ontario,[5] was sent to discover a route to the south, but he accomplished nothing of great moment.

Talon was quick to assure Colbert that all these expeditions were costing the Crown not a sou. He blandly informed Colbert that St Lusson, after taking possession of the Indians' lands for the King of France, had duly handed the lands back to the Indians and received in return packs of beaver pelts.[6] All that this really meant was, of course, that his "exploration" parties were also fur-trading expeditions and that they were proving to be very profitable.[7] Before his final departure from New France in 1672 Talon, with the consent of the newly appointed governor, the Comte de Frontenac, sent out another expedition led by Louis Jolliet, to locate the river, called Mississippi by the Indians, and said to flow far to the south. This was to prove to be the most momentous expedition of all; one that led to the ruin of Colbert's plans for the colony.

Since, with the Iroquois menace removed, the way was open for the western nations to bring their furs to Montreal, and also for Talon's exploration and trading parties to voyage far into the interior, by the same token it was safe for others to follow Talon's example. Enterprising fur-traders soon began going upriver to meet the Indians and obtain their furs before they got to Montreal. Merchants such as Jacques Le Ber, one of the wealthier men in the colony, began obtaining seigneuries at the western end of the island of Montreal, there to establish trading-posts. Talon's nephew by marriage, François-Marie Perrot who, through Talon's influence, had obtained the post of Governor of Montreal in 1669, followed suit and obtained a seigneurial grant of the large island that today bears his name at the junction of the Ottawa and St Lawrence rivers. There he established a trading-post to forestall the Montreal fur-traders. When they protested, he did not scruple to use force to make them desist. Faced with this form of competition, the merchant fur-traders in the colony began sending canoes loaded with trade goods to the Indian villages. Many of the seigneurs and *habitants* began to follow suit. As this forestalling competition grew apace the trade moved steadily westward, and bases were soon established in the heart of the continent, usually at or near the Jesuits' missionary posts, since these last were established wherever the

Indians congregated in large numbers. Thus, Sault Ste Marie and Michili-mackinac became the main fur-trade centres, and from these advanced bases the Canadian traders fanned out in all directions, moving with the Indians during their fall and winter hunting to obtain the furs almost as soon as they were trapped.

These men now spent a year or two at a time, and even longer, in the west, and then hired Indian canoemen to help them transport their furs to Mont-real. By the early 1680's they had established wintering-posts at the western end of Lake Superior, over the northern height of land among the Assini-boine tribes around Lake Winnipeg, and along the headwaters of the Mississippi. The farther the traders went the more avid seemed the Indians for trade goods, and the more furs could these intrepid voyagers obtain. Wherever they went they extended French influence until all the tribes in the basin of the Great Lakes were welded into a commercial alliance with New France. Inevitably, there were political undertones to this com-mercial alliance; to maintain it the French traders had to aid their com-mercial partners against their enemies, for the Indians had little under-standing and less respect for neutrality. Thus these fur-traders frequently went on war parties and became adept in the use of the scalping-knife.

The lure of profit proved irresistible to ever-increasing numbers of the more vigorous and adventurous French settlers until, by 1672, their numbers were estimated at three to four hundred, and seven years later this figure was doubled. Before long seigneurs were complaining, not only that it was impossible for them to get their seigneuries cleared and settled, but that they were losing many of their *censitaires* who had been unable to resist the attraction of the western fur trade. Many of the seigneurs them-selves began sending their sons out to the west to increase the family's fortunes.

The voyageurs who hired out to Montreal merchants to take a canoe load of trade goods to the west and return with a load of furs were paid 1,000 *livres* for the trip and they were allowed to take a few goods to trade on their own account. When they returned to the settlements they had money jingling in their pockets, and tales of the great distances they had travelled, the hardships they had endured, and the blood-tingling sights they had seen among the strange western tribes. When the more spirited of the youth in the colony compared such a wild, free life as this, dangerous and harsh though it undoubtedly was, to the arduous, seemingly endless, task of converting virgin forest into arable land, it is small wonder that so many of them abandoned the axe and the plough for the canoe paddle and the musket. Thus the very men who were most needed in the colony to implement Colbert's plans for economic development, the physically fit and those possessed of initiative, were drained away from the labour force.

These *coureurs de bois*, although in some ways an economic and social liability, were yet a unique group, purely Canadian in character, owing as much to the influence of the North American environment as to their French heritage. By roaming the forest and sharing the Indian nomadic hunter's life they acquired his skill with paddle and snowshoe, his mastery over the raw forces of nature. They learned to speak the Indian languages, to live and think like the Indians, to understand them, and what was more, to respect them. This was easier for the French to do than for the Dutch or English because the personal values of the French were closer to those of the Indians than were those of these other colonials. The French, like the Indians, wanted material things mainly to get more enjoyment out of life; they were not much concerned with storing up worldly goods. Both were motivated by a strong desire to earn the respect of their fellows for what they were rather than for what they possessed; and wealth, in any form, was regarded as merely an adjunct of personal worth, not as a worthy end in itself. Both had a very strong sense of personal honour and both had a mortal fear of being regarded by their fellows as wanting in qualities regarded as honourable. With these basic values in common, the French, since the days of Champlain, had maintained an easy rapport with the Indians that the English, both of the Hudson's Bay Company and of the colonies to the south, had never been able to equal.

The *coureurs de bois*, by their close contacts with the Indians, also acquired certain of their peculiar character traits; their native Latin exuberance became tempered by the Indian's stoicism, their Christian morality by the natural penchant of the Indian for cruelty. They not only learned to endure hardship and intense physical pain without flinching, schooling themselves in fact to endure it, but they also came not to flinch from inflicting it on their foes when the occasion seemed to demand it. Within the colony itself the forest was slowly pushed back and European institutions always remained firmly in control, but the river flowed past the doorstep of every house on every seigneury in the colony. Thus, it could hardly be said that New France had a frontier at all; that is, a line separating the civilized settlements from the wilderness. The environment of the frontier was, in fact, all pervasive in the colony.

Although the French early voyaged far into the west, established permanent posts, and claimed these distant lands for the French Crown, yet they could not be said to have occupied the west, anymore than the seamen of New England occupied the Atlantic ocean in their voyages to Europe, Africa, and the West Indies. In fact, the *coureurs de bois* more closely resembled the New England seamen than any other single group. Like seamen, the *coureurs de bois* left Montreal with cargoes of goods in their frail craft, voyaged great distances to exchange their goods, then returned with a cargo for their employers and received their pay. Like seamen they left their families at home and they were frequently accused of having a wife in every Indian village. Once they returned to Montreal they behaved much as sailors are said to behave. The Baron de Lahontan, an officer in the colonial regular troops in the 1680's, remarked on the similarity. He wrote:

> The Pedlers call'd *Coureurs de Bois*, export from hence every year several Canows full of Merchandise, which they dispose of among all the Savage Nations of the Continent, by way of exchange for Beaver-Skins. Seven or eight days ago, I saw twenty five or thirty of these Canows return with heavy Cargoes; each Canow was manag'd by two or three Men, and carry'd twenty hundred weight, *i.e.* forty packs of Beaver Skins, which are worth an hundred Crowns a piece. These Canows had been a year and eighteen Months out. You would be amaz'd if you saw how lewd these Pedlers are when they return; how they Feast and Game, and how prodigal they are, not only in their Cloaths, but upon Women. Such of 'em as are married, have the wisdom to retire to their own Houses; but the Batchelors act just as our *East-India*-Men, and Pirates are wont to do; for they Lavish, Eat, Drink, and Play all away as long as the Goods hold out; and when these are gone, they e'en sell their Embroidery, their Lace, and their Cloaths. This done, they are forc'd to go upon a new Voyage for Subsistance.[8]

Not all, but many – and these the more conscientious royal officials – saw clearly the dangers in this situation and sought vainly for some means to rectify it. When Colbert asked Jean-Baptiste Patoulet, *Commissaire de Marine* at Rochefort and Talon's one-time deputy, for his views on what needed to be done in Canada, Patoulet replied that means would have to be found to curb the *coureurs de bois*; otherwise the aims of the French in North America could never be achieved. He stated:

> These headstrong men are vagabonds who do not marry, who never work at clearing the land which should be the main task of a good colonist, and who commit an infinity of disorders by their licentious and libertine way of life. These men, living continually like Indians go twelve to fifteen hundred miles above Quebec to trade for furs that the Indians would themselves bring to our settlements. Their eagerness for gains that profit them not at all, owing to their dissoluteness, leads to indignities and vileness which ruins the good opinion that the Indian peoples should have of our nation, moreover the corruption of their morals is a grave obstacle to the inconceivable pains that the missionaries take to instruct the pagans in the knowledge of our Gospel.[9]

The clergy fully supported these views. Yet the missionaries also inadvertently served French economic and political interests. By establishing their missionary posts in the west they served as liaison officers between the Indians and the officials at Quebec, helping to keep the tribes friendly to the French. They also served as advance agents for the fur trade, as the establishment of good relations by the missionaries pre-disposed the Indians to trade with the French. Since both the missionaries and the fur-traders had to go among the Indians to achieve their ends, it was not long before the missionary posts and trading-posts were established side by side. Inevitably, however, the interests of the missionaries and the fur-traders came into conflict. To the missionaries chastity was the ideal pre-marital state, but to the Indians this was a novel idea, and one that had little to recommend it. Nor did it have much appeal to many of the fur-traders who frequented the Indian villages. Compared to more recent times the seventeenth century was a licentious age, but in the settlements of New France, at mid century at least, the dominant position of the clergy and their followers had imparted a very puritanical aura to society. As late as 1663, for example, a *habitant* of Montreal was fined ten *livres* at the behest of the curé, for ploughing his fields on a Sunday.[10] Many of the fur-traders, once out of the colony, reacted against this puritanism and attendant prudery by taking full advantage of the Indian girls' lack of inhibitions. In fact, some of the Jesuit missionaries claimed that this was one of the great lures for young men to leave the settlement for the roving life of the *coureurs de bois*.

Father Carheil, the Jesuit missionary at Michilimackinac at the turn of the century, declared that this situation had become so bad that the *coureurs de bois* and *voyageurs** hired Indian girls in preference to men on their voyages to and from Montreal. They defended the practice on the grounds that these girls could do a man's work, and would cheerfully do such chores as cutting fire wood and doing the cooking; moreover, they accepted lower wages. Father Carheil, however, was convinced there were other reasons. He charged that there was "a continual flux and reflux of these prostitutes who go from one mission post to another without stop, causing the most enormous and horrible scandal in the world."[11] Thus, when the missionaries tried to persuade the Indians to live according to the moral teachings of the Church, the Indians were quick to ask, why, if the Christian way of life was so superior to that of the Indian, did not the French themselves adhere to it. In the face of this the clergy sought by all means to keep the French and the Indians apart. They were forced to admit

---

* By the end of the century a distinction was being made between those who voyaged to the west without the sanction of the authorities, *coureurs de bois*, and those who had this approval, *voyageurs*. Prior to this, however, in the contemporary correspondence and official documents they are all referred to as *coureurs de bois* without distinction.

that the greatest obstacle to the conversion of the Indians to Christianity was their association with lay Christians.

For these reasons the Jesuits were among the strongest supporters of Colbert's policy for the development of New France. Both he and they wanted nothing more than to keep the French from voyaging to the Indian villages in large numbers. Yet they could not combine their forces to curb the practice, for toward no group was Colbert as hostile as to the Jesuits. In his official instructions to all the governors and intendants sent to New France he stated that the clergy in general and the Jesuits in particular had too much power in the colony and were eager for more. Nothing, apparently, could convince him that the clergy were not continually trespassing in the sphere of royal authority, that is, of his authority. The royal officials in the colony were, from the highest to the lowest, under his control, obliged to obey his orders, and it appears that he would have been satisfied with nothing less for the clergy.

There were, however, other complicating factors; among them the general relations between state and church in France at this time. In the latter half of the seventeenth century a struggle was in progress between the supporters of the Gallican movement, who wanted a national church virtually independent of Rome, and the ultramontanists, who desired a supranational church under the control of Rome. Louis XIV vacillated between these two forces, attempting to play off the one against the other; thus the separation of powers between church and state was not only ill defined but in contest. The Jesuit order was, of course, avowedly ultramontane; and here lay one of the roots of the trouble.

The consequences of this struggle for New France were well exemplified in the establishment of a bishopric of Quebec. Monseigneur Laval, although the bishop *at* Quebec, was not bishop *of* Quebec but rather of Petraea, *in partibus infidelium*; hence he was directly under the Vatican. This state of affairs irked Louis and Colbert, and they began pressing Rome to establish a bishopric of Quebec with the Bishop suffragan of the Archbishop of Rouen.[12] According to the Concordat of 1517, the King of France nominated all senior ecclesiastics in the kingdom, who were then appointed by the Pope, but the Vatican claimed that the Pope had sole jurisdiction over the clergy in pagan countries and, since the Canadian missions had been founded to convert the pagans, the Bishop of Quebec should be directly under Rome, not under an archbishop controlled by the King of France. Colbert, however, stated, "to tell the truth that reason seems to us to be but a feeble pretext and the real reason is that they hope to separate the clergy of New France from the church in France, which they do not wish to strengthen."[13] Colbert argued that the Canadian clergy had always been under the Archbishop of Rouen. He pointed out that the people of the colony were all natural-born French and he grossly exaggerated their numbers to strengthen his case, claiming that there were twenty to thirty thousand French resident in New France, and only some two hundred Indians, thus the colony was clearly French and not a pagan country converted to the faith; hence, to make the Bishop of Quebec independent of Rouen would be a breach in the established order of the French church.[14] The Vatican, however, stood firm. Louis and Colbert finally had to give way, and it was not until 1674 that the independent diocese of Quebec was established.

Another factor in the conflict between church and state was Colbert's belief that France must have a larger population to provide the labour force needed to strengthen the economic sinews of the nation. He bitterly resented what seemed to him the hordes of clergy in the land who, it was estimated, consumed one-quarter of the country's wealth but contributed, he thought, little of tangible value. He betrayed his views in a memoir discussing the reasons for the great wealth of England and Holland, both much smaller in population and resources than France. "There are," he wrote, "no monks in Holland or England." The fact that the clergy were celibate also distressed him and he declared that they "not only shirk the labour which would aid the common good, but also deprive the public of all the children whom they could produce to serve useful and necessary functions."[15] For these reasons, then, he was determined to keep the clergy in New France under firm control and his suspicious, hostile attitude prevented any alliance of church and state to further his economic policies.

Talon's first disagreement with the Jesuits in New France seemed, however, to belie all Colbert's suspicions. Informed by the Minister that a large number of immigrant families would be sent to the colony in 1666 and that he should have land cleared ready for them to begin work as soon as they arrived, Talon made ready to provide this land by the simple expedient of sequestering a large part of the Jesuits' seigneury at Notre Dame des Anges, land which they had held for forty years, had gone to considerable expense to clear and bring under cultivation, and on which they intended to settle more colonists. The Jesuits protested Talon's action in restrained language, but when the Intendant declared that it was an affair of state in which not religion but the King's interests were involved they immediately desisted, declaring, "we desire nothing more than to demonstrate to you that we are very submissive and very obedient subjects of the King, and your very humble servants."[16] This incident made clear that the Jesuits were far removed from any desire to challenge the royal authority, exercised by the intendant, in temporal matters; in fact it is difficult to see how even Colbert could have expected a greater degree of clerical submission to the royal authority.

On the question of trading brandy to the Indians, however, the clergy were adamant. Colbert, aware that the fur trade offered a very profitable outlet for surplus French brandy, was enfuriated by the attempts of the Canadian clergy to prohibit this trade. Talon, during the first years of his intendancy made no attempt to rescind the existing ban on the trade, and Tracy was firmly opposed to it; in fact, Tracy informed Colbert that nothing was so necessary as to curb the trade and he asked that a minimal amount of brandy be shipped to the colony. The *habitants* of Trois Rivières and Cap de la Madeleine were of the same opinion; they petitioned the Sovereign Council to stop the trading of brandy to the Indians to prevent the terrible disorders that it always produced. Tracy, accordingly, had the Council issue an *arrêt*. In 1668, however, after Tracy had returned to France and after Talon had begun to take an active part in the fur trade, he had the Sovereign Council rescind the ban and grant freedom to trade brandy with the Indians openly with the one ineffective proviso that they must not be allowed to get drunk. From this point on relations between Talon and the clergy were embittered.

In November 1668 Talon returned to France and was replaced by Claude de Bouteroue. He had stayed in Canada a year over his stipulated two-year term. For the last two years he had been importuning Colbert to be recalled, claiming that his health was suffering in Canada's severe climate and that family affairs in France required his urgent attention. While in France, however, he continued to interest himself in Canadian affairs and before he had been away a year he was reappointed intendant of New France. This time, however, Talon was determined to have things in the colony more his own way. He particularly requested that clergy be sent out who would be more complaisant, "who would not be troublesome or bedevil the people's consciences. One cannot," he emphasized, "stress this point enough for it is essential to the development of the Colony which suffers greatly on this score."[17]

Colbert was in complete accord, and the decision was now made to have the Récollet order, the most austere of the Franciscans, re-established in Canada. In May 1669 Father Allart, the Provincial of the order, and three of his friars were ordered by the King to embark for Quebec on the first available boat. It was not, however, until the following year that they arrived in the colony, where Bishop Laval had been ordered by Louis and Colbert to see to it that they were granted the lands and buildings that had formerly belonged to the order. The Récollets had been the first missionaries in New France, arriving in 1615, followed by the Jesuits in 1625. In 1632, when the colony was returned to France after its capture by the Kirke brothers, the Jesuits returned, but Cardinal Richelieu refused to allow the re-establishment of the Récollets, who were then quick to blame the Jesuits for this refusal. They now accepted with enthusiasm the King's and Colbert's orders to cross to Quebec, although their chief function was to serve as a foil against the Jesuits and Bishop Laval. They were to be used by the state in its struggle to reduce the church to subservience, and their future conduct in the colony made it plain that they did not object to this role, since it resulted in the favour of the royal officials. This was, in many ways, unfortunate; there was quite enough friction among the different groups of clergy in the colony without adding to it; and the Récollets proved to be anything but circumspect, or even adroit, in the difficult role contrived for them by Talon and Colbert.

Talon also requested that in his new commission he be given more extensive powers than he had enjoyed before, maintaining that in a post so far removed from the seat of royal power, where the presence of the monarch could not make itself felt, an intendant could not have too much authority. He also suggested that a Canadian aristocracy be created by granting him eight blank letters of nobility. This, he claimed, would enable him to form a small group who would be especially obligated to the King, and hence more devoted to his service. Colbert, however, rejected this suggestion out of hand, noting in the margin of Talon's memoir that such an innovation would merely establish a provincial royal court,[18] and there was no group for whom Colbert had greater contempt than courtiers. But he did look with more favour on Talon's suggestion that he be provided with two or three *lettres de cachet*, which would enable him to ship back to France any persons whom he judged to be acting in a manner prejudicial to the King's service and the good of the colony.[19] Whether or not Talon obtained these *lettres de cachet* is not known. If he did he appears not to have used them, but as he had pointed out, the mere knowledge that he had them would have a salutary effect among the colonists.

Talon's appetite for power was growing, and what is more, seems to have been strengthened by what it fed on. Consequently upon his return to Quebec he quickly became embroiled in acrimonious disputes with Courcelle, who had always been of the opinion that the governor of the colony rather than the intendant should have the dominant position, and the power, in the colony. To some extent this conflict between the two men was a clash of personalities. Courcelle was of the old nobility, a veteran soldier accustomed to giving orders and taking them only from his social equals and military superiors, not from civilians of the *noblesse de robe* whom he regarded as his inferiors in every way. He had always been on good terms with Tracy, but Talon's seemingly excessive powers and arrogant bearing he could not abide. In a larger sense this conflict was an expression of the changes taking place in the social framework of France; the old feudal nobility being supplanted by the new, rising class of career men, the men of wealth and talent, the nobility of the robe.

In 1669, when Courcelle had complained of the attitude of Talon's temporary successor, Bouteroue, Colbert had curtly informed him that a man in his position had to be tolerant of the faults of others, and make the best possible use of their good qualities in order that the King's intentions for the colony might be carried out. Shortly after his return to Quebec in 1670 Talon informed Colbert that the Governor appeared to be very jealous of the confidence the Minister had manifested in his, Talon's, abilities and became very annoyed whenever he failed to agree with him. Colbert impressed on Talon the need for them to forget their differences and co-operate, but the following year Talon complained that Courcelle treated him as his inferior, almost as a valet, and did much to hinder his plans for the colony. Unfortunately, Courcelle's correspondence has not survived, and Talon's dispatches to the Minister give, of course, only his side of the dispute. The real root of the trouble, however, is perhaps revealed in a memoir from Patoulet to Colbert wherein he states: "M. Talon most humbly begs the King, above all else, either to release him or to let him remain in that country alone."[20] In other words, he wanted to have complete power in the colony, with no one to dispute his absolute authority. It may well be no accident that his recall to France, on grounds of ill-health, was issued by Colbert four months later, or that his subsequent pathetic attempts to obtain permission to return to New France in a menial capacity were denied.*

Certainly in one of the spheres that were properly the governor's and not the intendant's, namely, the relations with the Indian nations, Courcelle showed far greater ability than Talon ever allowed he had and won the respect of French and Indians alike. When, in 1669, a Seneca chief was murdered by three soldiers of the Montreal garrison, Courcelle took swift

---

* In 1681, when it was anticipated that the governor of New France, Frontenac, would shortly be recalled, well-informed men at the Court stated that Talon was eager for the appointment as governor. The following year, when La Barre received the appointment, Talon tried to persuade the minister to allow him to return to New France to found, entirely at his own expense, an alms house to care for paupers, aged Indians, and such like. At the court it was suspected that he wanted to be in the colony in the expectation that the newly appointed governor, or intendant, would not remain in the colony long, and he being on the spot would then have a better chance of being appointed to the one or other post. But whatever his motives, the Minister refused to entertain his proposal for the alms house. On the face of it, running a home for the aged, decrepit, and poverty stricken seems out of character for a man of Talon's abilities and character.[21]

action lest the Iroquois regard the incident as a *casus belli*. The three men were quickly apprehended, tried and executed, before a large group of Iroquois, come to Montreal to trade. The Iroquois were much impressed with the fact that the French had condemned to death three of their own men for the murder of one Iroquois, and the peace was preserved. The following year, however, the Iroquois began warring again with the Algonquins, killing several and taking some prisoners. The Algonquins immediately struck back. It looked as though hostilities would spread to all the tribes allied to the French and eventually to the French themselves. Courcelle ordered both sides to cease fighting and to return their prisoners. When the Iroquois showed no inclination to accept this order Courcelle threatened to march an army into their country. The western Iroquois defied him, confident that their villages were too remote to be reached by a French army. They haughtily replied: "The Governor threatens to ruin our country? We shall see if his arm is long enough to lift our scalps."

The following year Courcelle had a large flatboat built at Montreal, capable of transporting heavier supplies than canoes could carry, mustered fifty-six volunteers, and on June 2 set off up the turbulent rapids of the St Lawrence to show the western Iroquois that their country was not beyond his reach. Ten days later they were at Lake Ontario, to the great consternation of the Iroquois hunting-parties they met. He informed them that if they wished to continue warring with the Algonquins and to extend the war to the French as some of them had threatened, they were completely at liberty to do so; but if they did, he added, he would bring an army to Lake Ontario in large boats and destroy them. The Iroquois were so impressed by Courcelle's audacious move they ceased all talk of war and made their peace with the Algonquins.

When Courcelle and Talon left the colony in 1672 they could fairly claim that a great deal had been accomplished under their administration. The threatened renewal of Iroquois assaults had been effectively curbed, and the colonists could continue to clear their land and sow their crops without fear. Colbert's plans for industrial and commercial development had made a brave beginning; if some of these plans had foundered it is not to be wondered at. For them all to have been crowned with success would have been nothing short of miraculous. The most conspicuous achievement was the great increase in population. In 1663 it had been estimated at 2,500 souls. In 1669 Colbert commented how pleased he was that the population had increased by two-thirds since the colony was taken over by the Crown. Three years later the Bishop informed him that 700 children had been baptised during the past year and that he estimated there would be 1,100 more during the coming year. How the Bishop arrived at this estimate is not known. In any event, by 1673 the population had increased to 6,705. This increase, however, was not all total gain. Despite Colbert's insistence that only sturdy men and women, of good morals, be sent to the colony, it was inevitable that many would find the life too hard or would be unable to adjust to colonial conditions, and by 1672 the authorities were perplexed how to cope with the large number of mendicants in the towns. By 1680 they had an additional problem: how to provide for the increasing number of widows and orphans resulting from the marriages in the 1660's and 1670's of young women to men much their senior in years. Eventually, however, institutions were founded to care for those who could not care for themselves, for this was considered to be a proper responsibility of society.

By 1672 knowledge of the extent and geography of North America had been greatly extended. The whole basin of the Great Lakes and beyond was now considered to be French territory and the English of New York were becoming alarmed at this expansion.[22] So too was Colbert, and rightly so, for this drain of French strength into the interior was crippling his plans for the colony's industrial development. Moreover, this exodus became serious just at the time that Colbert was obliged to stop investing Crown capital in the colonies. In 1672 the war with the Dutch began, a war that Colbert fully supported, hoping that force of arms would do what French merchants, sailors, and industrialists had been unable to do, eliminate Dutch economic competition. With this war draining French treasure, Colbert bluntly stated that for the time being Canada and Acadia would have to fend for themselves; the Crown could allocate no funds at all for their development.[23]

Acadia managed somehow to survive, but only just. New France, on the other hand, continued to develop along lines quite contrary to those indicated as desirable by Colbert. The lure of the fur trade in the interior was the line of least economic resistance for the Canadians, and against this force all the directives from Colbert's paper-strewn desk could not prevail. By 1672 Colbert and his assistant, Colbert de Terron at Rochefort, had succeeded in establishing a thriving colony in Canada, then told it to stand on its own feet. This it proved well able to do and had, in fact, already begun to strike out for itself; but the direction it took was not the one Colbert desired.

CHAPTER 6

Conflict and Constitutional Development

Colbert had little difficulty in finding a successor to Courcelle. Two men were eager to be appointed Governor General of New France. One was M. de Grignan, son-in-law of Mme de Sévigné, whose letters are among the literary gems of the period. He sought the post to escape his creditors. The other was Louis de Buade, Comte de Frontenac, who sought the post for the same reason. Frontenac, who was a godson of Louis XIII, was very well connected at Court; his father and grandfather had served in the entourages of Louis XIII and Henri IV, and his mother was a member of the very influential Pontchartrain family. He had, therefore, little difficulty in obtaining the appointment.

Born in 1622, Frontenac had entered the army in his 'teens and served in several campaigns during the Thirty Years' War, as colonel of the *Régiment de Normandie*. Like so many of his class he lived extravagantly and was heavily in debt. To extricate himself from his financial difficulties he followed the time-honoured recipe of marrying an heiress, Anne de la Grange, daughter of a wealthy member of the *noblesse de robe*. But this availed him nothing, as his father-in-law, who had done everything in his power to prevent the marriage, disinherited his daughter. In 1669 he served briefly with the Venetian forces fighting the Turks in Crete. The Venetian commanding general, Francesco Morosini, one of Europe's leading soldiers, took an almost instant dislike to him and summarily dismissed him after he had been on the island only a few weeks. Three years later his creditors, who were about to seize all his properties, were dismayed to learn that he had been appointed Governor General of New France and that with the commission he had obtained an order from the Council of State which deferred his legal obligation to repay his debts during the King's pleasure.[1]

In his character and temperament Frontenac was not well suited for the post of governor of a small, struggling colony set in the wilds of North America. His greatest asset was his personal charm, a quality of considerable benefit to its owner when at the Court, but not by itself sufficient to enable him to cope with the problems of a frontier province. He was extremely vain, could tolerate any amount of flattery, could never admit that he was ever in error, and had a fierce temper that he could not control. He had been well educated, most likely at a Jesuit college, and was very skilled in his use of words. His chief difficulty, however, was that he was in effect a feudal anachronism, a product of the old nobility that had dominated in the provinces, led armies against the Crown on occasion, served no interests but its own, and was now being reduced to impotence by Louis XIV and Colbert. The positions of power and influence in the land were coming increasingly to be occupied by men of the new, rising class, the *noblesse de robe*: men of great ability such as Talon, Colbert de Terron, and Colbert himself. Frontenac was unable to comprehend these changes, and his irascible temper made it impossible for him to submit to them quietly. He could only behave like a feudal baron who would brook no opposition from those beneath him, and this was bound to bring trouble in the royal province of New France under the tight control of Louis XIV and Colbert.

This trouble, however, when it came, served to throw into a clear light the basic problem of government under a despotic ruler, in a province as remote as was Canada, benevolent despot though Louis XIV undoubtedly was. The King in France was above the law, and during Louis XIV's reign this was not disputed because his rule was not only efficient and reasonably equitable, but also distinguished by moderation. In short, he gave the people the sort of government that the majority wanted, or at least could endure. But Canada was three thousand miles removed from the King's surveillance, and communications were severed for three-quarters of every year. Yet someone had to exercise the royal power and it had to be made manifest to all the King's subjects in this remote province that the King's will had to be obeyed, without question. This, then, was the function of the governor general, and the problem was to appoint men who could exercise the function; embody this supreme power in the same moderate manner that Louis XIV would have exercised it. Such men of the noble class, with the requisite military training and ability, who could lead men in time of war and command the respect of the people were indeed scarce. More particularly were they scarce when France was at war, as she was in 1672, for such men naturally preferred to serve with the army in Europe where the opportunities for glory were greater and, what was more significant, the chances greater of being brought to the notice of the King for exceptional service or valour.

Thus it could easily happen that a man lacking the requisite qualities of intelligence, dignity, moderation, military ability, and skill in handling men of all classes would have to be appointed to govern Canada, and since he represented the person of the King there could be no apparent check to his authority. He had, in other words, to appear clearly to be above the law and answerable only to the King. Frontenac was soon to make it glaringly obvious that he lacked most of these essential qualities; hence Louis XIV and Colbert were faced with the difficult task of finding some means to prevent him abusing his authority. Detailed instructions, appeals to reason, and biting criticism were all tried, but without success. Finally, and reluctantly, the King and the Minister were forced to issue edicts that limited the absolute powers of the governor, restricting his authority to certain spheres of action, and granting clearly defined authority to other officials and bodies. In this way, then, under the benevolent despotism of Louis XIV Canada acquired a semblance of constitutional government and the governor general came to be placed squarely beneath the law, albeit the law of Louis XIV and his ministers. That this was actually more real than apparent was made plain when he refused to obey the King's edicts, and insisted on regarding himself as not being under the constraint of any law that allowed others to oppose his wishes. Once Louis XIV and Colbert became convinced that Frontenac would not submit to the law, he was recalled.

In a negative sense Frontenac deserves some credit for this constitutional development. Just as there would have been no Magna Carta without King John, there would have been no checks placed on the authority of the governor of New France had it not been for Frontenac's consistent and flagrant abuse of power. But the staunch opposition of the barons was also needed at Runnymede; and in New France, too, opposition to Frontenac's abuses was a prerequisite for edicts to be enacted to prevent him, and his successors, governing in a tyrannical fashion. This the other royal officials and the people of New France, of both high and low degree, were not afraid to provide.

This opposition began very shortly after Frontenac arrived in the colony, for he wasted no time in demonstrating how he expected to be treated by all. No sooner had his commission as governor been registered by the Sovereign Council than he was engaged in disputes with the Intendant who was waiting for the last ships to sail before returning to France. Talon, as *intendant de justice, police, et finance*, had always presided over the meetings of the Sovereign Council, but Frontenac was convinced that it was he, as Governor General and not a subordinate official, who should perform the functions of president. He insisted that in the records of the Council he be termed *"haut et puissant seigneur,"* rather than *"Monsieur le gouverneur,"* a title that had satisfied his predecessors. Talon, having maintained his dominant position throughout Courcelle's term of office, was not the man meekly to submit to Frontenac's demands; consequently there were some heated exchanges. Frontenac objected to what he considered to be the intendant's excessive powers in the general administration of the colony, and in his first dispatches to the Minister he asked that the granting of land concessions to seigneurs and the issuing of passports to leave the colony be his sole prerogative, not to be shared with the intendant. He informed the Minister that "as long as a governor here lacks the power to grant any favours and is almost without a function . . . he cannot gain much influence or esteem."

Within a few weeks of his arrival Frontenac organized a colonial Estates General, ostensibly to have the people swear an oath of fealty to the King. It was quite obvious, however, that his real purpose was to impress the people by introducing some semblance of the pomp and circumstance of the Court with himself playing the stellar role. There was nothing wrong with this, but he did carry it to rather ridiculous lengths. Instead of the customary three estates: clergy, nobles, and commons, Frontenac formed four estates: clergy, nobles, commons, and judiciary. Since the Estates General in France had last met in 1614, before Frontenac was born, he can be excused for failing to follow established custom; very likely no one could recollect what the custom had been. For the nobles, he had to make do with three or four gentlemen and the officers of his guards; the leading merchants and the syndic of Quebec formed the third estate and the members of the Sovereign Council along with the judge of the Quebec Prévôté court formed the legal estate. Jean Talon refused to have anything to do with the affair, declaring himself to be a little indisposed. He recovered the following day.

On October 23 the assembly took place in the recently completed Jesuit church. Frontenac began by making a speech filled with flattering references to Colbert and the glory of Louis XIV, to whom he later sent copies, and the oath was then administered. When a group of Huron Indians later asked Frontenac to enact the ceremony again for their benefit, he gladly obliged. Colbert, however, was not at all impressed when he read of these proceedings and he wrote to Frontenac, tersely telling him that the King had no intention of calling the Estates General lest it detract from the royal authority; therefore no more such meetings should be held in Canada.

To assert, on the basis of this assembly, that Frontenac desired to establish a form of representative government would be very far from the truth. Such a notion was contrary to his views and completely out of character, and if further proof were needed Frontenac supplied it when he explained to Colbert: "I never claimed thereby to form bodies that should subsist, knowing well of what consequence that could be."

In November Jean Talon sailed for France. Bishop Laval had left the year before to make financial arrangements for the new diocese of Quebec. Colbert experienced great difficulty in finding a suitable candidate to replace Talon, and it was not until 1675 that one was appointed. It was not until that year, too, that Laval returned to Quebec. Thus, for the next three years Frontenac shared authority with no one. To some extent, the troubles that ensued can be blamed on the fact that Colbert neglected to give any instructions on who was to perform the functions of the absent intendant. It had to be either the governor or the Sovereign Council, or the two working together, but Frontenac assumed from the outset that the intendant's powers devolved upon him, and under the circumstances there were good grounds for his assumption. But he cannot be excused for the manner in which he used these powers. In his official instructions he had been specifically informed that he must not interfere with the functions of the Sovereign Council, but merely keep a watching brief to ensure that they performed their duties conscientiously and competently. Should they be in any way remiss, he had been instructed only to point out to them the error of their ways; if they were to decline his advice then he was to report the matter to the King who would take the appropriate action. No sooner, however, had the last ships sailed for France than Frontenac began usurping the functions of the Council, having cases pending brought before him and rendering judgements. He also began issuing *ordonnances* to fix price ceilings on some commodities, something that previously had been done by the Council. It may well have been that he delivered sound verdicts in the cases he heard, despite the fact that he had had no training in the law, and it is clear that there was a need for legislation to curb the profiteering proclivities of the colony's merchants and tradesmen, but his high-handed actions stirred up active resentment and opposition among the members of the Sovereign Council.

When Colbert was informed of these developments he made it very plain to Frontenac that he had misused his authority. The Governor was bluntly told that he had no right whatsoever to meddle in affairs of justice, or in these legislative matters that were clearly the province of the Sovereign Council. The people of New France, wrote Colbert, were to be allowed as much freedom as circumstances allowed to run their own affairs without hindrance or interference. Far from being chastened by this rebuke, Frontenac was infuriated. He was infuriated even more to discover that the Minister had accepted his eminently sound suggestion to increase the membership of the Sovereign Council from five to seven, but had not left the choice of the new councillors to him. Instead, Colbert had chosen them himself. Previously, Frontenac had made it plain to the members of the Council that they held office at his pleasure and could be dismissed by him at will. Now it appeared that this means of cowing them was being taken away from him.

Nor was it only members of the Sovereign Council who were opposing Frontenac in his attempts to rule the colony in an arbitrary and despotic fashion. During the summer of 1673 and the following winter and spring, he became embroiled in a violent conflict with the Governor of Montreal, many of the residents of that town, and a group of the clergy. This conflict centred about the fur trade; hence it affected directly a large number of the colonists, humble *habitants* and well-to-do merchants alike. Contained within this conflict was also a much larger issue, a matter bearing directly on the fundamental policy of the French in North America. The basic issue, that of French expansion into the North American continent, would have had to be decided sooner or later, but Frontenac took the decision out of the hands of the King and the Minister and settled it without regard for any interests but his own.

The dispute began when Frontenac decided to establish a fur-trade post on Lake Ontario. In the summer of 1673 he ordered the people of Montreal and vicinity to provide a hundred and twenty canoes; then, in July, obliged four hundred of the *habitants* to accompany him to Lake Ontario as a bodyguard and to build a trading-post. That the post was intended to serve a commercial purpose rather than a political or military one is evidenced by its location. Frontenac chose a site in a bay at the mouth of the Cataracoui River – where the city of Kingston now stands. In times of peace it was well located to tap the trade of the Iroquois returning from their hunting-grounds to their villages on the south side of the lake, but as a military fort it was virtually useless since it could command only the area within musket range of its walls, and in times of war an enemy could easily bypass it and just as easily starve out its garrison. In fact, during any war with the Iroquois the fort was untenable, and in 1689 it had to be abandoned. The post could, however, serve as a staging base for other posts to be built farther west and the fur-traders of Montreal were quick to see this threat to their interests. Such a chain of posts through the Great Lakes with barques sailing between them, might drain the fur trade that normally flowed from the west by way of the Ottawa River to the warehouses of the Montreal merchants.

The *habitants* of the Montreal area were incensed at being obliged to provide canoes, then to accompany Frontenac to Lake Ontario and there build the post while he discussed trade arrangements with the Iroquois whom he had previously invited to come to confer with him. They were convinced that this *corvée*, and the others that were to follow to transport supplies to the new post, had been contrived to benefit Frontenac personally. Normally, *corvées* lasted only a few days each year for work that benefited the entire community. They regarded Frontenac's *corvées* as a gross imposition. By the end of the summer the people of Montreal were in a very hostile mood and inclined to do all they could to hinder Frontenac's fur-trade venture. In this attitude they were encouraged by the Governor of Montreal, François-Marie Perrot.

Up until this point, the people of Montreal had had little cause to be pleased with their local governor who had proved to be a very unpleasant person indeed. He had himself established a trading-post a few miles west of Montreal and he consistently abused his authority to serve his private interests; but he had never done so on the scale that Frontenac had now done. Since Perrot's own interests were threatened by the new post, which Frontenac had named after himself, he was every bit as opposed to it as were the people of his government. Since nothing draws two people, or groups of people, closer together than a third they both dislike, Perrot suddenly became quite popular in Montreal when he began to arrest men who had obtained hunting-licences from Frontenac and misused them by going to the Indian villages to trade furs illegally, thereby forstalling the Montreal traders.

Frontenac was quick to see that Perrot and the people of Montreal could seriously hinder his new enterprise. He therefore took steps to remove Perrot from office and at the same time show all concerned that opposition to his plans would not be tolerated. During the ensuing winter he deliberately provoked Perrot into actions that could be regarded as a defiance of his authority; then through the agency of an unwitting Sulpician priest of the Montreal seminary, the Abbé Fénelon, he invited Perrot to come to Quebec to settle the issue amicably. Perrot, accompanied by the Sulpician, duly went in good faith to Quebec at the end of January, only to find that he had walked into a trap of Frontenac's contriving. When he called on Frontenac at the Château St Louis, the Governor was waiting for him with some twenty members of his personal entourage. Before Perrot could say a word he was seized and imprisoned in the dungeons of the Château. The next day Frontenac instructed the Sovereign Council to interrogate Perrot and bring appropriate charges against him.

For the remainder of the winter and through the following spring and summer the Sovereign Council did little but wrestle with this case and with others that arose out of it. Meanwhile, with Perrot out of the way, Frontenac replaced the Town-Major of Montreal with a member of his own entourage, the Sieur de la Nouguère, who served as acting governor of the town and its environs. This ensured that any opposition to the fur-trade activities of Frontenac and his associates would be curbed. The people of Montreal did not take kindly to this, and when Perrot's wife circulated a petition declaring that the signatories were satisfied with her husband's government, she had no difficulty obtaining signatures. The Abbé Fénelon, who appears to have felt that he had been tricked by Frontenac into luring Perrot into a trap, lent Madame Perrot his support and subsequently, at Easter, preached a sermon in the Montreal parish church which some regarded as a thinly veiled attack on Frontenac. In his sermon he cited certain actions on the part of a civil governor that would clearly constitute an abuse of his authority, such things as forcing the people to perform *corvées* which served only his private interests, oppressing any who resisted his attempts to extort part of the profits of their legitimate commerce, persecuting royal officials who sought to defend the people against his extortions, and surrounding himself with sycophants. When Frontenac was informed of this sermon by one of his fur-trade associates, the Sieur de la Salle, he declared the sermon to be seditious and ordered Fénelon to be brought before the Sovereign Council for trial. When Fénelon appeared before the court he pleaded benefit of clergy and denied the right of the court to hear the case because as an ecclesiastic he could not be tried in a civil court unless his bishop ordered him to submit and appear. With Bishop Laval in France, this was impossible, and when other members of the clergy were brought before the court to give evidence they too pleaded benefit of clergy and refused to testify. The Sovereign Council had never been faced with such a situation before, and its members were clearly at a loss what to do.

They found themselves in a similar predicament with Perrot. At least one member of the Council, and the senior councillor at that, the Sieur de Villeray who had had disputes with Frontenac earlier, supported Perrot. In fact, Villeray provided Perrot surreptitiously with legal counsel which he used with telling effect.[2] Only the fact that Frontenac threatened and bullied them without cease prevented the Sovereign Council dismissing the cases. Perrot stoutly maintained that he held a commission from the King, therefore he could not be tried by the Sovereign Council without its constituting an affront to Louis XIV. He also maintained, on better legal grounds, that, since Frontenac was his accuser and the members of the Council removable by him, they were merely the governor's agents and hence not legally empowered to sit in judgement on him.

Eventually, the Sovereign Council became more afraid of what the attitude of the King would be, were they to persist in the trial of Perrot and Fénelon, than they were of Frontenac should they not. Despite the latter's threats and imprecations they finally voted to refer both cases to the King. Perrot and Fénelon were sent to France on Frontenac's orders to answer for their alleged crimes. He also sent his secretary to ensure that the Minister heard his side of the story. Along with them went the Sieur de Lotbinière, recently appointed to the Sovereign Council by Colbert, ostensibly on private business, but it would have been most unusual indeed had he not gone to the Court while in France and given his account of events to the Minister. In any event, Colbert had Perrot sent to the comfortable seclusion of the Bastille for three weeks to make public amends for his affront to the royal authority vested in the Governor General. He was then allowed to return to his post as Governor of Montreal on condition that he apologized to Frontenac who was ordered to accept the apology without more ado. For his part Frontenac was ordered to treat Perrot with greater respect in future. This reinstatement was tantamount to a moral victory for Perrot and the people of Montreal who had supported him against Frontenac. The import was not lost on them. The Abbé Fénelon was ordered not to return to New France, and it was understood that his indiscretion had blighted his chances of ecclesiastical advancement. This made it clear that the clergy were not to interfere in civil matters. Frontenac was informed by the Minister that his attempts to bring a member of the clergy to trial had been *ultra vires*, that he had no authority over the clergy, and that such matters should be left in the hands of the bishop. The very most that he could do in cases involving the clergy was to order an offending cleric to return to France.

Frontenac's high-handed actions did, however, have certain beneficial effects. In an attempt to prevent their recurrence Colbert increased greatly the power of the Sovereign Council by granting its members royal commissions and decreeing that in future all appointments to the Council, including the posts of attorney general and recording clerk, would be made directly by the King. This meant that the governor could no longer use the threat of dismissal to make the Sovereign Council bow to his will.

At the same time the Minister appointed an intendant for the colony, Jacques Duchesneau, a man who had had some fourteen years experience in the royal service, and empowered him to act as presiding officer of the Sovereign Council. There was thus now a clear-cut separation of the powers of the governor, the intendant, and the Sovereign Council. This *Déclaration* of 1675 went a long way to prevent the governor of the colony exercising despotic power.[3]

Three years later, when Perrot arbitrarily imprisoned a judge in Montreal for having ordered the arrest of a *coureur de bois*, the Sovereign Council decided to take action but Frontenac, who had formed an uneasy alliance with Perrot to further their fur-trade activities, forbade them to intervene, ordered the judge imprisoned for two months, and refused to release him until he had paid a 200-*livre* fine. The Sovereign Council protested this and other arbitrary actions of the Governor, whereat he charged that their protests were tantamount to sedition. Colbert, however, took a markedly different view, and a royal edict was sent forbidding local governors to imprison or fine anyone without specific orders from the governor general or the Sovereign Council.[4] Colbert accompanied this edict with instructions to Frontenac that the King wished him clearly to understand that he was not to order the arrest of anyone for civil or criminal offences, nor to order the local governors to arrest anyone, but to leave this function entirely to the established courts. Only in cases of sedition and treason could the governor general take the law into his own hands and, Colbert tartly added, "such things hardly ever happen."[5] Thus, again as a result of Frontenac's despotic actions, legislation was enacted to guarantee the people of New France against arbitrary arrest. In England that same year, 1679, and under somewhat similar circumstances, Parliament passed the Habeas Corpus Act. At first glance it might seem strange that a divine right monarch such as Louis XIV, and the English Whigs, should enact similar decrees, but in fact both sought the same end, to prevent the abuse of power.

It was, however, one thing for Colbert and Louis XIV to issue edicts designed to ensure good government in New France; it was quite another to make a man of Frontenac's background and temperament abide by them. What is really significant about these conflicts is, not so much that Frontenac behaved as he did, but that the other colonial authorities, and most particularly the Sovereign Council, refused adamantly to submit to his violent attempts to reduce them to subservience. Although they were subjected to great abuse, they eventually defeated him and succeeded in maintaining their prerogatives, and with them, rule by law.

Another influential group in the colony whom Frontenac succeeded in antagonizing was the clergy, with the exception of the Récollets and the female orders. The disputes that ensued between the Governor and the clergy cannot be regarded as a simple conflict between the secular and the clerical authorities; personalities played too great a part. In any case, if there had ever been any question which should dominate the other, clerical or secular authority, it had already been clearly settled in favour of the Crown. The clergy did, however, serve as a convenient whipping-boy for Frontenac. He was very quick to seize on any incident that would give him occasion to complain to the Minister of the actions of the clergy and to claim that he had effectively prevented them abusing their authority. This, of couse, was very pleasing to the Minister, and Frontenac was clearly aware that it would be. The Minister's bias against the clergy also afforded the Governor ample opportunity to blacken the reputation of any laymen in the colony who opposed him by declaring them to be under clerical influence. Guilt by association was very real to Colbert.

The main issues around which conflict between the clergy and the

Governor centred were the old recurring ones of the brandy trade with the Indians and a new one which arose out of Colbert's scheme to civilize the Indians and thereby increase the working population of the colony. In 1669 Colbert, writing over the King's signature, had enunciated this "Frenchification" policy exhorting the bishop to have as many Indian children as possible raised and educated in the colony in order to create of them and the French a single people, this being the most important task that the clergy could possibly perform. Two years later he instructed Talon to "endeavour by every possible means to encourage the clergy . . . to bring up in their communities as many Indian children as possible, so that by being educated in the maxims of our religion and in our customs they, along with the settlers, may evolve into a single nation and so strengthen the colony." This policy, however, was not new. As early as 1636 the Jesuits had attempted to educate Indian children and introduce them to European ways, but with no success whatsoever. The restraints of civilized society had no appeal – just the reverse, in fact – for these wild, free children of the forest. Bishop Laval, the Sulpicians, and the Récollets made similar attempts with an equal lack of success. The Ursuline nuns fared a little better over a thirty-year period; they succeeded in training seven or eight Indian girls who eventually married Canadians, but this was a long way from fulfilling Colbert's expectations.

In the light of this long experience the clergy came to the conclusion that the policy was not only impracticable but detrimental to all concerned. They had early learned that when the Indians and the French lived in close proximity each tended to acquire the worst traits of the other, and they did their best to keep them apart. This, of course, was the antithesis of Colbert's policy and the Minister became convinced, not that his policy was impracticable, but that the clergy desired to keep the Indians isolated purely in order to maintain their own influence over them. He was further persuaded of this when Frontenac agreed with him, maintaining that the Indians would be readily assimilated were it not for the Jesuits' opposition to the scheme. He further claimed that the Jesuits wished to exclude the French from contact with the Indians in order to monopolize the fur trade.[6] In 1685, after Colbert's demise, the Marquis de Denonville, then Governor of the colony, informed the Minister that the policy of "Frenchification" of the Indians had no hope of success. Apart from a few plaintive comments by Frontenac during his second administration nothing more is heard of the issue. The "Frenchification policy" died with Colbert, but while he lived Frontenac took full advantage of the Minister's prejudice to belabour the clergy.

The dispute over brandy was a more serious matter because more people and interests were involved. The clergy, led by Bishop Laval, were adamant in their opposition to the sale of brandy to the Indians, as were some of the leading merchants in the colony – La Chesnaye and Le Ber, for example – and such senior officials as Tracy, Duchesneau, Pierre Boucher, and subsequently the Chevalier de Vaudreuil, Meneval the Governor of Acadia, Denonville, and the Intendant Champigny. Fur-traders such as Greysolon du Lhut and Louis Jolliet also voiced their opposition to the brandy trade. In New York, too, the officials strove to curb it, once they had seen its effects on the Iroquois.[7] Others in the colony, however, were just as strongly opposed to the imposition of any restraints on the sale of brandy. This group ranged in its membership from *coureurs de bois* and tavern-keepers to Talon, Frontenac, La Salle, La Mothe Cadillac, and Colbert himself. It is not without significance that these men all had a vested interest in the fur trade, nor that far greater profits could be made by trading brandy than any other commodity.

In 1668 Talon had had the existing edicts forbidding the sale of brandy to the Indians rescinded and the clergy had immediately intervened, maintaining that the issue fell within their province since it affected the morals, not only of the Indians, but of those who supplied them with liquor, and constituted a mortal sin. Bishop Laval had declared the matter a reserved case and ordered that those known to have traded brandy to the Indians be refused absolution. Colbert admitted that the clergy's stand was correct in principle, but he claimed that it was bad in practice because it would harm French commerce without achieving the ends desired by the clergy. He was strongly of the opinion that the Indians would stop at nothing to get liquor and, if the French refused it to them, they would go to the Dutch traders at Albany, there to imbibe protestant heresy along with English rum. "The Bishop and the Jesuit fathers," he had earlier stated, "without reflecting that prudence, not to mention Christian charity, requires that one should close his eyes to a lesser evil in order to avoid a greater one, or to achieve an end that transcends the evil, refuse to alter their views in this matter."[8]

Frontenac was quick to agree with the Minister's views and he claimed that the attitude of the clergy was another example of their usurping the royal authority vested in the governor general. He also maintained that the seriousness of the problem had been grossly exaggerated and that the Indians got drunk no more readily than did the Dutch or English, and no one pretended that it was a sin to sell liquor to them. Anyone who disagreed with Frontenac on this issue he declared to be under Jesuit influence, which, of course, damned them in the eyes of Colbert.

The clergy were not without influence at the Court, and in 1678 the King gave orders that twenty of the leading men in the colony should be called together to give their views on the issue. Since Frontenac was empowered to select the members of this so-called "Brandy Parliament" and Colbert sent his written views on the question, making it very plain what decision he wanted them to render, the outcome was easy to predict. One of the leading merchants, Aubert de la Chesnaye, who was not chosen to serve in this assembly, stated at the time that Frontenac chose only men who had a vested interest in the brandy trade and manipulated them "as a man in his position could easily do."[9] This was not strictly true, since five of the twenty members of the assembly declared themselves opposed to the trading of brandy to the Indians on religious, moral, and economic grounds; Louis Jolliet, the explorer, and Jacques Le Ber, reputed to be the wealthiest fur-trader in the colony, both declared that anyone caught taking liquor into the Indian villages should be hanged. But the majority view was that there should be no restriction on the brandy trade.[10]

The following year Louis XIV issued an edict which put an end to the dispute for the time being. He forbade anyone to carry liquor to the Indians in their villages, but allowed it to be sold to them, in moderate quantities, in the French settlements. At the same time the King ordered the Bishop to withdraw his interdict. The clergy well knew that Frontenac and those who shared his views could all too easily evade the intent of this edict, but they had to accept it without a murmur.

In some of their disputes with Frontenac the clergy found an ally in the newly appointed Intendant, Jacques Duchesneau, but it was Frontenac who was largely responsible for this alliance. An honest man, Duchesneau was also stubborn, and consequently became embroiled in disputes with Frontenac soon after his arrival. This naturally caused him to gravitate towards those others who were at odds with the Governor, until Frontenac found arrayed against himself what he labelled a cabal, consisting of the Intendant, the clergy, the Sovereign Council, and many of the leading merchants in the colony.

The latent hostility came to a head in a series of dramatic clashes between Frontenac and the Sovereign Council during the winter of 1678-79. Although Colbert had made it very plain in the King's *Déclaration* of 1675 that the intendant, and not the governor, was to preside over the meetings of the Sovereign Council, Frontenac could not abide this relegation of himself to a subordinate role in the Council's deliberations. To make matters worse, the Intendant and some of the councillors were very quick to make plain to him that his position in the Council was little more than that of an honorary councillor. On occasions when the Intendant was absent from the Council meetings and Frontenac tried to take over his duties, the Council insisted that it was not he but the senior councillor who was empowered to "ask for the opinions, collect the voices and deliver the judgements." Eventually, unable to submit to such treatment any longer, Frontenac on a very flimsy pretext demanded that he be styled Chief and President of the Council in its records and public notices. He also claimed the conclusive voice in its deliberations and that he should preside over the meetings in the absence of the intendant. This seemed to the suspicious councillors to be an attempt to usurp the functions of the intendant and to dominate the Council. They refused to entertain any such proposals, despite Frontenac's angry threats. Throughout the winter and spring of 1679 the fight continued while the normal business of the Council was neglected. The members of the Council refused to give way an inch, resting their case squarely on the King's *Déclaration* of 1675.

Finally, at the end of June, Frontenac gave the councillors one week to change their attitude or be treated as guilty of disobeying an order of their Governor General who represented the King. When they still refused, he issued orders to the Attorney General, the Sieur d'Auteuil, and two of the councillors, Villeray and Tilly, to retire from Quebec and reside at specified seigneuries in the country until the ships sailed for France in the autumn; they were then to go to France to answer personally to the King for their defiance of the orders of the Governor General. This harsh action did not have the desired effect. The remaining councillors refused to function as a Council, declaring that they could not do so since their membership was not complete. At a subsequent private meeting of the sitting and exiled councillors they proposed a compromise whereby they would consent to Frontenac's assuming of the rank, titles, and powers that he had demanded, but only under protest; this last, they stated, to avoid their contravening the *Déclaration* of 1675. They were determined to maintain the letter and spirit of that edict for, were it to have been in any way weakened, the Sovereign Council would once again have been subservient to the arbitrary will of the governor. Frontenac was equally determined to destroy the intent of the *Déclaration* and regain the powers that he felt should rightfully have been his: he therefore rejected their proposal, left for Montreal, then continued on his customary summer trading-trip to Fort Frontenac.

Before returning to Quebec in the autumn he had had time to reconsider, and the tone of the dispatches from the Minister that he found waiting for him at Quebec was not reassuring. Colbert had severely reprimanded him for squabbling with the clergy over the honours he was to receive when he attended mass at the cathedral in Quebec. Such things were considered very important in the stratified society of Louis XIV. Colbert had earlier upheld Frontenac's demands to be accorded the honours due his rank but Frontenac had subsequently offended everyone by demanding honours not accorded any other provincial governor in the kingdom. He had also been curtly informed that he would answer to the King if he continued to levy fines and imprison people arbitrarily as he had been doing. Moreover, the ships were about to sail for France carrying full reports of recent events from all concerned. He therefore decided to moderate his attitude and now agreed to leave his demands on the Sovereign Council in abeyance until the King could render a decision. Meanwhile, the exiled councillors were allowed to return and take their places at the council table, on condition that the dispute not be mentioned by anyone. He did subsequently attempt, by means of a subterfuge, to have the rank and titles he demanded inscribed in the records of the Council, but this was discovered by the Intendant and the Council forced him to back down.

There the matter rested when the ships sailed for France, bearing with them the senior councillor, the Sieur de Villeray, going to the Court on Frontenac's orders to account for his alleged defiance of the Governor. Auteuil, the Attorney General, and Tilly, who had also previously been ordered to go to France, were excused the voyage by Frontenac. Auteuil was let off on grounds of ill-health, an excuse that Frontenac scoffed at. He died a few days after the ships had sailed. Tilly was excused because, as he had done during the Perrot case a few years before, he had turned craven under Frontenac's threats and blustering and had informed Frontenac privately that he was not in accord with the stand taken by the others and did not want to be held accountable for it.

A replacement now had to be found for the deceased Attorney General. Duchesneau, aware for some time of the poor state of Auteuil's health, had earlier obtained a blank commission from the Minister for the post. The councillors agreed with him that Auteuil's son, who was a graduate in law from the University of Paris and a member of the bar of the *Parlement* of Paris, was the only suitable candidate and despite Frontenac's violent protests the Council registered his commission. This was a victory for the Council, and with young Ruette d'Auteuil as Attorney General Frontenac could expect even stronger opposition than in the past, for Ruette d'Auteuil claimed that Frontenac's harsh treatment had hastened his father's demise.

The following year, in October 1680, when the ships from France were seen making their way up the river there must have been a great deal of suspense until they docked and the seals were broken on the dispatches from the Court. The Sovereign Council, to their undoubted relief and satisfaction, had been upheld by Colbert and Louis XIV and Frontenac roundly condemned for his conduct. He was informed in the strongest terms by the King that he had acted completely contrary to the royal edicts, decrees and proclamations, and in particular his claim to act as presiding officer of the Sovereign Council was in flagrant disregard of the *Déclaration* of 1675. The King then reiterated in the clearest possible terms that Frontenac was not to retain in his possession the minutes of the Council meetings as he had done in the past, or to collect the voices of the councillors, or deliver the judgements, as these were the prerogative of the intendant. The Governor was also condemned for having ordered the Attorney General and two councillors into exile from Quebec.

In his dispatch Louis XIV declared that New France "runs the risk of being completely destroyed unless you alter both your conduct and your principles," and he then went on to say:

> All the corporate bodies and nearly all the private individuals who return to this country complain of clear-cut cases of ill treatment meted out to them in a manner quite contrary to the spirit of moderation which you should exercise in the maintenance of peace and good order among the people, all as enjoined in my orders and dispatches. My revenue collectors complain that trade is being lost and destroyed by the *coureurs de bois*, that they receive no protection and that you permit neither the departure of the ships at times when they could leave, nor freedom of navigation on the rivers without your permits and passports. The Bishop and his clergy, the Jesuit fathers and the Sovereign Council, and in one word, all the public bodies and private persons, they all complain.[11]

Colbert, in his dispatch, informed Frontenac that the King had taken so serious a view of the whole matter that he had studied the evidence in the disputes himself and was convinced that Frontenac alone was responsible for all the trouble. He added, however, that the King had allowed himself to be persuaded by Frontenac's friends and relatives that he would not behave in such a manner again and had agreed to permit him to retain his post for another year. Colbert stated bluntly that he did not think Frontenac was capable of mending his ways and in this he was to prove all too correct.[12] Meanwhile, word quickly circulated at the Court that Frontenac would soon be recalled, and the senior officials began receiving soliciting letters from men eager to take his place.[13] Frontenac and the Sovereign Council had thus, between them, forced Louis XIV and Colbert to clarify further the administrative and judicial system of the colony. An even more clear-cut separation and limitation of powers than had existed before was the end result.

Duchesneau, however, now found himself in an awkward position. Although Colbert and Louis XIV had restricted the authority of the governor and greatly enhanced that of the intendant and the Sovereign Council, yet they could not allow subordinate officials to attack the governor general with impunity, no matter how well grounded their position might be. The governor general represented the King, Louis XIV, and there was always the fear that such defiance of a governor general by his subordinates, no matter how wrong he might be, might somehow lead to attempts to curb the power of the monarch himself. Thus Duchesneau was informed by Colbert and Louis XIV that he had to submit to the governor in all things. The most that he could do, should the governor attempt to usurp the intendant's functions, was to register a protest and submit a report to the Minister. On no account could an intendant resist a governor who represented the authority and person of the King. Louis XIV reserved to himself the right of judging and remedying affairs of this sort.[14]

What the King and Colbert really wanted was a system wherein the governor general was supreme in his relations with subordinates, but not so supreme that he could act as he pleased rather than the way the King and his Minister desired. They wished the governor, the intendant, and the Sovereign Council to co-operate, each performing certain functions. Such a system could only work when these officials behaved with moderation and common sense. Frontenac had proven himself quite incapable of behaving in this wise, hence Colbert and the King had been forced to contrive what could be regarded as an incipient constitution for New France, but they shrank from its implications and rationalized their attitude by blaming Duchesneau for much of the trouble.

For Frontenac it appears to have been impossible to admit, least of all to himself, that he might have gone too far and, in view of the King's and Colbert's attitude, that it might be wise to behave more circumspectly in future. In a letter to his friend the Maréchal de Bellefonds he revealed himself to be quite unchastened, convinced that he was a much-abused man, long-suffering, and possessed of infinite patience in the face of provocations that were insufferable for a person of his rank.[15] Thus, with the intendant confirmed as presiding officer of the Sovereign Council, with the other members of this body gloating at their victory over the Governor and with the Attorney General, in particular, vengeful at the treatment meted out by Frontenac to his father, there was bound to be more trouble.

Within a few days of the arrival of the dispatches from the Court confirming the powers of the Sovereign Council this body began extending them by taking action which tended to undermine the powers of the governor. Instead of acting in a mere judicial and legislative capacity they now began exercising executive functions, not at the behest of the Governor but in defiance of him. On October 13 they began waging a campaign against the coureurs de bois at Montreal. One of the councillors, the Sieur de la Martinière, was delegated to investigate complaints which had been received against Perrot, the Governor of the island, who, now supported by Frontenac, was reported to be mistreating anyone who interfered with, or

criticized, his illegal fur-trade operations. The town bailiff had been arbitrarily imprisoned, some of his goods seized, and soldiers quartered in his
house because he had dared to arrest certain *coureurs de bois* who happened
to be in Perrot's employ. Other citizens of Montreal had been assaulted
and their property destroyed for opposition to Perrot's attempts to garner
the lion's share of the fur trade.

By this date the western fur trade was dominated by two rival organizations, that of La Salle, supported by Frontenac, and that of the Montreal
merchants, including the Sieurs de la Chesnaye, Le Ber, and Charles le
Moyne, the wealthiest men in the colony.[16] Martinière was associated with
this latter group; thus Frontenac had good reason to fear that any investigation of fur-trade irregularities would be aimed at his associates rather than
against his rivals. During the three weeks that Martinière spent at Montreal he arrested several *coureurs de bois* and seized considerable amounts of
contraband goods. The following spring, when the Council proposed to
renew this drive against those who flouted the edicts governing the fur
trade, Frontenac put every obstacle in their path. The Sovereign Council
refused to be deterred; they sent Martinière, accompanied by the Attorney
General, to the upper colony. When they returned to Quebec in June, after
making a thorough investigation, they preferred charges against Perrot and
the Sieur Boisseau, agent of the Company of the Farm which held the
monopoly on the purchase of beaver pelts and moose hides. Boisseau was
also one of Frontenac's fur-trade associates, and Frontenac claimed vociferously that the charges brought against Boisseau were a flagrant attack
on his authority. The Council riposted by accusing Frontenac of impeding
justice by the intimidation of witnesses. They even went so far as to request
Frontenac to absent himself from the hearings because "of the protection
that he accords to the said Boisseau in everything."[17] Finally, once they had
gathered all the evidence they could, they sent it to the King to prevent
Frontenac using his authority to quash the case. The following year the
Minister dismissed Boisseau from his post, recalled him to France and then
had him sent to the Bastille.[18] Once more, the Sovereign Council had defeated the Governor.

That year, 1681, Frontenac received another warning that unless he
changed his ways he would be recalled. Louis XIV again made it very plain
how he expected a governor of New France to comport himself and, more
significantly, that he had been forced to conclude that Frontenac was quite
incapable of abiding by the instructions and orders that he had received.
The King wrote:

> I admonish you to banish from your mind all the difficulties that you have

created so far in the execution of my orders; to behave with good-natured moderation towards all the *habitants*; to strip yourself of all the personal animosities which up till now have been almost the sole incentive of all your actions; nothing being more inconsistent with the duty which you have to discharge for me in the position that you hold. . . . I see clearly that everything gives way to your private enmities, and that which concerns my service and the execution of my orders is rarely the sole motive of your actions.[19]

In reply Frontenac protested that he was innocent of all such charges, declaring: "Your Majesty will plainly see that I have never had to endure more than when I have been made to appear violent and as a man who would disturb the officers of justice in the duties of their office." He went on to accuse Duchesneau of having deliberately goaded and provoked him with slanderous accusations and calumnies. It must be said that there was a grain of truth in this last statement, but it ignored all the slanderous accusations and calumnies that he had been levelling at the Intendant all this while. But Frontenac really went to the heart of the matter when he claimed that the real source of the trouble was the fact that Duchesneau had found a means to "gain complete control over the proceedings of the Sovereign Council."[20]

This last statement demonstrated clearly that Frontenac could not comprehend the newly defined function of the governor general of New France, despite the fact that Colbert and Louis XIV had so carefully and patiently explained it to him not once, but several times. It was perfectly true that Duchesneau now had control over the proceedings of the Sovereign Council, but it had been Colbert who had delegated this authority to the intendant. That Frontenac was either too proud or too obtuse to grasp this essential fact made it quite apparent that there was no hope at all of his accepting the limitation of his powers imposed by Colbert and Louis XIV. This fact alone must have made it obvious to the Minister that there was no alternative but to recall Frontenac. Then, finally, he made his own recall imperative by arbitrarily ordering the Attorney General to cross to France to account to the Minister for what Frontenac regarded as an insolent and captious attitude. "That which determined me," he explained to the Minister, "is the way that he has induced the Council to persist in their affronts against me at every meeting held since the adjournment."[21]

The mere fact that he had sent the Attorney General to France, after being most severely admonished for having done the same to Villeray, the senior councillor, not long before was bad enough. What made it immeasureably worse was that Auteuil was thus enabled to give Colbert and the King a first-hand account of Frontenac's assault on, and arbitrary imprisonment by force of, Duchesneau's sixteen-year old son, not to mention the Intendant's valet as well. The instigator of this last fracas was again Boisseau, whose own case was at the time being heard by the Sovereign Council. Encountering Duchesneau's son and valet in the street, Boisseau, according to young Duchesneau, called him foul names and threatened to thrash him. Duchesneau's son was reported to have replied in kind. When the incident was reported to Frontenac he demanded from the Intendant an explanation of his son's conduct. The Intendant then sent his son, escorted by his valet, his son's tutor, and his secretary to the Château St Louis where, instead of humbly apologizing to Frontenac for offending someone who enjoyed the Governor's protection, he demanded an apology from Boisseau. At this Frontenac flew at the lad in a blind rage and began flailing at him with a cane until others in the room intervened. Young Duchesneau and his escort then fled. When they reached home the Intendant immediately barricaded his house and armed his servants, preparing to use force should Frontenac send his guards to arrest his son.

When Bishop Laval heard of this he immediately intervened to prevent things getting completely out of control. Frontenac was determined that Duchesneau's son and servant should be surrendered to him to deal with as he saw fit, and Duchesneau was equally determined that they should not. Laval finally persuaded Frontenac to hold his hand and Duchesneau to agree that his son and servant should go to the Château, accompanied by the Bishop and some of the senior ecclesiastics, to be interrogated in their presence by the Governor. Frontenac grudgingly agreed to this, but he at the same time insisted that the Intendant's servant should be handed over to him unconditionally, whereat Duchesneau committed his valet to the royal gaol to forestall the Governor. Despite the fact that he had agreed to Laval's suggestion and that young Duchesneau had accordingly gone to the Bishop's palace to be ready to go with Laval to the Château at any time, Frontenac sent one of his officers to the palace to demand that the youth be handed over. Bishop Laval felt obliged to obey this direct order. Duchesneau's servant was then forcibly removed from the royal prison by Frontenac's guards and lodged in solitary confinement in a cell in the Governor's Château. A month later young Duchesneau was released by Frontenac, apparently little the worse for wear, but his arrest and confinement and that of the servant had been completely contrary to the royal edict of 1679 and the Minister's particular instructions, which had forbidden the governor general or a local governor to imprison anyone arbitrarily except for sedition or treason. At the next meeting of the Sovereign Council Frontenac was requested to explain why he continued to hold Duchesneau's servant prisoner without preferring charges preparatory to bringing him before a court for trial. Frontenac blustered and stormed that they were being insolent and he threatened to report them to the King. After much heated wrangling, and despite Frontenac's furious denunciations, the Council turned the tables on him by declaring their intention to send a full report on the matter to the Minister.

Shortly before the ships sailed for France bearing the Attorney General, copies of the deliberations of the Sovereign Council and the reports of all concerned in these incidents, Frontenac outdid himself by arbitrarily imprisoning one of the members of the Sovereign Council, the sixty-three year-old Sieur Damours, for a period of six weeks. Again, the Damours incident was an example of Frontenac's inability to control his violent temper. The previous April Damours had obtained a passport from the Governor to send a canoe to his concession at Matane on the lower St Lawrence, and also a barque once the river was ice-free. In mid August the barque returned, and Damours went to the wharf to see it unloaded. While there, he was arrested by one of the Governor's guards and conducted to the Château. There in front of the members of his household, Frontenac demanded to know why Damours had sent a ship downriver without a passport. Damours explained that he had obtained a passport for a canoe and a barque. Frontenac declared that it had covered only the canoe. At this Damours, not troubling to conceal his contempt, begged Frontenac's pardon, stated that he had regarded the passport as covering both, and added that he had always understood the King had given his subjects the freedom to "go without hindrance to the lands that he had granted them."[22] This rather insolent rejoinder touched a raw nerve, for it was perfectly true that Frontenac had been ordered to desist from his practice of requiring the people to obtain a passport, or permit, from him before travelling about the colony on their lawful occasions. He rushed to the door of the hall, shouted for his guards, and when they appeared he stormed at Damours, telling him that he would learn in prison what the King's intentions were. With that Damours was lodged in the cells of the Château.

When the Sovereign Council convened the following Saturday, despite Frontenac's protests, they entertained a written request from Damours, presented by his wife, that he be informed of the charges against him and brought to trial. Frontenac maintained that it was no concern of the Council, but this body had by now constituted itself a watchdog to guard against such excesses on the part of the Governor. As the inquiry proceeded, it became clear that it was not Damours but Frontenac who was on trial. After gathering all the evidence they could they ruled that it, too, should be sent to the Minister. The Sovereign Council had neatly outmanœuvred Frontenac by trying Damours on the charges that Frontenac had himself made and which were clearly untenable. Frontenac dared not send Damours to France on such a flimsy pretext and when he eventually released him from custody he thereby tacitly admitted that he had been in the wrong.

Late in the autumn the Attorney General, accompanied by Denis Riverin, the Intendant's very able secretary, arrived at the Court. They were closely interrogated by Colbert's son, the Marquis de Seignelay, now in charge of Canadian affairs. Louis XIV gave orders that he was to be informed of all that had transpired. Despite the best efforts of the Comtesse de Frontenac and her husband's influential friends and relatives at the Court, his case was clearly hopeless. His violence against the teen-aged son of the Intendant and against a member of the Sovereign Council, not to mention another of the King's subjects, the Intendant's valet, could in no way be condoned. But what must have seemed far worse to the King and his Minister was the effect these events would be likely to have on the Canadian people: the Governor's guards and the Town-Major's squad of archers marching through the streets of Upper Town, from the Château St Louis to the Intendant's house, then to the Bishop's palace and later to the riverside quays to arrest persons of such consequence; the Intendant hastily barricading his house, arming his servants with pikes and swords to stand off the Governor's guards. The sight must have caused a great stir in Quebec, and, when word of it spread losing nothing in the telling, throughout the rest of the colony. One thing was very clear, the royal authority had been demeaned. There was no possible alternative now but to recall both Frontenac and Duchesneau. In March 1682 the Abbé Tronson, superior of the Sulpicians in Paris, wrote: "There will be changes made in Canada this year. They are convinced that the good of the country demands it."[23] On May 9 letters recalling Frontenac and Duchesneau were issued. Six months later they were both on their way back to France.

Frontenac's first régime has been described as disastrous, and in many ways it undoubtedly was. Yet there can be no doubt that it was productive of much that, in the longer run, was to prove beneficial. Constitutional safeguards and courts of law are only established to meet a need; a need arising out of human frailties. Yet these constitutional safeguards are not necessarily forthcoming when there is a need for them, and courts of law are not always made independent of the executive power. That both these developments took place in New France to the degree that they did went far to provide the people in the colony with a type of government that sufficed for their needs and met with their approval. That it differed both in principle and practice from the types of government developing elsewhere is not really relevant. Suffice it to say that the disputes and turbulence of Frontenac's administration provoked a response, both in Canada and France, that went far to prevent the like occurring again.

CHAPTER 7

Western Expansion

While the disputes between Frontenac and the Sovereign Council were raging at Quebec other, and more dangerous, conflicts were brewing outside the confines of the colony. This period 1672-1682 saw Colbert's long-range policy for the economic development of the colonies in America shattered, and his immediate plans for its implementation abandoned. He and his successors, however, continued to espouse the policy down to the end of the century, but their doing so was little more than a gesture of despair, a refusal to face the fact that the policy was moribund and a new, positive policy to meet altered circumstances required. A new policy did, in fact, emerge; but it was one imposed by circumstances and events in North America, and to some extent in Europe. It was the policy of men in a canoe hurtling down rapids in a river untravelled before; all that could be done was to avoid the boulders in midstream and the deadly whirlpools, hoping that clear water lay somewhere ahead. There was danger here, excitement, and the sense of getting somewhere in a hurry. It was a reckless policy, but admirably suited to the Canadian temperament.

It was not entirely an accident that Colbert's policy was wrecked during Frontenac's régime, but he certainly was not alone, or even chiefly, responsible for the course of events. When Talon returned to France and no intendant was sent to take his place, most of the economic developments begun in the colony under his direction were quickly abandoned. But here again, the absence of an intendant was not the sole cause of their collapse. The war with the Dutch and the consequent abrupt termination of capital investment in the colony by the Crown were the main reasons why Canada's economic development, along the lines mapped out by Colbert began to founder and the new, unbidden, policy to take command. In other words, it was not state paternalism that stifled economic development, or initiative, in New France, but its sudden cessation.

The ship-building industry, which had shown some promise, failed to develop owing to high labour costs and the reluctance of Canadian merchants to invest their own limited funds in overseas trade in wartime. In 1673 Frontenac complained bitterly that Canadian workmen had "their heels on the necks of the habitants" and anything they did cost three times as much as in France. For this reason, those who had any interest in maritime trade to France or the West Indies had indicated that they would prefer to buy ships in France or Holland rather than have them built at Quebec. Yet, at the same time, ships from New England were calling at Quebec seeking cargoes of flour and ship masts. When the Dutch war ended in 1679 two to four ships a year sailed from Quebec for the Caribbean but the Sieur Patoulet, Intendant in the West Indies, complained that the timber, peas, flour, and salted fish they brought were either of indifferent quality or cost more than the same goods produced locally, and that the amount of sugar consumed by New France annually was barely cargo enough for one ship. In fact, by 1682, only seven or eight ships a year called at Quebec from France, laden mainly with wine, brandy, and small goods for the fur trade. Two or three of these ships took on bales of fur as cargo, and the rest returned empty. The domestic market for many manufactured goods was too small to make their production worthwhile. Tar, for example, cost twice as much to produce in the colony as to import from France. Although the *habitants* continued to produce some for their own use, in 1673 the tar furnaces at Baye St Paul, which had been damaged by severe earth tremors, ceased operations. The following year Talon's brewery closed down. The beer it had produced, although good, was too expensive, and the Canadians showed a marked preference for imported wine.

Frontenac and Duchesneau, for once, were in agreement. They both declared that a much larger population was needed in the colony to provide an adequate market and reduce costs, before industry and overseas trade could be expected to flourish. Colbert had been in too much of a hurry to get these things established. Had emigration to the colony been maintained at the same rate as in the years 1665-1671 and royal subsidies to the infant industries continued, then they might have survived. But when both emigration and subsidies, the two props that supported the colony's economic development, stopped, collapse was inevitable. This does not mean that trade and industry ceased entirely in New France. Small ships continued to be built for fishing in the Gulf to supply the home market. Saw mills were established on most of the seigneuries to provide lumber for local building purposes, and the *habitants* made their own homespun cloth. But all this was little more than domestic industry, or village industry, at best. It was certainly a far cry from the economic activity that Colbert had envisaged.

It is ironic that Colbert had been eager for war with the Dutch to remove their threat to his schemes for the economic development of France and the overseas empire, for this war did far more harm than the Dutch could have done. The trouble was that the French war aims were not achieved, the Dutch economic threat remained, and Colbert's economic plans were severely curtailed as a consequence of French military expenditures.

Although the economic activities of the colony had been reduced to a primitive level, a rather advanced social and administrative system had been established in New France. Moreover, many of the settlers would not be satisfied with a bare subsistence standard of living. Thus the colony remained dependent on the profits of the fur trade to provide the funds needed to pay the costs of its administration, its numerous social services, and the maintenance of a relatively high standard of living for the people. Colbert was fully aware of the benefits accruing from the fur trade; he had no desire to reduce these benefits in any way, but he was aware of the dangers inherent in a single staple economy, particularly of a luxury article which was at the mercy of the vagaries of fashion. What he wanted was to keep the fur trade under control to prevent its strangling other economic activities that would eventually, he hoped, provide a sounder basis for the colony's economy.

When, in 1674, the *Compagnie de l'Occident*, to the joy of the Canadian merchants, was finally liquidated, Colbert obliged the tax farmers, Oudiette and associates, to undertake to market all the beaver skins and moose hides produced in the colony. They also received the monopoly on the trade in all furs at Tadoussac, and no one was allowed to trade with the Indians in a vast area on the north shore of the St Lawrence centred on the Saguenay River. This Company of the Farm had to pay the Crown 350,000 *livres* a year for these monopolies but the Ministry of Marine fixed the prices the company had to pay for beaver in Canada. At first the price was set at 4 *livres* 10 *sols*, regardless of quality; then in 1677, because too much poor-grade beaver was being brought in, a scale of prices according to quality, ranging from 5 *livres* 10 *sols* for greasy beaver to 3 *livres* 10 *sols* for dry beaver, was introduced. These, however, were not the prices received by the fur-traders; when they brought their furs into the company's office at Quebec, or at Montreal when an office was finally established there in 1695, the beaver pelts were sorted as to quality, then weighed in bundles of twenty, thirty, up to a hundred. The company clerk deducted one-quarter of the gross value as the company's *quart*, or commission, and paid the Canadian trader the balance, not in cash, but in bills of exchange one half payable in two months' time, the other half four months later. French merchants, who came to Canada in the summer to buy furs and then returned in the autumn, received bills of exchange payable half three months from date of issue and the balance three months later. It is fair to assume that many of the *habitants* would not be in a position to wait this long for their money and would sell their furs, or their bills of exchange, at a discount to the wealthier merchants. Moreover, all beaver pelts had to be brought into the company's office before October 20 in order that they could be baled and loaded on board the ships before the close of navigation. Since furs had to be carefully stored to prevent damage by rodents and moths,* the merchants who had such storage facilities were in a position to buy beaver that reached Montreal or Quebec after the October deadline at a considerable discount.

The establishment of fixed prices for beaver had the same effect on the fur trade as a guaranteed price for such commodities as butter in more recent times. In the 1670's the need to limit the quantity of beaver fur was not apparent and supply and demand were fairly well balanced, but towards the end of the century, just at a time when the market for beaver in France was declining, the amount of this fur being exported from Canada began to attain astronomic proportions until the Minister of Marine, at his wits end how to stem the avalanche, threatened to abandon the colony entirely. Despite this, however, the Crown made sizable profits from Canada in the seventeenth century. In 1685 the beaver monopoly was leased for ten years to another tax farmer, Fauconnet and associates, for 500,000 *livres* a year, and even during the war years in the last decade of the century the expenses of governing and defending Canada were less than this, and in most years they were far less.

Although Colbert could hardly have imagined all the latent perils in the beaver trade, yet he did see clearly that it had somehow to be kept under control, and this was among the main responsibilities of the governor and intendant. They had to keep the fur trade in the central colony and stop the Canadians abandoning their farms and fishing-boats to voyage into the west to obtain furs from the Indians in their villages. The governor, the intendant, indeed all royal officials, and the clergy were forbidden to take any part in the trade for their personal profit. The governor and intendant in particular had, like Caesar's wife, to be above reproach in this respect; they had to see to it that neither their servants nor any members of their households engaged in the trade.

* In the warehouses the furs were stacked on large, flat metal plates suspended by long rods or chains from hooks set in the high ceilings, this to keep the furs several feet clear of the ground, safe from rodents.

Frontenac, however, held different views on the subject. In the summer of 1673 he established his trading-post, Fort Frontenac, at the eastern end of Lake Ontario. While the resentful *habitants* of Montreal were clearing the site and raising the walls of the fort, he conferred with the four to five hundred Iroquois (his estimate), come at the invitation he had sent them earlier. Frontenac himself appears not to have realized that the Iroquois made no attempt to oppose the building of this fort on their hunting-grounds, not because they approved of it, but because they were then in no position to do anything about it. They were being hard pressed in their war with the Andastes and Mohicans, and they embarrassed Frontenac by adroitly making it incumbent on him to furnish them with military aid in their war. They had, however, little alternative at the time but to trade with the French at Montreal because the Anglo-French war with the Dutch had prevented supplies reaching New York and the Albany traders' warehouses were empty. Later in the summer the Dutch recaptured New York and held it until the following year, again preventing supplies reaching Albany. Thus the Iroquois, for the first two years after the construction of this post, were obliged to trade with the French, and Fort Frontenac was much handier for them than was Montreal. Had, however, the Albany traders not been temporarily eliminated from the fur trade by events in Europe, then it is unlikely that the Iroquois would have taken enough furs to Fort Frontenac in the subsequent years to have paid the high cost of its maintenance. It would then have served only as an *entrepôt* and a base for trade with the Algonquin tribes farther west. In fact, this was to prove to be its main function in any event, and the fur-trading community of Montreal, from the outset, was very much aware of the dangers this would pose to their own trade with the western nations. It was for this reason that they showed such marked sympathy for their local governor, Perrot, in his conflict with Frontenac.

When Frontenac informed Colbert of the establishment of the new post, the Minister was anything but enthusiastic. He informed the Governor that he wanted the Canadians concentrated in villages in the central colony, and not encouraged in this fashion to become scattered about in distant wilderness outposts. In defending his actions Frontenac made grandiose claims for the benefits that the fort would confer on the colony, none of which would bear a close scrutiny, then made a temporary arrangement with two Montreal merchants to stock the post with trade goods. At the same time he gave his full backing to Robert Cavelier, Sieur de la Salle, who crossed to France and, with the support of influential people at the Court, obtained Fort Frontenac and the surrounding lands on seigneurial tenure. By the terms of this concession La Salle was required to clear the land, maintain a garrison of twenty men for two years, build a church within ten years, and maintain a chaplain at the post in the meantime. He was, just like any other seigneur, to grant sections of the seigneury to *habitants*, and it was specifically stated in the terms of the concession that all *habitants* on the seigneury had the right to trade for furs with the Indians. La Salle, however, made no attempt to establish settlers or to clear more land than was required to grow a few vegetables for the men at the post. All that he was interested in was the fur trade, and in this his chief associate was Frontenac who used the authority of his position to further La Salle's ventures in the western fur trade. In fact, every summer now, until the Iroquois turned hostile, Frontenac voyaged to Fort Frontenac with a dozen or more canoes of goods to trade with the Iroquois.[1]

Frontenac, La Salle, and their associates were now able to monopolize the fur trade of the Lake Ontario area and in 1676 they built another fort at Niagara, again without Colbert being informed of what was taking place. Fortunately for the Montreal fur-traders the Iroquois trade represented only a small part of the total western fur trade; the bulk of the furs coming down to Montreal was provided by the Ottawa middlemen. Yet Fort Frontenac and the post at Niagara, with the sailing vessels that La Salle had built at Fort Frontenac, served as *entrepôts* to tap the trade with the tribes west and north of the Iroquois; tribes that up till then had always traded with the Ottawa middlemen or Montreal *coureurs de bois*. The danger was very real that La Salle and his associates would, before long, be in a position to monopolize the entire western fur trade, and their subsequent actions made it plain that this was their aim. To protect themselves the Montreal traders now established a permanent base in the Ottawa country, at Michilimackinac, strategically located to tap the trade of the northwest, whence came the better quality furs.

In this fashion the colony became divided into two factions, that of Frontenac and La Salle and their associates, and that of the leading Montreal traders. Now the bulk of the trade was carried out in the west, necessitating an ample supply of trade goods and several months' time for the trip, the actual trading, and the return voyage to Montreal. Capital was needed for this, hence the little men, the ordinary *habitants*, were squeezed out of the trade except in the role of *voyageurs* under contract to transport goods for the leading merchants to the west and return with the furs. As the trade moved even farther west, more and more men were required for this task, and by 1679 the Intendant Duchesneau reported that some five to six hundred Canadians were off in the west and the entire fur trade controlled by "three or four hands." It was this rivalry between Frontenac's group and the Montreal merchants that was behind much of the conflict between the Governor and the members of the Sovereign Council, some of whom – like Martinière – were directly engaged in the fur trade and some

closely related to Frontenac's trade rivals. In fact, it was the economic expression of the struggle for power between the Canadian *bourgeoisie*** on
the one hand and the Governor General and La Salle on the other; the one
group permanently resident in Canada, the other striving for quick profits
to be spent on their return to France, once enough had been amassed.

Ironically, it was Colbert himself who allowed the flood gates to French
western expansion to be opened. This came about as the result of events
in North America and intrigue at Versailles. In the spring of 1674 Colbert commented that the discovery of a water route from Quebec to the
southern ocean, wherever it might be, would be of inestimable value to
Canada which, as he put it, "being so far north, allows ships to enter only
during four, five or six months of the year." An ice-free, year-round port,
at the mouth of such a river leading to Canada would open up entirely
new possibilities. Three months after Colbert made this comment, Louis
Jolliet returned to Quebec from his voyage down the Mississippi to within
a few days' journey of the Gulf of Mexico. Here seemed to be the route
that Colbert desired; moreover, Jolliet reported that it flowed through a
vast area where the unforested fertile prairies were ideal for settlement,
and the numerous Indian tribes had an abundance of furs that they were
eager to trade for European goods. When, however, Jolliet petitioned the
King to be allowed to establish a settlement in this country of the Illinois
nation he was curtly refused. Colbert declared that the population of the
colony in the St Lawrence valley would have to be greatly increased before
there could be any thought of new settlements in these distant parts. The
King cautioned Frontenac:

> Concerning these new discoveries, you must on no account encourage them
> unless there be a great need and some obvious advantage to be derived from
> them. You must hold to the maxim that it is far more worthwhile to

* The term *bourgeoisie* is used for lack of a more appropriate one. The term was
not used in the seventeenth century in this context, and indeed these Canadian
merchant fur-traders were not truly *bourgeois* in the sense that the term came
to be used in the nineteenth century. The names of some of these men are known:
Le Ber, Le Moyne, La Chesnaye, Martinière, *et al.*, and at a later date Denis
Riverin; but a good deal more research is needed to discover exactly how many
men comprised this group, the extent of their commercial activities, the amount
of capital they disposed of, their social and economic aims, and whether their sons
carried on the family business. From the evidence so far available it appears that
the founding of a fortune in the fur trade was regarded as a stepping-stone into
the ranks of the nobility, the Le Moyne family being a case in point. They
might best be compared, perhaps, with the emerging planter aristocracy of
Virginia.

occupy a smaller area and have it well populated than to spread out and
have several feeble colonies which could easily be destroyed by all manner
of accidents.[2]

Frontenac and La Salle, however, knew that a fortune in furs awaited
those who first established posts among the tribes in the Mississippi valley.
In 1676 they had built their post at Niagara, and the following year La
Salle crossed to France where, with the backing of Frontenac, the advocacy
of their influential friends at the Court, and by skilfully disguising his real
aims, he obtained what had been denied to Jolliet.[3] On May 12, 1678, La
Salle received official sanction to explore the Mississippi valley and discover
whether the river provided a route, as there seemed reason to believe, as
far as Mexico. As a means to this end he was permitted to build forts
wherever necessary in the new lands on the same conditions as obtained
at his concession of Fort Frontenac. The undertaking had to be accomplished within five years and entirely at his own and his associate's expense;
he was expressly forbidden to trade for furs with the Ottawas or any of
the other tribes who traded their furs at Montreal, but to defray the costs
of the enterprise he was granted the privilege of trading for furs in the
southwest, in the lands referred to as Cibola.*

The granting of this concession doomed any lingering chances there might
have been for Colbert's North American policy. The Minister had granted
permission to La Salle to establish posts in the west and engage in the fur
trade as a means to an end, namely, the discovery of a river route to the
southern ocean where it might be feasible some day to establish a warm-
water port connected with Canada and perhaps a base for the conquest of
Mexico; and all at no cost to the Crown. But to La Salle and Frontenac,
discovering the mouth of the Mississippi was not the end, but the means,
to engross the fur trade of half the continent. In 1678 La Salle returned from
France, and by December he was at Lake Ontario accompanied by the
Sicilian soldier of fortune, Henri Tonti. The following November they built
a post at the mouth of the St Joseph River at the foot of Lake Michigan; a

* Cibola was little more than a mythical kingdom, sought by the early Spanish
explorers, which was reputed to contain seven cities wealthier than Mexico
City. It was located on the high plateau between the Little Colorado and the
Rio Grande and occupied by the Zuni Indians who lived in *pueblos*, or towns,
constructed of *adobe*. The officials in the French Ministry of Marine, when
drawing up La Salle's commission, appear to have used the name Cibola to mean
the area south and west of the Great Lakes.

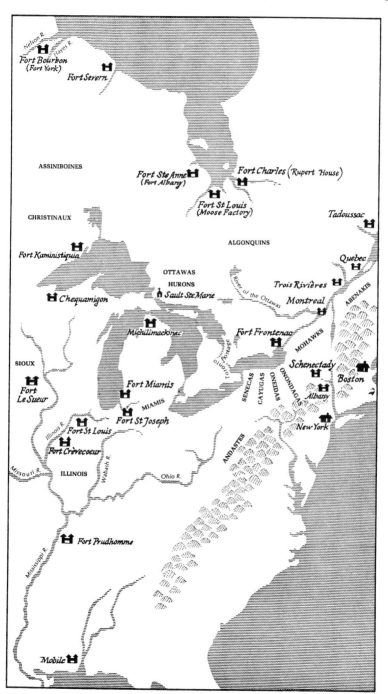

few months later Fort Crèvecoeur was built on the Illinois, then Fort Prud-
homme on the Mississippi below the Ohio. It was his intention to ship the
furs down the Mississippi and to France through the Caribbean, bringing
in supplies the same way, thus obviating the long voyage by canoe to
Quebec City, then by ship down the St Lawrence and across the Atlantic.[4]
This would have made the fur-trade posts in the Illinois country completely
independent of New France.

Meanwhile, from these bases La Salle and his associates were able to
monopolize the fur trade of the Illinois and Miamis tribes who, lacking
canoes, had previously traded with the Ottawa middlemen. Now, when
Frontenac issued permits to anyone to travel into the west he specifically
stated that the holders were forbidden to do any trading in the area of La
Salle's concession. La Salle himself, with Frontenac's sanction, granted
permits to trade in this area as a means to discharge some of his heavy
debts. Any *coureurs de bois* found in the region south of the Great Lakes
without either Frontenac's or La Salle's sanction had their trade goods confiscated. Not satisfied with the establishment of this illegal monopoly La
Salle sent his men to trade north of the Great Lakes, where better quality
beaver was to be obtained.

At the same time as La Salle was establishing his fur-trade posts in the
southwest, Daniel Greysolon, Sieur du Lhut, a cousin of Henri Tonti, was
at the headwaters of the Mississippi. On July 2, 1679, in the great village of
the Nadouecioux, he set up the arms of France, claiming these lands
traversed twenty years earlier by Radisson and Groseilliers for Louis XIV.
This mighty Sioux nation was, like the Iroquois, the inveterate enemy of
the Algonquins and had forced these latter tribes to leave the Lake Superior
area to settle at Lake Huron, where they were safe as long as the Iroquois
remained at peace. It was Du Lhut's aim to effect a permanent peace settlement between the Sioux and the Ottawas, Assiniboines, Crees, and Saul-
teurs; open the vast area west of Lake Superior to trade as La Salle was
doing to the south; then push westward to discover the western ocean.
The Sioux, however, were too proud and warlike to entertain any serious
thoughts of living at peace with their ancient enemies, and the Ottawa tribes
were equally suspicious of the French overtures to the Sioux.

Du Lhut sent three of his men westward with a Sioux war party. How far
they went is not known, but they returned the following summer with
some salt which came, they were told by their Indian guides, from a great
lake, twenty days' journey to the west, whose waters were not fit to drink.
This convinced Du Lhut that the western ocean was within reach, and in
June 1680 he crossed over the low height of land from Lake Superior to

the Mississippi, but abandoned his plans to voyage west when he learned that Father Hennepin, a Récollet with La Salle's men, and two other Frenchmen, had been captured by the Sioux earlier that summer and were being kept by them as slaves. He now travelled down the Mississippi, instead of to the west, located the Sioux who held the French captives, and obtained their release. For this action he received little thanks. La Salle, in a lengthy memoir to the Minister accused Du Lhut of engaging in illicit trade with the western tribes and of claiming to have been the first to explore the country of the Sioux when La Salle's men had earned this honour.[5] Most of the accusations that La Salle levelled at Du Lhut could, with greater justice, have been made against himself.

In 1681 Du Lhut crossed to France to plead, like Jolliet, for a seigneury in the new lands he had discovered, and like Jolliet without success. He returned, briefly, to the Sioux country in 1683 but then confined his activities in the west to the lands of the Assiniboines and Ottawas north of the Great Lakes. Thus La Salle was allowed to enjoy his monopoly of the Mississippi fur trade unchallenged. The rival Montreal traders, meanwhile, with their main base at Michilimackinac, spread out to the west and north, over the lakes, swamps, and rivers of the Canadian shield until they reached the open prairies of the Lake Winnipeg region.

As the number of men deserting the colony for the west steadily increased, Colbert issued new edicts forbidding all trade with the Indians beyond the confines of the colony, but they had no effect whatsoever. The Intendant Duchesneau suggested that the situation might improve were permits to be issued for some ten, fifteen, or twenty canoes a year to be allowed to go to the west to trade, granting the permits to Canadian families in turn according to need. Colbert, to everyone's surprise, seized on this suggestion. He had come to realize that the problem could not be solved by threats of punishment; there were by this time far too many *coureurs de bois* to punish them all for breaking the law. In 1681, with a gesture almost of despair, he issued two edicts, one granting an amnesty to all *coureurs de bois* who returned immediately to the colony, the other initiating the *congé* system suggested by Duchesneau. Up to twenty-five of these *congés*, or licences, could be granted jointly by the governor or intendant each year, and no one was to receive a *congé* two years in succession.

Those who received *congés* did not have to go to the west themselves, they could hire canoemen to go for them; each *congé* allowed one canoe with three men to go upcountry to trade. The recipients could also sell their *congés* if they wished, and it was not long before they were changing hands for ten to eleven hundred *livres* each. The Minister was quick to realize that good use could be made of this, and eventually it became customary to order the governor to grant two or three *congés* to the hospitals or to men who required capital to establish some industrial enterprise. In short, they served as a form of colonial taxation. Their main purpose, however, along with the amnesty, was to persuade the six hundred-odd *coureurs de bois* in the west to return to the colony and engage in more useful enterprise such as agriculture, fishing, or lumbering, while waiting their turn for a *congé*, or to be hired by somebody who had obtained one. By these means, it was hoped, not more than seventy-five men at a time would be absent from the colony.

Frontenac declared that this new policy would quickly put an end to the trouble. Events proved otherwise. Rumours spread quickly in the colony that an amnesty was forthcoming and, before the royal edict granting it was registered by the Sovereign Council, some sixty canoes manned by nearly two hundred men hurriedly left for the west. Duchesneau morosely remarked that these men could spend the next few months trading in the west, then return, avail themselves of the amnesty, and be in a state of grace with the law. In fact, the *congé* system had been introduced too late for there to have been much hope of its having the desired effect. Unscrupulous governors, and the coming need for military measures in the west, made all such measures futile.

The Intendant, Duchesneau, maintained that Frontenac was in league with some of the *coureurs de bois* and through them carried on a lucrative trade for his own account. Frontenac accused Duchesneau of the same thing and declared that he did not dare take too severe measures against these outlaws lest they take refuge in the English colonies and divert the western fur trade to Albany and Philadelphia. A good deal of fur was smuggled by the French traders to Albany because the merchants there paid nearly three times as much for beaver as did the Company of the Farm; moreover, they paid in hard cash, not in post-dated bills of exchange. The Company of the Farm maintained that merchants from Albany came up to Chambly on the Richelieu to obtain furs and were well supplied by the Montreal merchants and by Frontenac himself, who shipped furs to Albany from Fort Frontenac, by way of the Oswego and Mohawk rivers.

Although this smuggling was carried out in defiance of French government policy, the colony derived considerable benefits from it. The merchants were rendered more prosperous thereby and some of them invested part of their profits in such enterprises as lumbering, fishing, and commerce. Currency was always in short supply, so much so, in fact, that until the Intendant de Meulles inaugurated his famous card money in 1685, beaver pelts were a much-used medium of exchange. Moreover, during the period 1675-1685, twice as much beaver was shipped to France as the French market could absorb. Had the surplus not been diverted to New York, the French market would have been flooded with beaver much sooner than it eventually was. In fact, if anyone had cause to complain at this illicit trade it was the Hudson's Bay Company, not the French Company of the Farm, for had it not been for the supplies of superior English trade goods, duffel cloth, strouds, and Brazil tobacco, obtained at Albany, the French traders would have been much harder put to it to prevent the Algonquin tribes from trading at the recently established Hudson's Bay Company posts.

This English company had begun to take form in 1666 when two Canadian renegades, Radisson and Groseilliers, interested a select group of London businessmen, influential courtiers, and members of the Royal Society in the possibility of profits to be made trading with the Indians for furs in Hudson Bay.[6] Early in the century Henry Hudson and Thomas Button had sailed into the Bay searching for the North-West Passage to the western ocean; thus England had claims to the area based on prior exploration. In 1668 this London group had sent out one ship, the *Nonsuch*, which wintered in the Bay and returned with enough furs to convince those who had put up the money that the enterprise was worthwhile. They immediately decided to invest more capital and press suit through the usual Court channels for a charter that would grant them all the lands around the Bay and sole right to the trade therein. On May 22, 1670, the charter was issued by Charles II to the eighteen associates, incorporated as the "Governor and Company of Adventurers of England trading into Hudson's Bay."

Fortunately for this fledgling company, relations between the Courts of England and France were at this time very cordial. The Dutch were the common foe and the fleets of England and France were combined under the command of the Duke of York. The English were permitted to trade with the French West Indies, and Colbert appeared not at all disturbed by the establishment of English posts in Hudson Bay. In fact, he informed Colbert de Croissy, ambassador to the Court of St James, that the projected voyage of Van Heemskerke to Hudson Strait to claim lands for France in that area was in no sense intended to harm English interests, and Louis XIV would give the King of England every satisfaction should the French appear to trespass on territories claimed by England. "This makes it very clear," Colbert informed the ambassador, "that no disputes nor difficulty can possibly arise in this connection."[7]

Thus it was that the English were able to consolidate their bases in the second of the three great entrances to the northern half of the continent. To the south they had regained the Hudson River entry-way from the Dutch. The French in the St Lawrence valley lay between the two. As yet, there was enough elbow room between them but it would not be long before the French began to feel the pressure, and this pressure forced the French to expand westward to outflank the English posts to north and south.

In fact, the Intendant of New France, Jean Talon, was already disturbed by the presence of the English at Canada's back door and in 1671 he sent Paul Denis, Sieur de St Simon, Father Albanel, S.J., and Sebastien Pennara overland to the Bay to explore the area, claim it for France, and induce the Indians to trade with the French. They found the English posts deserted and duly took possession of the country in the name of Louis XIV. In 1674 Father Albanel returned to the Bay to found a mission. He also had instructions from Frontenac to persuade the Indians to stay away from the English heretics and do their trading either at Tadoussac or with the Ottawa middlemen. This time when he arrived at Charles Fort in James Bay, Albanel found it occupied. Governor Bayly, failing to reciprocate Colbert's earlier sentiments, sent Albanel a prisoner to England. This marked the beginning of the struggle between the fur-traders of the Bay and those of Montreal; a struggle that was to endure until well on into the nineteenth century. In this contest the English had the advantage of cheaper trade goods because it cost far less to transport them by sea to the Bay posts than it cost the Montreal merchants to transport goods by sea from France and then by canoe to their western posts. The English had better quality cloth and the black Brazil tobacco that the Indians preferred, but the French had better axes, knives, gunpowder, and gun flints. The French also had another advantage that the English were never able to overcome: far more skilled and enterprising traders who spoke the Indians' languages, knew their ways, were prodigal with their brandy, and took their goods to the Indians' villages thereby saving them the long canoe journey to the Bay, through the bleak lands where game was scarce. Once at the Bay posts the trade was done "through a hole in the wall," with little ceremony or bargaining. This compared very unfavourably in the Indians' view with the free and easy ways of the French who would smoke, drink, joke, and haggle until the Indians had completed their trading.

It was, then, the *coureurs de bois* whose way of life Colbert so greatly deprecated who proved the most effective weapon to combat this English threat from the north. They established trading-posts on the river routes to the Bay, intercepting the Indians and prevailing on them to save themselves the long journey to the English posts. Even Duchesneau, who was bitterly opposed to western expansion, was obliged to give ground. In 1681 he informed Colbert, "the only way to prevent [the English] succeeding in what is harmful to us in this respect would be to drive them out by armed force, since the Bay belongs to us; or at least if it is not desirable to go to this extremity, to construct forts on the rivers that flow into the lakes in order to hold the Indians there."

But while the authorities in France and New France were wondering how best to cope with this northern threat, a much more serious menace to the entire French position in North America arose to the south. French expansion into the west had developed while, and because, the Iroquois were at peace. Were they to turn hostile, then Fort Frontenac and the staging post at Niagara became untenable and the French routes to the west, both the Lake Ontario and the Ottawa route, would be in danger of being severed. French communication lines were flanked by the Iroquois along most of their length, and in the event of the Iroquois turning hostile the French would have to run the gauntlet from Montreal to the Mississippi.

All that had kept the Iroquois docile for so long was their war with the Andastes and the Mohicans. As long as these tribes remained hostile, the Five Nations had sullenly to watch the French expand into lands they either regarded as properly theirs, or otherwise coveted. Each year, when Frontenac met them at Fort Frontenac, they gave every appearance of being subservient to him and he was easily convinced that he could exert great influence over them; but events were to show that it was not so much a case of Frontenac's keeping the Iroquois docile, but of the Iroquois appearing so. Frontenac, owing to the profits to be made in trade with the Iroquois, not to mention the smuggling of furs to Albany that he was accused of engaging in, had a vested interest in maintaining good relations with them. The Iroquois, however, were in a somewhat more advantageous position here, for whenever it suited them they could cease to trade at Fort Frontenac and take their furs to Albany. In purely trade relations Frontenac was more dependent on the Iroquois than they were on him; but politically and militarily the Iroquois were dependent on the neutrality of the French as long as their war with the Andastes and Mohicans endured.

Then, in 1676, the whole basis of the peaceful relations between the French and the Iroquois was shattered.[8] In May of that year the Andastes suffered heavy losses in a surprise attack by a force of Virginia frontiersmen. At this the Andastes sued for peace with the Five Nations, quit their lands in the Susquehanna valley, and were assimilated by their old enemies. They then began to ravage the Virginia frontier settlements. And at the same time that the western Iroquois received this great adjunct to their military strength, the eastern Iroquois also were freed from the intermittent attacks of the Mohicans. For some reason that is not clear this Algonquin tribe made its peace with the Iroquois, deserted the French alliance, and allied itself with the English and Dutch at Albany.

That the balance of power in North America had been tilted against the French was quickly made plain. The Jesuit missionaries now reported that the Iroquois, particularly the Senecas and Cayugas who previously had appeared well disposed towards the French, were threatening to attack both the French and their Indian allies. And it was just at this critical juncture, when the French had to be prepared to counter any Iroquois move, that La Salle began building his posts in the Illinois country, an area that the Iroquois had once held and were determined to regain. The French now claimed sovereignty over the lands of the Illinois and Miamis nations and were thereby obligated to afford these tribes military aid against their enemies. In a giant leap the French had advanced their commercial empire to the heart of the continent and outflanked the Iroquois, without realizing what the consequences must be. The rival expansionist aims of the French and the Iroquois made a clash inevitable. Yet, despite the reports reaching Frontenac from the Jesuits in the western missions, the Récollets at Fort Frontenac, and the Sulpicians at the Bay of Kenté, that the Iroquois were preparing to strike back, there is no evidence that he appreciated how dangerous the situation really was. He consistently reported to the Minister that all was well, that the Iroquois were completely subservient to him. There was no indication in his dispatches to the Court that any serious threat to French interests in the west existed or even seemed likely.

Then the long-pending storm finally broke. In September 1680 an Iroquois army six to seven hundred strong invaded the Illinois country. Upon receiving word of their approach the Illinois sent their women and children some fifteen miles away for security and made ready for battle. Their chiefs were anything but sanguine of the outcome; many of their warriors were away hunting and those who remained had only bows and arrows, whereas the Iroquois were armed with muskets.

According to Henri Tonti's account of events, the Illinois chiefs prevailed upon him to approach the Iroquois to discuss a peaceful settlement of their differences. He received a flesh wound for his pains, but the Iroquois were sufficiently disconcerted to learn that the French were allied with the Illinois that they agreed to enter into negotiations. During the ensuing uneasy armistice, Tonti and his companions slipped away, abandoning the Illinois. After enduring great hardships they reached Michilimackinac in the spring. There they learned that the Iroquois had attacked and destroyed the Illinois village. According to accounts which later reached Quebec, a Récollet friar had been killed and several hundred Illinois, mostly women and children, taken prisoner. Shortly afterwards a Miamis village was also attacked, and a number of prisoners taken. The following year the Senecas threatened to extend the war to the Ottawas, using as excuse the murder of one of their chiefs by an Illinois warrior in an Ottawa village.

The seriousness of the situation in the west was now apparent to everyone in New France. The Intendant, Duchesneau, stated that the Iroquois's policy was clearly to conquer the western nations one at a time: first the Illinois, then the Miamis, then the Ottawas. This accomplished they would control the western fur trade and divert it to Albany, with themselves playing the role of middlemen. It was therefore essential, he declared, to reduce the Iroquois to their former submission or destroy them. The leading men in the colony shared this opinion; they stated that the Iroquois were determined to break the French hold on the western fur trade and would strive to keep the French inactive by diplomatic means while they conquered the allies one at a time. They, too, were convinced that only a very strong stand could deter the Iroquois: the threat of force and, if that did not suffice, then the use of it.

Frontenac, however, rejected this firm policy. He attempted to appease the Iroquois. He sent one of his officers with a canoe load of trade goods to the Senecas to placate them for the murder of their chief in the Ottawa village and to ask them to confer with him the following spring or summer at Fort Frontenac. He assured them he would compel the Ottawas to render full satisfaction for the crime. This gesture merely incited the Iroquois to further acts of aggression. They now began pillaging French canoes wherever they encountered them. They even forced their way into Fort Frontenac and pillaged its supplies. Upon hearing of this, and a third-hand Indian rumour that the Iroquois had threatened to attack him should he go to Lake Ontario to confer with them as he had stated he would, Frontenac refused to stir from Montreal.

It was at this juncture of events, in July 1682, that Frontenac received the dispatches from the Court. They contained his dismissal and recall to France. Not, ironically enough, for his weakness in the face of the Iroquois threat – Louis XIV and the Minister had as yet no knowledge how serious this had become – but for his maladministration in civil affairs and his use of force against any individuals who opposed his arbitrary government. Upon receipt of his dismissal, any hope that he might have been prevailed upon to take firm action to meet the crisis facing the colony vanished. His aim now became to prevent open hostilities with the Iroquois before he left the colony so that he could later claim to have left Canada in peace and allow his successor to take the blame for whatever ensued.* When, in mid

* Upon his arrival at the Court he submitted a memoir to the Minister in which he presented a very distorted picture of events prior to his departure from the colony, making it appear that he had left New France secure and in no danger from the Iroquois. Then after fighting had broken out, he declared that he had

August, delegates from the Ottawa, Huron, and Miamis nations came to Montreal to plead for aid against the Iroquois, Frontenac informed them that he intended to confer with the Five Nations at Fort Frontenac to settle the dispute and he would then "reproach the Iroquois" for their attacks on the Illinois and Miamis. When the allies declared their intention to retaliate in kind against the Iroquois attacks he pleaded with them not to do so but to await the outcome of his conference. They returned to the west very dissatisfied, convinced that they could expect no aid from the French and that their best hope for survival lay in coming to terms with the Iroquois.

Frontenac now turned his attention to the colony's defences, which were virtually non-existent. The few old forts built in Courcelle's day had crumbled into ruins, none had been built in the new seigneuries, Montreal had no wall about it of any sort. From Trois Rivières to Montreal the settlements could have been devastated by a few hundred Iroquois. In the time remaining to him before he left the colony he could do no more than indicate a few sites in the exposed areas near Montreal where forts should be built. It remained for his successor to build them. In the light of this, and of Frontenac's failure to take any action, it was small wonder that the aggressiveness of the Iroquois grew by leaps and bounds. After incorporating the Andastes into their own ranks and obtaining a plentiful supply of arms from Albany they were at the peak of their strength.

In September, while Frontenac was still at Montreal, the Sieur de la Forest, commandant at Fort Frontenac, arrived with a deputy from the Onondagas. This chief, Tegannissorens, stated that, in response to Frontenac's request brought to them the previous autumn by the Sieur de la Marque that the Iroquois should confer with him at the fort, he had gone to Cataracoui along with delegates from the other four nations. Not having found Frontenac there, he had come on alone, being assured by La Forest that the Governor would be at Montreal. He requested Frontenac to go in his barque to Ochuguen at the mouth of the Onondaga River to confer with their chiefs. He declared that the Iroquois had no desire to wage war with the Ottawas, Hurons, or Miamis, and asked Frontenac not to believe all the rumours to the effect that they were about to march against the Illinois.

In reply Frontenac stated that he was unable to go to Ochuguen that year to confer with them. He declared that he was delighted to hear that the Iroquois were so peaceably inclined but he also asked why they would not agree to end their war with the Illinois. What answer, if any, Tegannissorens made to this is not recorded. Although Frontenac already knew

known how to keep the colony at peace during the ten years of his first administration but that his successors had plunged it into a needless war.

that he had been recalled to France, he asked the Iroquois not to take any action before he had discussed the whole issue with them the following spring.

If Frontenac actually believed Tegannissorens' protestations of the Iroquois's peaceful intentions, he was the only responsible person in the colony who did. Everyone else was convinced that this embassy was merely a rather obvious gambit in the Iroquois policy, which was to drive the French out of the western fur trade by crushing their allies one by one, just as they had previously conquered the Hurons, the Andastes, the Mohicans, and other tribes. Their ambitious plan depended for its success on one thing – preventing any intervention by the French, for it was only the French who could unite the intended victims and organize a concerted attack on the Iroquois villages. Thus they would do everything in their power to keep the French inactive, and make all manner of promises; then, when the western allies of the French were crushed and there was no longer any great danger of a concerted attack on the Iroquois villages, they would launch their entire strength against the French settlements. The first step in this plan had already gone into effect; the Illinois and Miamis were under attack and had already suffered heavy losses. Once these tribes were crushed it would be the turn of the Ottawas; if the Iroquois succeeded in seizing hold of Michilimackinac they would then be able to dominate the Great Lakes, and the French hold on the western fur trade would be destroyed. This was the consensus of opinion in the colony. Father Jean de Lamberville, the Jesuit missionary with the Onondagas, who was very loath to see hostilities begin between the French and the Iroquois since this would have ended his years of missionary endeavour, wrote to inform Frontenac how serious the situation was:

> Several times they have insulted the French without being called to account, and this has led them to believe that the French are afraid of them. They gain every year from our losses; they crush our allies and make Iroquois of them; they do not hesitate to say that, after adding to their own ranks from those we have abandoned, and strengthened by those who would have been able to aid us in waging war against them, they will descend *en masse* on Canada and overwhelm it in a single campaign.[9]

The whole Great Lakes area now smouldered with war and preparations for war. War chiefs in the Iroquois longhouses told of past wars against the French and the older Algonquin foes; young braves boasted of the deeds they would surely do. Years of long pent up rancour and blood-thirst made them all the more determined to settle accounts once and for all. They were already at war with the Illinois and Miamis; there was grave danger that the Ottawa nations would be crushed, or to avoid it, would secede from the French alliance which seemed of little benefit and join forces with

CUL—E

the Iroquois against the French. Were this to occur, the fur-trade economy of New France would have been ruined and, in the colony's virtually defenceless state, concerted attack by the Iroquois and northwestern tribes would have overwhelmed it. All that would have been left of Louis XIV's province in the St Lawrence valley would have been mutilated corpses and smouldering ruins.

This, then, was the situation that faced the Canadians in 1682 when Frontenac and Duchesneau were recalled. The rapid expansion into the west was now being challenged by the Iroquois. Behind this foe was the challenge of the English fur-traders of New York, Pennsylvania, and Virginia, and behind them the commercial rivalry of England. The fears expressed so often by Colbert that French expansion into the interior of the continent would jeopardize everything that the French had struggled to establish in North America were now seen to be very real. Even without this expansion the threat to New France would still have been there, but the central colony would at least have been in a better posture for defence. As it was, the French could not save the situation by abandoning their posts in the west, for their allies would have construed this as total abandonment of them to the fury of the Iroquois. Frontenac had already gravely weakened the alliances with the western tribes by his futile attempts to appease the Iroquois. All Colbert's policies, instructions, and edicts to the contrary, the French now had no choice but to consolidate their hold on the west for they had given too many hostages to fortune. They were, in fact, astride a tiger and it would have been fatal to try to dismount.

CHAPTER 8

Challenge and Inadequate Response

Before Colbert could recall Frontenac and Duchesneau, their successors had to be found. Although it was not as difficult in the 1680's as it had been fifteen years earlier to find men willing to accept such appointments, it was still by no means easy to get capable men. Thus, for the post of Governor General of New France a member, not of the feudal aristocracy but of the *noblesse de robe*, Le Febvre de la Barre, was chosen. Born in 1622, the same year as Frontenac, he had been trained in law rather than in the army; he had served as Intendant of Paris during the Fronde, and later in the provinces. Subsequently he was appointed Governor of Cayenne in French Guiana, where he showed a conspicuous lack of military ardour in conflicts with the English. He was essentially a man of weak character, too easily imposed upon by others, who sought to hide his lack of moral fibre with displays of bravado.

It proved somewhat easier to fill the vacant position of intendant. Jean Talon appears to have been eager for the appointment, but he was passed over in favour of the Sieur Bégon, a member of the Colbert family. Then, at the last moment it was decided to send Bégon to the West Indies and his brother-in-law, Jacques de Meulles, Sieur de la Source, was chosen for New France in his stead.

It was not only in New France that changes were being made. In the Ministry of Marine Colbert's son, the Marquis de Seignelay, had been placed in charge of Canadian affairs in 1681, and on the death of Colbert two years later he succeeded as Minister of Marine. Although Seignelay had been given a very thorough training in all aspects of naval and colonial administration and was a man of considerable ability, yet he was not the man that his father had been. Whereas Colbert possessed a detailed knowledge of all affairs in the departments under his charge, there were many gaps in Seignelay's knowledge. When, for example, a decision had to be made on the spheres of authority of the Canadian officials, Seignelay scribbled a note in the margin of the abstract, requiring the *commis* to inform him how Canada was governed. He also showed a cavalier attitude toward the responsibilities of his office, and as his father complained, had a tendency to leave important matters to the last minute. Relying on his quick, facile mind he then dispatched them swiftly but without giving them sufficient thought. Colbert remarked sadly to Colbert de Terron "it is impossible that he will become really competent unless he changes this manner. . . . I fear nothing so much as this facility of his for it causes him to have a good opinion of himself and to be content with this superficial knowledge of things which will never make him a capable man."[1] Unfortunately, Colbert failed to change his son's character, and after Colbert's death policies came to be framed and decisions made in a very haphazard manner.

Before La Barre and de Meulles sailed for New France they were, however, carefully briefed by Seignelay. He made it plain to them that their main task was to restore order in the colony and prevent a recurrence of the vicious squabbling that had caused so much trouble. On Seignelay's orders de Meulles read all Colbert's dispatches, edicts, instructions, and letters to Frontenac and Duchesneau and made abstracts of the pertinent passages to obtain a clear idea of the respective spheres of authority and responsibility of the governor and intendant. In his official instructions de Meulles was informed, in a very firm manner, that on no account was he to engage in any disputes with the governor. This, the instructions emphasized, the King regarded as most essential for his service and the good of the colony, "where the people have suffered much in the past because of the divisions of those having the principal authority." To make doubly sure, Louis XIV himself briefed La Barre, impressing on him that Frontenac and Duchesneau had been recalled because their intemperate conduct had been prejudicial to the royal service and the well-being of the colony. La Barre was left in no doubt that he had to govern himself, and the colony, by quite different maxims from those of his predecessor in office.

Neither Louis XIV, nor Colbert, nor Seignelay, however, realized that something far more serious than the disruption of the civil government now threatened New France. In his official instructions La Barre was informed that past experience had shown that the Iroquois could only be restrained by fear of the French but that they had recently committed acts of violence and unless checked might become more audacious. La Barre therefore was instructed to take a force of five to six hundred Canadians to Lake Ontario, to show the Iroquois that their villages could be attacked should they not restrain themselves. He had also to stop the Iroquois warring with the Illinois and neighbouring tribes, but he was not to attack them except as a very last resort, and then, only if he were certain that such a war could be concluded swiftly and to the French advantage. There was no awareness here of the magnitude of the Iroquois threat, or of the defenceless state of the colony.

When the ships bearing La Barre and de Meulles arrived at Quebec early in October 1682, after seventy-eight days at sea, they received a rousing welcome. The cannon began firing as fast as the gunners could load and reload, the greenish-black gun smoke drifting upriver on the fresh north-east wind. Even before the ships had dropped anchor, the leading citizens came aboard to pay their respects to the new Governor and Intendant, while from the terrace of the Château St Louis Frontenac was able to watch these proceedings with not a little chagrin. But when La Barre and de Meulles lowered their gaze from the cannon and the stately buildings on the crest of the steep cliff, they saw at the water's edge little but piles of charred debris. Two months previous, on August 4, fire had broken out among the warehouses of Lower Town while the bulk of the merchants were away at Montreal. Two-thirds of the homes and warehouses had been destroyed, some fifty-five buildings in all, with much of their contents.

This disaster emphasized the continual danger of fire in the colony's three main centres of population. As yet, most of the buildings were constructed of wood and those few built of stone had cedar shingle roofs which could all too easily take fire from chimney sparks. But the worst menace was the carelessness of the people who dumped hot ashes in the street, knocked out their pipes among wood shavings, or carried burning coals from one house to another on a shovel. The Sovereign Council had enacted laws forbidding all these things, but their enforcement proved difficult. Thus fires, if rarely as disastrous as the conflagration of 1682, were all too frequent in the colony.

Although La Barre had been well informed of the faction fights in the colony, he was still taken aback at the intensity of the passions that had been aroused. He informed the Minister shortly after his arrival that perhaps after the ships had sailed, removing Frontenac and Duchesneau from the scene, things might calm down, but he feared that it would be a year or more before calm was completely restored. What came as a much greater shock, however, was to discover the imminent danger in which the colony stood from the Iroquois. This was made amply apparent in the documents that Frontenac turned over to him, telling of the most recent hostile actions of the Five Nations. La Barre wasted no time. He called an assembly of the leading men in the colony, who were well informed of the facts of the case. The Bishop, three Jesuit fathers, the Superior of the Sulpicians at Montreal, the Governor of Trois Rivières, the leading seigneurs and fur-traders, and the Intendant; twenty-two in all, met in this *ad hoc* assembly of notables at Quebec on October 10 to give the Governor the benefit of their views and advise him on what should be done. Had he known, when offered the appointment as governor of the colony, what these men would have to say, La Barre might well have thought twice before accepting.

They stated unanimously that for the past four years the English at Albany and New York had done everything possible to induce the Iroquois to attack New France. The only thing that had deterred them, the assembly declared, was the fear that while they were attacking the French settlements the western nations would unite and destroy the Iroquois villages. Thus, the Iroquois had entered into negotiations with Frontenac, but only to dissemble, hoping to keep the French inactive while they attacked the western tribes one by one. They had already seriously weakened the Illinois and were likely to destroy this nation completely in the near future. This done, they would go on to destroy the Miamis, the Ottawas, and the Jesuit mission at Michilimackinac, making themselves masters of Lakes Erie, Huron, and Michigan. With the French driven out of the west, and their allies destroyed or scattered, just as in earlier years the Hurons, Andastes, Mohicans, and Abenakis had been crushed and scattered, they would then have won the western fur trade and could fall on the French settlements at their leisure.

The only way this chain of events could be prevented, the assembly declared, was by a show of force, and if that did not suffice, then a full-scale campaign against the western Iroquois would have to be undertaken. The colony, it was stated, could muster one thousand men able to bear arms and travel by canoe, but were they to undertake such a campaign the fields would go uncultivated and famine would result. They therefore appealed to the King to send two or three hundred regular troops to guard the river entrances to the upper colony, garrison Fort Frontenac, and escort food convoys to Lake Ontario. One hundred to a hundred and fifty indentured labourers would be needed, they stated, to aid the men who stayed behind to get the crops in and harvested. Funds would also be needed to build a storehouse, to convoy adequate supplies to Fort Frontenac, and to build two or three barques on Lake Ontario. It was essential, they declared, were a campaign to be undertaken that it be pressed with vigour and not as had been done seventeen years earlier when the Iroquois had been frightened but not really harmed. This time, five hundred men would have to be sent against the Senecas and another five hundred against the Onondagas, to remain in the Iroquois country long enough to hunt them down and destroy them piecemeal. There was, however, the possibility that were the Iroquois to see troops and war supplies arrive from France they might decide it would be prudent to abandon their aggressive policy. The assembly declared that they had become increasingly bold of late only because the French had not reacted to their aggressive acts. As no troops had been sent from France they believed the King had abandoned the colony to its fate.[2]

De Meulles, in his dispatch to the Minister reiterated what the assembly had said, emphasizing that the Iroquois were not the barbarians that people imagined but were indeed exceptionally astute in the field of power politics. He stated that the embassy they had sent to Frontenac a short time before was a good example of their tactics, being designed to deceive Frontenac and at the same time to discover what his reaction to their attack on the Illinois was likely to be. The sole aim of the embassy had been to make sure that they would not have to fight more than one enemy at a time, this having always been their policy; and were they to be allowed to continue unchecked, they would destroy their enemies one by one and eventually succeed in making themselves masters of North America.[3]

While La Barre was penning his dispatch to the Minister, expressing the same views as the Intendant and appealing for troops and supplies, three hundred Nipissings, one of the Ottawa nations, arrived at Montreal seeking refuge. Their chiefs went on to Quebec to ask that they might be given land among the French where they could be secure from the Iroquois, who, they reported, were preparing to attack the Hurons. La Barre now informed Seignelay he was making preparations for a campaign the following year, and intended to winter in the Iroquois country to prevent them recouping their strength. He was quite confident that he would have everything under control in short order, provided the King supplied the men and funds he had requested. His mere presence, he declared, had given the Iroquois something to think about. "They know of me," he stated, "before they have met me, for the English have informed them that I gave them a very rough time when I waged war in the West Indies. But," he added, "you must be convinced that what I have requested is absolutely necessary and that without aid the country is lost."[4] To gain time he sent a canoe, loaded with presents, to the Iroquois to invite them to meet with him at Montreal the following June. He hoped that this might cause them to defer their threatened assault on the Ottawas until he was in a position to attack them.

The evidence and future events were to prove that the assessment of the situation by La Barre, de Meulles, and the members of the special council was essentially correct. They erred, however, in holding the English chiefly responsible for Iroquois aggressiveness. Although they were certainly eager to have the Iroquois divert the western fur trade to Albany and encouraged renegade *coureurs de bois* to establish themselves in the province and hire out to Albany merchants, the close ties between James II and Louis XIV caused the officials at Whitehall to caution the Governor of New York not to do anything that would give Versailles cause for complaint.[5] The French in Canada also gravely underestimated the forces needed to subdue the Five Nations. Seventeen years had passed since the Iroquois had last attacked the French settlements and memories of the horrors of that war had perhaps grown dim. Moreover, in that war the western nations of the Iroquois confederacy had not attacked the colony, being themselves too hard pressed by the Andastes. Now, the French had to face all five nations of the Iroquois confederacy, numbering over 2,500 warriors, well armed with English muskets, while New France could muster only a thousand men. Moreover, the Canadians, despite the King's orders to Frontenac, repeated year after year, to train them in the use of arms, were without weapons and were no match for the Iroquois in forest warfare. These odds had to be redressed by the French allies who together greatly outnumbered the Iroquois. Were the French to succeed in destroying some of the Iroquois villages, these allies would be quick to respond. This was really the only hope the French had to curb the Iroquois swiftly and avoid a long drawn-out war that would inevitably do incalculable damage to the French settlements. Yet action had to be taken soon; the longer it was deferred the more aggressive the Iroquois became and the more inclined became the French allies to submit without a fight. La Barre and de Meulles had done all they could under the circumstances. The next move rested with the Minister of Marine.

In addition to taking active steps to cope with the menace from the southwest, La Barre showed an immediate awareness of the threat to French control of the western fur trade posed by the English traders in Hudson Bay. He granted trading *congés*, without troubling to have them countersigned by the Intendant, to Du Lhut to trade at Lake Nipigon, to Durantaye for Michilimackinac, and to the Sieurs St Germain and Argenteuil for Lake Abitibi. It was intended that they would block the river routes to Hudson Bay and persuade or prevent the northern Indians going there to trade. Judging by the amount of fur subsequently traded at the Bay posts, they had little success, and some in the colony were quick to inform the Minister that La Barre was not only issuing *congés* wholesale but had a financial interest in this trade. La Barre denied the accusations and asserted that he was merely striving to carry out the King's instructions to prevent the English becoming firmly established in the Bay.

These instructions clearly indicated a change in attitude on the part of the French government. Ten years earlier Colbert had indicated that France would not contest the English claims to the areas where they had established posts in the Bay. Now they were inclined to do so; but they had left it too late. In December 1674 Radisson and Groseilliers, disgruntled with the treatment they had received from the Hudson's Bay Company, crossed to France on Colbert's invitation and promise of reward. The Minister then sent them to Quebec to discuss with Frontenac how best to deal with the situation in the Bay but, as Radisson put it, "being arrived at Quebec, we found that jealousy and interest which some persons had over those that had the absolute command at that time of the trade in Canada, and whose creatures were employed for new discoveries, ordered things so that the Count de Frontenac, the Governor, took no care to perform what we had been promised he should have done for us."[6] Groseilliers remained in Canada, but Radisson returned to France and after taking part in a campaign in the West Indies crossed again to England, ostensibly to bring his wife to France. While there he tried to restore himself to favour with the directors of the Hudson's Bay Company but without success. By now almost a regular cross-channel commuter, he returned once again to France in October 1679. When he approached Colbert and Seignelay they had nothing but harsh words for him, but Bellinzani, Colbert's assistant in commercial matters, put him in touch with the Quebec merchant, La Chesnaye, who was in Paris endeavouring to gain a charter for a company to trade in Hudson's Bay. This charter was finally granted in 1682. Meanwhile, La Chesnaye, assured that the charter would be forthcoming, returned to Quebec to organize the company. After one more trip to England and further fruitless discussions with the Hudson's Bay Company, Radisson borrowed 200 *livres* from Bishop Laval's agent in Paris,[7] and then crossed to Quebec, arriving there in September 1682.

When La Chesnaye applied to Frontenac for an exit permit for the vessel he had fitted out to go to the Bay, the Governor refused to grant it on the grounds that they might run afoul of the English "which would perhaps cause strife and wrangling." La Chesnaye did, however, obtain a permit for Radisson and Groseilliers to return to France by way of New England on a ship belonging to the Governor of Acadia. They wintered at Acadia, and in the spring La Chesnaye sent a fifty-ton barque loaded with trade goods to pick them up. This done they sailed to Hayes River in the Bay where they captured the trading-post and ship of a New England interloper. Some time later they took prisoner John Bridgar, recently arrived Governor for the Hudson's Bay Company, and his men. Leaving eight men at their own post, they sailed back to Quebec on the New England ship, taking its crew and Bridgar with them, and a "couple of thousand weight of beaver."

When Radisson had given his account of what had taken place in the Bay, La Barre and de Meulles found themselves perplexed as to what to do. La Barre, shortly after his arrival at Quebec, had encouraged the colony's merchants to join with La Chesnaye to contest the English company's hold on the Bay fur trade. Six of the leading merchants had done so, and the *Compagnie de la Baye du Nord* was formed. La Barre was aware that the aims of this company were approved by the government in France, but it seemed to him that the actions of Radisson and Groseilliers amounted to little more than piracy.

He therefore ordered the release of the New England trader, Benjamin Gillam, his ship and his crew, and also the Hudson's Bay Company man, John Bridgar. In addition, La Barre obliged Radisson and his associates to pay Gillam 1,000 *livres* damages, but when the *commis* of the Company of the Farm at Quebec demanded that La Chesnaye and Radisson pay the *quart* on the 2,000 beaver pelts that Radisson had brought back from the Bay, La Barre and de Meulles intervened. La Barre referred this matter to Colbert and gave it as his opinion that the Company had no right to collect the *quart* on beaver that "came from farther than the shores of France," particularly in view of the risks they had run and the losses they had incurred.[8] The answer from Seignelay, received the following year, made it plain that the French government was determined to contest the English hold on the Bay. La Barre was sternly rebuked for releasing Gillam's boat since this served to strengthen English claims to Nelson River.[9] La Barre tartly replied that he had assumed His Majesty would have taken it ill were he to have declared war on the English in Hudson Bay.[10] Since Seignelay had neglected to send any orders or instructions in 1683 concerning French policy in the Bay, or anywhere else for that matter, La Barre had reason to resent Seignelay's remarks.

In 1684 the Quebec company sent two ships to the Bay, commanded by the Sieur de la Martinière, a member of the Sovereign Council. Unfortunately, they were delayed en route. When they arrived at Nelson River they discovered that Radisson had arrived ten days earlier and, quite in character, was once again in the employ of the Hudson's Bay Company.* Radisson and the English took the Canadians prisoner, seized the furs they had traded, valued at over 400,000 *livres*, then destroyed the post. Martinière, after vainly protesting to the Hudson's Bay Company men, established a new post farther south on the Hayes River. He was only able to obtain from the Indians beaver to the value of 20,000 *livres* because the English traded their goods at much lower prices than could the French. After abortive attempts by both parties to capture each other's posts, the

---

* In 1685 Radisson once again sought to betray his English employers and transfer to French service, but Seignelay would have none of it. That Radisson was able to switch allegiance from France to England and back again as many times as he actually did was a truly remarkable accomplishment, surpassed only by the fact that he eventually died quietly in his bed, aged seventy-four.

Quebec men left the Bay on July 15 to return home. En route they captured a small Hudson's Bay Company barque with a cargo valued at 20,000 *livres*, evaded capture themselves by a larger English vessel, and reached Quebec on October 7.

The members of the Quebec company had invested 120,000 *livres* in the Bay enterprise, and the loss of the past winter's trade of furs to the English was a cruel blow. De Meulles pointed out to the Minister that the English in the Bay had a strong company behind them whereas the French had only a few merchants, but that they were willing to carry on both by way of the Bay and inland, along the rivers flowing into the Bay, in an attempt to stop the English drawing off the trade of the entire Lake Superior basin. The members of the company petitioned Seignelay for a warship of twenty to twenty-four guns to give them protection against the English pirates and French renegades. This request was ignored, but they did receive from the King a thirty-year concession on the lands at the mouth of the Nelson River and the right to establish three posts inland on the main rivers flowing into the Bay.

The French government was willing to allow the Canadians to contest the English hold on the Bay, but it was not willing to give the Quebec merchants the active support they required in the unequal contest. But what was far worse, what crippled the Quebec company's chances far more effectively than the actions of the Hudson's Bay Company men, was the Minister's decision that all furs taken at the Bay had to be brought to the bureau of the Company of the Farm at Quebec where the customary *quart* would be deducted; this, despite the fact, as La Barre had pointed out, that the Nelson River was closer to France than it was to Quebec by sea. The isolated posts in the Bay could not be made an integral part of New France; they had to be exploited and controlled directly from Europe as the English had demonstrated. Vested interests in France would not allow of this, and the Canadian *Compagnie de la Baye du Nord* with its very limited resources was unable to compete with the Hudson's Bay Company. From this time on the French were able to hinder the English in the Bay only by outright aggression and by their more effective inland traders, but they were unable to drive the English out of the Bay. This meant that the English had gained effective control of another of the main entrances to the interior of the continent.

In Acadia, too, the French were being hard pressed by the English, but in a different way. In 1678 Frontenac had, on his own initiative, appointed Michel le Neuf, Sieur de la Vallière, Governor of Acadia. Vallière was not given a royal commission, indeed the Minister of Marine appears not to have been aware that Frontenac had even made the appointment. Meanwhile, Vallière served without pay, but once established at Beaubassin he found ways to recompense himself. New England fishermen from Boston and Salem frequented the rich fishing-grounds along the coasts of Acadia in large numbers and dried their fish on its shores. Vallière sold them licences to fish in these waters at five pounds per vessel. To facilitate matters he commissioned a New England merchant, John Nelson, to issue the licences at Boston. The number of New England fishing-boats greatly exceeded that of the French and Acadians; they drove the latter away from the better fishing and drying areas, even seizing their boats on occasion. In fact, the French fishermen were treated as interlopers, and the Acadian fishing-trade was monopolized by New England, with the connivance of the French governor.

The fur trade, too, was in their hands; they traded directly with the Indians at the mouth of the St John River and elsewhere along the coast, maintaining warehouses at Port Royal for the purpose. The furs that Vallière obtained from the Indians farther inland he sold to the Boston men. The supplies needed by the Acadians at the scattered settlements along the coasts were furnished by Boston merchants who also helped themselves to cargoes of coal at Cape Breton. Thus, to all intents and purposes, Acadia was a colony of Massachusetts rather than of France.

The French government was, however, vaguely aware that conditions in Acadia left much to be desired, and early in 1682 a Huguenot merchant of La Rochelle, Bergier, in partnership with three bourgeois of Paris, Gautier, Boucher, and de Mantes, were granted fishing and trading rights in Acadia.[11] It was hoped that this company would succeed, where individuals had failed, in exploiting the resources of the province, establishing trade with France, New France, and the West Indies, and bringing about a sizable increase in population. When the clergy of the *Missions Etrangères* in Paris got wind of this they protested vigorously,[12] mortally afraid of any Huguenot establishment in the areas served by their clergy. But their protests were of no avail.

Bergier established a base at Chedabouctou on the south coast of Acadia and reported that there were ample supplies of trees suitable for masts, and oak for ship planking. He quickly found, however, that his company had small hope of commercial success as long as he had to compete with the New England men. The Minister of Marine now began receiving memoirs complaining of their depredations and of the support they received from Vallière. Bergier pleaded for naval aid to drive the English out of Acadian waters and to stop the Salem pirates seizing French ships. The Minister failed to provide the 130-ton frigate that the company had requested, but in March 1684 a royal edict was issued declaring that any foreign vessels found fishing or trading for furs within the confines of the French company's concession would be seized and confiscated.

Bergier promptly seized eight New England ships, loaded with fish and furs, and took their captains to La Rochelle where they were brought before the Admiralty Court. Two of the English captains were able to produce licences issued by Vallière and were released. Bergier was ordered to take them back to Acadia at his own expense and make restitution of their barques and their cargoes. The six others lacked licences and admitted they had known of the French edict before leaving Boston. The confiscation of their ships was upheld, despite loud protests from New England. Unfortunately for the French, if force was to be used the New England men were in much the stronger position. They promptly seized four French ships in reprisal, and the Acadians no longer dared put to sea.[13]

Bergier's frequent detailed complaints of Vallière's depredations eventually had the desired result. Upon investigation it was discovered that Vallière had never been commissioned by the Crown as Governor of Acadia and, in view of his reprehensible actions, in April 1684 he was summarily ordered to cease exercising a governor's powers. Unfortunately the man now appointed as Governor of Acadia, François-Marie Perrot, was as much a rogue as Vallière. In fact, the main reason for Perrot's appointment was the desire to remove him from his post as Governor of Montreal where his actions had caused vigorous complaints. He had, however, too many friends with influence at the Court to be deprived of all office; thus, he was, in the usual manner of bureaucracies, merely given this new appointment. He was also given a free hand in Acadia. The province still remained nominally under the authority of the Governor of Quebec, but La Barre was informed that, owing to the difficulty of communications which prevented anyone at Quebec knowing conditions or circumstances in Acadia, he was not to issue any orders to Perrot.[14] De Meulles had proposed to overcome this problem by building a road from Quebec to Acadia, but Seignelay declined to furnish the twenty to thirty thousand *livres* the Intendant had estimated it would cost.

Thus, the removal of Vallière brought about no real improvement in Acadian affairs, and before long the same sort of complaints were voiced against Perrot. Nor was Bergier, the chief complainant, himself without sin. In 1684 La Barre declared that Bergier and Company were making no real attempt to provide the supplies needed by the Acadian settlers, who were still obliged to obtain all their needs from Boston. By 1687 the Minister was unable to ignore the complaints against Perrot any longer and dismissed him from his post. He remained in Acadia, however, and continued his abuses, despite warnings from the Minister to desist or learn what it meant to incur the King's serious displeasure. Ironically, it was New

England freebooters who succeeded in solving this problem where the
Minister of Marine had failed. In May 1690 two English pirate ships landed
at Port Royal, sacked and burned the settlements, murdered some of the
settlers, and took Perrot prisoner. He was subsequently rescued by a French
privateer and taken to France, where he died the following year.

Although Perrot was succeeded as Governor of Acadia by an honest and
competent man, Louis-Alexandre Desfriches, Sieur de Meneval, the province still languished as a result of French neglect, and its considerable
assets continued to be exploited by New England men. The *Compagnie
de la Pêche Sédentaire* stated that the main source of weakness in the
colony was the dissoluteness of the settlers, many of whom had obtained
huge concessions by false pretences, some having frontages of over one
hundred and fifty miles, and that they made no attempt to develop their
lands but spent all their time trading with the Indians and debauching the
Indian girls. The company stated further that there was no one in the
colony capable of dispensing justice equitably, those empowered to do so
being decrepit, ignorant, and corrupt. The Marquis de Denonville, who
succeeded La Barre as Governor of New France in 1685, confirmed this
statement, declaring, "there all is confusion, disorder and debauchery with
the Indians who complain that their girls are being seized. The entire fur
trade goes to the English who are more the masters of that country than
we are ourselves."[15] Not until the outbreak of hostilities in 1690 between
England and France did any marked change take place, and then only because France had to prevent the province falling completely into the hands
of the English. That it did not was more a sign of New England's military
ineptitude than of French initiative.

While these squabbles were taking place in Acadia, others were beginning
in Quebec, forming a discordant background noise in a minor key to the
sombre rumbling of war in the west. Within a few months of their arrival
in the colony de Meulles and La Barre began bickering. The Intendant
accused the Governor of attempting to usurp his authority in the Sovereign
Council, of interfering in matters of justice, and of serious malversations in
the fur trade. As a result of the earlier dissension Seignelay was quick to
give credence to de Meulles's charges; then he just as quickly accepted La
Barre's explanations. De Meulles, who was a born intriguer but not a
very clever one, eventually went too far. He suggested that the governor's
powers be considerably reduced and his own enhanced. Seignelay nearly
exploded when he read de Meulles's dispatch. His reply was scathing: "I
am convinced that a man who is capable of entertaining such a notion, and
proposing it lacks the wisdom needed for a post such as you hold and I

advise you to think a little longer another time on what you write me."
De Meulles dared not answer the Minister back. He could only wait for
an opportunity to prove to the Minister that he had been right, and he did
not have to wait long for the Governor to give him the opportunity.

In the spring of 1683 the Iroquois replied to La Barre's request that
their delegates come to Montreal to confer with him. They informed him
haughtily that he must come to them if he desired a conference. La Barre
and de Meulles were convinced by this that nothing less than a large-scale
assault on the Iroquois villages would bring them to reason. In early June
they sent a barque to France, post-haste, to apprize the Minister of the
seriousness of the situation and to obtain the King's sanction for a war
with the Iroquois. At the same time they made an almost frantic appeal
for six hundred trained troops with good officers, a thousand muskets, as
many swords, and all the other munitions and supplies needed for a campaign. La Barre closed his dispatch to the King by declaring: "I will perish
at their head or destroy your enemies, as soon as I am in a position to undertake the task."

Shortly after the barque had left, a merchant ship arrived at Quebec. It
brought no dispatches from the Court but it did bring a personal letter for
La Barre which must have made the situation appear almost hopeless. This
letter informed him that Frontenac had given the Minister definite assurance
that, before leaving the colony, he had negotiated a satisfactory peace
settlement with the Iroquois.

This may help explain why Seignelay, at this juncture of events,
showed so little concern for Canada. In April he was at Toulon, the
Canadian dispatches not yet attended to. They awaited his return. At the
end of May they still had not been dealt with, but it was hoped he would
find time to attend to them while accompanying the King on another trip.
He neglected, however, to take them with him, and since he did not return
to Paris until the end of July it was by then too late to deal with them
before the Canadian convoy sailed. The Sieur de la Garde, a *commis* in the
Ministry of Marine, did what he could, but without the Minister's approval
it was not much.[16] A dispatch for the King's signature was drafted on
August 5 and eventually sent off along with one hundred and fifty Troupes
de la Marine, hastily recruited in the back alleys of Rochefort.

Meanwhile, La Barre and de Meulles were writing further desperate dispatches, pleading for men, arms, funds, and orders. La Barre declared that
with five hundred good troops he would invade the Iroquois country, winter
there, and destroy them in the space of a year, but without troops he could
do nothing; and without the Minister's orders, he added, he could take no
action. He therefore decided to temporize and try to avert an open clash
with the Iroquois, whose war parties were now attacking not only the

Illinois and the Miamis but also the Ottawas. He sent men he could depend on to reinforce the western posts. He also sent Charles le Moyne, who was greatly respected by the Iroquois, to Onondaga to try to persuade the Five Nations to send delegates to Montreal that summer to confer with him.

Not without difficulty, Le Moyne induced their chiefs to go to Montreal where La Barre was liberal with presents, but the only assurance he could get from them was that they would try to restrain their warriors from attacking the Ottawas and Hurons. When he demanded to know why they were warring with the Illinois, the great Onondaga war chief, Tegannis-sorens, replied: "They deserve to die; they have shed our blood." All that La Barre could hope for now was that the situation in the west would not get worse before the Minister realized that the colony had to have aid, and soon; but events in North America would not wait on the convenience of a Minister at Versailles.

Early in November, after La Barre had reconciled himself to the fact that for some unaccountable reason he would receive no orders, instructions, or funds and supplies of any sort that year, the royal frigate *La Tempête* arrived at Quebec with the King's dispatch and the hundred and fifty Troupes de la Marine. This did little to strengthen La Barre's position. Only one hundred and twenty of the troops were fit for service. Of the thousand muskets sent, seven hundred and forty proved to be worthless and had to be sent back; instead of light brass cannons, heavy iron ones without carriages were sent, useless for forest warfare, and of the thousand swords, six hundred were found to be broken on arrival. Nor could La Barre derive any comfort from the King's dispatch of August 4, drafted by the *commis* La Garde. It contained no meaningful orders or instructions, only pious declarations that war would be very bad for the colony; therefore La Barre had to pacify the Iroquois by diplomacy. He was, however, to use his own discretion, and if war were absolutely necessary then he had to defeat the Iroquois swiftly and decisively, forcing them to accept terms which would end their interference with the French fur trade. In short, La Barre had to avert a war without the necessary men or supplies. After reading it, he must have realized that no matter what he did, he would be blamed for anything that went wrong and, under the circumstances, little was likely to go right.

The following May 1684, when a Seneca chief arrived at Quebec to assure La Barre that his nation desired nothing but peace with the French, La Barre was very skeptical, and his suspicions were quickly confirmed. While this Seneca was still at Quebec, four *coureurs de bois* arrived from the west bringing word that the Iroquois had attacked Fort St Louis in the Illinois country. La Barre was immediately urged from all sides to launch a full-scale assault on the Iroquois. The colony's merchants had over 300,000 *livres'* worth of trade goods in the Ottawa country alone and they feared that were Fort St Louis to fall, as it might well have done already, the Iroquois would turn north to attack the Ottawas with their full strength. Word was later received that the garrison at Fort St Louis had beaten off the Iroquois assaults, but the commanders of the western posts and the Jesuit missionaries among the Ottawa nations all declared that unless war were carried to the Iroquois villages the west would be lost. Father Garnier, however, the Jesuit missionary with the Senecas, and Father Lamberville with the Onondagas, were strongly opposed to the French warring with the Iroquois.[17] Such a war would, of course, have gravely imperilled their heroic efforts to christianize these nations. Much seemed to depend on whose missionary work was being threatened.

But in the colony everyone was hot for war, and La Barre, although beset by grave misgivings, began making hasty preparations for a campaign with the meagre forces he had available. Orders were sent to Durantaye, commandant at Michilimackinac, and to Du Lhut, to bring as many *coureurs de bois* and allied Indians as possible to Lake Ontario to join the force that La Barre would bring from Montreal. By July 16 the available troops and militia, nearly eight hundred men, were assembled at Montreal where they were joined by 378 allied Indians. But, as the moment for departure drew near, La Barre began to quail at the thought of leading this ragged army through the wilderness into the enemy's country, against a foe that cared nothing for the rules of war. In a frantic last-minute effort to delay events he sent off letters to the Governors of New York and Massachusetts, informing them of his plans and appealing to them to furnish no aid to the enemy. He insisted on waiting for their answers, but after ten days he had to give way to pressure from his subordinates. With obvious trepidation he gave the order to set off, and the motley force began slowly portaging its way up the St Lawrence. When they reached Lake St Francis, La Barre received word from Father Jean de Lamberville at Onondaga that the Senecas were willing to give him satisfaction, but that if he persisted in attacking any one of the Five Nations they would all unite their forces, destroy him and his army, then lay waste to the French settlements. The Iroquois braves were, Father Lamberville stated, declaring that the French must have "a great desire to be stripped, roasted and eaten and that they will see if their flesh, which according to them is saltish on account of the salt the French make use of, be as good as that of their other enemies whom they devour."[18]

At this, what little stock of courage La Barre retained seeped away. He rushed on ahead of his forces to Fort Frontenac and sent word back to

Father Lamberville that he would be willing to negotiate a peaceful settlement. A few days later he sent the Sieur le Moyne to Onondaga to arrange the preliminaries. For the ensuing fortnight he waited impatiently for word from Onondaga, while the officers and men grew sullen at the turn events had taken. Before long rations ran short, then the men began to sicken at an alarming rate with fever. It was the dread tertian ague.* La Barre sent five hundred of his men and two hundred of the Indian allies, who had so far escaped the contagion, to La Famine on the south side of the lake where they could eke out their supplies with fish and game. But when he crossed the lake, upon receiving word that the Onondagas would meet him, he found the men there laid low with fever. He himself was not spared long. When Le Moyne, also ill and barely able to walk, arrived with the Iroquois envoys and a sizable escort of warriors, they were quick to appreciate that the French were at their mercy. One word from the Onondaga war chiefs and none of the French would have lived to see Montreal again.

It was under these conditions that the Onondaga spokesman, Hotréouati, contemptuously dictated terms to a French governor who was barely able to stand. He stated that the French had no justification for warring with the Senecas. The Miamis they would spare, but the Illinois they would destroy or perish in the attempt. He warned La Barre that he feared for the lives of his men in the lands of the Iroquois; therefore he would be well advised to take them back to Quebec where they could sleep in safety. To these terms, couched in insulting phrases, La Barre could only reply that the Iroquois must cease pillaging French canoes in the Illinois country, but Hotréouati vouchsafed nothing and La Barre dared not press the point.

The next day the French dragged themselves back to Fort Frontenac. La Barre sent a message to Durantaye, who had reached Niagara with one hundred and fifty *coureurs de bois* and over five hundred Ottawas, ordering him to return to Michilimackinac. The Ottawas had been reluctant to accompany Durantaye and when they learned what had taken place at La Famine, what little faith they had in the French was seriously diminished. Many of La Barre's men died before reaching Montreal, and the disease swept through the colony. The expedition had served only to weaken the colony's meagre forces, discourage the Indian allies, and persuade the Iroquois that they had little to fear from the French.

In France, meanwhile, the Minister had, in April, finally turned his attention to the affairs of Canada. The responsibility for the aggressiveness of the Iroquois he placed squarely on La Barre's shoulders; giving a strange

---

* The tertian ague is better known as Spanish influenza, the dread disease that swept through Europe in 1919, leaving thousands dead in its wake.

twist to the charges of de Meulles, Seignelay declared that La Barre's grant-ing of an excessive number of *congés* had incited the Iroquois to retaliate against the influx of French in the west. He reiterated the statements made in the King's dispatch the preceding year, that war would be very bad for the colony. La Barre was to oblige the Iroquois to remain at peace with the French and their allies without resorting to force. If, however, war was absolutely necessary he was to undertake it only if he could be absolutely sure of complete success with one campaign. Orders were given to raise an-other four companies of Troupes de la Marine for service in Canada, but the King's dispatch then stated, "I again repeat that I trust you will not need them for a war with the Iroquois, which would be very prejudicial to the well being of the colony and could never serve any useful purpose."

Then, in July, La Barre's urgent dispatches, telling of the Iroquois attack on Fort St Louis, expressing the fear that Fort Frontenac would be next and that Quebec itself might soon be in danger, reached the Court. Although the Sieur de la Salle, then in France, declared that these reports were all false, the Ministry of Marine was jolted out of its lethargy. Garrison troops at Brest were rushed to Rochefort to take ships to Canada, and officers at the latter naval base became very worried lest they be selected for the ex-pedition.[19] The Minister, in the King's dispatch, now gave his approval of La Barre's decision to attack the Iroquois and declared that the troops being sent should enable him either to destroy the Iroquois completely or at least to impose his terms on them. The dispatch then went on to say "no matter what advantage you might obtain for the glory of my arms, even though the entire destruction of the barbarians might result from the con-tinuation of this war, you must prefer to make peace, which will restore calm to my subjects and enable you to strengthen the colony by the means indicated to you in all my previous letters." When La Barre reached Mont-real after his campaign, more dead than alive, he could fairly claim that he had followed these instructions to the letter.

It could not be asserted that La Barre would have exercised better judge-ment had he waited for the reinforcements he had requested to reach him before launching his campaign. The ships bearing them did not leave Roche-fort until late in August, and for a while it was feared they would not get away in time and would have to wait until the following spring. Moreover, instead of the three hundred troops promised, only two hundred were sent, and without proper arms, supplies, or funds for their pay. They added little to the colony's strength. By spring of the following year no funds remained for the pay of these troops, and the Intendant was obliged to release the men to find employment, and their keep, as best they could in the towns and on the farms. Owing to the death of so many of the militia, during and after La Barre's campaign there was a shortage of labour and many of the troops found employment; but by early June, when the crops had been planted, the *habitants* no longer needed casual help. De Meulles, faced with a desperate situation, solved it by an ingenious innovation. He made his own money out of packs of playing cards, by simply writing the denomination, and affixing his signature on the face. He also issued an *ordonnance* declaring that these notes would be redeemed as soon as the ships arrived with specie from France; meanwhile the paper money had to be accepted at face value.

This card money proved very successful indeed, and for much longer than the summer of 1685. There had always been a serious shortage of currency in the colony – all manner of foreign coins circulated but were continually drained off to France or Albany – and beaver skins were an awkward medium of exchange. In 1676 Duchesneau had proposed the issuing of 93,000 *livres* of coins to circulate only in Canada, but Colbert had vetoed the suggestion by claiming that when the colony produced enough goods through trade and industry, currency would be attracted into the colony.[20] This desirable end had not yet been achieved, and de Meulles's card money filled a long-felt need. It proved so useful a device that from this time on the intendants had continual recourse to it. Although the Minister of Marine constantly demanded that the outstanding card money be redeemed and no more issued, no sooner would it be called in than circumstances would make it expedient to issue a fresh lot. Thus, an emergency led to a genuinely useful monetary system; one that, on the whole, worked well for several years.

At the same time as he performed this unique service for the colony, the Intendant also sent a very detailed account to the Minister of La Barre's campaign, maintaining that the Iroquois would have been completely crushed had not the Governor preferred to negotiate a dishonourable peace settlement. He criticized everything that La Barre had done; held him to blame for everything that had gone wrong, even for the epidemic that had struck the army; claimed that the officers had been on the verge of mutiny and had almost taken over command and gone on to attack the Iroquois; that the Indian allies were now about to declare war on the French; that the colony was virtually lost; and that despite all this, he remained on the best of terms with the Governor.[21]

La Barre, for his part, made no attempt to give a false picture of the situation. In his report to the Minister on his campaign and the treaty he had made with the Iroquois he gave a strictly factual account of events. He did not, of course, blame himself, but circumstances, for the sorry outcome. He stated that a campaign against the Iroquois was a far more difficult undertaking than those who had urged it on him had ever imagined. The transporting of an army and supplies to Lake Ontario was in itself, he stated, an extremely difficult task. Gone now was all the bluster of the previous year. Instead of promising to crush the Iroquois in one year, given five hundred regulars, he now declared that the task would require a large body of troops and several years of hard campaigning, during which time the security of the colony would be continually threatened by Iroquois raids.[22]

When Louis XIV and Seignelay received the Canadian dispatches, and the terms of La Barre's treaty, they immediately recognized that French prestige had suffered a humiliating defeat. At a time when France was the most feared nation in Europe, a painted savage in the North American wilderness had dictated terms to one of Louis XIV's provincial governors. The King and his Minister now, for the first time, took a close look at the situation. Seignelay was able no longer to maintain his attitude that the threat to Canada was not there, in the hope that it would then go away.

Someone, of course, had to be held responsible for this sorry state of affairs, and La Barre was the obvious choice. The next ship to Canada brought his recall. De Meulles likely gloated when he read in the King's dispatch: "I have no cause to be satisfied with the treaty made between the Sieur de la Barre and the Iroquois; his abandoning of the Illinois has displeased me greatly and it is that which has determined me to recall him."

There can be no question but that the decision to recall La Barre was justified. He had demonstrated his incompetence beyond all doubt. Moreover, his health was shattered and when he sailed for France in 1685 no one expected him to survive the voyage. But he had at least made an attempt, however ineffectual, to cope with the Iroquois threat, and if it did nothing else his failure forced the Minister to face the facts and take more effective measures to cope with it. One thing was now abundantly clear. If French interests in North America were to be safeguarded against the Iroquois threat in the west and the Hudson's Bay Company threat in the north, more effective measures would have to be taken. Large military forces would have to be employed, more competent men placed in charge, and more authority and greater freedom of action given them.

CHAPTER 9

Denonville's Response

It could not be said that Seignelay was incapable of learning from experience. To replace La Barre he now selected Jacques Réné de Brisay, Marquis de Denonville, Brigadier and Colonel of the Queen's Dragoons; a man in whom he personally had great confidence and who was generally regarded as one of the better officers in the kingdom. He also gave orders for the raising of five hundred additional Troupes de la Marine and one hundred and fifty *engagés* for Canada. Denonville personally supervised the recruiting and equipping of the ten companies and found himself over 6,000 *livres* out of pocket as a result. His care for their discipline and well-being, as well as his meticulous attention to detail, is evidence of his capabilities as a commander. That he inspired confidence is attested by the fact that several officers on half-pay volunteered to serve with him as sergeants on the understanding that they would be recommissioned when vacancies on the establishment occurred.

Before sailing from La Rochelle in June 1685, Denonville asked that he be allowed to take forty extra men to replace those who would likely not survive the voyage. The request was turned down by the Minister, but it at least served to indicate that the casualty rate for an Atlantic voyage on a troop ship was estimated to be about the same as for a battle. Denonville wisely chose to sail on a merchant ship, as he was accompanied by his pregnant wife and his daughters. Sailing with him was Jean-Baptiste de la Croix de St Vallier, a young priest of Grenoble who had been appointed to succeed Laval as Bishop of Quebec. Father Dudouyt of the Missions Etrangères at Paris was of the opinion that St Vallier was too young, too austere, and too much the perfectionist for the Quebec see, but being well connected at the Court and not wishing to be a bishop in France, he had been given the Canadian appointment. Before many years were out the Canadian clergy were pleading to have their new Bishop removed, and Laval, who remained at Quebec, was to refer to him as a scourge sent by

God to punish everyone for their sins. Even Denonville, who was a deeply religious man, must have been taken aback when St Vallier delivered him a lengthy lecture on the manner in which his daughters should comport themselves. One also wonders how these girls reacted to the diatribe on female vanities and the injunction against dancing with members of the opposite sex.

On August 1 Denonville and his family reached Quebec in good health. Toward the end of the month the King's ships arrived, and Denonville's fears for the condition of the men were borne out. On one of the ships sixty men had died of typhus and scurvy and another eighty were more dead than alive. At the Hôtel Dieu the sisters, aided by the other clergy, set up cots in every available space in the hospital, in the chapel, the outbuildings, and in tents in the courtyard. By the time the second troop ship unloaded its dreadful freight they had over three hundred fever-stricken, delirious men to care for.

Although the Hôtel Dieu had an enviable reputation for caring for the sick, the state of medical knowledge in that age was rudimentary to say the least. In fact, the best hope of recovering from a serious ailment was to give the medical profession as wide a berth as possible. The sovereign remedies for disease were purges and bleeding. In 1676, for example, when the Superior of the Montreal seminary, M. de Bretonvilliers, was stricken with a severe pain in his right side, accompanied by fever and violent headaches, he was bled six times. When this did not have the desired effect, the patient instead becoming distinctly weaker, he was thoroughly purged. To everyone's sorrow, he died two days later. The good sisters at the Hôtel Dieu, however, reported that the most successful of all the remedies they tried with the stricken soldiers was bleeding at the temple. Many of them, for whom there had appeared to be no hope, were, they claimed, quickly cured with this treatment. Many more, however, were too far gone.

As luck would have it, among the passengers in this convoy was one Michel Sarrazin, master surgeon, who was to gain international recognition as a surgeon, doctor of medicine, and scientist. He was immediately pressed into service. The following year he was appointed Surgeon-Major to the regular troops in the colony. In addition he developed a large private practice, counting all the colonial notables among his patients. In 1699, in recognition of his contribution to knowledge in the fields of botany and zoology he was, along with Sir Isaac Newton, elected a corresponding member of the *Académie Royale des Sciences*. He compiled a catalogue of over two hundred Canadian plants with extensive notes on their pharmaceutical properties, determined after careful experimentation. He also submitted articles on the flora and fauna of Canada, after very careful dissections. The one animal that defeated him was, it almost goes without saying, the skunk. He was forced to abandon his attempts to dissect and study its anatomy because, he noted, "it had a dreadful smell, capable of making a whole canton desert."[1]

There were several other competent doctors and surgeons in the colony. In fact, New France was singularly well served in this respect, having had at least ninety-six practitioners of the healing arts in the second half of the century. Many of them, however, appear to have had few qualifications and more likely than not were mere herbalists, or barbers who had mastered the knack of slitting a vein and mixing a draught of Glauber's salts, one of the common remedies of the age. Some forty-two citizens of Montreal had enough faith in master-surgeon Estienne Bouchard to contract with him in a pre-paid health-insurance scheme. For a fee of five *livres* each a year, they and all members of their families received medical care until completely recovered from all accidents and ailments except the plague, smallpox, leprosy, epilepsy, and lithotomy. The Hôtel Dieu in Montreal had a similar contract for the inmates of their hospital with master-surgeons Jean Martinet de Fourblanche and Antoine Forestier. For a fee of 75 *livres* a year they contracted to visit the hospital wards to treat the patients, all charity cases, every day; each for three months in turn.[2] For the soldiers in the Troupes de la Marine there was an arrangement similar to the present-day Blue Cross Plan; a deduction was made in their pay regularly by the intendant to cover the cost of any medical treatment they might need and he made a supplemental grant to the hospital from the colony's general funds for each soldier treated. In the 1690's, during the war with the English and the Iroquois, these funds proved inadequate to pay the cost of treating all the casualties. Knowing that the Minister would not sanction any additional grants to the hospital, the Intendant Champigny and Frontenac, the Governor, gave the hospital considerable financial aid out of their own pockets.

As late as September 1685 there were a hundred troops still in hospital at Quebec with some of them dying every day. Denonville filled the gaps in the ranks from among the hundred and fifty *engagés* who had been sent with the troops. He found that the troops sent previously added little to his military establishment; many had succumbed to the earlier influenza epidemic and of the rest a quarter were not fit for service of any sort. When the ships returned to France they took back with them forty-four men who would never be of any use for military or other duties. Denonville was also greatly perturbed to discover that there was no magazine at Quebec where arms and powder could be stored in safety and that the King's stores were in a shocking state of confusion. Upon demanding an accounting Denonville discovered that de Meulles had been trafficking in these goods for his own profit. This was quickly stopped by placing triple locks on the warehouse, requiring the attendance of himself, the intendant, and the commissary to open the door. When de Meulles showed no inclination to mend his ways Denonville reported his malversations to the Minister, and the following year de Meulles was summarily dismissed from his post and ordered to return to France.

In 1686 the arrival of Jean Bochart de Champigny to replace de Meulles made Denonville's task considerably easier. Although this was the first appointment in the royal service that Champigny had held, he proved to be an exceptionally able man. A member of one of the older and wealthier families of the *noblesse de robe*, he was a personal friend of Denonville, which was one reason for his having been given the appointment. It was thereby hoped to avoid a recurrence of the bitter divisions that had vexed New France in the past. In this respect the Minister was not to be disappointed, much to the surprise of many in the colony. Like Denonville, Champigny was deeply religious, but by no means subservient to the clergy; when the wishes of the bishop or his clergy came into conflict with royal policy Champigny would not give way to them an inch. He was, in fact, a man of very strong character; when he felt strongly about something he could be extremely caustic, even to the Minister himself. One thing, however, appears markedly lacking in his make-up: namely, humour.

In the Sovereign Council there was no friction at all between the Governor and the other members. Denonville attended its meetings as infrequently as possible, and then only when the Council requested him to give an opinion. He asked the Minister to allow him to absent himself altogether as, not being a lawyer, he felt that his opinions would contribute little of value to the Council's deliberations, and besides he had more than enough to do without attending these meetings. The Minister, however, decided that this might establish a bad precedent and Denonville was instructed to attend whenever he was asked, and give his opinion.

That Denonville was not merely trying to shirk his responsibilities is made very plain by the fact that he accomplished more for the colony in a few months than his predecessors had achieved in as many years. Within a few weeks he had travelled from one end of the colony to the other, observing everything. He saw very quickly that sweeping reforms were badly needed, not only in military affairs and the civil administration, but also in Canadian society itself. He was appalled by the debauchery prevalent among Canadian youth, their total lack of discipline or respect for authority. From the moment a Canadian youth was big enough to handle a gun, his father dared not lay a hand on him. This condition was, he stated, worse among the seigneurs' families than the *habitants* and it stemmed largely from the fact that they were allowed, and encouraged, to spend most of their time hunting, or off on fur-trading expeditions where they lived like savages, without the restraint of parents, curé, or civil authorities. Another social evil was the excessive number of taverns. Every rogue and idler in the colony had but one ambition; to open a tavern and so avoid labour on the land. He had noted some seigneuries with only twenty homes, and half of them taverns. Trois Rivières, with twenty-five houses, had eighteen to twenty grog shops; and Quebec and Montreal were, he stated, just as bad.

To rectify these social evils he declared that he intended to take stern measures. Cabarets were to be strictly regulated and the seigneurs held responsible for those on their lands. Men living debauched lives would, from now on, receive corporal punishment publicly. To rectify the state of idleness in which the women and girls lived during the long winters, with nothing to occupy their time except keeping warm, he took steps to have hemp and flax sown in all the seigneuries so that the women could eventually weave cloth. He clearly implied that he, rather than the devil, would find work for idle hands in future. De Meulles had complained that six girls sent to the colony to teach Indian girls at the school run by the Sisters of the Congregation how to weave, knit, and make lace, had proved to be street-walkers picked up in La Rochelle. The sisters refused to have them, and de Meulles declared that he would have sent them back to France but for the fact that they would be easy to marry off. Champigny and Denonville took a sterner attitude. They decided to send several notorious prostitutes of Quebec and Montreal back on the first ships. They made the mistake, however, of informing the Minister of their intentions and he forbade it on the grounds that this constituted no punishment and might, instead of acting as a deterrent, serve to encourage others to adopt their reprehensible way of life. In this respect, too, the colony was expected to look after its own.

Much stricter regulations governing *congés* for the western fur trade were introduced. Whereas Frontenac and La Barre had granted these permits in large numbers to their friends and associates, Denonville limited the number to twenty-five and granted them all to poorer families who had been excluded from such favours in the past. He thereby made enemies of some of the more influential families in the colony. He also asked the Minister not to send any more "gentlemen" to the colony. What was needed, he said, was men who would put their hands to the plow and the mattock, not indigent nobles who merely added to the colony's problems. At the same time he also appealed to the King to grant pensions to certain impoverished noble families who were living a miserable existence after having served the Crown and the colony well during their more active years.

The King eventually agreed to allow Denonville to grant them up to 300 *livres* but instructed him to see to it that no one not of noble birth adopted the nobles' mode of life.

Denonville saw clearly, however, that these measures did not go to the root of the trouble. What was needed was an opportunity for the young Canadians to exercise their abundant energies and talents in more constructive ways. For many of them, life on the land had little attraction. "The Canadians," he wrote, "are all big, well built and firmly planted on their feet, accustomed whenever necessary to live on little, robust and vigorous, very obstinate and inclined to be dissolute, but quick witted and vivacious." For such as these a military career would have great appeal. He therefore recommended that a few companies of regular troops be recruited in the colony with Canadian officers, and used to garrison forts in the west. He later suggested that the sons of Canadian seigneurs be sent to France to serve in the King's guards or other regiments. In 1687, the King granted six blank commissions for the Troupes de la Marine to be issued by Denonville and the Intendant to Canadians, with the strict injunction that the recipients must be gentlemen. From this time on the officer corps of the Troupes de la Marine was made up very largely of Canadians, for the experience of the war years showed that they made far better officers, under Canadian conditions, than did the officers sent from France.

Another problem that Denonville tackled in a constructive manner was education. He obtained the King's consent and a 400 *livres*-subvention to establish a navigation school at Quebec to train Canadian youths as pilots. Louis Jolliet, the discoverer of the Mississippi, subsequently became instructor at the school. There was a chronic need for river pilots at this time, as well as for accurate charts of the St Lawrence. Many ship captains refused to bring their vessels farther than Ile Percé or Tadoussac, whence goods had to be trans-shipped in schooners to Quebec. Although Jolliet had charted the St Lawrence and in 1686 the King made him a·grant of 300 *livres* for this work, the Minister sent a master navigator, the Sieur Deshayes, to Quebec with Denonville to make new charts. Deshayes, however, was taken ill, and the charts were eventually made by Franquelin who also mapped a large part of North America. Several years later, in 1693, Canadian youths were being sent to France for training as navigators and they were given every inducement to serve in the navy. Some Canadians did receive commissions in the French navy and performed valiant service indeed, Le Moyne d'Iberville being among the more outstanding of this number.

Then, as now, providing for the education of Canadian children created a serious problem. This was the responsibility of the clergy, who never had adequate funds or enough qualified teachers. The girls were, of course, educated by the nuns, the Ursulines and the Sisters of the Congregation, and they likely received as good an education as they would have received in France. Religious instruction was strongly emphasized; then the basic subjects, reading, writing, arithmetic, and Latin, and also some rudimentary chemistry and botany for the preparation of simple remedies. Such things as needlework were also taught; but perhaps most significant of all, the girls were trained to have pleasing manners and to be good conversationalists.

At Quebec and Montreal, schools for boys were attached to the two seminaries and there was the Jesuit College in Quebec and a Jesuit Latin school in Montreal providing higher education. In 1686 Bishop St Vallier undertook to have school teachers trained in the colony, and the Minister gave him every encouragement. It is interesting to note that in the schools under the jurisdiction of the Seminary at Quebec, "streaming" of the students was insisted on. The students were divided into groups according to the progress they made, and no student was allowed to advance to the next group until he had mastered the work of the group he was currently in. The curriculum was quite rudimentary: reading, writing, Latin, the catechism, civility, contracts, and arithmetic.[3] Owing to the limited facilities at the Petit Séminaire at Quebec only thirty students could be admitted; any who showed a lack of ability or application were obliged to withdraw to make way for others who were eager for the opportunity. The head of the mission in Paris declared in 1687: "It is far more worthwhile to have only a few students, and that they be good ones."[4] And at Quebec M. Brisacier declared that they could not accept more than thirty students. He admitted it was shameful not to admit all the boys who had both the desire and the capacity to learn, but they could only do so much and this much they were determined to do well.[5] In short, they regarded the maintenance of high standards as essential.

For the sons of *habitants* an alternative to tilling the soil was provided by the technical school founded by Bishop Laval at St Joachim in 1684. Here youths without means were taught a useful trade: carpentry, cabinet-making, masonry, wood-carving, and iron-working, among others. Before long, Canadian-trained craftsmen were turning out work of very high quality. Working with white pine rather than the hard woods commonly used in Europe, the cabinet-makers produced excellently proportioned furniture. The same white pine was used for panelling churches and the wood-carving employed in the churches and homes was of an exceptionally high quality, exhibiting a baroque exuberance in keeping with the Canadian temperament. The wrought-iron work was of equal quality. Such simple things as door hinges, window screens, and steeple cocks were frequently works of great artistic merit.[6] And perhaps most important of all, these things were housed in homes and churches done in the architectural style of northern France but modified into a functional style unique to Canada, as typical of the country and as æsthetically pleasing as the Queen Anne style architecture later adopted in New England.

Some aspects of housing in New France, however, were not at all to Denonville's liking. He objected strongly to the prices currently being charged. Nine thousand *livres* without the land for quite modest houses, and fourteen to fifteen thousand for ones of a "reasonable" size, seemed to him to be exorbitant. As for the Château St Louis where he resided, he reported that it was crumbling into ruins and, being constructed entirely of wood, could burn to the ground at any time. But in this respect it differed not at all from the rest of the town where the citizens piled the winter's supply of firewood around the walls of their homes. To make matters worse, during the dry summer weather and the cold winter months when the wells dried up or froze solid, water supplies for Upper Town had to be transported from the river in buckets. La Barre had had work begun on a deep well, but the available funds had become exhausted before an adequate water source was reached. The urgent need for its completion was made manifest in 1686 when the Ursuline's convent and chapel burned to the ground. Twelve years later, however, there was still no adequate water supply in Upper Town.

The Intendant was more fortunate than the Governor in the accommodation afforded him. The King had agreed to purchase Talon's idle brewery for conversion into a *Palais de Justice*. De Meulles had begun this work and his successor, Champigny, saw to its completion. Despite constant grumbling from the Minister at the seemingly endless bills, Champigny had the building turned into quite a handsome edifice containing his own living-quarters, a chamber for the Sovereign Council with the necessary service rooms, storerooms, and cells for the detention of prisoners awaiting trial or punishment.

One of Denonville's first actions upon his arrival was to put those of the troops who were fit enough to work building a palisade around Montreal as a security measure. When, a few years later, the danger of Iroquois attacks increased, many people living nearby began to move into the town for safety. This afforded those owning vacant land inside the walls an irresistible opportunity to reap large profits, and prices quickly began to soar. Such developments, however, were frowned on by the authorities and the Intendant promptly ordered that no one would be permitted to retain more than one *arpent* of land within the town walls. Those retaining this much vacant land had to build a masonry house with a stone chimney within a year of the date of the *ordonnance*; those failing to do so forfeited their land to the seigneurs of the island and received not more than 200

livres per *arpent* compensation. The Intendant at the same time decided
to embark on some town planning. When the streets had last been sur-
veyed in 1672 by Dollier de Casson they had varied in width from thirty
to eighteen feet. Champigny considered the narrower streets to constitute
a fire hazard and he ordered that all the streets were to be widened to thirty
feet. They also had to be repaired, pot-holes filled, stumps and boulders
removed, and bridges built over the streams. This work had to be undertaken within a month or the property-owners would be subject to a ten-
livre fine, plus the cost of the labour, hired by the town authorities to do
the work for them. The local judge and the Intendant frequently issued
ordonnances requiring householders in the towns to clear the streets in
front of their homes of snow in winter and rubbish the rest of the year.
Cellars also had to be cleared of offensive rubbish on pain of a ten-*livre* fine.
Other regulations attempted to solve the parking problem and to curb the
tendency of sleigh and wagon-drivers to show scant respect for the safety
of pedestrians. In Montreal, at least, it appears that "Plus ça change, plus
c'est la même chose."

Had Denonville and Champigny not had to cope with external threats to
the colony, threats that endangered its very existence, they would undoubtedly have had greater success in coping with these social problems.
But their most urgent task was to curb the Iroquois aggression and cope
with the Hudson's Bay Company's threat to the fur trade. In his instructions to Denonville the Minister had stated that his principal aim must be to
remove the fear of the Iroquois menace by humbling their pride. He had
to maintain a firm and vigorous policy toward them and make them understand that they would "have everything to fear if they refused to submit
to the conditions he imposed on them." How Denonville accomplished
this, by diplomacy or by war, was left entirely to his discretion, and he
quickly concluded that it would have to be war. He saw very clearly that
New France was caught in giant pincers, the English in Hudson Bay
forming one jaw, and the English of New York allied with the Iroquois
forming the other. The fate of the colony was reduced to a question of time;
it required time to make the colony secure against attack, yet if the French
did not humble the Iroquois quickly, the west would be lost. And with
every month that went by, this danger increased.

Within a few weeks of his arrival in the colony Denonville began making
active preparations to cope with these threats. From the outset he was ably
assisted by the Chevalier Louis-Hector de Callières, who had been sent out
in 1684 to replace Perrot as Governor of Montreal. Callières, a brother of
François de Callières, one of Louis xiv's four private secretaries and a very

able diplomatist, was to play a leading role in the history of New France during the next two decades. Thirty-six years old when he arrived in New France, he had spent twenty of those years on active military service. He was a competent commander, inclined to be a martinet and possessed of an irascible temperament which was not improved by frequent attacks of gout. He had a capacity for rubbing people the wrong way and was more feared than respected by his subordinates. He was clearly better suited for a military than a civil post, but the duties of a governor of Montreal at this time required a military man rather than a subordinate civil administrator. Certainly he and Denonville were in complete accord on what measures were needed to defend the colony.

One of the first recommendations that Denonville made to the Minister was that the main threat to the security of the colony could very effectively be removed were Louis XIV to purchase the province of New York from James II. The likelihood of this occurring was, however, very remote. At this time French and English commissioners were busily seeking to negotiate a settlement of the two countries' competing claims in North America, to the dismay of the Spanish, who feared any rapprochement between France and England, and who were already perturbed about La Salle's ill-fated attempt to establish a colony in the Gulf of Mexico.[7] Denonville warned the Minister that Hudson Bay was not big enough for both the English and French. It was, he stated, impossible to supply the French posts in the Bay by an overland route from Quebec, and any arrangement whereby both countries had establishments there would work to the disadvantage of the French since their rivals would offer twice as much to the Indians for their furs; but, he added "if the price of our goods were equal to that of the English, we would certainly have the preference because our ways suit the Indians much better than do those of the English who fear and rebuff them."

Despite the opposition in England of the anti-French party composed of "zealous Protestants," and the Spanish ambassador, a treaty of neutrality in North America was negotiated in London. Before Denonville received word of this, and the resulting orders that the subjects of the two Crowns were not to commit acts of hostility pending a definite settlement of their territorial claims in America, he had decided to settle the Bay problem in what seemed to him the only effective way.

In the spring of 1686 he sent an expedition of one hundred and five men – thirty French troops with their officers and batmen commanded by the Chevalier de Troyes, and sixty Canadians led by Pierre le Moyne d'Iberville and two of his brothers, Jacques de Sainte Hélène and Paul de Maricourt – overland from Montreal to James Bay. De Troyes later had some rather harsh things to say on the Canadians' lack of discipline and their disinclination to take orders, but it is doubtful if he and his troops would ever have reached the Bay without them, for this wilderness route entailed incredible hardship. Once there they exceeded their instructions, which were rather vague and likely deliberately so. They took the three English posts at the foot of the Bay by force and along with them fifty thousand prime beaver pelts. Among the English prisoners taken was John Bridgar, who had been brought to Quebec in the like circumstances before. This was some recompense for the loss the Canadian company had suffered at English, or rather Radisson's, hands two years previous. Despite the outraged cries of the Hudson's Bay Company and the protests of Whitehall, the French refused to relinquish the posts and they still occupied them when war broke out between the two countries in 1689.

Denonville must have wished that it were possible to deal with the threat from the south as expeditiously. The more he studied that situation the worse it appeared. He knew he lacked adequate forces to resolve the Iroquois problem swiftly, yet the longer he delayed the more the situation deteriorated. If he appealed for more troops and arms he had no surety they would be forthcoming, and by the time they did arrive the Iroquois might well have driven the western tribes out of the French alliance and into a commercial alliance with New York. Colonel Thomas Dongan, the aggressive Irish Catholic Governor of New York, who had served in the armies of Louis XIV before the Stuart restoration, was taking active measures to seduce the Ottawa tribes. He had also persuaded several *coureurs de bois* to turn renegade and work out of Albany. He stoutly maintained that all territory south of the Great Lakes belonged to the English Crown and that Albany traders had every right to trade with the Indians north of the Lakes. At the same time he enforced a strict monopoly for Albany of the English fur trade; the residents of the other provinces, even of other towns in New York province, were rigorously excluded from the trade. This policy was, of course, bitterly resented by those excluded, and some New England officials declared that New York was as much to be feared as were the French.

In 1686 the Albany merchants, spurred on by Dongan, sent several traders guided by Canadian renegades to Michilimackinac where they gave much more merchandise for furs than the Montreal traders ever had. This proved a great temptation to the Ottawa middlemen to forget their age-old hatred for the Iroquois and enter into a commercial alliance with them and the Albany men. They were all the more inclined in this direction out of resentment and fear at the weakness displayed by the French in the face of Iroquois aggression in recent years. Moreover, the Iroquois were showing their contempt for the French by pillaging their canoes wherever they encountered them. Durantaye, the commandant at Michilimackinac, and the Jesuit missionary, Father Enjalran, had to exert all their influence to prevent this alliance taking effect. It was only with great difficulty that they persuaded the Ottawa and Huron chiefs to go down to Montreal the following winter to confer with Denonville. There they were more impressed with what he had to say than they had been with Frontenac's tergiversations and they agreed to abide by the French alliance. It was clear, however, that it would take more than fine words to hold them for long.

Denonville was kept fully informed of Dongan's designs by the Jesuit missionaries in the Iroquois centres and by an agent he had sent to New York to report on what was going on. He thus learned early that Dongan, encouraged by the commercial and near political success of the first expedition, planned to send another and larger one to Michilimackinac. He had persuaded the Senecas to return several Huron and Ottawa prisoners, recently captured, to draw these nations out of the French alliance and into Albany's economic orbit. This convinced Denonville that the only way to prevent the loss of the western fur trade and mass assaults by all the Five Nations on the French settlements was to wage a preventive war on the Iroquois during the coming summer.

He was, however, fully aware of the terrible risks for both the army and the colony that an invasion of the Iroquois country would incur, particularly with the colony in its virtually defenceless state. Yet he dared not begin building forts in the seigneuries to provide security for the *habitants* for two reasons: time would not allow of it, and he feared that were he to do so the Iroquois would anticipate him and attack the settlements before he could attack them. He informed the Minister that two armies were required to quell the Five Nations swiftly by attacking them on both flanks: one army to attack the Senecas in the west, the other to attack the Mohawks in the east and at the same time frighten the English at Albany into inactivity. With the villages on the flanks destroyed, the two armies could then march on the three central villages, ravage them, and make it impossible for any of the nations to afford succour to the others. But he did not have the forces at his disposal for such a campaign and he dared not wait any longer in the hope that they would be sent him. All he could do was attack the Senecas, the most distant, powerful, and aggressive of the Five Nations, with the forces he had and hope for the best; for not to do so clearly meant losing the west by default and inviting them to attack the French settlements.

If careful planning alone could have ensured a successful outcome to the campaign, then New France would have had nothing to fear. To keep the Iroquois, and Dongan, guessing as long as possible, Denonville carefully masked his preparations. Supplies were sent to Fort Frontenac well ahead of time. The pre-fabrication technique, to be much used in North America in later years, was employed in the building of flatboats to transport the troops; boards were cut to size, then stored away out of sight, ready to be assembled quickly at the last moment. It was, however, impossible to maintain complete secrecy, and the Onondagas, suspecting that something was afoot, proposed a conference at Fort Frontenac to settle recent incidents peaceably. Denonville agreed to the meeting, hoping to lull them into a false sense of security. This was a ruse the Iroquois frequently used themselves. When Father Jean de Lamberville, residing with the Onondagas, came to Quebec to arrange for this conference, Denonville did not divulge his intention to attack the Iroquois. Had he done so, this missionary, who was bitterly opposed to war with the Iroquois, would have refused to return to Onondaga and be a party to the deception. His failure to return would have further aroused the Iroquois suspicions. Were they then to have massed a few hundred warriors in ambush at the rapids along the St Lawrence, they could have caused very heavy casualties and likely disrupted the expedition. There was also the danger they might attack the settlements with part of their forces while the army was out of the colony. Thus the Iroquois had to be deceived as long as possible.

Very detailed instructions were sent to the commanders of the upcountry posts. Tonti and the Sieur de la Forest were ordered to march as many Illinois warriors as they could muster to the south of the Seneca villages, where they would be ready to attack the Senecas as Denonville's force drove them before it. Durantaye was ordered to station himself and his men at the Toronto portage, and Du Lhut likewise at Detroit, to intercept the Albany traders who were expected to voyage to Michilimackinac. All the *coureurs de bois* in the west, and as many Ottawas and Hurons as could be induced to join them, were to muster at Niagara and await further instructions. Adequate supplies were sent to the western posts, and the Jesuit missionaries with the Ottawas, who strongly favoured the campaign, served as liaison officers, passing on Denonville's orders.

By early June all was ready. The troops and militia were mustered at Montreal, 832 Troupes de la Marine and over nine hundred Canadian militia. While the final preparations were being made, the first of a convoy of eight ships neared Quebec after a record crossing of thirty-three days. It brought eight hundred more Troupes de la Marine and Philippe de Rigaud, Chevalier de Vaudreuil, the newly appointed commander of the regular troops in the colony. When Vaudreuil learned that a campaign was about to begin, weak though he was from the voyage, he rushed to Montreal to join it, without even waiting for his baggage to be unloaded. It was, however, impossible to incorporate these new troops in the expedition.

On June 13 the army left Montreal. The following day it was joined by four hundred allied Indians, many of them Christian Iroquois from the Jesuit mission at Sault St Louis and the Sulpician mission close by Montreal. These warriors were allied to the French, mainly owing to their religious ties; they had long resisted all the blandishments of the Five Nations and the governors of New York to return to their old villages. Naked except for breech clouts with animal tails attached, antlers or horns on their heads, bronzed features painted with black-and-red bars and flashes and their bodies with crude drawings of animals, their nostrils and ears pierced with metal rings and spikes, they provided a striking contrast to the regular troops in their pale-grey uniforms with red or blue facings.

Merely to get this army to Lake Ontario was a major undertaking; for much of the way the river, hurling itself across a spur of the Canadian Shield, was turbulent with rapids and cascades. The men had to portage their supplies around these long stretches while the Canadians dragged the flatboats up the surging currents. Some three hundred of them suffered leg injuries. An Iroquois ambush here would have been dangerous in the extreme. At the Cedars Rapids the Intendant went ahead with fifteen canoes loaded with supplies to get everything prepared at Fort Frontenac so that the army could move off again with the minimum of delay.

Several Iroquois lurking along the river were captured by the advance scouting parties. At Fort Frontenac Champigny invited the so-called Neutral Iroquois of Kenté, and a group of Oneidas who were returning from a hunting-trip, to come to the fort for a feast. Once inside the palisade they were made prisoners. He used this stratagem because he lacked enough men to take them by force, and they had to be taken lest they warn the enemy of the army's approach. On June 29 Father Lamberville arrived at the fort, alone. The Onondaga chiefs, by now informed of the size of Denonville's force, had declined to accompany him. Lamberville, however, was very bitter at the turn events had taken, for it put finis to his missionary efforts. On July 1 Denonville reached the fort with the army, and the following day the Neutral Iroquois of Ganneious were taken by force, bringing the total number of prisoners to some fifty men and one hundred and fifty women and children.

These Neutral Iroquois were actually members of the Cayuga nation who had retired to the north side of the lake for safety during their war with the Andastes. They were, in fact, neutral only when it suited their convenience, and Denonville regarded them as a danger to his lines of communication. Moreover, they would serve as hostages should any of the French be taken prisoners during the campaign, and might well be the means of saving some of the French from a horrible death at the stake. But although the French had good reason for taking all these Iroquois prisoner, the fact remains that the method used by Champigny to capture two groups of them was a very dubious one.[8]

The day after the army's arrival at Fort Frontenac the Sieur de la Forest arrived from the Illinois country with word that the Illinois warriors had declined to march against the Senecas, fearing an attack on their own villages. This greatly reduced the chances of a really damaging blow being struck against the enemy. La Forest had, however, some encouraging news. Two parties of Albany traders had been captured by Durantaye and his men before they had reached Michilimackinac. The French renegades who had served as guides were later given a summary trial by Denonville and then shot, *pour encourager les autres*. Thus, Denonville's foresight and careful planning had effectively quashed this dangerous threat to French control of the western fur trade.

On July 4 the army embarked again and began skirting the south shore of the lake. This kept the Iroquois guessing which of their villages would be attacked, making it difficult for them to consolidate their forces. On the morning of the tenth the disembarkation point was reached. Just as the boats and canoes put in to shore, out of the morning mist appeared a fleet of canoes. Oars and paddles were dropped, muskets primed. All was anxious quiet for a few moments. Then came shouts of recognition and relief. The canoes bore the *coureurs de bois* and Ottawas, led by Durantaye, Du Lhut, and Nicholas Perrot, punctual almost to the minute.

Four hundred men were left to garrison a redoubt at the landing point, quickly built to protect the boats, canoes, and supplies for the return journey. Were they to have been destroyed by the Iroquois, few of the French would have seen Montreal again. For the better part of two days the army now marched through the forest in suffocating heat. In addition to their weapons the men had to carry thirteen days' food supplies on their backs. Three rivers had to be crossed, and it was expected that the foe would be waiting in ambush at any or all of them. The first two defiles were crossed with no sign of the enemy. Denonville planned to camp for the night at the third river barrier, close by the Seneca villages. As they neared this ravine, however, the scouts returned to warn that they had found tracks of a large party nearby.

In the van of the army were the *coureurs de bois* under Callières. The Indian allies were spread out on the flanks; the main force of the Troupes de la Marine and militia in the rear. Suddenly a ragged volley was poured into the advancing forces from the flanks. The Canadians and some of the Indian allies immediately took cover and returned the fire. This sudden rattle of musketry, the screams of the wounded, and the shrill warcries of the Indians caused panic among the regular troops. Even some of the officers threw themselves to the ground in fright. Denonville and Vaudreuil quickly rallied them and drove them at the double to aid the advance battalion. At this the Senecas turned and fled, throwing away their muskets and blankets to speed their flight.

Among the trees the pall of acrid gun smoke slowly lifted, revealing thirty-eight lifeless bodies; twenty-seven Senecas, five Canadians, one regular, and five Indian allies. Six Canadians and five regulars were wounded; among them was Father Bruyas, Jesuit missionary at Michilimackinac. It was subsequently learned that the Senecas had had seven hundred and fifty warriors in the action in two groups, and another three hundred in a well-fortified stockade nearby. Two days after the action the allied Indians brought in some Illinois captives of the Iroquois and a Seneca chief, too old to flee, who informed Denonville that forty-five Senecas had been killed in the skirmish and sixty badly wounded. Father Bruyas discovered the chief had acquired the faint rudiments of Christian belief from the Jesuits once resident there; his Indian captors were therefore persuaded to kill him mercifully with a swift blow of a tomahawk rather than by slowly burning him to death.

The French forces, too worn out by their march and the excessive heat to pursue the enemy, camped where they were. The Indian allies, who had been counted on to pursue the foe and cut down as many as possible, preferred to deal with the dead. They hacked the bodies of the fallen Iroquois into quarters for their cooking-pots. The Ottawa tribesmen, who had fled at the first musket shot and then returned when the action was over, particularly distinguished themselves here, to the great disgust of Denonville and his officers. Denonville was also disenchanted by the conduct of the Troupes de la Marine during the affray and he later wrote to Seignelay: "I have written you nothing about the wretchedness of our soldiers the day of our attack on the Senecas. What can one hope to accomplish, Monseigneur, with such men as these?"

The next day the army cautiously advanced on the Seneca villages only to find them deserted. The longhouses, the food *caches,* and the adjacent cornfields were now systematically destroyed. It took the army nine days to do it. It was estimated that 350,000 bushels of standing corn and 50,000 bushels of dried corn were destroyed. At the village of Gannouata they found a post bearing the arms of England which Governor Dongan had had placed there in 1684, and as Denonville commented, "contrary to all right and reason . . . it being indubitable that we discovered this country and took possession of it, moreover for twenty consecutive years we have had Fathers Fremin and Garnier resident there." To rectify the situation the Seneca lands were duly claimed for Louis XIV by prior right of exploration and conquest. But Denonville was under no illusions that anything less than occupation of the territory would validate the claim.

By the time the work of destruction was completed it proved impossible to go on to attack the Cayuga villages. The terrain was too difficult and the men were falling ill at an alarming rate with dysentery. The Ottawa allies began to slip away before the work was done, brazenly criticizing the French for warring on cornfields rather than on the Iroquois. The army now made its way back to the boats; the wounded were sent directly to Fort Frontenac and the rest proceeded to Niagara where Denonville had a log fort built on a point of land where the Niagara River empties into Lake Ontario. It was intended to forestall Dongan's plans to establish a fort there to guard a trade route from Albany to the northwest tribes. Denonville also hoped that it would serve as a base for the Ottawa tribes to harass the Senecas should they re-establish their villages. While the fort was being built Denonville gave the men a half-day off, a group at a time, to visit the great falls, ten miles distant. Leaving at the fort a garrison of a hundred men under the command of the Sieur de Troyes, Denonville brought the army back to Montreal, arriving on August 13.

The campaign had lasted exactly two months. It had entailed little fighting and few casualties, but very great hardship. Denonville himself was completely worn out by his exertions; he had had no rest during the entire campaign or the weeks of preparation that had preceded it. His health was seriously impaired in consequence. When he came to assess the results, he acknowledged that the campaign had accomplished about what he had anticipated, which was not as much as he had hoped for, or what the situation had demanded. But all concerned now realized what it entailed to take an army into the canton of the most distant and powerful of the Iroquois nations. If nothing else, Denonville had prevented, for the time being at least, the Iroquois and the English of New York breaking the French hold on the western fur trade. This in itself was no mean feat.

CHAPTER 10

The Iroquois Response

When Denonville, upon his return to Quebec, took stock of the situation he found it none too reassuring. His campaign had hurt the Senecas but it had not reduced their fighting strength materially. They could be expected to strike back. The threatened defection of the western allies had been prevented, but only for the time being. That threat could be renewed. In fact, all that Denonville had really gained was time; time in which to try to convince the Minister of the need for yet greater forces. For the alternative to overwhelming the Iroquois in one swift campaign was a long-drawn-out war of attrition, a war that the French would be unlikely to lose, but one that would cause terrible destruction to the French settlements. Denonville bluntly informed the Minister: "The colony situated as it is, I must tell you once again my Lord, that to sustain it properly requires that you do not put your hand to the task half heartedly." He declared that a hundred determined Iroquois could lay waste to all the seigneuries above Trois Rivières; then asked that another eight hundred trained troops and one hundred and fifty recruits be sent. "I strongly doubt," he added, "that I am asking you for enough."

At the time he wrote, Iroquois war parties had begun to attack the outlying French settlements, burning barns and homes, cutting down the *habitants* in their fields. A supply convoy sent to Forts Frontenac and Niagara got through without incident but was ambushed on its return journey; eight men were killed and one taken prisoner. But the cruellest blow of all, one far worse than anything the Iroquois could inflict, was an epidemic of smallpox and measles, brought by the ships from France, that swept through the colony. Before it subsided the population was decimated; over a thousand persons had died, out of a total population – including the troops – of just over eleven thousand.[1] One-quarter of the troops who survived were incapacitated, and the ranks of the militia and of the Mission Iroquois were also depleted. Denonville found that his effective forces were weaker now than they had been when he arrived in the colony.

Before his campaign Denonville had received orders from Seignelay to send all the male Iroquois he managed to capture to France to serve in the galleys, as sturdy oarsmen were always in short supply. Denonville had grave misgivings as to the wisdom of this; hence he retained twenty-two of the fifty-eight warriors captured to use as bargaining agents in future negotiations with the Iroquois. He also requested the Minister to see to it that those sent to France be well treated and returned to Quebec immediately should they be needed. Seignelay subsequently assured him that these prisoners would lack for nothing, and there is no doubt that galley rowers were relatively well treated; they were well fed and well housed, and kept healthy and strong, because they were of no use if ill or feeble. In fact these Iroquois prisoners, when they reached Marseilles, received preferential treatment, and compared to the way they treated their own prisoners they had little cause for complaint. The fact remains, however, that in complying with his orders and sending these men to France for whatever purpose, Denonville made a serious error in judgement. The danger of their succumbing to disease during the Atlantic crossing, or later in France, was great, and any value they had as oarsmen was greatly exceeded by their value as hostages and for bargaining with the Iroquois in future negotiations. Denonville's enemies later made much – too much – of it.

Meanwhile Denonville and Champigny were kept busy coping with internal problems. Fortunately, the colony was not short of food, in fact there was enough of a surplus of wheat to allow of exports to France and the West Indies, but many of the people lacked the wherewithal to buy food or anything else. The *coureurs de bois*, having spent most of the summer in the Seneca campaign, had brought no furs down to Montreal, and Iroquois war parties had subsequently blocked the Ottawa route to Michilimackinac. This interruption in the fur trade affected all other economic activity and threw many in the three towns out of work. It was imperative that the previous year's take of furs be brought from the west; otherwise the colony would be in a desperate situation. Denonville therefore sent a large force of the Canadians who had served in the militia during the Seneca campaign to the Ottawa country. To recompense them for their services in the campaign, Champigny allowed them to take five hundred *livres* in trade goods each. When informing the Minister of this breach in the regulations governing *congés*, Denonville and Champigny explained: "if all the furs were to be lost the country would be ruined. Nothing is more to be desired than a safe return hence we have felt it necessary to do everything possible to bring this about."

And in the colony itself, Iroquois raids and disease had left many widows and orphans in their wake. Montreal, Trois Rivières, and Quebec were flooded with poor wretches reduced to begging at street corners. At the same time, when work was available some able-bodied men and women either refused to work or demanded exorbitant wages. In short, there were deserving and undeserving poor. By April the problem had become really serious and the Intendant was obliged to take action. He had the Sovereign Council establish a Bureau of the Poor in the three towns – Quebec, Trois Rivières, and Montreal – each run by a local committee of responsible citizens. In the country districts similar committees were to be established, composed of the local *curé* and two *habitants* elected by the parishioners. Now, anyone seeking charity had to apply to their local Bureau and if work could be found for them they had to take it at the wages decreed by the committee. In each town or parish a lady committee member visited all the homes at least once a month to solicit money, food, and clothing. The aged and ailing poor were to be sent to the hospital for care or treatment or placed in the care of more well-to-do relatives. Children of poor families were to be placed in service, care being taken to obtain the best terms possible for them, duly notarized. Tools and materials were to be provided for those with a trade, and tavern-keepers were strictly forbidden to purchase these items from the indigent.

This legislation clearly implied a recognition of the principle that society was responsible for the well-being of all its members. There was, of course, no trace of the Calvinist concept that poverty was a sin; no stigma was attached to it, but there was a clear understanding that it was a social evil that had to be rectified. The chief aim was to help the poverty-stricken to help themselves; those who could not help themselves received aid, those who could but would not were to be punished, and the directors of the Bureaux were empowered to have such worthless individuals put in gaol or in the stocks, on a bread-and-water diet.[2]

While the Intendant was trying to cope with this social problem Denonville and Callières were desperately striving to bolster the defences of the colony. In all the exposed seigneuries stockades were built where the *habitants* could take refuge in case of attack. This, however, was not accomplished without difficulty. The *habitants* resented being called out for this *corvée* and they stubbornly refused to take adequate precautions against surprise attacks. However, after a few of them had been killed and several farms burned by an estimated two hundred marauding Iroquois, Callières commented, "these raids . . . have made our *habitants* recognize the need for fortifications."

During the winter Fort Frontenac and the new fort at Niagara had been besieged by Iroquois war parties. At Fort Frontenac the cattle had been killed, the outbuildings burned, and the fort itself frequently endangered by flaming arrows. The garrisons at both forts, unable to hunt or fish for fear of being cut down, had been living on a diet of flour and salt pork; scurvy claimed its victims. Of two hundred and forty men in the garrisons of the two forts, one hundred and eighty perished.[3] This made it all too obvious that such posts on the borders of the enemy country were a liability in time of war; they had proved to be nothing but prisons at best and tombs at worst for their garrisons who were unable to harm or obstruct the movements of the enemy in any way. Moreover, it required several hundred men to convoy supplies to them in safety. As the Intendant Champigny later pointed out, the expeditions required to supply these forts might just as well be used to attack the Iroquois villages instead. Denonville was now forced to conclude that Fort Niagara would have to be abandoned, but he was very reluctant to abandon Fort Frontenac since Sébastien le Prestre de Vauban, the greatest military engineer of the age, had sent plans for the construction of a genuine fortress to replace the original trading-post.[4]

In the spring of 1688, when winter relaxed its bitter grip on Canada, the feeling of release and well-being that usually ensued was this year tempered by anxiety and fear. Now the increasing warmth of the sun, the ice moving majestically down the free-flowing river, the deepening green of the forest above the brown earth, all held a dreadful promise: that of swift, savage attacks by Iroquois war parties. Denonville realized that the forts being built in all the seigneuries were inadequate protection. The men had to get their crops in and tend their cattle. The fields were spread out and surrounded by bush; hence the *habitants* needed a corps of troops to protect them against ambush while they worked. The only solution that Denonville and Champigny could see was to change radically the colony's land-tenure system and concentrate the people in fortified villages instead of allowing them to remain on their isolated, exposed homesteads along the river. Such a revolutionary scheme required time and a surcease from attacks. Moreover, the *habitants* could be counted on to resist any such move with vigour. The Governor and Intendant asked the Minister to send royal edicts ordering that the village scheme be inaugurated, with heavy penalties for any who refused to obey. But they also declared that it could not be done while the immediate threat of war hung over the settlements. Denonville stated: "The interest of this colony is to have peace; it would be advantageous at any price."

Peace, however, could be ensured in only two ways: by crushing the Iroquois, or by negotiating a settlement with them. Only the former method could ensure an enduring peace, but Denonville was forced to conclude that it would require an army of four thousand men and two years' supplies. The Minister, however, had been unable to persuade Louis XIV to send the eight hundred regulars that Denonville had earlier requested; only three hundred could be spared, for France was again on the verge of war, this time with half of Europe arrayed against it. "You must arrange things," Seignelay stated, "in such a way that the forces you have will suffice and His Majesty is persuaded that with your ingenuity and your capacity, and by reinforcing the soldiers with the *habitants* and the friendly Indians you will find the means to prosecute this war with advantage."

Denonville was now driven to the conclusion that there was no alternative but to try to negotiate a peace settlement. Even with the additional three hundred troops, he had fewer men than had been available two years before, owing to the ravages of disease and the necessity of sending a party of Canadians to Hudson Bay to reinforce the posts captured earlier from the English. He therefore sent four of his Iroquois prisoners to their villages to invite the chiefs of the Five Nations to confer with him. Despite the best efforts of Governor Dongan of New York, the Onondagas, Cayugas, and Oneidas were persuaded by Father Lamberville to send delegates to Montreal. Denonville here showed himself to be a very skilled diplomat. He made it difficult for the Iroquois chiefs to refuse to negotiate by stating that although he wanted peace it would not be easy to arrange since Dongan maintained that the Iroquois were his subjects and could make no treaties without his mediation. This hurt the pride of the Iroquois, and their spokesman, Hotréouati, hotly denied the allegation, declaring that they held their lands directly from the Great Spirit, had never been overcome in war by either the French or the English, and wished to be friends of both the French and the English without acknowledging either of them as their master. "I have," he declared, "two eyes, I regard on two sides the two trees of the peace for the three nations; I extend my two arms, the one towards Montreal, the other towards Albany."

After much diplomatic manœuvring, a preliminary peace treaty was arranged during which hostilities were to cease and arrangements to be made for a general peace conference at Montreal the following year to include the Five Nations, the French, and all the tribes allied with the French. It was agreed also that there would be a general exchange of prisoners. Denonville requested the Minister to send back the Iroquois prisoners in the galleys and have every care for their health and well-being. And at Albany, Sir Edmond Andros, recently appointed Governor of New England and Lieutenant-Governor of New York after Dongan's recall, informed the Iroquois in September that they were to cease attacking the French since the King of England had signed a treaty with the French forbidding them to invade English territory or in any way harm his subjects. He clearly implied that the Iroquois were British subjects and their lands under British sovereignty. This the Iroquois did not openly question as long as it suited their convenience.

Denonville's preliminary peace treaty appeared, on the surface, to have removed the threat to New France, but he was well aware that this was more apparent than real. The main issue in dispute, control of the western fur trade, and the even more fundamental issue, whether the wealth of the interior should go to Europe by way of the St Lawrence or the Hudson River, had merely been deferred for the time being. To the north in Hudson Bay, however, the French now held all the posts at the Bottom of the Bay. De Troyes's expedition had cost the Hudson's Bay Company an estimated £50,000 in damages, plus the £20,000 a year in trade carried on at these posts. The company had managed to retain its post on the Nelson River and, with the signing of the Anglo-French Treaty of Neutrality in November 1686, the English "adventurers" hoped to force the Canadians to abandon their posts by enticing the Indians to trade at Nelson River and at a new post it was intended to establish at the Bottom of the Bay.

But the French had other ideas. They were determined to retain and consolidate their hold on the Bay. To them the Treaty of Neutrality implied that the English were not to interfere with their trade in that area. Denonville was convinced that naval power was the only effective means to control the Bay, and in Pierre Le Moyne, Sieur d'Iberville, he found the man capable of utilizing this power. Until his death in 1706 Iberville, third son of Charles Le Moyne of Montreal, was the scourge of the English, not only in Hudson Bay but also in Newfoundland, along the Atlantic coast, in the Gulf of Mexico, and in the West Indies. A born leader of men, raised on the Canadian frontier, brave, utterly ruthless, and extremely enterprising, he performed astounding feats. He could well be compared with such men as Francis Drake or Cortez. Against such a man as this the hired servants of the Hudson's Bay Company had little chance; by comparison they pale into insignificance.

It was Iberville, along with his brother Ste Hélène and forty men, whom de Troyes had left in command at the posts captured at the Bottom of the Bay in 1686. The following year Iberville captured the English supply ships while reinforcements were sent overland from Canada. All that was left to the English was their post at the Nelson River. Iberville then returned to Quebec, conferred with Denonville, and was sent to France to obtain naval support. The Minister concurred with their views and Iberville was given command of one of the fastest sailing ships in the French navy, the two-hundred-ton *Soleil d'Afrique*, to escort the *Compagnie du Nord's* supply ships from Quebec to the Bay. However, before the convoy could sail from Quebec in June 1688, Denonville was obliged to order the Sovereign Council to defer, for the second time, the paternity charges preferred against Iberville by a girl in Montreal.[5] This awkward matter shelved, Iberville set sail. During the ensuing winter in the Bay he blocked the English attempts to establish a post at the Albany River, and with scurvy as his main weapon captured their ships, crews, and supplies. The French hold on the posts at the Bottom of the Bay was now secured, and when news of Iberville's feats reached England the Hudson's Bay Company began to experience difficulty in obtaining ships and competent captains. Financially, too, the company had suffered severe losses. Although handsome dividends were paid in 1688, 1689, and 1690 before the full extent of the damage inflicted by Iberville was known, the dividend of 1690 was the last the company was to pay until 1718.[6]

And while this was taking place to the north, Denonville was taking full advantage of the peace treaty just signed with the Iroquois. He sent supplies to the western posts and instructed the commandants to be on their guard against surprise attacks. At the same time, the garrison at Niagara was withdrawn and the fort burned. It had proved its uselessness beyond all doubt. He also sent Callières to France to make clear to the Minister the realities of the situation, and to submit their proposals for what they regarded as the only means by which the colony could be made secure short of a hideous, long-drawn-out war of attrition with the Iroquois. Their scheme was quite simple: the conquest and occupation of New York. They maintained that it could be done with less than half the force required for the crushing of the Iroquois, and with New York occupied by the French the Five Nations would have no alternative but to accept any terms the French cared to impose on them. All that was required for the enterprise, they stated, was two expeditions, one of eight hundred men from Canada to capture Albany, destroy it and the nearby settlements, then return to Quebec with the prisoners; the other, a maritime expedition, to consist of six frigates and twelve hundred men, to go directly from La Rochelle to capture Manhattan Island, then, using New York as a base, ravage the coast as far north as Boston. This done, the land forces could threaten from the rear the Iroquois who, with their source of arms and supplies removed, would have no recourse but to capitulate.

This was indeed a bold scheme, yet were it to have been properly executed it would have had an excellent chance of initial success. At this time New York's defences consisted of nothing but a crumbling wall at the southern tip of Manhattan Island, to protect a battery of guns more likely to harm those who fired them than those fired at. Whether or not the French could have held the province for very long is debatable, but once in control they might well have held it long enough to make the Iroquois abandon their aggressive schemes. Perhaps the most amazing thing of all was the fact that Louis XIV eventually adopted the proposal in principle.

By this time, however, Denonville was worn out by his exertions, by anxiety, and particularly by his apparent failure to convince the Minister of the very real danger in which the colony still stood. He had done all that had been humanly possible and he feared that it was likely not enough. With his fundamental honesty, he blamed no one for this but himself and he now informed Seignelay that the situation required the King's intervention and his replacement by "a man more capable than I." Callières, upon his arrival at the Court, was quick to solicit the governor general's post for himself, should Denonville be granted his recall. The King acceded to Denonville's request and ordered that he be appointed to the agreeable sinecure post of assistant-governor to Louis XIV's grandson, the Duc de Bourgogne, as reward for his services. To replace him the King chose, not Callières, but a man who, aided by his friends and relatives at the Court, had for years been waging a persistent campaign for the Canadian appointment: the Comte de Frontenac. By 1689 memories of his disastrous earlier administration had faded among the officials in the Ministry of Marine and his own plausible accounts of events had gained credence by constant repetition in the right quarters.

In the meantime Denonville could only wait upon events: wait for the ships to return from France with news of the war rumoured to be raging there, perhaps with more troops and adequate funds for the colony's defence, perhaps with his successor; wait anxiously for the Canadian *voyageurs* to return from the west with the furs so urgently needed to alleviate the distress in the colony; wait for word from the Iroquois when they would come to ratify the peace treaty. The *habitants*, however, felt no such anxieties. The absence of the Iroquois allowed them to sow their fields in peace and they quickly abandoned their earlier precautions against surprise attack as the need no longer seemed to exist. In the absence of Callières, Vaudreuil took over the command in the Montreal area and he was not the stern disciplinarian that Callières was. Instead of living in crowded discomfort, but in security within the stockades, the *habitants* were once again back on their isolated homesteads.

Spring became summer and still there was no word from the Iroquois. In June three merchant ships brought news of the war in Europe, but of the King's ships, with the sorely needed funds, supplies, orders, and the Iroquois prisoners, there was not a sign. The officers and men in the regular troops now became a source of anxiety. The officers were disgruntled at being stuck in Canada while a major war was being fought in Europe with all its opportunities for glory and promotion. Moreover, they had not been paid for some months. Champigny had to resort to all manner of devices to provide food for the men. The officers, owed over 50,000 *livres*, he prevailed upon to manage as best they could, but some of the junior NCO's refused to obey orders, claiming that the officers were pocketing the men's pay. On July 6 Champigny, in a dispatch to the Minister, remarked with considerable understatement, "We await, my lord, with much impatience the honour of your orders for this year." While he wrote this dispatch the ships for Canada were still in La Rochelle Harbour, and the Intendant of the naval base there was frantically trying to round up crews. They eventually got away on July 23 bearing dispatches, dated March 20 and May 1, for Denonville and Champigny, informing them that France was at war with the Hapsburg Empire, Spain, and the Dutch Netherlands; that a revolution had occurred in England where William of Orange was in control and that the English colonies would likely declare for him. No troops and less funds were available for Canada; hence Denonville was required to guard against attacks from the English colonies and negotiate a firm peace with the Iroquois. The King and Seigneley also made it plain that they were completely satisfied with Denonville's conduct of affairs to date.[7]

After these dispatches were written, however, a radical change in French policy had occurred. For a time Louis XIV had hoped to restore James II to his throne and prevent England entering the coalition against France. It was for this reason that the proposal for an assault on New York had been initially shelved. On May 1 Seigneley wrote to Denonville, "although his Majesty considers this proposal to be sound, he does not think that it would be convenient to execute it at present." But James II's forces, fighting to secure a bridgehead in Ireland, had little success, and on May 17 England declared war on France. Louis XIV and Louvois immediately decided to concentrate French naval and military strength against England, and Denonville's proposal for the conquest of New York was reconsidered. The plan of campaign finally adopted, however, bore little resemblance to the original, and there was little hope of it succeeding. It was a case of too little and too late. Instead of two striking forces, one going by sea and the other overland from Montreal, there was now to be only one from Canada, with a naval diversion of two warships off Manhattan Island to attack from the sea when the Montreal force of nine hundred Canadians, after capturing Albany and proceeding down the Hudson River, was ready to assault New York. This plan, to enjoy any success at all, required the complete co-operation of the French naval officials at Rochefort, the Atlantic weather, the inhabitants of New York province, and the Iroquois. The mere fact that New France would have been left virtually defenceless for several months, an open invitation to the Iroquois, should have sufficed for the rejection of the mad scheme.[8] But it was ordered put in operation, and on June 7

Frontenac received his instructions as Commander-in-Chief. The Canadian convoy bearing Frontenac and Callières, escorted by the two warships needed for the New York attack, was scheduled to sail by June 14 at the latest. It did not leave La Rochelle until July 23; hence it ran into strong westerly winds, usual at that time of year.

Other ships, however, sailing to other ports, had not been so long delayed. As early as March 1, when the St Lawrence was still ice-locked, ships from England had carried word to Boston of the Revolution and the King's flight to France. The officials in Boston and New York were quick to grasp the implications, and by April rumours were circulating that England and France were at war. A few weeks later a ship brought official word that a state of war existed. The Iroquois were quickly informed. At this, all thought of ratifying their treaty with the French instantly vanished. In their earlier wars they had had to fight alone; this time they believed they could now count on the active military support of both England and her colonies. Bronzed runners sped back and forth along the forest trails linking the villages of the Five Nations. At the great council fire at Onondaga the war chiefs quietly made their plans, and from Albany came fresh supplies of arms and ammunition.

But of all this New France knew nothing. Denonville and Champigny were still anxiously awaiting the ships from France, storm-tossed on the Atlantic, and some word from the Iroquois when they would come to Montreal to ratify the peace treaty. All was quiet in the colony. The Canadians, waiting expectantly for the fur brigade to arrive from the west, were hard at work getting in the harvest, only too glad that there was no sign of the Iroquois. But in Albany, on August 16, Messrs Philips and Van Cortland wrote to the Secretary of the Privy Council in Whitehall: "The Canton Indians above Albany hearing of war between England and France are gone to fight the inhabitants of Canada."[9]

On the night of August 4 a violent hailstorm swept across Lake St Louis and over the island of Montreal. Under its cover an estimated fifteen hundred Iroquois warriors crossed the lake undetected by the sentries in the forts, then dispersed in small bands among the homesteads at Lachine. At dawn they struck. The *habitants*, asleep in their homes, were awakened by the terrible warcries shrilling in their ears. Doors splintered under the blows of tomahawks, and the hideously painted savages burst into the houses. Women and infants were hacked down and mutilated along with the men. More were taken prisoner to provide sport later at the torture stake. Houses and barns went up in flames. Those who escaped the first terrible onslaught fled to the nearby forts where they should have been all the time.

Some of the survivors reached Montreal bringing fragmentary, incoherent reports, making it appear that the enemy were everywhere at once in over-whelming numbers. Denonville gave the only order he could under these circumstances. Everyone was to take cover in the forts. Vaudreuil with three hundred men was sent to strengthen the garrisons. Taking his orders to get everyone within the forts too literally, he refused to allow one of his officers to lead an attack on a large group of Iroquois reported to have become blind drunk on the liquor found in the homes. His slow-wittedness prevented the French striking what might well have been a very damaging counter-attack on the Iroquois.

Once at Fort Roland in the stricken area Vaudreuil sent word back to Denonville asking for more men. Eighty were immediately dispatched but were ambushed when within sight of the fort. The officers in the fort pleaded with Vaudreuil to be allowed to go to their aid, but he refused, claiming that his orders were to remain in the fort. Only a handful of the trapped detachment reached safety. Of the rest, some were killed, more captured. Toward evening the Iroquois recrossed the lake. That night the men in the forts could see the faint glimmer of their fires on the south shore, and rightly guessed that the Iroquois were celebrating their victory by burning some of their prisoners slowly to death.

It was a long time before any true estimate of the losses and destruction could be made. For months afterwards men, women, and children, assumed dead, reappeared after making good their escape. Meanwhile, the first exaggerated reports had gained credence. Only twenty-four of the *habitants* were actually killed at Lachine. Some seventy to ninety were taken prisoner, and it has been reliably estimated that forty-two of them never returned; they were either killed or, having been adopted into Iroquois families, chose to remain. Of the seventy-seven houses in the area, fifty-six were destroyed.[10] The colony was to suffer much heavier losses in later assaults, but this was the first for many years, and the sudden ferocity of the attack spread terror everywhere.

During the remainder of the summer and well into autumn, until the cover of the forest leaves had gone, small Iroquois war parties struck at the settlements, killing the unwary, burning barns and homes, slaughtering cattle. Denonville now decided that Fort Frontenac would have to be abandoned; he needed all the men available to defend the settlements; he could not spare the few hundred needed to convoy a winter's supplies to this post which, as Champigny remarked, "to speak the truth is a prison for the confinement of the garrison, it can hinder the comings and goings of the enemy only when they venture within musket range." On September 24 orders were sent to the garrison to return to Montreal after destroying the fort to prevent the English occupying it.

The Iroquois, however, did not have things all their own way. A scouting party of twenty-eight Canadians under the Sieurs du Lhut and Mantet fought a brisk engagement with an Iroquois war party on the Lake of Two Mountains at the western tip of the island of Montreal. Eighteen of the Iroquois were killed and three taken prisoner, without loss to the Canadians. The three prisoners were brought back to Montreal. In the Place Royale the Mission Indians tortured them to death, *au petit feu*. As the towns-people in the crowded square watched the long-drawn-out agonies of their foes they came to realize what their own people who had been captured must have had to endure; what they themselves would suffer should they be captured by the Iroquois. In this war no quarter would be asked or given, and this dictated its tactics: the sudden attack from ambush; swift flight if the enemy appeared in too great strength; fight to the death if escape were impossible. Anything to avoid being taken alive.

While the *habitants* of the Lachine area were still mourning their dead, the entire colony was given cause to rejoice. The Canadians sent upcountry two years before to bring down the furs now returned, their canoes loaded with 800,000 *livres'* worth of furs; more than had ever reached Montreal at one time. The clerks of the Company of the Farm had to work long hours to get them sorted and baled and the letters of exchange made out. The merchants' shelves were rapidly cleared of the few goods remaining, for the supply ships from France still had not arrived. Many were now wonder-ing if they would come at all. War with England and the Dutch could all too easily mean the capture or sinking of the Canadian convoy on the Atlantic. Finally, in mid October, two months overdue, they reached Quebec. There could be no thought at so late a date, even if the Iroquois assault had not made it totally unfeasible, of any large-scale invasion of New York. No one could hold its commander in any way to blame when the plan was abandoned.

As the ships sailed into the basin the cannon on shore fired the usual salute and everyone in the town rushed to the docks. Denonville and Cham-pigny were not on hand; they were still at Montreal striving to strengthen the defences in the exposed areas. But the senior clergy and the members of the Sovereign Council were there. The ships in June had brought reports that Frontenac was to return as Governor. The clergy had been warned by colleagues in Paris and at the Court to mask their feelings and show no chagrin upon his arrival. When their old adversary came ashore they did their best, but Frontenac was under no illusions concerning their true feelings.

Upon being informed of the Iroquois attacks he decided to go to Montreal at once, but he insisted on an escort suitable to his dignity. He compelled the leading citizens of Quebec and a large number of *habitants* to accompany him as bodyguard. Heavy rains and the necessity of having several boats caulked delayed his departure for a week. The seven-day trip in foul weather could hardly have caused this large escort to view his return with enthusiasm. But at least he made it plain from the outset that whether they liked it or not, he was their Governor and he intended to be obeyed.

At Montreal Frontenac lost no time in quarrelling with Denonville and Champigny. When he learned that orders had been sent for the destruction of Fort Frontenac he was furious and immediately ordered a detachment of three hundred men to proceed to the fort to countermand the order. Denonville and Champigny protested strongly against this decision, but to no avail. The Canadians ordered to make up the detachment made their opposition very plain, and this Frontenac blamed on the lack of discipline that had been allowed to develop in the colony during his absence. Before the detachment got very far, however, they met the garrison bringing word that the fort was destroyed. With great alacrity they returned to Montreal. Frontenac was enraged by this turn of events and in his first dispatches to the Minister he expounded at length on Denonville's sins of omission and commission. The troops and *habitants* were, he claimed, worn out by constant Iroquois raids. The destruction of Fort Frontenac he regarded as criminal, claiming it to be the only thing that had prevented the English gaining the western fur trade, that it was the western allies' only safe retreat from the Iroquois and essential for the colony's defence. None of these claims would bear a close examination. The general prosperity resulting from the arrival of the fur brigade he dismissed with the comment: "This abundance delights only a few merchants and a small number of individuals who have a share in it, but the colony as a whole is thereby neither richer nor more content." And the havoc wrought at Lachine he exaggerated out of all proportion, claiming that over two hundred men, women, and children had been killed out of hand and over a hundred and twenty taken prisoner.

These first dispatches of Frontenac's went on the ship that took Denonville back to France. They were clearly contrived to make the conditions in the colony upon his arrival appear as black as possible. On the other hand, those who had served with Denonville made no attempt to blame him for the initial defeat inflicted by the Iroquois in this war that was to last another ten years. Denonville himself, however, was no courtier; he made no attempt to reply to Frontenac's charges. For everything that had gone wrong in the colony he accepted the entire responsibility, and the blame. For the things that had gone right he gave credit to his subordinates whenever possible and to God when it was not. When he left Quebec in November his departure was deeply regretted by many, not least by Champigny who must have had serious misgivings concerning his future relations with Denonville's successor.

Yet it was as well that Denonville went. He took his responsibilities very seriously indeed and the state of his health made it doubtful how much longer he could have borne them. Moreover, he no longer had confidence in his ability to cope with the problems that the outbreak of full-scale war created. He was, in some ways, a rather tragic figure with a touch of Hamlet about him. Although he left the colony immediately after the Iroquois had scored an initial victory in a war that was to endure almost to the end of the century, this should not be allowed to obscure all that had been accomplished under his government. He had led the first French assault against the western Iroquois, thereby raising French prestige from the depths to which it had sunk under his predecessors; the attempts by the Governor of New York to divert the western fur trade to Albany had been blocked, and the French hold on the posts in James Bay had been maintained. Last, but far from least, Denonville made an honest attempt to inaugurate some badly needed social reforms. Had he not been so preoccupied with the threat to the colony's security he would likely have accomplished much more in this field, but he did at least succeed in providing careers in the French forces for the sons of Canadian seigneurs. That they gave such a good account of themselves is, in some measure, a tribute to his sound judgement.

CHAPTER 11

Border Raids and Sea-Borne Assaults

In the autumn of 1689, with England and France at war, and following the mass assault on New France by the Iroquois, it was obvious to all the senior officials in the colony, with one notable exception, that there now could be no negotiated peace settlement with the Iroquois. Whether Louis XIV and Seignelay liked it or not, it had to be all-out war. The Five Nations had to be subdued or New France would be. Nor was there much hope of doing this, with the forces available, in one quick campaign. The colony had to mobilize all its resources for defence and for a long war of attrition. The west had to be held and the Indian tribes retained in the alliance against the Iroquois, or at least their defection to the Iroquois and Albany prevented. At the same time the colony had to guard against the possibility of attack by land and sea from the English colonies, for they, with their many ships, could well muster forces to attempt in reverse the strategy that Denonville and Callières had advocated in their proposed attack on New York.

Frontenac, however, had other ideas. While in France he had vociferously maintained that he was the one person who understood the Indians and knew how to deal with them, and that they both feared and respected him. He had easily convinced himself of this and he subsequently claimed that he had, through this personal influence over the Iroquois, maintained the colony at peace for ten years and that as soon as he was recalled his successors had embroiled the colony in a damaging and unnecessary war. All that was needed to prove these assertions was to have the Iroquois informed of his return and for them to accept his terms for peace. And this, early in November, he set out to do. He sent three of the Iroquois prisoners, who had served in the galleys and been returned to Quebec, back to their villages to invite the chiefs of the Five Nations to meet with him in the spring to arrange a peace settlement.

Champigny was of the opinion that this move was a mistake. He could see no reason why the Iroquois would agree to any terms that would be acceptable to the French now that the English were fully engaged in the war. His view proved to be correct. The Iroquois spurned Frontenac's offer and at the same time ravaged the French settlements at La Chesnaye and on Ile Jésus near Montreal, killing many of the *habitants*. Frontenac could not admit that he had misjudged the temper of the Iroquois, or that he had overestimated his influence upon them; he therefore blamed the failure of his attempted negotiations on anonymous persons in the colony who had themselves communicated with the Iroquois. Who these persons were, or why they desired to see the Iroquois attacks continue, he neglected to mention.

When the Ottawas heard of Frontenac's attempt to enter into negotiations with the common enemy they became very disturbed. They remembered only too well his attempts to appease the Iroquois during his first administration, and his refusal to offer them any aid in the face of threatened Iroquois attacks. As they saw the situation, any peace settlement between the French and the Five Nations would merely allow the latter to concentrate their full strength against the western nations. To forfend this, one of the Ottawa tribes now entered into negotiations with the Senecas, and in February three of their chiefs went to a general council of the Five Nations at Onondaga to settle the terms of the treaty in the presence of representatives from Albany. At this meeting the Ottawa delegates agreed to use their best efforts to induce the other Ottawa nations to break with the French and enter into a commercial and military alliance with the Iroquois and the English.

It would be unjust to lay all the blame for this development on Frontenac's shoulders. The Ottawas, like all the Indian nations, were impressed by strength and had contempt for any show of weakness. During the preceding ten years the French had not demonstrated their ability to curb the Iroquois and the devastation wrought at Lachine undoubtedly impressed the Ottawas. But under these circumstances Frontenac chose a singularly unpropitious moment to try to negotiate with the Five Nations. It led both them and the Ottawas to believe that the French were weak; to the one an enemy who could be destroyed and to the other an ally who could not be trusted.

It was, however, a few months before word of these developments reached Quebec. In the meantime Frontenac was busy with other matters. Upon his return to Quebec from Montreal he began what, on the surface, appeared to be merely the indulging of his old penchant for wrangling with the Sovereign Council. Most of its members had held office during his first administration and they had been instrumental in having him recalled in disgrace. By a series of adroit manœuvres that exemplified the gulf separating a man long accustomed to pitting his wits against courtiers at the Court of Louis xiv and these less sophisticated colonial officials, he obliged the Sovereign Council to eat humble pie and go to unprecedented lengths in protocol when he attended the meetings. Now, upon his arrival at the intendant's palace for a meeting of the Council the captain of his guards entered first and announced him. The Intendant then had to clear the chamber and delegate two councillors to go to the head of the stairs to receive the Governor and escort him to his place in the council chamber, whereupon business could be resumed. By this means he gained the moral ascendancy and nipped in the bud any tendency there might have been to treat him, the representative of the King, with less respect than the office he held demanded.

Having made his point, Frontenac gave the Sovereign Council little cause for complaint for quite some time. In fact, as far as civil affairs were concerned his second term in office was far more tranquil than had been his first. There were several reasons for this: his earlier dismissal had been a sobering experience and, like Charles ii of England, he had no desire to go on his travels again, particularly since he had been stripped by his creditors of most of his property in France and now had to depend on his salary and perquisites of some 24,000 *livres* a year to support himself, as well as his wife in France. Moreover, this time he had serving with him three men of great abilities and exceptionally strong characters: Champigny, Callières, and Vaudreuil. All three had powerful friends and relatives in France. Callières, in particular, could not be offended since his brother, one of Louis xiv's private secretaries, had the ear of the King.

Another reason for the lack of conflict in Quebec was the war being waged at the other end of the colony in the Montreal area. For the best part of three months after the mass assault on Lachine, Iroquois war parties infiltrated the settlements, struck swiftly, then vanished like wolves into the forest leaving behind smoking ruins where once a home had stood and, in the ashes, the mutilated, scalped bodies of the *habitant* and his family. Try as they might, the Canadians and regular troops were unable to forfend these attacks. Not until the trees were stripped bare of their foliage, whereupon the Iroquois warriors were obliged to turn their attention to hunting food for the winter and to trapping for the furs needed to purchase supplies at Albany, was there any surcease.

There was, however, another enemy who could be reached; one whom the Canadians held largely responsible for their suffering: the English of

New York. For some time they had been eager to give this foe a taste of the war that had been unleashed on Canada. It was also believed that the destruction of Albany, which maintained a tight monopoly on trade with the Iroquois, would deny the enemy its supplies of arms and ammunition, at least temporarily. Moreover, there was good reason to believe that Albany could be destroyed with a fraction of the forces that would be needed to attack the Iroquois villages. Certainly in the English colonies it was expected that Albany would fall were the French to attack it. In fact, in October 1689, Edward Randolph had written from Boston to the Bishop of London: "I have certain intelligence that the French mean to attack Albany in January, when the lakes and rivers are all frozen. I doubt not that they will take it unless orders arrive from England to prevent them."

Had the authorities in Canada but known it, an invasion of New York in even moderate force could have wrought havoc, for both that province and New England were in a state bordering on anarchy. The revolution in England had spurred disaffected elements in these colonies to try to seize control from the royal officials. In the port of New York a revolutionary junta led by Jacob Leisler did gain control. In Albany, however, officials loyal to Sir Edmond Andros refused to join Leisler's party, although many in the town would have supported him. This bastion of the northern frontier was thus divided within and isolated from without. Frontenac, however, when he decided to launch a winter attack on the English, did not concentrate his forces against Albany. Instead he mustered three small war parties to ravage the English border settlements at three widely separated points, from the Atlantic coast to upper New York.

In bitter January cold the war parties assembled at Montreal, Trois Rivières, and Quebec. The Montreal party, consisting of 114 Canadians and 96 allied Indians, mostly from the Iroquois missions at Sault St Louis and Mount Royal, were led by Nicolas d'Ailleboust de Mantet and two of the Le Moyne brothers, Ste Hélène and Iberville. For several days they marched south through the snow-laden forest, dragging their supplies on toboggans. When they were within striking distance of both Albany and the smaller settlement of Schenectady the officers debated which to attack. One of the officers who had visited Albany argued strongly in favour of falling on it, but Frontenac's orders specifically stated that Schenectady was to be attacked because it could be taken with less risk.[1] And so Schenectady it had to be.

At midnight they were close by the village stockade. They found no sentinels on guard and one of the gates ajar. The Canadians and Indians slipped silently inside. At each of the thirty-odd houses six or seven men posted themselves, their arms primed. It was Lachine all over again. A shrill warcry suddenly shattered the cold stillness of the night. The doors were smashed open. Men, women, and children were hacked down as they struggled terrified out of their warm beds. At a few houses the doors resisted the blows of tomahawks long enough for the occupants to seize their weapons and make a stand. Fires were quickly set to the walls and shingle roofs. The occupants either died in the flames or were slaughtered as they broke out. Before the first savage fury of the attack subsided, sixty of the settlers had been killed. The Mayor of Albany wrote shortly after "The Cruelties Committed at said Place no Penn can write nor Tongue expresse; ye women big with child ripped up and ye children alive thrown into ye flames, and their heads dashed in pieces against the Doors and windows."

The Canadians lost one of their men and one Indian ally. Some fifty to sixty of the settlers somehow escaped death in the initial assault and had their lives spared. Most likely their homes had been attacked by the Canadians rather than by the Indian allies who would spare no one. In one of the houses thirty Mohawks were found, but because Frontenac had given specific instructions that any Iroquois encountered were not to be harmed, they were allowed to go free, causing disgruntlement among some of the Nipissing warriors in the war party. The homes of a few residents, who had been instrumental in saving French prisoners from the Mohawk torture fires in the past, were not touched. The others that were still standing were put to the torch. The surviving prisoners were then divided into two groups. Twenty-seven men and boys, along with fifty horses loaded with plunder, accompanied the Canadians on the long march back to Canada. Some twenty-five others, not fit for that journey, were turned loose. Most of them eventually reached Albany stark with terror, their limbs badly frozen. And in the forest clearing on the banks of the Mohawk River, grey mounds of ashes and the smoke-blackened stone pillars of fireplaces made ugly scars in the surrounding whiteness, where Schenectady once stood.

This swift assault marked the inauguration of a Canadian form of offensive warfare. Regular French troops could not have carried it out as the Canadians had done. Courcelle's campaign of twenty-four years before had proved that. Nor could the English colonials wage this type of warfare. For success it required men who could live in the wilderness and strike swiftly like Indians; who could march great distances on snowshoes in the bitter, morale-destroying cold, carrying their meagre supplies; and who would go into the attack at the end of a journey that in itself was a severe test of a man's endurance. This the Canadians had proved they could do, when they were led by their own kind. Unfortunately, their virtues as irregular guerilla fighters were offset by their lack of discipline, their dislike for orders, their insistence on pleasing themselves. These failings appeared on the return journey to Montreal. By the time the party was nearing the French settlements some of the men were straggling far behind. The Indian allies went off to hunt, and forty of the Canadians pushed on ahead of the main party. When almost within sight of Montreal eighty warriors from the Mohawk villages, a war party raised by the thirty Mohawks spared at Schenectady, caught up with the stragglers, taking nineteen of them prisoner.

While this was occurring the other two war parties were marching southeastward towards the New England frontier. By March 27 the Trois Rivières party of twenty-five Canadians and an equal number of Indians, led by the Sieur Hertel, reached Salmon Falls, a settlement of three small stockaded forts near Portsmouth on the Atlantic coast. As at Schenectady, no watch was being kept. At dawn the three forts were attacked simultaneously. Caught in their beds, thirty-four of the settlers were killed in the first swift attack. Another fifty-odd, mostly women and children, were taken prisoner. The isolated farms round about were burned, the cattle slaughtered. When· a scout reported that militiamen from Portsmouth were approaching, Hertel gave the order to retire. Slowed down by their prisoners, they made a stand at a river, killed and wounded several of their pursuers, then slipped away. They had inflicted losses on the enemy out of all proportion to the size of their own force.

Nor were these the only losses that New England had suffered at the hands of the French and their Indian allies. Privateers from Port Royal had already captured a goodly number of fishing-vessels, and the Acadian Indians were harassing the frontier settlements continuously. In 1689 they had captured an English fort at Pemaquid and several blockhouses in the area, killing some two hundred settlers. When word was received of the destruction of Schenectady, followed by that of Salmon Falls, the Governor and General Council of Massachusetts appealed to the neighbouring colonies for aid in an attack on Port Royal. By the end of April an expeditionary force of eight ships with seven to eight hundred men had been raised under the command of Sir William Phips, recently arrived from England.

The times could not have been more propitious for the assault. Acadia was too remote from Quebec to expect any assistance from that quarter, and in the entire province there were only ninety Troupes de le Marine: twenty-five in garrison at Chedabouctou, the rest at Port Royal. Some of these men were too old and infirm to be of any use and there were only some forty serviceable stand of arms for all of them.[2] Nor was this the worst of it. Dissension was rife in Port Royal where the judge, the Sieur des Goutins, and La Mothe Cadillac, one of the worst scoundrels ever to set foot in North America,[3] were continually scheming to undermine the authority of the Governor, Meneval.[4] By the autumn of 1689 this situation had become so bad that Meneval pleaded to be recalled. He warned that if Seignelay refused him he would quit his post at the first opportunity, come what may, "preferring a hundred times to spend three years in the Bastille than a single week here."⁵

It was not surprising, then, that when Phips's ships arrived at Port Royal Meneval offered no resistance but capitulated on being offered honourable terms. In fact, he likely regarded Phips more as a God-sent liberator than an enemy. After the capitulation, however, he had cause to wonder. The terms he had accepted allowed himself and his garrison to march out of the fort with the honours of war and take ship to France or Quebec; the churches were not to be touched, and freedom of religion was allowed to the Acadians, who were also guaranteed the security of their property. After the surrender these terms were dishonoured. The New England men began systematically pillaging the homes, warehouses, and churches. The latter they also desecrated. When everything in the settlement worth taking had been loaded on the ships they returned to Boston, leaving no garrison to occupy the captured post, and taking Meneval prisoner with them.⁶ As part of his share of the loot Phips seized all Meneval's personal effects and furnishings, silver, books, table linen, bedding, wine, and clothing, not even excluding four pairs of linen drawers, four pairs of silk garters, and a dozen night caps, four of them edged with lace.⁷ Not until the end of December did Meneval, despite Phips's vigorous opposition, succeed in obtaining his and his two servants' release from Boston gaol, along with a court order for the return of his effects and passports to cross to Europe.⁸

The easy success of this venture, and the fact that it had been such a profitable one, more than paying the cost of the expedition, decided the General Court of Massachusetts to press for an assault by all the colonies on Canada. The attack on Salmon Falls by Hertel's party, while many of the men in the district were off at Port Royal, lent vigour to their intentions. The neighbouring colonies were asked for assistance in the godly design, and to finance it a form of joint-stock company was established. Those who subscribed money for the fitting-out of the expedition were to be repaid out of the rich plunder to be provided by Quebec, whose churches were filled, it was believed, with gold and silver idolatrous ornaments. The men taking part were, of course, to get a goodly share of the plunder, but any remaining, once the charges had been paid, was to go half to the province and half to the stockholders.⁹ The province had little difficulty raising funds or men.

And while this was taking place in Boston, to the north the Sieur Hertel's war party had just joined up with that from Quebec under the Sieur de Portneuf, comprising fifty Canadians and four to five hundred Abenakis. Hertel sent most of his men back to Quebec with some of the prisoners.

The majority of these unhappy wretches, however, had to be left with their Indian captors, but some of them were subsequently ransomed by the French and brought to the security of Quebec where they were well treated. Meanwhile, Portneuf's joint force made its way slowly through the wilderness, living off the land and pausing for days at a time to hunt. This delay also served to let the alarm on the English frontier abate. Toward the end of May, two months after Hertel's attack at Salmon Falls, they came within sight of Fort Loyal on Casco Bay. Thirty men of the garrison sallied out to attack what they took to be a few marauding Indians. When they realized their mistake it was too late. The Abenakis fell on them from all sides. Only four men managed to escape back to the fort.

Portneuf now disregarded Frontenac's strict orders not to attack strong points, only isolated settlements. He laid siege to the main fort where the settlers from the surrounding district had taken refuge under cover of darkness. Trenches were dug, European fashion, up to the walls of the fort, and mines laid. At this the garrison surrendered. The cannons were spiked, the fort itself destroyed, and the farms for five miles around put to the torch. Three to four hundred people along the frontier fled to the safety of Portsmouth. By June 23 the Canadians were back at Quebec with four or five prisoners. Again, the bulk of the captives had had to be left to the mercy of the Indians, who killed the wounded and any others who could not keep up with them on the march.

Throughout New England and New York these savage attacks had spread terror, fear of their recurrence, and the desire for revenge. Frontenac claimed that the English would now be deterred from joining with the Iroquois for combined attacks on Canada. In fact, the raids had the opposite effect. Throughout the northern provinces the colonial assemblies met to join with Massachusetts and New York in planning an assault by land and sea to destroy the French menace once and for all. But in New France the success of these raids was like a tonic. At last the enemy had been made to feel what Indian warfare was really like. Some in the colony, however, had reservations. The Intendant voiced their misgivings when he declared, in a dispatch to the Minister, that the Canadians and Indians should have been united in one strong striking force for an attack on Albany, which he claimed could then have been destroyed. He added: "If this blow had been struck against Albany we would have seen the Iroquois greatly humbled, because it is from there that they obtain all the succour they need, being out of reach of Manhattan and Boston, particularly during the winter." The Governor of New York and the Crown officials in New England were in agreement with Champigny. The Governor of New York pleaded with the other provinces to aid in the defence of the northern frontier and declared:

I need not relate unto you of how great import the preservacon of this place is, being the only bulwark and safeguard of all Their Majesty's plantacons on the main of America, and if, for want of strength, the French should assault and gain Albany how farr your Government and all the English Colonys on both sides of us would be endangered, you can easily judge. For we have nothing but that place that keeps our Indians steady to us, and the loss of that must be the loss of them, and the loss of them must be the loss of all the King's interest on this continent.

The Massachusetts officials were of the same mind. Albany, the Governor and Council of Massachusetts declared, was "the hinge upon which in great measure the weight of our present New England affairs doth turn." In fact, for the duration of the war the English colonial officials lived in constant dread lest the French destroy Albany. In 1698 the Governor of New York, the Earl of Bellomont, stated that had the French attacked this key base "with half the number of men that they had provided at Montreal they could not (humanly speaking) have failed to take it . . . and it is more than probable that [the Iroquois] would have revolted to them upon such a loss and disgrace. God be thanked for the province's escape."

From a tactical point of view Frontenac's border raids had been a success; losses had been inflicted on the enemy at slight cost to the French and the initiative in the war appeared to have been regained. Strategically, however, it was another story. It was the Iroquois and the Albany merchants and officials who were the real foes of Canada, and neither of these had been in any way harmed. Nor had the English colonies as a whole been seriously damaged by the raids; their ability to strike back had not been impaired. In fact, the raids merely spurred them on to far greater efforts than they would otherwise have undertaken.

While the English colonies prepared to wage war Frontenac, refusing to admit that his influence over the Iroquois was not what he claimed it to be, sent another peace embassy to the Five Nations. This one met with a warm reception. The interpreter and Canadian canoemen were tortured to death, the officer in command, the Chevalier d'Au, was savagely beaten, then turned over to the English. The Ottawas, however, had had much greater success in their negotiations with the Five Nations. During the winter Durantaye, the commandant at Michilimackinac, sent word to Quebec that the Ottawas would soon be lost to the alliance and would likely turn on the French. Frontenac, hard put to it to explain this turn of events to the Minister, declared that it resulted from the abandonment of Fort Frontenac.

In an attempt to forestall the allies' defection, as soon as the Ottawa River was free of ice he sent a detachment of 143 men, convoyed part way by thirty more, to Michilimackinac with liberal presents for the Ottawas. Two days out from Montreal they ran into an Iroquois ambush. Eight Canadian *voyageurs* were killed. Some of the officers were for turning back, but the commander of the party, the Sieur de Louvigny, refused. He led sixty men in a counter-attack and caught the enemy unawares. Pouring a sudden volley into the Iroquois from close quarters, they charged into the enemy midst. The Iroquois fled in panic. Only four of their canoes got away, many of the men wounded. Some thirty others were killed on the spot; four were taken alive, two men and two women.

When the party reached Michilimackinac the Ottawa ambassadors were preparing to leave for Onondaga to ratify their treaty with the Iroquois. It was only with great difficulty that they were dissuaded. This issue was not finally settled until the French, playing on the Indian blood-lust, induced some of the Ottawas to assist in torturing one of the Iroquois prisoners to death. Even then French policy might not have prevailed but for the fact that this prisoner proved unable to bear the pain as the red-hot irons were held to his flesh. Instead of singing his death-song and hurling back the taunts of his tormentors he screamed in agony and begged to be spared. The Ottawas regarded this craven display with contempt and deemed him unfit to die a warrior's death. The French immediately urged them on with the cry: "*à la chaudière.*" The poor wretch was quickly dispatched, his butchered carcase boiled and eaten. After this there could be no thought of an embassy to Onondaga and the Ottawas agreed to go to Montreal to confer with Frontenac. It had been a close thing, but French policy had prevailed, for the time being.

In mid August over five hundred Indians from all the upcountry nations in the French alliance came down to Montreal. When Frontenac met them in a general council they made very plain their lack of confidence in his policy. A Nipissing chief who had accompanied the French in the attack on Schenectady spoke bitterly of Frontenac's orders on that occasion. He reminded Frontenac that the thirty Mohawk warriors in Schenectady who had been spared on his orders had later pursued the French, capturing several of them. What could have been a severe blow to the Mohawks, had these warriors been killed, had been translated into a loss for the French. He could not understand why, at a time when the Iroquois were ravaging the French settlements, the French refused to strike back, but instead sent peace embassies to the Five Nations. He demanded that Frontenac explain his policy. Le Baron, a Huron chief, exhorted the French to press the war against the Iroquois as well as against the English. When the Mission Iroquois demanded to know why the Ottawas had themselves been negotiating with the Five Nations, an Ottawa chief bluntly declared that since the French were striving to negotiate a separate peace with the enemy, they had had to look to their own interests, and to try to prevent the Iroquois turning full strength on them alone.

Frontenac had no alternative but to disavow his attempts to appease the Iroquois. It had merely encouraged them and he had come dangerously close to losing control of the entire west. He now promised that he would not enter into any negotiations with the Iroquois without the participation of the western allies; meanwhile he swore to press the war against the Five Nations until they sued for peace, and he called on the allies to do the same. With this the allies appeared to be satisfied and the next few days were devoted to feasting and the trading of the furs the allies had brought with them.

On September 4, while the allies were still at Montreal, a small force of Albany militia and Iroquois struck at the settlement south of Montreal, destroying the farms and cattle, killing over fifty *habitants* and regular troops working on the harvest. Serious though these losses were, they were nothing to what had been intended. This raiding party of one hundred and fifty men, led by Captain John Schuyler of Albany, had formed part of an army of militia from all the northern English colonies which, along with a large force of Iroquois, had been raised to capture Montreal while a fleet from Boston went by sea to capture Quebec.

Fortunately for New France, the English colonials found that it was one thing to plan a massive assault on Canada, quite another to carry it out. When the militia assembled at Albany they proved to be far fewer than the 855 agreed upon by the provincial commissioners. The leaders quickly began quarrelling, provisions and canoes were lacking, and some of the men came down with smallpox. At this the western Iroquois hurriedly withdrew, and most of the militia used it as an excuse to turn back. John Schuyler persuaded twenty-nine Albany militia and a hundred and twenty Iroquois to press on, but the attack that was intended to tie down the bulk of the French forces at Montreal, while the Boston fleet took Quebec, ended as a quick raid and swift withdrawal.

A month later, while Frontenac and Champigny were still at Montreal, preparing to settle the troops in their winter quarters, the town-major of Quebec received word from the Abenakis of Acadia that an enemy fleet was in the Gulf. He immediately sent word to Frontenac, and a canoe down-river to reconnoitre, then called in all the *habitants* near Quebec to dig trenches and strengthen the newly built log palisade at the rear of the town. The citizens with homes and the merchants with warehouses along the river bank hurriedly transported what they could of their goods and possessions up the steep cliff, hoping to find shelter in Upper Town. The sisters of the Hôtel Dieu dug a pit in their garden to bury their silver and altar vessels and then made ready to move to nearby Lorette. When word came that the enemy fleet had passed Tadoussac, there was near panic. Everything depended now on time, on whether the Boston fleet would reach Quebec before Frontenac arrived from Montreal with the troops.

Fortunately, Frontenac had been about to leave for Quebec when he first received word of the enemy's rumoured approach. He and Champigny left at once by canoe. The next day came word confirming that the fleet was off Tadoussac. Frontenac immediately sent orders to Callières to bring every available man, regular and militia, to Quebec in all haste. At Trois Rivières he paused only long enough to order the militia there to leave at once for the threatened capital. Four days after leaving Montreal he arrived with two to three hundred men. He found that the Sieur Provost, the town-major, had already sited the cannon and done much to strengthen the defences. The spirits of the people rose considerably when they learned that more men were on their way. To maintain morale he strode about, exuding confidence, and forbade anyone to leave the confines of the town.

Three days later, on the Sunday evening October 15, the Boston fleet, commanded by Sir William Phips, dropped anchor off the Ile d'Orléans. It numbered thirty-four sail, bearing twenty-three hundred sailors and militia. Early the next morning they moved upriver with the tide. A little before ten a pinnace flying a white flag put off from the flag ship bearing an envoy, Major Thomas Savage. When the pinnace reached shore the Sieur Provost was there with two sergeants who quickly blindfolded the Major and conducted him up a steep path to the Château St Louis. All the way up a squad of a dozen men pressed in on him, making him think he was being pushed through a dense crowd. Shouts from the men, barked orders from the sergeants, and the laughter of some ladies come to watch the spectacle impressed on Major Savage, as was intended, that the people of Quebec were not at all perturbed by the New England fleet.

At the Château St Louis Frontenac, the Intendant, the Bishop, and the senior officers were waiting, dressed as though for a royal levée; the officers in dove-grey uniforms with gold and silver lace at throat and wrists, plumed hats, their hair powdered and curled. When the blindfold was removed Major Savage was shaken to find himself in this "stately Hall full of Brave Martiall men." Their proud expressions as they regarded him in stern silence was even more disconcerting. Visibly impressed, the Major meekly asked that he be permitted to discharge the commission given him by his Admiral, then handed to Frontenac an ultimatum.

Couched in severe phrases by the four puritan preachers who were members of Admiral Phips's council of war, the document began: "The warrs between the two crownes of England and France doth not only sufficiently warrant; But the destruction made by ye french, and Indians, under your command and Encouragement upon the persons and Estates, of their Majesties subjects of New England, without provocation on their part, hath put them under the necessity of this Expedition for their own Security and satisfaction." It then went on to demand the immediate surrender of the colony's forts, stores, and military establishment within the hour, failing which Quebec would be taken by force of arms.

The time it took to make a hurried translation of this document allowed Major Savage to regain his composure. He now took a watch from his pocket, handed it to Frontenac, and rather imprudently announced that, it then being ten o'clock, he must have an answer by eleven, no later. Stung by this effrontery, Frontenac brusquely replied that he would not keep the Admiral waiting. Indicating his officers, who were angrily declaring that Phips and his men were mere pirates and hence this envoy deserved to be hanged out of hand, he demanded of Major Savage if he really believed that these gentlemen would consent to their Governor's accepting such terms. The Major then asked for a reply to the ultimatum in writing, whereat Frontenac made his ringing rejoinder: "I have no reply to make to your general other than from the mouths of my cannon and muskets. He must learn that it is not in this fashion that one summons a man such as I. Let him do the best he can on his side as I will do on mine." With that Major Savage, greatly to his relief, was reblindfolded and conducted back to the pinnace.

Frontenac's proud challenge was, to say the least, disconcerting to the New England men. It had been expected that the bulk of the colony's troops would be engaged at Montreal by the Albany forces and Quebec taken without a fight. By the time Phips's council of war convened to consider the French answer, the tide had ebbed and no landing could be attempted that day. Toward evening the sound of drums and fifes could be heard approaching Quebec; then great cheers rolled across the water from the town. It was Callières with another five to six hundred militia from Montreal. Frontenac now had over two thousand men available – several hundred more than Phips could deploy. The prospects for the Boston men looked grim indeed. There could be no thought of a protracted siege. It was so late in the season they had to take Quebec within a fortnight, three weeks at the most, or run the risk of being trapped by the freeze-up. Were that to happen they would be fortunate if they were able to surrender to the French before being massacred by the Indians.

The odds, then, were all on the French side. They had only to wait for the New England forces to attack them in their prepared positions, parry the thrust with their superior forces, and wait for the enemy to go home. And at this period military thinking strongly favoured defensive tactics over the offensive; the aim was, not to win a decisive victory, but to avoid defeat and, at all costs, avoid heavy casualties.[10] This last was of particular importance to the French. With war raging in Europe there was slight hope of replacements being sent from France, hence Frontenac had to husband his forces.

Phips did have one advantage: mobility. He could move his troops by ship and attempt a landing above or below Quebec. Thus Frontenac could not be sure where the main assault would come until Phips actually committed his main forces; he therefore had to guard against feints and diversionary attacks. The most vulnerable part of Quebec's defences were the heights to the rear of the town, and here Frontenac sited eight cannon to cover the landward approaches, with some smaller pieces on the rear slope close by the palisade. The east side, facing the St Lawrence, had several batteries and the road leading up the cliff to Upper Town had been hastily barricaded at several points. To the north, facing the basin and the St Charles River, the steep cliffs fell away from the beach, leaving ample room for manœuvring on the flats below. At low tide the St Charles River could be forded at two points, but Frontenac had several cannon sited to cover these crossing places. In fact, considering the forces available on the two sides, Quebec was virtually impregnable.

But the New England men, having come this far, had at least to make an attempt on the enemy stronghold. On the Tuesday, morning, one boat tried to land on the Beauport flats, across the St Charles from Quebec, but the weather was rough and the *habitants* of Beauport drove the boat back with a brisk fire. The next day, however, twelve to thirteen hundred men were landed at La Canardière on the flats, under the command of Major John Walley. Their plan for attack was to march to the St Charles and ford it under cover of the fleet's cannon fire, while the smaller ships landed the army's field guns and supplies on the Quebec side. At the same time, some of the larger ships were to bombard the town from the St Lawrence. When the main force was across the St Charles and beginning the assault up the hill to Upper Town, these ships were to land two hundred men on the left flank to attempt to storm the cliff. Other of the ships were to sail upstream to attempt a diversion above Quebec to draw off some of the defending forces.

The chief weakness in this combined operation was that it required perfect timing and co-ordination. Both qualities were markedly lacking in the attacking forces. The St Charles could be crossed only at low tide, which occurred at four in the afternoon and four in the morning. When it turned, the tide rose three feet in an hour to a maximum of seventeen feet.[11] This meant that the army had only two hours to get across and once across it could not retreat. Moreover, they had to carry out this manœuvre under cannon fire, with the French drawn up ready to attack them once they had struggled across.

Highly trained regulars might have done it, disspirited amateurs clearly could not. When Walley's forces marched over the swampy, brush-covered terrain towards the forbidding cliffs on the other side of the St Charles they were assailed by parties of Canadians who kept up a galling fire. Instead of coming into the mouth of the St Charles to provide covering fire, the Boston ships cannonaded the town, doing little damage apart from frightening the poor sisters of the Hôtel Dieu half to death. Some of the sisters, however, had the wit to gather up twenty-six cannon balls that fell in their garden and take them to the French batteries "to return to the English." The day wore on and the ships still did not put in to aid the army. The weather was bitterly cold and the men had to camp for the night without blankets, in clothing still damp from the landing. Next morning their situation was grim. For rations all they had was a couple of ship's biscuits each, and the rum supply was exhausted. Major Walley marched the men closer to Quebec, beating off small parties of Canadians who kept sniping from cover. High tide was at nine in the morning, but at first light the ships recommenced cannonading the town until they received several hits and retired. When the tide rose again that evening they still did not land any supplies for their army. And across the St Charles they could see the main French forces drawn up, waiting impatiently for them to attempt the crossing. Again the men, with smallpox now spreading in their ranks, were faced with a night in the open. The officers decided that they would have to get their troops back to the ships to recuperate; then, if circumstances allowed, attempt a landing elsewhere.

The next morning the ice on the stagnant pools was thick enough to bear a man. The Canadians continued their constant harassing fire throughout the day, inflicting some casualties. Shortly before dawn, an attempt was made to get the army off, but as soon as the ships' longboats put in to shore all order and discipline vanished. The separate companies became a mob of desperate struggling men, fighting to be first off. Walley, seeing no hope of restoring order and getting all the men away before daylight revealed their plight to the French, ordered the boats away.

That day, October 21, they spent beating off Canadian attacks, while across the St Charles the French forces stood waiting, quite unaware of the enemy's miserable condition. Shortly before midnight the boats again put in to shore, and again the men, frantic to get away, fought and clawed their way into the boats nearly swamping them. But somehow, under cover of darkness and a heavy rain that had sent the Canadians to seek shelter, they managed to get away. They left behind five of their six small cannon, a quantity of ammunition, and a drum.

Later in the day a council of war was held on the flagship. A landing at Lower Town was suggested, but the officers all knew that the men were not up to it. On October 25, after a violent storm, sail was raised and the fleet slipped downstream, out of sight of Quebec. The next day some prisoners taken by the fleet on its way up the St Lawrence were exchanged for those taken by the Canadians in the border raids; then the New England men made haste for home. Many of them failed to reach Boston; one ship was wrecked on Anticosti Island and at least two others were lost at sea. And when the ships finally reached port the smallpox that had ravaged the men quickly spread through New England, causing heavy loss of life. Although their losses from enemy action had been slight – Frontenac claimed they had suffered over five hundred casualties, but Phips admitted to only thirty dead and this seems closer to the truth – yet the failure of the expedition and the losses from disease in its wake proved to be a crippling blow to New England. The shareholders received no return on their investment. On May 6 the following year Governor Henry Sloughter of New York wrote: "The whole country from Pemaquid to Delaware is extremely hurt by the late ill managed and fruitless expedition to Canada, which hath contracted £40,000 debt and about 1,000 men lost by sickness and shipwrack and no blow struck for want of courage and conduct in the Officers, as is universally said and believed."[12]

When it was certain that the Boston fleet had fled, there was great rejoicing in Quebec. The colony had emerged virtually unscathed from the most dangerous threat in its century's existence. This first attempt by the English colonies to conquer New France in two swift combined campaigns had failed dismally. The enemy had organized this great expedition and been beaten back at a cost to the French of only six or seven killed and some dozen wounded. It was to be a long time before they would try the like again.

Meanwhile, on November 5 a solemn *Te Deum* was sung in the cathedral, and the chapel recently built in Lower Town was now named Notre Dame de Victoire. And at Versailles, when word was received of the repulse of the New England assault, Louis XIV ordered a medal struck to celebrate the occasion, with the inevitable beaver in the design and the legend, *Kebeca liberata M.DC.XC – Francia in novo orbe victrix*. But had the attack on Montreal occurred in sufficient strength, and Phips's fleet arrived at Quebec earlier, as had been intended, it might well have been a different story. In fact, a more apt legend for Louis XIV's commemorative medal might well have been: *Fortuna a Deo amatus juvat.*

CHAPTER 12

War and Trade

Once the first jubilation at the withdrawal of the Boston fleet had subsided, the people of New France had to face another cruel foe: hunger. The previous spring the King's warehouses at Montreal had burned down, destroying all that had remained of the supplies for the troops. The Iroquois and heavy rains had ruined much of the crops and only three out of eleven supply ships from France reached Quebec before the freeze-up. The price of wheat rose to fifteen *livres* the bushel, and of other foodstuffs there was little or none to be had. By spring the people were grubbing in the fields for gleanings; this and fish were all that kept them alive.

In fact, the spring and early summer of 1691 were the worst in living memory. As soon as the forests turned green two large Iroquois war parties, numbering nearly a thousand warriors, descended on Montreal and ravaged the farms from the western tip of the island to the Richelieu River. The regular troops and militia had to stand helplessly by for lack of ammunition. In desperation the Intendant finally ordered the lead eavestroughs and window-mouldings stripped from the houses to be melted down for bullets. Before the Iroquois army finally retired, over a hundred men, women, and children had been killed or captured.

When Champigny toured the upper colony he was profoundly moved. In his dispatch to the Minister he wrote:

> I found the people living above Trois Rivières in a state of great misery and the whole countryside ruined by the enemy, with the exception of the area around Boucherville and close by the forts, to which all the *habitants* have been forced to retire. This prevents them working on their distant fields or raising cattle except in very small numbers owing to the limited space within the fort walls. They dare not venture out because of the enemy who appears from time to time. What is even more grievous is the number of *habitants* crippled in the war and the poor widows who, having lost their husbands in the fighting, have difficulty obtaining bread for their children.

Fortunately the ships arrived from France by mid July that year, but no sooner had badly needed supplies been sent on to Montreal than reports came in that an army was again being mustered at Albany for the invasion of Canada. As it turned out the early reports were exaggerated. It was not an army that was descending the Richelieu towards the French settlements but another raiding party, made up of 266 Albany militia led by Major Peter Schuyler, along with 146 Mohawks and Mohicans. Callières had sufficient warning to muster 600 regulars, a detachment of Canadian militia, and a body of Mission Indians. Crossing to the south side of the St Lawrence, he stationed 160 of this force, the élite of the regulars with some of the militia and allied Indians under the command of a veteran officer the Sieur de Vallerenne, near Chambly to check the enemy's advance from this direction. The bulk of the forces remained encamped at Prairie-de-la-Magdelaine.

Three days passed with no sign of the enemy's approach. The night of August 10-11 it rained heavily, and in the militia camp the sentries took shelter. At dawn the enemy silently moved down on the sleeping men; then charged in among them inflicting heavy casualties. The regulars encamped nearby, hearing the din, rushed up. Before they were fully aware of what was going on they were met by a fusillade from the Canadian camp. Their losses were heavy. The surviving officers quickly rallied them and they pressed home their charge, putting the enemy to flight.

The Albany forces, retiring swiftly along the Chambly road, suddenly found themselves faced by Vallerenne's detachment. They halted, and for a few moments there was silence as the forces took stock of each other. Then, seeing that they had the advantage of numbers, the Albany militia and their allies charged in. Vallerenne waited until they were within pistol range before giving the order to fire. Several in the front rank of the charging foe were felled, the rest fell back, and the Mohicans withdrew entirely. A second charge was driven back by a volley from the disciplined troops, who then came in from front and flanks. At this some of the Canadian militia fled but were quickly rallied by their commander, Le Ber du Chesne. A savage hand-to-hand fight ensued with sword, knife, tomahawk, and clubbed musket. For over an hour the bloody struggle went on before Schuyler's men and the Mohawks began to give ground, then turned and fled. Vallerenne's men were too exhausted to think of pursuit. They had barely the strength to carry their dead and wounded from the blood-trampled forest roadway.

Schuyler later admitted to losing thirty-seven killed and having thirty-one wounded, but claimed to have killed some two hundred of the French. For their part the French admitted forty-five of their men killed and sixty wounded. In one dispatch Frontenac stated that the enemy had lost over three hundred killed; in another he reduced the figure to 120 killed and left on the field. The French losses had been due largely to the carelessness of the Canadian militia in not maintaining a proper watch. Had it not been for the steadiness of Vallerenne, the French losses would undoubtedly have been greater and those of the Albany forces negligible. Although the French suffered the heavier casualties, the Albany men had taken enough of a mauling that they did not venture near Canada again until the war ended, much to the dissatisfaction of their Iroquois allies.

Although the Canadian militia lacked the discipline needed for pitched battles, they had by this time served their apprenticeship in guerilla warfare. They had, of necessity, become as skilled in the stealthy war of ambush and surprise attack as the Iroquois themselves. Now, when Iroquois war parties descended on the colony they encountered the Canadian militia and Mission Iroquois waiting for them at the river crossings. After a few such encounters, and knowing that if taken alive the torture fires awaited them too, they became more circumspect. Nor was it only when they invaded the French settlements that they suffered losses. Callières and Vaudreuil were sending out war parties of their own to ambush the Iroquois on the edges of their own country, in their hunting-grounds and at their fishing-places. In 1692 the Ottawas and Hurons brought forty-two scalps to Montreal to claim the thirty *livres* scalp bounty. All told, it was estimated that over a hundred Iroquois were killed and forty-four taken prisoner that year. Other parties struck at the New York frontier, and blond scalps were frequently brought back to Montreal. So severe were these attacks that the exposed frontier settlements began to be abandoned. In March 1692 the Commander-in-Chief and the Council of New York had to issue an order that all men capable of bearing arms who had fled the vicinity of Albany were to return within a fortnight.[1] It failed, however, to bring them back or stop others leaving.

This mode of warfare was costly in equipment as well as men, and the Intendant Champigny began to receive sharp criticism from the Minister for what was regarded at Versailles as excessive military expenditures. To a considerable degree this criticism was occasioned by the changes that had recently taken place in the Ministry of Marine. Seignelay had died on November 3, 1690, and been succeeded by Louis Phélypeaux de Pontchartrain, a kinsman of Frontenac. Pontchartrain had asked not to be given charge of the Department of Marine, because he knew nothing of its affairs and had his hands full with the Ministry of Finance. Louis, however, had insisted because there was no one else in whom he had confidence. A hard-pressed man of modest talents, Pontchartrain's chief concern was somehow to provide the vast sums needed to prosecute the war in Europe. He begrudged every *livre* that was allocated to the war in Canada. Being fully occupied by domestic problems, he left Canadian affairs in the charge of the Intendant of Commerce, Jean-Baptiste de Lagny, who happened to be a friend of Frontenac's. As the costs of the North American war steadily mounted, rising to over 200,000 *livres* a year, it was the Intendant Champigny rather than Frontenac who was raked over the coals by the Minister.

In 1693 Pontchartrain informed the Intendant that unless he curbed these excessive expenditures he would run the risk of having to foot the bill himself. This was more than Champigny could tolerate, and he informed the Minister in blunt language and in great detail why military operations in America were so much greater than in Europe and why they could not be reduced "unless it were decided to abandon the colony completely and leave it a prey to its enemies." He explained that every war party had to be equipped with canoes or snowshoes, arms, ammunition, food, and clothing. Parties were sent at frequent intervals by Frontenac to Acadia, the Illinois country, Michilimackinac, and beyond. "If all this," wrote Champigny in anger, "and an infinity of other things could be done without expense in a new country half ruined by war, it would be a most admirable secret which, with all my heart, I wish I had been able to discover in order to satisfy His Majesty and please you."[2] A provincial intendant, no matter how provoked he might be, no matter how much he might feel himself to be in the right, could not write with impunity in such language to a minister. Champigny had enemies in the Ministry of Marine; his friends in Paris now began to fear that he would soon be dismissed from his post.

Between Frontenac and Champigny, apart from occasional clashes of personality which the Intendant managed to keep under control, there were two main sources of conflict, both stemming from their differing views on colonial policy. Champigny was a firm believer in the policy originally formulated by Colbert, to diversify the colony's economic activities and curb the tendency of the fur trade to absorb too much of the available supplies of capital and labour. Frontenac had no objection to the policy of economic development within the colony, provided it did not in any way curtail the trade in furs. He was of the opinion that the central colony should serve merely as a base for this trade in the west, but he overlooked one significant factor: the market in France for beaver was not expanding, whereas the amount of fur being exported from Canada was. In fact, the market was contracting as hat-makers found ways to manufacture hats with cheaper materials than beaver fur: rabbit fur, lamb's wool, and llama fur from Peru. When the Company of the Farm began to complain vociferously that it was being inundated with beaver, mostly of a poor grade, and that it had huge stocks which it could not dispose of at any price, the Minister of Marine was forced to take notice. In his dispatches to Frontenac and Champigny he ordered them to stem this flood of fur by limiting the number of Canadians who went upcountry to trade.

The Intendant was eager to comply and he did his best to make sure that only twenty-five *congés* were issued each year, but at every turn he was circumvented by the Governor. Even when the colony was besieged by Iroquois war parties and every man was needed to defend the settlements, Frontenac persisted in sending parties of over a hundred men to the western posts. Ostensibly, these parties served a military purpose, to garrison the posts and carry ammunition and supplies to the allies to enable them to press the war against the Iroquois. In fact, however, some of the officers in these military detachments used the supplies to trade for their own profit. Nor did they serve any real military function. Once the convoys reached Michilimackinac or the Illinois posts, the men then proceeded farther west in small parties to trade in the Indian villages and establish new posts far in the interior. The Indians were now under continual pressure to trap furs, not only during the winter when the pelts were at their prime, but all year round. The result was that the Indians had little time for war parties against the Iroquois and the bulk of the furs was made up of poor-quality summer-killed pelts that the squaws had not been able to dress properly.

Politically, too, Frontenac's fur-trade expansion policy had pernicious results. Since the days of Champlain, first the Hurons and then the Ottawas had served as middlemen for the tribes farther west, many of whom lacked the materials for canoes and were dependent on the Ottawas to transport their furs to Montreal in exchange for French trade goods. The Hurons and the Ottawas had built up a vast commercial empire in the heart of the continent, based on their commercial alliance with the French.[3] But now, Frontenac's military detachments, instead of cementing the alliance with the western tribes by combining with them in attacks on the Iroquois, were disrupting it. In their eagerness to get cheap furs they voyaged over a thousand miles north and west of Michilimackinac to obtain them from the Assiniboine tribes who had previously traded with the Ottawas, thus eliminating the latter nation as middlemen. Worse still, many of them voyaged to the headwaters of the Mississippi to trade with the mighty Sioux nation who, for as long as men could remember, had been the hereditary foe of the Ottawas. In their clashes with the Sioux, the Ottawas now found their enemies armed with French muskets. They complained even more bitterly when they discovered French *coureurs de bois* among the Sioux war parties. The Ottawas had long valued the French as commercial partners. When the French became trade rivals, and aided their enemies in war, the basis of the alliance crumbled. The Iroquois were quick to take advantage of this, and their subtle overtures to the Ottawas were to come at a most awkward time for the French.

Frontenac's military strategy was also strongly criticized by the Intendant and Callières. The *petite guerre* policy of harassing the Iroquois and the English settlements with small war parties had had considerable success, but like all wars of attrition it was very costly in both men and material. Moreover, the French war aims were very complex. The worst thing that could have happened would have been the total destruction of the Five Nations: their presence, in strength but not too great strength, was essential to the economic and political security of New France. In 1694 Callières explained this quite succinctly to the Minister. He stated that they must on no account crush the Iroquois completely, but should merely reduce them to a point where they could not attack New France but were still sufficiently strong "so that the fear that our Ottawas might have of them will always serve as a barrier to prevent them going to the English to obtain cheaper merchandise." Were the Iroquois to have been removed from the south side of Lake Ontario and the St Lawrence, the western fur trade would have gone to Albany and Philadelphia rather than to Montreal. Here, indeed, was a paradox: the Iroquois were at one and the same time the greatest menace and the certain safeguard of New France.

As early as 1693 Callières and Champigny were urging that the time had come to launch a full-scale invasion of the Iroquois cantons to destroy their villages and food supplies. They believed that this would deprive the enemy of the means to wage aggressive war and oblige them to accept terms. Whether they were correct in this assumption, or whether the Iroquois strength needed to be drained further by attrition before such a campaign would force them to accept, and what was more important abide by, French conditions for peace is a moot point. Certainly Callières's opinion, since it was he who was directing the war against the Iroquois, carries weight.

Champigny was particularly eager for a change in strategy because, as it was, the Canadian *habitants* in the militia units were doing most of the fighting and suffering heavy casualties. This sorely distressed the Intendant. He maintained that the regular troops could be employed to greater advantage in the war and the militiamen used more sparingly. To him the *habitants* were the colony's greatest asset; they had families to support whereas the regulars, who were not allowed to marry, were expendable. Their losses could be made up by reinforcements sent from France. In 1691 he complained to the Minister:

It is very aggravating for the poor *habitants* of this country to find themselves continually ordered out for a war when the majority of the soldiers are not; they have never yet refused to march, but they, as well as their families are reduced to such a miserable state, I believe it to be urgent that they be employed in some other manner for fear of disheartening them completely and casting them into the depths of despair. It was apparent to me during my last trip that some of them were very discontented at always being called out while many of the soldiers remained working.

Yet Frontenac and his subordinate officers can hardly be blamed for using the Canadian militia for war parties since the Troupes de la Marine had proved themselves to be of little use in guerilla warfare until they had had several years' experience of voyaging long distances by canoe, living off the land, and fighting as individuals rather than as drilled mass units. In fact, during the closing years of the war, of fifteen hundred regulars Champigny declared only some two hundred were fit for service with these war parties, but seven hundred could be utilized in a large-scale campaign where flatboats would be used for transport. "There is no gainsaying," he admitted, "that these are very wretched soldiers and that the *habitants* are worth incomparably more in the war, for voyages and for other duties." It was, none the less, the officers in the Troupes de la Marine, many of them Canadians, who led the war parties.

The regular troops were used mainly to garrison the forts, to work on the fortifications being constructed at Quebec, and as a labour force on the land and in the towns. In fact this latter function was their main one, leading to gross abuses that the Intendant strove to curb with little success. The system of allowing the troops to work in civilian occupations had begun as a temporary expedient under de Meulles. The soldiers, of course, much preferred this life to military duties, and the seventeenth-century method of paying the troops lent itself to abuse. There was no elaborate accounting system; periodically a pay parade was held, the Intendant or his deputy at Montreal counted heads, and the captain of each company received a lump sum to pay those present and accounted for. The officers became very adept at learning when a pay parade would be held and then, and only then, their companies were always up to strength.

There was always, and more particularly in wartime, a chronic labour shortage in the colony. Since there were no barracks in the colony, the troops not on garrison duty in the forts were billeted on the people. These men could earn much more by working for the *habitants* on the farms and in the towns than they received in military pay. Many of the officers were quick to take advantage of this. They themselves were poorly paid; captains received the equivalent in present-day money of only some $100 a month and thus they would release their men to work as civilians provided they did not object to their officers pocketing their military pay.

None of them did; the officers were able to see to that. Thus, all too frequently, when the men were needed for military duties they were not available.

Champigny eventually, in a moment of anger, suggested an ingenious solution to the problem; namely, marriage. He declared that the best way to curb the abuses and have the Troupes de la Marine serve the military functions they were intended for would be to marry them all off to Canadian girls, discharge them, and make them settle down on the land. After a few years of this they would become *habitants*, fit for military service in the militia, and the King would be spared the cost of their maintenance. This scheme was, of course, far too radical to be entertained seriously.

When Frontenac's subordinates began urging him to undertake a full-scale campaign against the Iroquois, he refused at first to hear of it. He maintained that it would strip the colony of its forces and leave it open to a devastating enemy attack. Then, early in January 1693, he ordered a raid on the Mohawk villages. Like Courcelle's campaign a quarter of a century earlier it proved to be a near disaster, and for much the same reasons. The force, comprising 625 men, reached the Mohawk villages without incident. Most of the warriors were off hunting, and no resistance was offered. The villages were burned and then the small army began the return journey, taking with them three hundred prisoners, mostly women and children. A few days later, over five hundred Mohawks and Albany militia caught up with them. After a brisk engagement in which the French suffered twenty-four casualties, they continued their retreat, threatening to slaughter their prisoners if they were impeded. But what the enemy was unable to do the weather accomplished. A sudden thaw made the ice on Lake Champlain treacherous. Food supplies had run out, and all but fifty-eight of the prisoners had to be released. When the cache of food left on the east of the lake for the return journey was reached, it was found to have been spoiled by the rain.

With no food and a hundred miles to go to the French settlements the men faced starvation. Four Indians and a Canadian were sent to bring aid but it took them five days to reach Montreal. Callières immediately sent 150 men with supplies, but before they reached the stranded army some of the men had died of hunger and exposure, and the rest were boiling their moccasins for broth. Eventually the survivors staggered on to Montreal, many of them completely incapacitated by the ordeal. No more winter campaigns were attempted; Callières was now convinced that they were too risky.

The raid was not, however, without results. It had been a rude shock to the Mohawks and it had come at a critical moment. For some time the

Iroquois had been disgruntled because the English colonies were leaving the fighting to them and they taxed the Governor of New York severely over it. They demanded to know not only why New York was not engaged in the war but why the other colonies were not fighting the common foe. This was a question that Governor Fletcher of New York was putting to the governors of New England, Virginia, Maryland, and Pennsylvania. When he asked them for aid in defending the northern frontier, all he got for answer was a curt refusal from some provinces and "good wishes" and a few bills of exchange for modest sums from the others. He was even more incensed when some of these bills of exchange were dishonoured upon being presented for payment. In mid June 1693 Fletcher wrote, "if our Canton Indians, who seem to stagger and are enclined to make peace with the French of Canada, through want of those usual supplys and presents which this poor Province cannot longer support itself under, and they should be induced to make up a separate peace, the ruin of the whole country would unavoidably ensue." He was not then aware that, while he wrote, a chief of the Oneidas was at Quebec, sounding out Frontenac on the possibility of a peace settlement.

At the same time, the Iroquois approached the Ottawas and Hurons, suggesting a separate peace and commercial alliance. This Iroquois proposal was clearly aimed against the French. To the dismay of Louvigny, commandant at Michilimackinac, and the Jesuit missionaries, the northern tribes proved all too receptive to the Iroquois overtures. Callières and Champigny were both convinced that the Iroquois embassy to Frontenac was intended merely to frustrate any plans the French might have had for a full-scale campaign against the Iroquois villages. Both the Governor of Montreal and the Intendant were firmly of the opinion that such a campaign would have to be undertaken the following year, 1694, to prevent the French losing control of the west, let alone to put a stop to the Iroquois attacks on the colony. When, in September, 426 recruits for the Troupes de la Marine arrived at Quebec, bringing the total strength of the regulars to over fifteen hundred officers and men, Champigny began having flatboats built for the campaign he hoped would be launched the ensuing year. Frontenac, however, insisted that he must have another five hundred regulars before he could undertake it.

In Acadia, too, the situation was not good. The province had long suffered from neglect on the part of the Ministry of Marine, and the destruction of Port Royal by Phips in 1690 had been a harsh blow. In fact, the only things that prevented Acadia being seized and held by New England were the bitter hostility of the Indians toward the English, the willingness of some Boston merchants to sell arms and supplies to the French garrisons whenever the ships from France failed to arrive,[4] and New England's lack of adequate forces to occupy the province.

In 1691, the Sieur de Villebon had been appointed Governor of Acadia. He established himself not at Port Royal, but at a post near the mouth of the St John River and devoted his time to fur-trading. Two veteran officers, the Sieur de Villieu and the Sieur de Montigny, were detached from the Troupes de la Marine in Canada and sent to command the regular troops in garrison at Fort Nataxouat on the St John River. Within a year of Villebon's appointment many complaints were received by Champigny from the *habitants* and seigneurs of the province. Villebon, in his determination to monopolize the fur trade, dealt with them harshly. What was in some ways worse, he retained for his own use part of the presents and supplies sent from Quebec for distribution among the Abenakis. Villieu also complained that Villebon was defrauding the regular troops of part of their supplies and consistently refused to furnish any aid to the war parties Villieu was sending out against the English settlements. Champigny tried to get to the bottom of these charges, which were too frequent and came from too many sources to be ignored, but it proved impossible to do anything effective from Quebec.

Under the circumstances it is small wonder that the Acadian tribes began to negotiate with the Massachusetts authorities for a peace settlement and a trade agreement. This dismayed the French in both Acadia and New France, for were these tribes to be lost to the French allegiance then all of Acadia to the Gulf of St Lawrence would be lost too. Despite, however, the efforts of Villieu and Father Louis-Pierre Thury, the French missionary at Penobscot, the Abenakis signed a treaty at Pemaquid in August 1693 with the Massachusetts authorities. Fortunately for the French a wave of religious hysteria was then sweeping over New England and the authorities were too engrossed with the detection, trial, and destruction of witches to take advantage of their opportunity to drive the French out of Acadia. The French were thus able to mend their political fences and induce the Abenakis to break with the English. In July 1694, led by Villieu, they ravaged the English settlements to within forty miles of Boston, killing over two hundred settlers. Two years later the English threat was greatly diminished with the arrival of Iberville in the Acadian theatre of war. Commanding two frigates, he took supplies to the fort at the mouth of the St John River and, after a short combat, captured a New England 24-gun frigate. He refitted his prize, put a crew on board, and proceeded to Pentagouet where he was joined by 240 Abenakis led by the legendary Baron de St Castin, who was as much Indian as French, and the Sieurs de Villieu and Montigny, with twenty-five Troupes de la Marine. On August

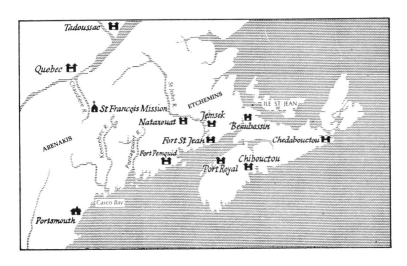

3 : Acadia.

14 they anchored off the English fort at Penobscot. Iberville sent the commander, Captain Chubb, a summons to surrender and received the boastful reply, "That if the sea was covered with French vessels, and the land with Indians, yet he would not give up the fort."[5] St Castin sent word to the garrison that, if they delayed surrendering until an assault was launched, his Indians would give no quarter. This, and five mortar bombs thrown into the fort, caused Captain Chubb to change his mind. His drums promptly beat the *chamade*, and he accepted Iberville's terms. The fort was surrendered, and the garrison of ninety-two men marched out, to be transported to Boston and exchanged for French and Indian prisoners held there. The fort's fifteen cannon were removed, the plentiful supplies of arms and ammunition given to the Indians, and the fort destroyed.[6] The results of this campaign were considerable: French prestige among the Abenakis, Canibats, and Malekites rose immeasurably, and these tribesmen now renewed their attacks on the English settlements as far as Andover, within twenty-five miles of Boston. With the Penobscot base destroyed, the Acadian fishermen were less liable to attack by New England privateers and at the war's end the French were able to advance their claims for the Acadian border to the Kenebec River.

Throughout the war, the French and the English had been able to injure each other in this area, but neither side had forces sufficient to hold the conquests they made. The New Englanders had destroyed Port Royal early in the war, and subsequently ravaged the French settlements at Beaubassin, after the hapless Acadians had surrendered on assurance that their homes and farms would not be damaged,[7] but the English settlements had suffered far worse at the hands of the Indians allied to the French. Now, just before the war's end, Iberville had ensured French dominance of the disputed border area by his capture and destruction of Penobscot. But this dominance was asserted by French naval power and the Indian allies; had the French had to depend on the Acadian settlers alone the province would have been England's for the taking. In 1686 the French population of Acadia had been 885, in 1693 it was just over a thousand, and in 1701 it was still only 1,734. That was the true measure of French weakness in Acadia.

At the northern periphery of the French empire, meanwhile, in Hudson Bay, much the same pattern of attack and counter-attack was taking place with the control alternating between the French and the English and neither able to exclude the other or dominate in the Bay for very long. The Canadian *Compagnie du Nord*'s attempts to control the fur trade of the Bay from Quebec, either by means of overland routes or by sea, had not been successful. By 1690 it was plain that this was to be chiefly a naval contest, fought by ships operating out of ports in England and France and trading directly between the Bay and these ports.

In that year, 1690, Iberville had forced the Hudson's Bay Company men to burn their post at the mouth of the Severn River and retire to York Fort on the spit of land between the Nelson and Hayes rivers. The French then controlled the Bottom of the Bay and England held only the one post, York. In that year, too, the Hudson's Bay Company made its first direct attempt to extend its influence into the interior of the continent. On June 12, 1690, young Henry Kelsey set off from York Fort with an Assinipoet chief and travelled as far as Lake Winnipeg, and likely beyond to the northern plains along the Saskatchewan. His aim was to establish relations with the inland tribes, to try to induce them to end their inter-tribal warfare, hunt beaver instead of each other, and bring more furs to the English posts by the sea. In 1692 he returned to York Fort. It is difficult to see that he had accomplished very much. Kelsey's journey is significant chiefly because he was the first Englishman to penetrate the interior, but it was to be a long time before English traders again ventured far inland.

The following year the Hudson's Bay Company sent three ships to the Bay. The Canadian company sent one. The English ships arrived first, captured the French post at the Albany River, and took the winter's catch of furs: 31,441 beaver pelts. When the Canadian ship arrived it could do nothing but destroy the other French posts at the Bottom of the Bay to prevent them falling into English hands. The total loss to the French was estimated by Iberville to be 200,000 *livres*. They had been driven completely out of both James and Hudson Bays. The English company was now supreme, but this achievement came at a time when the beaver market in England and on the continent was glutted.

Despite the state of the market, Iberville was convinced that the contest in the Bay was worth while and that the Nelson and the Hayes rivers were the source of prime pelts. In 1694 he obtained the Minister's approval for another attempt to seize the Bay posts. With two frigates he sailed from La Rochelle on May 10 for Quebec. There he enlisted 104 Canadians and six Mission Iroquois on a profit-sharing basis. They were to get half the profits of the trade until July 1697, half of anything seized from the English on land or sea, and they were allowed to trade one hundred *livres'* worth of goods for their own account. On such a basis these Canadians were willing to endure more and risk more than were the meagre-salaried servants of the Hudson's Bay Company. In early August they left Quebec. On September 24 they reached the Hayes River and laid siege to York Fort. Three weeks later Governor Walsh surrendered the fort. Captors and captives alike suffered severely during the ensuing winter; twenty of Iberville's men and several of the English died of scurvy. The following September, leaving the Sieurs de la Forest and de Martigny in command of the fort, renamed Bourbon, Iberville sailed to La Rochelle with 60,000 *livres'* worth of prime beaver.

The Hudson's Bay Company, however, still held the posts in James Bay, and in 1696 their ships reached Hayes River just two hours before Sérigny, one of Iberville's brothers, arrived from France with two small supply vessels. There was no hope of relieving the fort with the more powerful English ships commanding the river mouth. Sérigny sailed away to avoid capture, and the French garrison in the fort had no choice but to surrender. Once again, the English controlled the Bay; and once again superior sea power had effected it.

In Europe, meanwhile, England and France, both exhausted by the long war, were negotiating for peace. Both countries were, however, anxious to have control of the Bay before the negotiations were concluded. One French diplomat remarked that it would be well to recapture York Fort before the peace treaty was signed and decide later whether to hold or abandon it. Were the English to retain it at the war's end, he noted "we will never put foot there again and it is perhaps not unimportant to have the best beaver, or at least to deprive the English of it."[8] In 1697, both the French and the English sent out strong naval forces to settle the issue. Iberville was at this time in Newfoundland. After his capture of Penobscot on the borders of Acadia he had waged a swift and successful campaign in Newfoundland, destroying the English fishing-stations and seizing all the ports except Bonavista. Before he could consolidate his victories by driving the English out of the island entirely, his brother Sérigny arrived at Plaisance with the French ships and orders from Pontchartrain. Iberville was instructed to sail to Hudson Bay with the *Pélican*, mounting forty-four guns, and the *Palmier*, *Profond*, *Violent*, *Esquimeau*, and *Wasp*, recapture York Fort, and garrison it with one hundred men to make sure it was securely held this time.

The Hudson's Bay Company sent out the *Hampshire* with 56 guns, the *Dering* with 36, and the *Hudson Bay* with 32. On July 8 Iberville's squadron left Plaisance. The *Esquimeau*, a thirty-ton brigantine, was lost in the icefields in Hudson Strait. The supply ship *Profond*, a poorly armed *flûte*, was caught by the English ships. The crew put up a fight, but their ship was badly battered and they ran it on the ice. The English ships then sailed off, believing the *Profond* to be wrecked. Meanwhile, Iberville in the *Pélican* had reached York Fort on September 4. The next day the English ships hove in sight, and Iberville sailed out to give battle: one ship against three, 44 guns against 114.

The English were confident that they would finally settle accounts with their old foe and ensure, once and for all, their hold on the Bay. Captain Fletcher on the *Hampshire* bore down on the *Pélican*, the other two ships following in line astern. Iberville daringly held his course, and the *Hampshire* luffed into the wind to avoid collision. The *Dering* and *Hudson Bay* were then badly battered by the *Pélican*'s broadsides before the *Hampshire* could bring her guns to bear. The battle raged for over two hours. Then, with the *Hampshire* and *Pélican* sailing side by side, guns blazing, the two captains on their quarterdecks raised glasses of wine to each other in a gallant toast. That courtesy observed, a crashing broadside ripped into the *Hampshire*. The ship staggered, then suddenly sank on a shoal, taking her crew with her. At this the *Dering* made off, and the *Hudson Bay* struck its flag, only to founder during the night in a storm.

Next day the *Wasp*, *Profond*, and *Palmier* arrived. Iberville landed cannon and mortars and began bombarding the English fort. The garrison refused to surrender until Iberville threatened to launch an assault and warned that no quarter would be given. Governor Bayly again rejected the summons, but his garrison could see no good reason why they should lay down their lives for the directors of the Hudson's Bay Company, comfortably abed in England. They refused to continue the fight. On September 13 Bayly surrendered the fort.

And while these English and French seamen had died in battle on the icy waters of Hudson Bay, English and French diplomats were disputing in the Dutch town of Ryswick. On October 1, seventeen days after the

surrender of York Fort, the peace treaty was signed. By its terms the situation in Hudson Bay was to revert to that existing when war had been
declared. This would have required the English to hand over the posts at
the Bottom of the Bay, which they still held, and the French to hand over
York Fort. In fact, neither side made any attempt to adhere to these terms;
both retained what they held at the war's end. This included the £20,000
of furs that Iberville took with him to La Rochelle when he returned in
November. As late as 1701, when war once again had to be resorted to in an
attempt to settle Europe's problems, the dispute over Hudson Bay had not
been reconciled by the commissioners appointed for the task. If anything,
however, the French got the better of the many exchanges, for the posts
at the Bottom of the Bay were vulnerable to pressure from Canada and, as
Iberville maintained, the Hayes and Nelson rivers produced the prime furs.[9]

While a handful of French and Canadians in Acadia and Hudson Bay were
gaining the upper hand against heavy odds, in Canada and the west things
were not going well at all. When the Iroquois heard that troop reinforcements had reached Quebec and that flatboats were being constructed at
Montreal they hastened once more to send an embassy to Frontenac to
discuss peace terms. Champigny and Callières were convinced that they
were deceiving Frontenac, and he was equally convinced that his policy
had finally succeeded in bringing the Iroquois to accept his terms. Callières,
in a dispatch to the Minister, stated that the Iroquois aim was to keep
the French inactive in order to garner a good stock of furs, draw the western
tribes into a commercial and military alliance, and then reopen the war
against Canada with renewed vigour.

   Frontenac attempted to take advantage of the cessation of hostilities to
achieve one of his more cherished aims: the restoration of Fort Frontenac.
Despite the Minister's instructions that the fort should not be restored because every one familiar with the country advised that it could serve no
useful purpose in wartime and would merely be a drain on the colony's
strength, in 1694 Frontenac organized an expedition for the purpose. Just
as it was about to leave Montreal a dispatch arrived from the King ordering
Frontenac to provide a hundred Canadians to accompany Iberville to
Nelson River in Hudson Bay. Although Frontenac was extremely resentful
of Iberville and lost no opportunity to criticize him, even accusing him
of incompetence and lack of valour, he dared not ignore this order; and so
the Canadians, who were far more eager to accompany Iberville than restore
Frontenac's fort, went off to Hudson Bay to capture York Fort.

   At Michilimackinac, meanwhile, Louvigny, the commandant, managed
to persuade the Ottawa chiefs to go to Montreal to discover for themselves

that the Iroquois were deceiving them when they claimed that Frontenac was negotiating a separate peace with the Five Nations. A few days after these Ottawas reached Montreal, an Iroquois embassy also arrived, bringing thirteen French prisoners for exchange as part of the peace settlement. Despite all Frontenac's protestations, the Ottawas returned to Michilimackinac convinced that the Governor could not be trusted and that their only security lay in accepting the Iroquois offer of peace and a joint commercial alliance with Albany. Then, early in 1695, believing themselves secure from attack in the west, the Iroquois again began ravaging the French settlements. Yet Frontenac still refused to organize a full-scale campaign against them. He claimed that it might not succeed, that the enemy might attack the colony while the bulk of the colony's forces were away; hence it was better to remain on the defensive. His real reason for this procrastination, however, was his determination to restore Fort Frontenac, and this time he succeeded, despite explicit instructions from the Minister forbidding the move and orders to invade the Iroquois country instead. Seven hundred men were utilized in restoring the fort, and a garrison of forty-eight was left to hold it.

And while this was being done the situation in the west deteriorated. Now, the Hurons, the Ottawas, and also the powerful Fox and Mascoutin nations were negotiating with the Iroquois. These tribes were angered, not only by Frontenac's negotiations with the Iroquois, but by the fact that he had authorized a *coureur de bois* named Le Sueur to re-establish the old post at Chagouamigon where he traded fire-arms to their ancient foes, the Sioux. To them it appeared that the French were now allied with their old enemies, the Sioux and the Iroquois. The western tribes therefore decided to turn the tables on the French and ally themselves with the Iroquois against the French and the Sioux. French canoes en route to the Sioux country were stopped and pillaged to prevent them carrying arms to this old foe.

By 1696 the situation was so desperate, and the pressure from all sides to take action before it was too late so pressing, that Frontenac had to give way. On July 4 a French army of over two thousand men made up of regular troops, Canadian militia, and the Mission Indians left Montreal. Frontenac, now in his seventy-fourth year, insisted on accompanying it. The south side of Lake Ontario was reached without incident. When the army was a day's march from the enemy villages a red glow illumined the night sky some miles distant. Next day the army continued on into the heart of the enemy country, led by Callières on a horse he had had transported most of the way by flatboat to spare his gouty leg. To the rear was Frontenac, carried in an armchair. When the Onondaga villages were reached late in the afternoon nothing remained but ashes. The enemy had burned their bark huts and the stout stockade built with English help, and then had fled. Nothing remained to be done but destroy the surrounding cornfields and the caches of food. Vaudreuil, with six hundred men, went on to the Oneida villages to carry out the same task there. After three days of this destruction in the enemy country, the army returned to its boats and by August 20 was back in Montreal. The total casualties had been one very old Onondaga warrior too feeble to flee, who had been slowly burned to death by the Mission Indians, and four men lost to the French: three by drowning and one killed on the way home by a lurking Iroquois.

The campaign had proven to be little more than an arduous river voyage. Yet it sufficed to break the offensive spirit of the Iroquois and save the west for France. It had, however, been carried out not a moment too soon. Had Frontenac delayed another year it would likely have been too late, and had he waged the campaign two years earlier it would likely have had equal success. The Ottawas and Hurons had refused to aid the French in the campaign, but once they saw that their ancient foes were hard hit they immediately began sending war parties to harry them. All thought of a settlement between them and the Five Nations was now abandoned and the French alliance was restored. The Onondagas and Oneidas, their food supplies gone, were forced to appeal to the other three nations and to the English, who had little to spare. The Mohawk chiefs demanded of Governor Fletcher that the English combine their forces by land and sea for an assault on Canada. If this were not done, they declared, they would have to sue the French for terms.

Throughout the war the Iroquois had borne the brunt of the fighting; they had received little but broken promises from the English colonies. Nine years of war, combined with disease, had taken a terrible toll in their ranks. At the beginning of the struggle for the west their warriors had numbered some 2,800; by 1698 they were reduced to 1,320. Meanwhile, their principal enemy had gained in strength. Over six hundred reinforcements for the Troupes de la Marine reached Quebec between 1693 and the end of the fighting. In 1688 the white population of New France had been 10,523; by 1695, despite very heavy losses from disease and war, the population had increased to 12,786. But fortunately for New France the Iroquois had not been completely crushed. They now wanted peace, but a negotiated peace. Thus the negotiations were to drag on for another three years before a settlement was finally reached. And the Five Nations continued to serve as an effective barrier between the French allies in the west and Albany, forcing these western nations to continue to cleave to the French.

Ironically enough, the very thing that the French had been striving to save from Albany and the Hudson's Bay Company had now become a serious economic liability. In France the market was completely glutted with poor-grade beaver pelts. For the past six or seven years nearly four times as much of this fur had been shipped from Quebec as the market could absorb. By 1695 the Company of the Farm had three and a half million *livres* worth of surplus beaver that it could not dispose of at any price. The government in France had tried by every possible means to shore up the sagging market, but to no avail. Yet something had to be done to bring supply in line with demand. In 1697 the existing lease would expire, and under the circumstances it would have been difficult to get anyone to take over the Farm. This would have meant a loss of half a million *livres* a year to the Crown, already hard pressed financially by the mounting costs of war.[10]

The Minister's repeated orders to Frontenac and Champigny to curb the number of men going to the west had been of no avail. Champigny had certainly tried, but his efforts had been circumvented at every turn by Frontenac. In 1693 the Governor remarked in a letter to his friend de Lagny, who was in charge of Canadian affairs in the Ministry of Marine, that on orders from the King he had been obliged to grant several of the year's twenty-five *congés* to the Montreal hospital and to certain deserving persons designated, but that this would be of no consequence. "If," he wrote, "we have anyone else in such pressing need that we feel we should grant them some favour, we will let them go under the guise of a detachment."

By this time Pontchartrain had become convinced that the western posts served no useful military purpose and that the forces sent to them every year by Frontenac were responsible for the glut of beaver; every canoe load of goods sent to the west meant three canoe loads of furs coming back the following years. Thus, in 1696, with only a year left in the current lease of the Company of the Farm, Pontchartrain and Louis XIV made a drastic decision : to withdraw from the west almost entirely.

When Frontenac returned from the Onondaga campaign that had restored French influence and authority in the west he found a dispatch from the Minister waiting for him. It tersely ordered, in unequivocal terms, that immediately upon its receipt the office of the Company of the Farm was to suspend the acceptance of beaver pelts until further orders, and no more *congés* or permits for voyages to the west were to be issued under any pretext whatsoever. In October came another dispatch clarifying and amplifying this first order that had hit the fur-trading fraternity like a bombshell. The King now ordered that all the western posts, with the single exception of Fort St Louis in the Illinois country, were to be destroyed and the garrisons withdrawn. Fort St Louis was to be retained for purely military purposes; no beaver pelts were to be taken in trade there whatsoever. Merchants having furs or merchandise at the posts were to be allowed to send canoes to bring these goods back, but every precaution had to be taken to prevent them taking more goods upcountry with them.

Frontenac was extremely bitter at this turn of events. He informed the Minister that the edict meant the ruin of New France, asserting that once the French abandoned the western posts the allies would form an alliance with the Iroquois and Albany. He weakened his own arguments, however, by declaring that if the Sieur de Tonti were forbidden to trade for beaver at Fort St Louis, he and his associates would abandon it, as indeed they did four years later. Pontchartrain was quick to reply: "This argument seems very weak to his Majesty and it, more than anything else, has convinced him of the truth of the reports he has received that these posts were established to satisfy the greed of some of the officers rather than for the preservation of the colony."

Others in the colony quickly made their views known, and a flood of letters and memorials from Canada poured into the Ministry of Marine. Some few supported the new restrictions; most did not. Denis Riverin, one of the leading *bourgeois* in the colony, advocated abandoning the posts south of the Great Lakes but holding Michilimackinac and the other posts in the northwest. He pointed out that the Ohio and Mississippi valley areas produced only poor-grade furs that were a glut on the market; hence these areas were of no value to Canada. The territories north of the Lakes, however, should be held because they produced the prime-quality furs. He stated further that the English colonials could gain access fairly easily to the Ohio and Mississippi areas, but they could be kept out of the lands north of the Lakes. And even though it were possible to keep the English out of the southern regions by force of arms, why pour out blood and money, he asked, to deny to the English what was only a liability to France? In other words, he advocated that France withdraw to, and hold, the lands that were later to constitute the Dominion of Canada.

Even Champigny considered the new edict too sweeping. He advocated retaining the *congé* system and two posts, Michilimackinac and St Joseph-des-Miamis at the foot of Lake Michigan, but with much more stringent restrictions on the garrisons to prevent the old abuses. His proposals had much to recommend them but they proved to be merely academic, for the Minister gave way to the clamour from Frontenac and the fur-trade fraternity and modified the terms of the edict. In so doing he allowed all the abuses to continue and removed some of the beneficial features of the old system. Four posts were now to remain: Michilimackinac, St Joseph-des-Miamis, St Louis-des-Illinois, and Fort Frontenac, but the garrisons of these forts were forbidden to trade for furs. The ban on *congés* remained, but the Company of the Farm was ordered to accept beaver, at somewhat reduced prices. Since there was no way to ensure that the officers and men at these posts obeyed the new edict, it meant that the officers whom Frontenac appointed to command at these posts had a monopoly on the western fur trade.

Champigny tried to stop them taking trade goods to the west, but Frontenac refused to allow of any effective action being taken. When the Montreal merchants and their *voyageurs* in the west saw Frontenac's men flouting the King's edict, they too refused to obey. By October 1698 Champigny declared that a state of general disobedience ruled in the west and in the colony. Vast quantities of trade goods were smuggled out of Montreal at night, and Champigny remarked bitterly that the King's edict was regarded by everyone as a dead letter. By 1698 the surplus of beaver pelts in the company warehouses had reached one million *livres* weight, more than enough to supply the whole of Europe for ten years. In 1698 and 1699 the Company of the Farm sent representatives to Quebec to explain to the Canadians why a reduction both in the amount of beaver accepted and in price was essential. The Canadian merchants refused to accept their arguments, whereat the Minister declared that the colony must either accept the Farmers' terms or dispose of their furs in France themselves. The Canadian merchants, believing that the Farmers had been profiteering at their expense, rashly decided to assume the beaver monopoly. Along with it they had to take over the great mass of surplus beaver stored in France at a price of 700,000 *livres* and pay the Crown 240,000 *livres* a year. In October 1700 the new Company of the Colony was established, on borrowed capital; 50-*livres* shares were issued to allow all the colonists to share in the expected profits. Unfortunately, colonial optimism and self-confidence were no substitute for experience, acumen, and capital. Within a few years this grandiose enterprise was virtually bankrupt, and the Crown had to intervene.[11] It was to be a long time before the fur-trade economy was restored to health; not, in fact, until moths and rodents had solved the basic problem, that of the surplus beaver in storage.

In Europe, meanwhile, peace was breaking out. The belligerents were all exhausted, but some were more exhausted than others, and all were striving to gain a last advantage over the enemy before the final round of negotiations at Ryswick. William III of England was chiefly concerned with European dynastic issues, particularly that of the succession to the throne of Spain. He was, therefore, not eager to press colonial issues. The *status quo ante bellum* in North America would satisfy him. France, however, had gained an advantage here; all the English assaults on French possessions had been repulsed; Fort Penobscot on the border of Acadia had been destroyed; the frontiers of both New England and New York had been ravaged and forced back; the English outposts in Newfoundland had been destroyed and the island virtually conquered. Iberville had been sent to Hudson Bay with a strong force, and the outcome there was awaited with confidence. To gain an even stronger position and to forfend a rumoured English attempt to regain Newfoundland and attack Canada, in January 1697 de Lagny in the Ministry of Marine began drawing up plans for a large-scale naval expedition to protect Newfoundland against the anticipated counterattack, block the assault on Quebec by way of the St Lawrence and then, joined by Frontenac with fifteen hundred troops of the Canadian garrison, go on to ravage the coast of New England, capture Boston and New York, and devastate the settlements between there and Canada. The Marquis de Nesmond was given command of the naval force, consisting of thirteen men-of-war and four fireships. In April he received his instructions and orders to sail as soon as possible. In March a dispatch had been sent to Frontenac by way of Acadia warning him to be prepared to repel the expected English assault and to have a force of 1,500 men ready to join the fleet at Pentagouet as soon as Nesmond sent word that he was ready to attack Boston and New York.

These orders, making the whole enterprise appear delightfully simple, reached Quebec at the end of May. For the next several weeks there was frantic activity. The fortifications at Quebec were hurriedly strengthened; four hundred canoes were constructed for the expedition; and the necessary men and supplies organized. Then everyone waited anxiously for word of the enemy's approach and of Nesmond's arrival at Acadia. For over three months they waited, and nothing happened. Finally, on September 8 a dispatch came from Nesmond at Newfoundland to say that head winds had delayed his crossing and, the season being too far advanced for the projected campaign, he was returning to France. It is doubtful if the expedition, even had it had all the success anticipated, would have changed the balance of power in North America for long. It had been intended purely as a destructive pillaging expedition; the French forces would have been inadequate to conquer and occupy New England and New York. The mere fact, however, that they were able to mount such an expedition and the English were not indicates that at the close of hostilities the French were in the stronger position.

The following February the final act of the war between England and France in North America was played out when a delegation from Albany arrived at Montreal to inform the French that a peace treaty had been signed in Europe. They were anxious to apprize the French of this before any more war parties were sent against the New York frontier. With them they brought some French prisoners to effect an exchange, but to their chagrin all but two or three of the prisoners in Canada refused to return to the English colonies. Many of them were young children, ransomed by the French from their Indian captors. They had been cared for by the nuns or by private families. Most of them had been received into the Church of Rome and it was mainly for this reason that they refused to leave. It may also very well have been that life among the easy-going Canadians was much more to their liking than the bleak puritan atmosphere of New England and New York.

The Albany delegates were suspicious of this development. To make it quite clear that the prisoners were not under any restraint, Frontenac ordered them to appear before the Albany men for questioning, but they still remained adamant in their decision. Frontenac and Champigny, bearing in mind that there were several Canadian children held in the English colonies, finally agreed that all the prisoners under twelve should be obliged to return whether they wanted to or not. It was felt that children under that age were too immature to decide the religious question for themselves. The children concerned disagreed; when they were told they had to go back most of them ran away and hid. Frontenac had, reluctantly, to agree to round them up and send them to Albany at a later date. Those allowed to remain were, at his solicitation, granted naturalization papers by the Crown.

And in France a clerk in the Ministry of Finance made an entry of 2,808 *livres* in his ledger to cover the cost of clothing issued to fifty-two Canadians released from prison in England and sent to France.[12] They sailed for Canada with the next convoy. Who these men were, where or when taken prisoner, is not known; perhaps they were captured on the high seas, perhaps in Hudson Bay, or perhaps they were fishermen taken in the Gulf of St Lawrence or Acadia. Most likely they had long since been given up for dead by their families. With any luck they may have reached Quebec in time to assist in the *Te Deum* sung at the Cathedral to celebrate the return of peace. The people of New France had good cause to rejoice; they had more than held their own in this long, cruel war.

CHAPTER 13

Economic Development

Although the period from 1689 almost to the end of the century was dominated by the struggle for ascendancy in North America, absorbing French energies and resources, yet in New France there was considerable development in the economic spheres.[1] Despite heavy losses from disease and war the population expanded quite rapidly, to an estimated 15,000 by 1700. During these years the policy of the Crown remained that laid down by Colbert, to make the colony self-sufficient in the necessities of life. In 1687 Champigny and Denonville were instructed by the King, "this colony . . . will never be stable as long as it cannot subsist by itself, and the absolute necessities of life cannot be obtained from it."

The main obstacles to self-sufficiency in foodstuffs were the devastation to crops wrought by the Iroquois, the reluctance of the *habitants* to grow more than sufficed for their own needs, and the emphasis placed on wheat despite the fact that the soil and climate were unsuitable for this grain. Excessive rainfall and, in some years, plagues of caterpillars, frequently caused scarcity. Had it been possible to overcome the *habitants*' hostility to change and have them raise successfully the winter wheat developed in New France by the colony's outstanding botanist, master-surgeon Michel Sarrazin, then crop failures might well have been less frequent. Another difficulty arose from the fact that wheat, harvested in late summer, was not usually thrashed until mid winter, which meant that the amount available for the following year could not be estimated very closely before the last ships of the year sailed for France in November. Thus, the inten- dant, who had to provide seed grain and ensure that the wheat supply would be adequate for the troops and the civilian population, was faced with a difficult task. Under the circumstances, he was likely to over- estimate the amount of flour the colony would require from France for the year ahead. When there was a sizable surplus in the colony, as in 1694, he had to have it exported to the West Indies and to France to prevent the price in the colony subsiding too much and the *habitants* planting less the following year as a result.

Once the war was over and the menace of Iroquois attacks ceased, agriculture made rapid advances. New land was wrested from the forest, particularly around Montreal, as discharged soldiers took up concessions and the sons of *habitants*, who had remained on their fathers' farms for security reasons, began to clear land of their own. The decline in the fur trade also served as a stimulus to agriculture. Thus, the amount of wheat raised in the colony showed a remarkable increase during these years: from 100,971 bushels in 1688 to 160,978 in 1698.[2]

In some districts milling the wheat was often difficult. In winter, when slower-running rivers froze, and in a dry summer when the flow of water was insufficient, the mills could not operate. Where fast-flowing rivers or streams were lacking, as on the island of Montreal, windmills were built, but a lengthy period without a strong wind meant that the people had to boil gruel rather than bake bread. As early as 1680 Dollier de Casson, superior of the Sulpicians who were the seigneurs of the island of Montreal, proposed to build a canal from Lake St Louis to a small lake on the island out of which flowed the St Pierre River, parelleling the St Lawrence and flowing into it near the centre of Montreal. Not only would this canal, by diverting water from Lake St Louis, have increased the flow of the St Pierre, thereby allowing water mills to be built, but it would also have provided a safe water route for canoes around the dangerous rapids at Lachine. What de Casson proposed was, in effect, the Lachine canal. His superior in Paris, however, refused to allow the undertaking owing to lack of funds. De Casson refused to be discouraged and by 1689, with a large increase in population in the district, the need for more mills was very acute. He therefore proposed that the *habitants* of Lachine who had failed to pay their seigneurial dues should discharge their obligations by beginning work on the project. The Intendant Champigny issued an *ordonnance* to this effect on June 5, 1689, and a week later work began on the first canal in North America. De Casson estimated that it would take only two months to complete. This was later seen to have been dangerously optimistic. As it was, the Iroquois onslaught on Lachine of August 5, 1689, put a stop to it.

Eight years later de Casson began again. This time he wanted two canals: the original one, and another to divert a smaller river, the St Martin, into the St Pierre. After much discussion, in 1700 a self-styled, self-taught engineer, Gédeon de Catalogne, contracted to build the first of these for 9,000 *livres*. When the Sulpicians in Paris heard of this they feared that de Casson had taken leave of his senses. At this time Vauban was drawing up his plans for a system of canals to link all parts of France in one great water-route network, and some parts were being constructed, but the Abbé

Tronson in Paris was of the opinion that Catalogne was no Vauban. Unfortunately, he proved to be correct. Catalogne was unable to complete the work; he succeeded only in flooding some adjacent farmland and wasted 20,000 *livres* of the Sulpicians' very limited funds.[3] It is quite possible, however, that the canal, given proper direction, could have been built, and it would have proved very beneficial both as a safe water route and as a source of power, but the colony still lacked the capital and the professional talents needed for undertakings of this magnitude.

One of the worst problems with which the intendant had to cope derived from the fact that a large proportion of the colony's annual budget for the military and general administration was sent from France, not in cash but in merchandise. Much of it was intended for the troops, but the remainder he was expected to sell in the colony at a profit. With such a system the temptation was great for the intendant at Rochefort, who had charge of these supplies, to balance his own books at the expense of the colonies. Champigny and Frontenac frequently complained of short weight and poor quality in the flour and salt meat sent for the troops. One shipment, Champigny claimed, was so old and mouldy it appeared to have been salvaged from the supplies used on a campaign in some earlier war.

Another source of trouble was the merchants of La Rochelle. They had been granted a monopoly on the Canadian trade and in return were required to transport military supplies free of freight charges. They more than made up for this, however, by doubling the prices at which they sold their own goods in the colony. They also raised their freight rates from 50 to 120 *livres* the ton and their insurance rates to 20 per cent. These *marchands forains* not only sold goods wholesale to the colony's merchants; they also took a very active part in the fur trade. When they arrived in the summer they hired *voyageurs* to transport their trade goods to the west and upon their return in the autumn, or in the following year, paid them off, sold the beaver to the Company of the Farm, and took the other furs back to France to sell to the French furriers. When the western tribes came down to Montreal to trade their furs, they set up their stalls on the common and traded directly, in competition with the *habitants* and Canadian merchants. The Intendant de Meulles stated that they skimmed off the cream of the colony's trade, but he was prone to exaggerate. In any event it is difficult to say whether or not their activities were detrimental to the economic development of the colony. Some of them, for example, provided capital for such enterprises as the timber trade. A good deal more research is needed on this aspect of the colony's history before definite conclusions can be drawn.

Another group who sometimes engaged in this commerce were officers on naval vessels escorting ships to Quebec. In 1687, when the ships bringing Vaudreuil and reinforcements for the Troupes de la Marine made a record Atlantic crossing in thirty-four days, some of the captains and ships' writers set up stalls in the market-place at Quebec and sold off several tons of merchandise and wine. Some of this was wine and food not consumed during the voyage, but much of it the captains had brought specifically to sell, despite the fact that such commercing was not only strictly forbidden but regarded as highly improper for officers and gentlemen. One officer, a M. Guillotin, was reputed to have sold well over two thousand *livres'* worth of goods provided by his father-in-law, a merchant of La Rochelle.[4] It would appear that these naval officers were not the only ones to take advantage of their opportunities. Several years after Champigny's return to France it was reported on good authority that, with the connivance of a Quebec merchant, he had made 25,000 *livres* a year, twice his annual salary, by supplying the troops with articles of clothing on a repayment basis.[5]

The chronic problem of shortages and profiteering created another difficulty in the colony: one that caused a conflict over a fundamental economic and social principle; namely, price controls. Colbert had been strongly opposed to the old practice of fixing prices; had, in fact, been a firm advocate of the free-market principle, maintaining that free trade stimulated production and so established fair prices.[6] Pontchartrain, a remarkably humane man, viewed things differently; he had great concern for the members of society who suffered acutely while a free market adjusted itself. Here was a basic difference in outlook; Colbert concerned with the state of the economy, Pontchartrain with the state of society.

Champigny subscribed to Colbert's view and strongly advocated a free market in the colony, even in such times of shortage as existed in 1691. In a dispatch to the Minister he declared: "It is extremely important to allow freedom of trade if one wishes to attract merchants from France. It is only this freedom which will create abundance and abundance cheap goods." Pontchartrain, however, saw clearly that economic laws could be abused and he subsequently informed the Intendant, over the King's name: "It is a good thing to conserve the freedom that commerce requires but when the avarice of individuals goes too far and proves detrimental to the well being of the country it is necessary to curb it by every practicable means, even by legal sanctions, when other means fail."

Frontenac, too, did not share Champigny's views on economics. In times of chronic shortage the officers and men, the officials, and everyone on fixed incomes suffered severely from the attendant rise in prices. They demanded the protection of price controls. Economic theory did not butter their parsnips, and while a few months might be a very short time so far as the economic law of supply and demand was concerned, people could be reduced to extremes of misery in less time than that. Champigny claimed that he had inspected the retail merchants' books and found that they were making less than a 10 per cent profit on their goods. He blamed the high prices on the profiteering of the La Rochelle wholesale merchants. Frontenac, however, still maintained that there was no excuse for the price of meat being double what it had been before the war and he charged that two of his old foes in the Sovereign Council, d'Auteuil and Villeray, had bought up all the cattle in the vicinity of Quebec. He demanded that a meat market with rigidly controlled prices be established, but Champigny refused, claiming that it would be unworkable. Although the phrase "black market" was unknown in his day, this was clearly what he had in mind as the main reason why he thought the control of food prices would not be in the public interest. He finally settled the issue by calling an assembly of the leading residents of Quebec in order to hear their views. At this meeting, held in mid winter 1695, the consensus of opinion went against the Intendant. Bowing to the popular will, he established a controlled meat market in Quebec. The following year, when there was a shortage of grain and the *habitants* charged extortionate prices, he was obliged to abandon economic principle again and fixed the price at four and a half *livres* the bushel.

Second only to agriculture, in the stress laid on it by the Crown, was fishing. The King even encouraged the Governor and Intendant to engage in the industry themselves, the only commercial activity that was permitted them. Despite the best efforts of the Intendant, however, the industry by the end of the century could not be described as flourishing. The main reasons for this were the lack of capital needed to outfit fishing-vessels, the remoteness of the better fishing-grounds from Quebec and the even greater remoteness of export markets, the lack of salt supplies in the colony, and the greater attraction of the fur trade for most Canadians.

One man who did make a valiant effort to develop commercial fishing in the colony was Denis Riverin. Born at Tours about 1650, Riverin came to Canada as secretary to the Intendant Duchesneau, and a few years later he was appointed agent of the Company of the Farm. With capital provided by the Crown, being granted two fur-trade *congés* a year for three years, worth a thousand to eleven hundred *livres* each, he agreed to bring twenty skilled fishermen to Quebec from France to teach the Canadians the skills of the trade and to import the necessary equipment. Had it not been for the war Riverin would undoubtedly have had greater success, but New England privateers were a constant menace. In 1687 they captured the boat and equipment that Riverin had had sent from France. Despite this heavy loss he persisted and by 1689 he had twenty fishing-boats operating in the Gulf. When they returned with a good catch, other Quebec merchants were encouraged to follow suit. Fishing and trading stations were now established along the shores of the Gulf, on the Labrador coast, and in Newfoundland.

In 1699 the Sieur Vitré, a member of the Sovereign Council, received a Crown subsidy of four thousand *livres* and sent boats out for whales and porpoises. Two years later his ships brought back seventy whales, and the Canadians now began to give the Basques, who had regarded the white whales of the St Lawrence almost as their private preserve, some competition. Frontenac and Champigny were not so fortunate. In 1692, they went into partnership with two Quebec merchants, La Chesnaye and Pachot, obtained a boat that Iberville had captured from the English, and sent it off to Plaisance to get a cargo of cod, and from there to France for supplies. They expected to make a sizable profit, but before the year was out the ship was recaptured by the English and Champigny bemoaned the fact that he had lost four thousand *livres*.

The depredations of these privateers, who ventured to within fifty miles of Quebec, were a constant menace, not only to the fishing industry, but to the colony in general. In 1692 the *flûte St Jacob*, bringing supplies for the troops, was captured in the Gulf by a Boston privateer. Champigny, facing a thin winter since some eight to ten tons of supplies for his own household had been on board, estimated the total loss to be 200,000 *livres*. In 1694 two English brigantines cruised in the Gulf all summer and took another *flûte*, the *St Joseph*, bringing supplies to the colony, as well as a Quebec fishing schooner. The capture of the *St Joseph* represented a loss of nearly 300,000 *livres*. Some of the religious orders suffered heavily as their year's supplies had been on board. This, and other such losses,[7] greatly reduced the funds and supplies available for military operations, and Champigny became engaged in a bitter argument with the Minister over repayment. The Intendant insisted that the Crown must stand the loss, not the colony. The Minister maintained with equal vehemence that the colony had to tighten its belt and not expect the Crown to reimburse the colonial budget. Since the cost of much of the foodstuffs lost at sea had been deducted from the pay of the troops for their subsistence, Champigny persisted in demanding repayment and he won out in the end. In 1700 the Minister grudgingly gave in and the funds were duly credited to the colony's account.

The maritime war in Canadian waters was, however, not entirely one-sided. French and Canadian ships frequently took English prizes. One such capture was an English brigantine taken by the Sieur Aubert of Quebec while returning from a voyage to Bayonne in 1697. This prize was sold at Quebec for the tidy sum of 80,000 *livres*, and it resulted in a violent dispute between Frontenac and Champigny over the disposal of the proceeds. Frontenac overruled the decision of the prize court and the Intendant's rulings, then claimed a third share of the prize for himself. For the Governor to interfere in a judicial procedure in this fashion, and particularly to overrule an *ordonnance* of the Intendant, was very serious indeed, especially when there was a strong suspicion that he had done so for personal gain. The Minister was already out of patience with Frontenac for his refusal to abide by the restrictions recently placed on the fur trade. Both he and Louis XIV felt that this time Frontenac had overreached himself, and he received a very severe reprimand. His overruling of the Intendant's decision was declared to be completely *ultra vires*, and Champigny's *ordonnance* was upheld.

This incident marked a turning-point in Frontenac's career. A few years before, complaints against him to the Court had been summarily dismissed, and as late as 1695 his complaints of the Intendant's opposition to his policies had caused Champigny's friends to fear that he would shortly be dismissed from his post. After the Aubert case, however, the reverse was true. The Minister increasingly accepted the Intendant's recommendations and dismissed Frontenac's complaints. Frontenac sought to defend his actions in the ship-prize dispute by blaming it all on the machinations of the Intendant and his supporters at the Court who, he claimed, constantly slandered him. The Minister, however, scrawled in the margin of Frontenac's dispatch the terse, revealing phrase; "Il a tousjours mal fait."

One ship prize taken in the Gulf that caused no controversy was a New England ketch, taken in 1691 and carrying a very valuable cargo of salt. The lack of any native supply of this commodity was a serious handicap to the fishing industry. During the Onondaga campaign the army found some salt springs, and Champigny, when he heard of them, commented that were they only located closer to Quebec, the cod fishery would flourish. When he imported salt on the colony's account and sold it at slightly over cost to the fishermen to encourage them, the Minister took him severely to task for not realizing a much greater profit to augment the colony's funds. Had Colbert still been in charge it is unlikely that he would have been so short-sighted.

All in all, the fishing industry made some progress during this period, but it was confined largely to the domestic market. The Quebec fishermen could not compete on the French market with the fishermen from France. The cost of salt, of boats, equipment, food supplies, and the men's wages was far higher at Quebec than at the French ports; hence a catch cost them far more than they could sell it for. Only such specialized items as

CUL—H

eels could the Canadians sell profitably in France because Canadian eels had a much better flavour than the European variety and the river near Quebec abounded in them; as many as five thousand were taken in a day from one weir, representing ten casks full which sold at 25 *livres* the cask at Quebec. Unfortunately, smoked or pickled eels never became a staple of the diet in France, only a delicacy, although referred to by Frontenac as "the manna of the *habitants*."

The French at this time were not unaware that their North American possessions contained considerable mineral wealth. Ships called regularly at Cape Breton for cargoes of coal; samples were sent to the Royal forges in 1687 but they were found to be of mediocre quality. When the war intervened, interest in this source of fuel vanished. The same occurred with the porphyry on the island of St Pierre and the iron ore at Trois Rivières and Baye St Paul. Denonville and Champigny were very eager to have a forge established in the colony, if only to produce stoves which would remove the fire hazard of open fireplaces, as well as be a much more efficient means of heating. They had to admit, however, that the estimate of costs provided by the master iron-worker sent from France was frightening and only the Crown could undertake it, no one in the colony having that much capital.

The fire hazard of open, wood-burning fireplaces and cedar shingle roofs that needed only a few sparks to set them alight caused Denonville on one occasion to exclaim, "I am in state of continual alarm for my house and for the town." He and Champigny kept nagging the Minister to send out some tile and brick makers, and when Seignelay instructed them to have the powder magazine roofed with tiles they tartly pointed out that he was obviously unaware that there was not a single tile to be had in the colony. The following year, however, two Quebec *habitants*, Laudron and L'Archevêque, established a factory for the manufacture of bricks, tiles, and earthenware pots. The chief problem they had to face was the lack of skilled workers. Champigny pleaded with the Minister to have tilers, brick-makers, and potters sent out; he even suggested that if the Minister balked at the expense he could deduct the cost from the colony's funds. Whether or not they were sent is not known, but this factory did remain in operation until about 1700.

Although skilled workmen to make coverings for houses were in short supply, the people of New France at least had a master craftsman to make coverings for their heads. Monsieur Quenet, master hat-maker of Quebec, was doing so well that he returned to France in 1687 and engaged several more workmen. The Minister gave him every encouragement, paid his and his workers' fares to Quebec, and appointed him the official examiner to maintain the standards for the craft in the colony. Champigny was instructed to issue an *ordonnance* whereby anyone wishing to make hats had to prove his competence by producing a *chef d'oeuvre* in the presence of the Intendant or his deputy, which would then be judged by Quenet. It is unlikely that this duty took up much of the Intendant's, or of Quenet's, time.

One industry that did take up a great deal of Champigny's time was the production of timber and ship masts. There was more correspondence between the Intendant and the Minister over these products than all the other Canadian industries combined. The main reason for this was the vital need in France for ship planking, and more particularly for masts, once the outbreak of the war in 1689 cut off supplies from the Baltic. In the age of sail, masts were as vital a commodity to the maritime nations as oil in a later age. Without an adequate supply of masts ships became useless hulks, rotting in harbour, and a faulty mast could lose a battle. The best material for masts was the *Pinus sylvestris*, a tree which requires hot summers and very cold winters to ensure the slow growth, the proper proportions, and the retention of the resin that made for resiliency long after cutting. The most vital of all were main masts, which had to be some forty yards long and forty inches in diameter at the base. Only one tree in ten thousand was suitable for this purpose, and their price reflected their rarity.

The main source of these mast pines was the forests of Russia and northern Germany. The chief suppliers were the timber merchants of the Baltic ports, particularly Riga and Danzig. Smaller spars, however, came from Norway or Sweden. In times of war military operations could be seriously affected by lack of masts and spars; hence both England and France were eager to find a source in their American colonies.[8] It was for this reason that Champigny devoted so much time and energy to the establishment of the mast industry in New France. Just a few weeks after his arrival in the colony, in 1686, he reported that red pine trees suitable for masts had been found in abundance, and he had some cut ready to be shipped to the royal shipyards for inspection the following year.

Seignelay was very enthusiastic at the hope held out by Champigny. The French yards frequently had to make do with masts constructed from long strips of pine pinned together. Thus Seignelay demanded a detailed report on Canadian mast trees and sent out two master ship-carpenters to investigate. They found large stands of oak suitable for ship planking and at Mal Baie stands of red pine of twenty to twenty-eight inches diameter and of a quality they claimed to equal the best obtainable in Europe. To test the resiliency of these trees they felled one of the tallest they could find and let it crash down the mountain side. They reported that it bounded down the slope and landed at the bottom on its small end without breaking; which, besides being an interesting spectacle, appears to have proved its worth.

In 1686 a Quebec merchant, François Hazeur, in partnership with two merchants of La Rochelle, Jean Grignon and M. de Lorme, invested 50,000 *livres* in a sawmill at Mal Baie which employed thirty men and could produce 50,000 planks a year as well as masts thirty to thirty-five inches in diameter and seventy-five feet long. Other stands of oak and pine at Trois Rivières and Baie St Paul were found to be suitable for masts and ship timbers. At the latter place the Quebec Seminary had built a mill in 1685 which employed fifteen men and turned out 25,000 planks a year. Champigny gained expert help in 1690 when Samuel York, one of the prisoners taken at Casco Bay by Portneuf's raiding party, was found to be a master carpenter. He was quickly put to work at Baie St Paul cutting mast pines.

As to the quality of Canadian masts and timbers, reports varied. The experts continually being sent out from France all reported the quality to be excellent, and the Minister stated that the first masts received in the French shipyards were good enough. The Intendant Bégon at Rochefort, however, subsequently claimed that Canadian masts were of poor quality. Champigny stoutly denied it, hinting that Bégon was allowing his judgement to be swayed by the Pyrenees timber interests who had no desire to see Canadian masts enter the French market. Champigny also maintained that Canadian masts were not only of better quality than those from the Pyrenees but could eventually be supplied at far less cost, despite the excessive freight rates charged. Certainly in these early years they cost no more than did those cut in France since the Minister complained that they cost as much. Considering that this was an infant industry, requiring considerable capital outlay, high initial costs were to be expected. This proved to be as true in New England as in New France, and the English looked to this area for naval supplies out of wartime necessity, "with more regard to getting it than to price."[9]

At all events, Champigny made it abundantly clear that New France could supply masts and ship timbers of good enough quality at a reasonable cost. The market for these commodities was certainly there. All that remained was to get them across the Atlantic, and it was this problem that proved to be the most difficult to overcome, for not any ship could transport masts or long baulks of timber. What was needed was a *flûte*, a long, narrow cargo ship with a stern opening to allow the masts and timber to be taken into the hold, as they could not be loaded through a deck hatch. Moreover, the *flûte* had to reach Canada earlier in the summer and leave earlier than was the usual custom of ships sailing to Quebec, in order to return across the Atlantic before the onset of autumn gales. These wooden sailing-vessels were not stiff and rigid as are modern steel-plated hulls; they had play in their timbers which made them answer the helm in a rough sea almost like a live thing. But with a cargo of masts on board, a ship's hull was stiffened, as though in splints, and, with the constant strain from the thrusting of the ship's own masts under their large spread of canvas, they were less seaworthy in heavy weather. It is not to be wondered at, then, that the masters of the ships calling at Quebec frequently were reluctant to take the masts and timbers that were ready for export.

Every year Champigny complained strenuously about this state of affairs, and the Minister's usual reply was to have another master carpenter sent out to make a report. The Intendant protested that it was a *flûte* of six to seven hundred tons that was needed, not more paper work. Then, in 1693, the Minister made the awkward discovery that, of all the ships used for carrying supplies to Canada, only one *flûte* was of the right tonnage and dimensions to transport the masts. Top priority was given to masts on this vessel, even over the furs of the Company of the Farm, and in 1694 the King agreed to an annual grant of 8,000 *livres* to subsidize the industry. There could, however, be little hope of healthy development or profit in an industry when ninety masts were cut during the winter and too often the *flûtes* sent out for them could only take twelve. Yet despite all these difficulties the mast and timber industry did become established and Samuel York, when he returned to the English colonies in 1700, reported to Lord Bellomont that "ninety great masts are shipped yearly from the Bay of St Paul to France."[10]

The employment of this New England prisoner in the mast industry points up the serious shortage of skilled labour in the colony throughout the period. Before the advent of war in Europe Seignelay made an honest attempt, as had his father earlier, to provide some experienced tradesmen. He informed Champigny that such men were extremely loath to emigrate to Canada unless they were assured a much higher standard of living than they enjoyed in France. He managed to induce a few to go out but only after guaranteeing them a high salary and their passage back to France at any time, should they find Canada not to their liking. He instructed Champigny to see to it that they received the best of treatment in the hope that they would be persuaded to remain and train young Canadians in the skills of their trades. Under these circumstances it is not surprising that there were frequent complaints that artisans demanded outrageous wages and pleased themselves rather than their employers as to hours and conditions of work. Frontenac, for example, declared that these tradesmen had their heels on the necks of the *habitants*, charging three times as much for their services as was customary in France. And when Denonville was making estimates of the cost of fortifications at Quebec he informed the Minister that the work could only be undertaken if workmen were sent from France on a contract basis. To employ Canadian labour, he warned, would cost an infinite amount as an ordinary mason demanded three *livres* ten *sols* a day and a carpenter four *livres* ten *sols*; the equivalent in present day funds, as near as can be estimated, of $5.25 and $6.75.

One remedy for the shortage of unskilled labour was advanced by Ruette d'Auteuil, the Attorney General, who advocated importing negro slaves into the colony. Although French subjects could not be enslaved, since it was a basic concept that all Frenchmen were born free, there was no moral or legal objection to the enslavement of negroes. Thus the King gave his consent to Auteuil's proposal, but the Minister warned that in his opinion negroes would not survive the Canadian winters. In reply Auteuil pointed out that they survived in New England and he advanced the interesting notion that they would earn more than their keep were they to be clad in winter in robes of "dry" beaver pelts. In this way they would be able to survive and work in the cold and at the same time they would convert the "dry" beaver robes into "greasy" beaver, thereby doubling the value of the pelts. Champigny, however, was not impressed by this argument. He was convinced that the Canadian climate was unsuitable for negro labour. He suggested that any who disagreed could import a few slaves and prove him right at their own expense. Eleven years later, however, in 1700, Callières and Champigny asked that the officers in the colony should be allowed to import negro slaves to be employed as house servants, and the following year this permission was granted to all residents in the colony provided they could guarantee payment of the purchase price.

Had slaves been imported into the colony in any number they would have added just one more item to the colony's adverse balance of trade. Before the outbreak of war, ships came to Quebec from New England to buy grain whenever there was a shortage in the English colonies, but with the arrival of reinforcements for the Troupes de la Marine the export of this commodity ceased. Denis Riverin, in 1686, did send three ships with cargoes of wheat, flour, and peas to the West Indies, and Champigny did all he could to encourage this trade, but during the war years the colony rarely raised enough to feed itself, let alone a surplus for export. Pontchartrain, as had been Seignelay and Colbert before him, was at first eager to see this trade develop and, when some of the Quebec merchants showed some interest in shipping timber, barrel staves, and fish to the islands, he did all he could to encourage them. In 1695 he even informed the Intendant of the West Indies that sugar and rum would be admitted into Canada duty free. Since rum would have competed with brandy from France, this clearly indicates that he was eager to see the intercolonial trade develop. It is probable, indeed likely, that it was not Pontchartrain but de Lagny, the Intendant of Commerce, who was responsible for this policy. The latter was in charge of Canadian affairs at this time and Pontchartrain likely signed the dispatches drafted by de Lagny without more than glancing at them.

Trade with foreign colonies was, however, something else again. Colbert had encouraged trade, in all but furs, between Canada and the English colonies, but Pontchartrain was bitterly opposed to all foreign trade. With the war over, in 1699 a group of New York merchants suggested a mutual trade agreement. Callières, who had succeeded as Governor a few months earlier, and Champigny proposed that English cider and beer be exchanged at Quebec for French wines and brandy and that grain be traded according to need and supply in the French and English colonies. But the Minister, when informed of this, immediately vetoed the arrangement. He was afraid it would lead to the exchange of Canadian furs for English cloth and other manufactured goods, to the detriment of French manufactures.

Shortly after this injunction reached the Intendant, a ship from New York put in at Quebec with a cargo of flour, beer, and other goods. Champigny and Callières allowed the captain to dispose of his goods and take on a cargo of wine and brandy in exchange. When they informed the Minister of this they hastened to add that they would make it clear to the Canadians that trade with the English colonies was frowned on. This waiting until the horse was well clear of the stable before closing the door seems to have annoyed Pontchartrain intensely, for in the margin of Callières and Champigny's joint dispatch is the terse angry note: "Saisir et arrester tous sans miséricorde."

A few months after sailing from Quebec this same New York ship returned, and again the Governor and Intendant allowed it to dispose of its cargo in exchange for brandy. They excused their action on the grounds that since the New York captain had acted in good faith, they had not had the heart to turn him away. They hastened to add that they had warned him not to come again. Then, instead of showing remorse for their insubordinate actions, they had the effrontery to suggest to the Minister that, far from being forbidden, trade with the English colonies should be encouraged. "We are obliged to inform you," they wrote, "that this ship benefited the colony greatly, and if the matter were to arise again it would be fitting that we maintained this liberty, for if there is famine there and abundance here we could ship grain to them in exchange for their hard cash, of which this colony is entirely stripped." Pontchartrain, however, was not convinced. His marginal comment this time was: "Mal. C'est très mal."

This ban on trade with the English colonies gave rise, inevitably, to smuggling. Before the war the Company of the Farm had complained that vast quantities of beaver were smuggled to Albany every year. At that time the Albany merchants paid up to three times as much for beaver as did the French company; moreover, they paid in hard cash, not in post-dated bills of exchange. Since the Company's bureau in Quebec refused to accept beaver after October 20, rather than store it until the ships returned from France the following summer, merchants with beaver pelts on their hands after that date must have been sorely tempted to send them to Albany. It was, as Frontenac had pointed out, virtually impossible to stop this smuggling, since the Mission Iroquois of Sault St Louis were the ones usually employed to transport the furs. The colony did, however, derive considerable benefits from the smuggling. It brought much-needed currency into circulation, and provided the merchants with capital, which some of them – La Chesnaye for one – used in such enterprises as fishing and lumbering. It also enabled them to obtain the English cloth, strouds and duffels, that the Indians preferred to the more expensive and poorer-quality French woollens. Without this source of supply the western Indians would have been more likely to trade at the English posts at Hudson Bay than with the French at Michilimackinac.

The war, of course, put a stop to this traffic, but as soon as hostilities ceased in 1698 it began again. Callières did his best to stop it, posting guards on the Richelieu and farther south within the bounds of New York, but to no avail. The Mission Iroquois easily evaded them, and so did many Canadians. The Governor of New York tried to block this trade and with no greater success. He complained that Canadians were transporting not only furs but "great quantities of French silks and other goods to Albany from Canada which they convey to New York." Albany men were also voyaging to Montreal with goods, even taking horses and mares during the winter months for sale in New France.[11] It is easy to see now that intercolonial free trade would have been very beneficial to New France. It was not, however, so easy to appreciate this fact at the end of the seventeenth century.

Surprisingly enough, under Colbert and Seignelay trade policy had been quite liberal. They had realized that it would tend to strengthen the colony. Under Pontchartrain, however, the policy became increasingly more restrictive. He appears to have been able to see only that trade between Canada and the English colonies would benefit the English, otherwise they would not seek it, and anything that was good for the English was bad for the French. Even trade between Canada and the French West Indies was, in 1702, restricted to prevent them supplying each other with goods which might otherwise have come from France, and trade between New France and the English colonies was banned completely.

The extent to which the Canadian economy would have benefited had this export trade been fostered rather than prohibited can hardly even be guessed at. In any event the outbreak of war again in 1702 would have stopped it. Moreover, in the 1690's the drain of the war on the colony's energies and resources, and the overriding attraction of the fur trade, rather than Pontchartrain's short-sighted policies, were the greatest obstacles to the economic development of New France. It is rather ironic, however, that during the early years of the royal régime, when New France had little or no export trade to speak of, except furs, the government strove to encourage it by every means possible. Then, at war's end in 1697, when the colony was in a position to develop and expand its trade, which would have stimulated to some extent the entire Canadian economy, government policy sought to stifle it.

During the brief four years of peace between 1698 and 1702 the Canadian economy prospered as never before. Crops were good during these years, lumbering and fishing industries were showing considerable promise, occasioning comment in France.[12] The population was expanding rapidly, and more land was being put into production. In fact, it is possible that the Canadian economy was much healthier than is generally imagined. One reason for this is the nature of the historical evidence. When things went well there was little comment since this was expected; but when things did not go well then there was a spate of correspondence between the Intendant and the Minister of Marine. Thus it would be easy to be mis-led into believing that the Canadian economy was far less viable than it actually was. Once the ravages of war were repaired, and this did not take long, the Canadian people enjoyed a much higher standard of living than did most people in Europe. No one starved, no one needed to go hungry or ill clad, all had roofs over their heads, and fertile land was to be had for the asking by all who were willing to work. So conscious were the Canadians of these benefits of peace that when war again threatened it was suggested to the Minister that, in the event of renewed hostilities between England and France, neutrality should be observed in North America. "It is certain," wrote one memorialist, "that it would be infinitely more advantageous for Canada and should be preferred to war."[13] While it is true that the Canadians' relatively high standard of living was dependent very largely on the fur trade, subject to the vagaries of a single staple market, and a luxury staple at that, yet in this respect New France differed little from Virginia with its dependence on tobacco. All things considered, by the end of the century the Canadian people were relatively well off, and they knew it.

CHAPTER 14

Church and State

At the beginning of this period, in 1663, the State, in the persons of the King and his ministers, displayed a marked determination to suppress what they believed to be the excessive authority wielded by the clergy in New France. By the end of the period, in 1701, the royal officials in both France and New France no longer showed much concern over this issue, for the clergy in the colony were now manifestly subordinate to the authority of the State. This change did not occur overnight. It was, in fact, indicative of a change in the religious climate, not only of France, but of Europe. The flames of the religious wars had burned themselves out and now even the embers were growing cold. Then, as the politico-religious clamour in France, attendant upon the Jansenist, Gallican, and Huguenot controversies, began to subside, the religious outlook of Louis XIV underwent a change. His marriage to the pious Madame de Maintenon during the winter of 1683-84 symbolized and fostered this change. As religious issues ceased to disturb the political waters, Louis XIV became more concerned with his own religious well-being. His attitude was quickly reflected by the courtiers, and Versailles, previously noted for debauchery, now wore the air of a seminary – or so it seemed to one observer, Primi Visconti. Thus, it was no longer politic for royal officials to be too vehemently anti-clerical. The royal prerogatives still had to be guarded against clerical encroachment, but there was no longer anything to be gained by a great display of zeal.

When, in 1689, Frontenac was restored to favour at the Court and re-appointed Governor General of New France, the King's Jesuit confessor, Père la Chaise, was assured by Frontenac's friends that his attitude toward the clergy was quite different from what it had been during his first administration, and the Jesuits would henceforth have no cause for complaint.[1] This happy prospect was made all the more likely of fulfilment owing to the change in attitude of the clergy in New France. The almost fanatical zeal of the Jesuit missionaries of fifty years before had subsided. They no longer courted martyrdom at the Iroquois torture stakes; their *Relations* were no longer being published; they had, in fact, become political agents of the Crown, as well as evangelicals, among the Indian nations.

Of all the orders engaged in missionary work the Jesuits were, however, the only ones to have much real success. The Sulpicians had early established a missionary post at the Bay of Kenté on Lake Ontario among a group of Cayuga Iroquois, but by 1679 they had had to abandon it for lack of staff and funds. Frontenac sent Récollet friars to some of the western posts, but they served as little more than chaplains to the garrisons and the itinerant *voyageurs*. North of the Great Lakes the Jesuits stationed at Sault St Marie and Michilimackinac pursued their heartbreaking task among the Ottawas and the remnants of the Huron nation, but their progress was painfully slow, as they themselves admitted.

Farther south, in the Illinois country, the Jesuits also maintained missions, but they could not do a great deal for the thousands of pagans comprising the Illinois and Kaskaskia nations. In 1698, when the Iroquois attacks had ceased, Bishop St Vallier, full of zeal, sent three priests from the seminary at Quebec to minister to these nations. The following year Callières and Champigny allowed him to send two more. Then they found that most of the priests in the colony were eager to go; in fact, it began to look as though there would be a clerical exodus. The Sulpicians, when they requested permission to send missionaries to the west, were told by the Abbé Tronson, their superior in Paris, that they must remain in Montreal since to serve the people there was their primary obligation. Callières and Champigny, however, began to fear that, if the exodus of secular clergy were allowed to continue, the colony would be denuded of parish priests. The Jesuits, too, protested this development. They regarded the western nations as their private preserve and they refused to allow the newcomers to go among some of the Indian nations to give religious instruction, claiming that these tribes were attached to their missions.[2] Eventually, with the founding of Louisiana and the need to hold the tribes in the Mississippi valley in the French allegiance, there was more than enough for all the clergy to do in the southwest.

Far to the east, at Tadoussac, the Jesuits had long maintained a mission to serve the Montagnais, Papinachois, Mistassins, Outabitibecs, Algonquins, and other tribes. During the summer months a few ships called en route to Quebec and the Indians then came down the Saguenay to trade their furs. During the winter the place was deserted, as the Indians scattered in small nomadic bands throughout the mountainous northland, following the caribou. A more wretched, arduous existence it would be difficult to imagine, but the Jesuits chose to accompany these wandering hunting-parties into the wilderness; vermin, filth, disease, and starvation always with them. Despite almost incredible sufferings the missionaries had little success; the Indians of these regions lived an almost animal-like existence; they had to devote all their energies to the struggle with a hostile environment merely to obtain food. It was virtually impossible to impart to them the concepts of the Christian religion, and before the end of the century the missionaries were withdrawn to serve among more promising nations in the west. The Tadoussac mission had, however, enabled Father Albanel and some of his companions to gain a knowledge of the intricate water routes between the St Lawrence and Hudson Bay.

In 1683 when the Sillery mission became overcrowded, the Jesuits had established the St François de Sales mission for the Abenakis on the Chaudière River south of Quebec. By 1689 there were some six hundred souls in the village, all converted to Christianity, very loyal to the French and always ready, indeed eager, for war with their hated foes of New England. Farther east were the Jesuit missions at Pentagouet and Nanrant-souak in Acadia – the latter called Norridgewock by the New Englanders – founded in 1694. The tribes on the borders of New England, served by these missions, were maintained in the French allegiance by the Jesuit missionaries, by the legendary figure the Baron de St Castin, a one-time officer in the Carignan-Salières regiment who preferred the wild free life of the forest tribes who had adopted him as their chief, and perhaps most of all by their hatred of the English. In 1675 over four hundred Abenakis had been treacherously captured in time of peace by a New England force, some of the prisoners had been hanged, the rest sold as slaves in Boston. This the Abenakis, who retired temporarily to Sillery near Quebec, never forgave. During the ensuing years they were to be the scourge of the New England frontier and the main defence of Acadia. Here, more than anywhere else, the Jesuit missionaries, men such as Sebastien Rasle, were French political agents as well as missionaries.

Oddly enough, the Jesuits also had considerable success in converting the Iroquois to Christianity. Between the wars, during the years from 1665 to 1689, their missionaries worked tirelessly in the Iroquois villages and they eventually persuaded many of their converts to remove to New France where they became established on the south side of the St Lawrence, at the Sault St Louis mission across the river from Lachine. More and more converts removed there from the villages of the Five Nations, and in 1687 Governor Dongan of New York complained that the Jesuits had seduced some six to seven hundred to Montreal and added that more were "like to doe, to the Great prejudice of this Gov't if not prevented." In 1698 Peter Schuyler and Godfrey Dellius of Albany, after a visit to Quebec at the end of the war, stated that the Five Nations would be lost to the English alliance if the Jesuits were allowed to return to the Iroquois villages. They declared, "this wish for instruction in Christianity is the one thing that has made them leave their country for Canada." Here indeed was a convincing testimonial to the missionary work of the Jesuits.

During the war of 1689-1698 these Mission Iroquois performed valiant service for the French. Although they could not be relied upon in engagements with the Mohawks, whence the majority of their number originated, they harried the English settlements unmercifully and attacked the western Iroquois readily enough. They also rendered signal service in giving warning of impending Iroquois attacks. In all these actions they suffered heavy casualties. In 1692 Champigny declared they had lost by that date over one hundred and twenty warriors, killed and burnt alive. Despite all the blandishments of the Five Nations and the authorities at Albany, they refused to abandon the French. The English colonials had, then, some grounds for their view that the Jesuit missionaries were as much agents of French imperialism as they were of the Church.

Within the colony itself conflicts between members of the clergy and royal officials still occurred, but for the most part they were not so much clashes between church and state as conflicts between individuals. There were also conflicts between rival groups within the clergy, and when they occurred the royal officials quickly intervened to restore order. These conflicts indicate not any deep-rooted division between clerical and lay authorities, but rather that the French tended by nature to be a quarrelsome race, not given to compromise.

It certainly could not be said that the people of New France were priest-ridden. Just the reverse was true. Throughout this period there was a grave shortage of priests to serve the people in the colony. In 1665 there had been ten secular priests for a population of a little more than three thousand, by 1700 there were sixty-odd to serve an estimated 15,000 people. In 1683 de Meulles had reported that three-quarters of the *habitants* did not hear mass more than four times a year, that many of them died without benefit of the sacraments, and had little more understanding of the Christian religion than did the Indians who had never heard of it. And in 1701, Callières and Champigny pleaded for more clergy to be sent out from France.

It was, in fact, the lack of clerical influence in the colony that led to one conflict between the Bishop and the royal officials. The King, as well as the people of the colony, was very anxious to have resident priests established on a permanent basis in all the parishes. The Bishop of Quebec, however, could not see his way clear to do this to anything like the extent that the King and his officials desired. He maintained that the best way to utilize his limited resources was, not to establish priests in parishes on a permanent basis, but to have them all established at the seminary in Quebec and sent out on missions for extended periods throughout the colony. This also ensured that they were constantly under his control, and the royal officials suspected that his objections to the establishment of resident parish priests sprang from his reluctance to give up his complete authority over them. They also maintained that it would cost far less to maintain a resident priest than a roving one. The Bishop, however, maintained, and with justice, that in most parishes the tithes were insufficient to maintain a *curé*.

This question of funds inevitably led to conflict between the Bishop and the Intendant, both as to amount and manner of distribution. The priests maintained that they could not support themselves in a parish on less than 800 *livres* a year. An assembly of seigneurs, in 1680, declared that they could not and would not provide more than 500 *livres* a year. Frontenac agreed with the seigneurs. Bishop Laval had claimed, in 1678, that a *curé* required 600 *livres* a year and Colbert had rejected this out of hand, pointing out that there were over four thousand parish priests in France who had revenues of less than 200 a year.* Finally, in 1684, the King decreed that 400 *livres* a year would have to suffice for the *curés* in Canada. Since this was half as much as the priests themselves felt necessary, and a third less than the Bishop's figure, it is easy to see why the clergy showed little enthusiasm for the establishment of resident *curés*. It also helps explain the clergy's eagerness to undertake missionary work in the west in 1698.

Nor were the clergy able to derive much revenue from fees. In 1690 the fee for the publishing of the banns of marriage, the wedding ceremony, and the mass were fixed at six *livres*. In the country districts the fee for burials in a cemetery was six *livres*, and eight *livres* for high mass. Burial within the crypt of the church was always regarded as a mark of honour, but with the passing of the years space became short; thus, to discourage the custom, in 1690 the synod held at Montreal established fees of 120 *livres* for burial within church buildings at Quebec, 100 at Montreal, 60 at Trois Rivières, and 40 in country parishes. Children, however, were to be interred for half these rates.⁴ Vanity, even in death, now tended to be expensive.

By 1692 only two parishes had resident priests, and the Intendant recommended that the annual royal subsidy of 8,000 *livres* for the maintenance of the priests and the churches be withheld until the Bishop established at least twelve permanent *curés*. This threat appears to have had some effect, for the Bishop quickly established another three. The manner

---

* This, however, was a poor argument. The physical and spiritual condition of the rural clergy in France at this time was deplorable.³

in which the subsidy was to be doled out also caused controversy between the Intendant and the Bishop. The latter insisted that this sum should be paid directly to him to distribute as he saw fit, but the priests of the seminary objected strongly to the arbitrary manner in which he did it. Champigny recommended that it would be better were he to distribute these funds directly to the *curés*, making up the difference between what they received in tithes and what they required to subsist. A compromise was eventually reached, but the Intendant always maintained a close check on the disposition of the funds.

Before any new religious institutions could be established in the colony, the Crown had to be satisfied that there was a genuine need for them and that they were possessed of adequate revenues. When the Sieur Charon wished to employ his own wealth to establish a male almshouse at Montreal and had gathered about him a group of like-minded men who were willing to dedicate their lives and their personal property to the care of orphans, the indigent poor, the aged, the crippled, and all who were unable to care for themselves, the proposal was very carefully investigated before royal sanction was granted. Once this was given, control of the institution's finances was taken out of the hands of the donors and given to a committee composed of the Governor, the Intendant, and the Bishop.

The Intendant kept a close check on the endowments, revenues, and expenditures of all the religious orders. When the Bishop wished to see the Ursulines established at Trois Rivières, Champigny obtained instructions from the Minister requiring that adequate revenues be provided before royal sanction would be forthcoming. Similarly, when St Vallier, despite vigorous opposition from the Intendant, persisted in establishing a general hospital at Quebec to care for the indigent and the chronically ill, Champigny stopped him taking staff from the Hôtel Dieu to maintain the new establishment. Relations between the Intendant and the Bishop became strained, but Champigny refused to give way. It was his view, and the Minister's, that he as Intendant was responsible for the physical well-being of the people and he, rather than the Bishop, who would decide what the colony needed, and could afford, by way of social services. In these matters the clergy had to submit and take their orders from the state authorities.

The extent to which the clergy were under state control was made clear in 1698. In Lower Town of Quebec the church of Notre Dame de Victoire had been built partly at the expense of the local residents, who thereby expected that mass would be celebrated at a reasonable hour for the benefit of the older people who had difficulty climbing the hill to the Cathedral, particularly in winter. The Bishop declined to have mass said there after eight o'clock, and when the parishioners complained the Intendant insisted that it be said at eleven o'clock for their convenience.

In 1687 Champigny had informed the Minister that he would take steps to find out what revenues the priests received, the condition of the churches and presbyteries, "the manner in which the service was performed and the spiritual aids provided for the *habitants*." All this he very effectively did. Although he was a very religious man, considered by some to be on too good terms with the clergy, yet whenever royal authority over them was at issue he remained adamant.

The attitude of the people of New France toward religion is, of course, much more difficult to assess than is their attitude toward the clergy. The latter they rather took for granted and were inclined to pay as little as possible for all the services the clergy rendered. Any suggestion that the tithes should be raised they resisted with vigour, and they were very quick to appeal to the intendant whenever they felt they had a grievance. On the other hand, the clergy sometimes had to threaten to refuse the sacraments to those who neglected to pay the tithe, and in such instances the intendant supported the ecclesiastical authority.

At the beginning of this period many of the Canadian settlers had been very devout, puritanical in fact. With the great influx of immigants and troops the moral and religious climate changed; and, in the view of the clergy, not for the better. The clergy at Montreal, and the Bishop, frequently fulminated from the pulpit at the laxity of morals, the prevalence of an irreverent attitude, and female vanities which appeared to the puritanical to be scandalous. The ladies in the towns, however, insisted on dressing according to the dictates of fashions in metropolitan France, and Sunday mass was, of course, their best opportunity to display their wardrobes. Bishop Laval objected strongly to women appearing in church clad in luxurious garments, their hair elaborately coiffured, as though dressed for a ball and, what was far worse, revealing their naked arms and bosoms or "contenting themselves by donning transparent veils which served only to add lustre to such scandalous nudities." He ordered his priests to refuse the sacraments to any women who appeared dressed in this manner. Laval's successor, St Vallier, went further; he tried to stop the women wearing low-cut gowns in their homes. Needless to say, when the ladies had to choose between dressing according to the decrees of fashion or those of their bishop, the bishop's mandates were ignored. When the priests refused to administer the sacraments to them, protests were made to the Intendant and the Governor who were quick to intervene. When Frontenac complained to the Court of the clergy's strictures he received both the Minister's and the King's support. The Intendant Champigny, more sagaciously, referred the matter to the senior clergy in France who immediately brought pressure to bear on the Canadian clergy and obliged them to adopt a more tolerant attitude.

If the number of illegitimate children is any criterion, the morals of the colonists appear to have been relatively high. Between 1686 and 1700, for example, only eleven illegitimate children were baptized in Montreal. This, however, and despite the rapid increase in population after 1663, compares unfavourably with the forty-year period between 1621 and 1661 when only one child out of 674 baptized in the entire colony had been born out of wedlock. It must be remembered, however, that after 1665 there was a heavy influx of regular troops into the Montreal area, and such an event usually has an unsettling effect on morals. Then again, the number of children who died before being baptized, or who were conceived out of but born in wedlock is not known. Certainly the clergy were not inclined to be complaisant about such things. No more was the intendant, since foundlings were wards of the Crown and he had to provide the services of a wet nurse to care for them for a fee of 45 *livres* a quarter until they were eighteen months old, then he had to have them adopted by honest families.[5]

The seventeenth century was a superstitious age. Although in 1682 Louis XIV ordered that the prosecution before the courts of persons suspected of sorcery was to cease forthwith, many of the Canadians, particularly in the rural areas, still believed firmly in witchcraft, sorcerors, elves, and all manner of evil spirits, relics of a distant pagan past. Tales of werewolves and the famous *chasse-galerie*, a variation of the Faust legend, were recounted around the fireplace of a winter's night to generations of Canadian children; but these stories were as harmless as fairy tales. Persons suspected of being sorcerors, however, were regarded with fear, all manner of ills and misfortunes, personal and communal, were blamed on their activities, and the clergy were frequently called on to exorcise them with prayers, candles, and holy water. Individuals who today would be recognized as suffering from mental illness were then thought to be possessed of demons, and the clergy were at great pains to prevent innocent persons being accused of bringing the affliction on the sufferer by means of witchcraft. Those believed to have been sorcerors were, however, denied burial in sanctified ground.[6]

In the country districts, elves were frequently held responsible for mischief that today would be blamed on juvenile delinquents. The prevalence of these beliefs is indicated by the recipe widely used to curb the alleged depredations of elves in the *habitants'* stables. It consisted of placing a pail of cinders behind the stable door so that it would be upset when an elf entered. The elf then had to pick up the cinders piece by piece to remove all trace of his presence. By the time the task was completed the elf had neither energy nor inclination for his usual pranks. Very rarely did one return to a stable where he had had this experience. In the Montreal area a bucket of grain was used in place of cinders and it proved equally effective.[7] These beliefs and practices were harmless. Nothing ever occurred in New France to compare with the wave of witchcraft hysteria that swept through New England in the 1690's and died out only after nineteen men and women had been tried, found guilty of being in league with the devil, and hanged.

All in all, despite the frequent complaints of the clergy concerning morals, there is no evidence to indicate that the Canadian people were skeptical in matters of religion. Although the religious fervour of the earlier settlers had, by the end of the century, given way to a more secular outlook on life and the pleasures of this world come to have more immediate appeal than the contemplation of eternal bliss in the next, yet religious observance was accepted by all as meet and proper. Perhaps they took their religion a little for granted at times, since it was not threatened, but it was still a very integral part of the people's lives.

That a marked change in the religious climate of the colony had taken place by the last decade of the century is exemplified by a series of bitter disputes that arose in 1694. For a good many years the week preceding Lent, known as Carnival week, had been devoted to parties, balls, masquerades, and general roistering. In Talon's time Bishop Laval, supported by the more devout persons in the colony, had sought to check what he regarded as excesses committed during this period of organized frivolity. He had been made to desist by Talon and the Sovereign Council. During Frontenac's second administration the Governor sought to enliven the long winter months by staging amateur theatricals, culminating their activities in Carnival week. Some of the ladies of Quebec took part in these plays and all who had the entrée to the Governor's circle attended them.

At this period the more puritanical clerics still regarded the theatre as an agency of the devil and maintained that no one could even attend a play without thereby falling into sin. In France, however, only the *dévots*, the extremely devout, paid any attention to the fulminations of the clergy on this issue and, at the Court, plays were regularly presented for the diversion of the King and the courtiers. Thus, the clergy were obliged to be tolerant; but one play, first produced in 1664, had proven to be more than they could stand. This was Molière's *Tartuffe*, a biting satire on religious hypocrisy in general and the alleged hypocrisy of the *dévots* in particular. Although Louis XIV enjoyed the play's première, for political reasons he bowed to the storm raised by the clergy, and the play was banned by the Archbishop and the *Parlement* of Paris. In 1669, however, Louis had the ban lifted and the play was then performed to packed houses.

Despite the fact that there was no longer any legal obstacle to the performance of this play, when Bishop St Vallier learned that Frontenac and his players intended to produce *Tartuffe* he became convinced that the devil was loose among his flock and he had to stop it at all costs. He began by having a pastoral letter read in the churches of Quebec declaring that such plays could not be enacted without all concerned falling into mortal sin. This, however, was rather innocuous and not likely to deter the members of Frontenac's following. He therefore tried to stop the play by launching an attack on the Sieur de Mareuil who, he had been informed, was to play the leading role. He issued a *mandamus* publicly denouncing Mareuil for blasphemies and impieties, and denied him the sacraments.

Here, although the Bishop was on somewhat safer moral grounds, he ventured into a political quagmire. There can be no doubt that Mareuil was a rather unsavoury character but he enjoyed the protection of de Lagny, a very powerful official in the Ministry of Marine. At de Lagny's behest, and despite the Intendant's protests, Frontenac had, without displaying any enthusiasm, granted Mareuil a half-pay supernumerary commission in the Troupes de la Marine and maintained him as a member of his household. In October 1693, four months before the trouble really started, St Vallier had written to de Lagny to complain of his protégé's habitual drunkenness and loose conduct. He also stated that both Frontenac and Champigny had several times stated that they were very displeased with his behaviour.[8] Mareuil, however, feeling secure in the protection of de Lagny and Frontenac riposted to the Bishop's accusations by demanding a copy of the pastoral letter in which his honour and reputation had been impugned and that the identity of his accusers be revealed to him.

The Bishop replied two weeks later, on February 1, 1694, by bringing charges of impiety and blasphemy against Mareuil in the Sovereign Council. Since blasphemy was a civil offence the Council, over Frontenac's protests, instructed the Attorney General to investigate the case. Auteuil, always glad of an opportunity to embarrass the Governor, found that the case warranted a hearing, and on March 15 Mareuil was taken into custody for interrogation. Frontenac took strong exception to the Attorney General's handling of the case. He maintained that the entire proceedings were highly irregular, and it does appear that he spoke the truth when he declared that the Council was more incensed with the person accused than with his alleged crimes. During one session Frontenac lost his temper and made the serious mistake of declaring that, as chief of the Sovereign Council and Governor General of the colony, he could bring Auteuil to heel if need be. This gave the Attorney General an opening which he could not resist. He immediately quoted the Royal *Déclaration* of 1675 and the edict of the Council of State of 1680 as proof that Frontenac was exceeding his authority. He then declared that he took his instructions from the Sovereign Council, not from the Governor. Frontenac, whose blood was up, could not let this pass, and the sitting degenerated into a very heated altercation. Auteuil subsequently recognized that he had gone too far and he apologized to Frontenac for his offensive words.

The Bishop, meanwhile, made it obvious that it was not Mareuil's alleged impieties and blasphemies that he was chiefly concerned with, but Mareuil's role in the play *Tartuffe*. Encountering Frontenac and Champigny walking together in Upper Town, and acting apparently on a sudden impulse, he offered to give Frontenac one hundred *pistoles* – 1,110 *livres*, or roughly $2,000 in present-day money – if the play were not put on. Impulse or no, this appeared at first to be a very shrewd move, for Frontenac, to Champigny's astonishment, accepted the offer without demur. St Vallier wrote out a note for this sum on the spot, and Frontenac redeemed it the following day. In doing so he compromised himself.

Had Frontenac let matters rest there, much further trouble involving other people and raising fresh issues might have been avoided. Unfortunately, shortly after his profitable encounter with the Bishop he sought to put him in the wrong by submitting a request to the Sovereign Council that it appoint two of its members to investigate whether or not the plays that had previously been enacted were in anyway criminal, wicked, or vicious, prejudicial to the honour of God and his church, or harmful to the colony. Accompanying this request was a preamble stating that the King desired those to whom he had confided the government of his provinces to ensure that the clergy did not, on specious pretexts, extend their authority too far and institute a form of Inquisition. The members of the Council could have been in no doubt that the King and his ministers would see nothing wrong in amateur theatricals. Frontenac had cleverly put them in the position of being obliged to support him, and in doing so, implicitly hold the Bishop to blame for the controversy.

This action appears to have enraged the Bishop beyond endurance. He obviously had believed that his payment of money to Frontenac would end the matter and now felt that he had been tricked. He was later to demand of the Minister that the hundred *pistoles* be deducted from Frontenac's salary and paid over to the Hôtel Dieu and the Hôpital Général. At all events, St Vallier began flailing out at everyone who was even remotely associated with the Governor. He left Quebec for a visit to Montreal, stopped en route at Trois Rivières, and promptly placed an officer in the Troupes de la Marine under an interdict for keeping a mistress after having been warned to desist.

This officer, Desjordy, also enjoyed the protection of de Lagny and hence of Frontenac.

At Montreal St Vallier became embroiled with the Récollets, with whom Frontenac had close associations, and with the Governor of the town, Callières. Shortly after arriving in the town he attended a ceremony at the Récollet friary. As soon as he entered the chapel for the service he noticed that a stool reserved for the local Governor was in a more eminent position than the one he was to use. He promptly had it removed. When Callières arrived he, without a word, took his place at the *prie dieu* near the altar reserved for the Governor General on the occasions when he attended mass there. St Vallier took this as an intentional slight and, rising from his place, went over to Callières and told him he had no right to occupy a more eminent position than that of the Bishop. Callières, who could take offence every bit as quickly as St Vallier, curtly replied that he had every right to occupy it. At this St Vallier declared that he would leave the church unless Callières gave way. The Governor retorted that St Vallier was free to do so. At that the Bishop stalked out in a rage that boded ill for all concerned. After the service Callières, some of his officers, and a few others joined the friars for lunch in the refectory. Several ladies, among them the sister of the superior of the Récollets, entered during the meal and went about the tables with pouches, imitating the mendicant friars. With the food they had thus obtained in jest they held an impromptu picnic in the refectory garden.

A few days later St Vallier returned to the assault. He ordered the Récollets to remove both the stool normally used by Callières and the *prie dieu* reserved for Frontenac. The Récollets were quick to comply, but when Callières heard of it he had the stool and *prie dieu* replaced, declaring publicly that he would place a sentry over them if any objections were raised. At this, St Vallier placed the Récollet church under his interdict. The Jesuits and Sulpicians, who had long resented the presence of the mendicants, could not resist gloating; they now began to treat the Récollets like pariahs. Meanwhile, the Bishop had returned to Quebec, leaving Montreal in a state of great excitement. Champigny did all he could to effect a reconciliation but neither the Bishop nor Callières would budge an inch. For two months the Récollets complied with the Bishop's stringent order, but when all their appeals to him were rejected they finally defied him, reopened their church, and began celebrating mass for the public. Regardless of the injustice of the case they had now put themselves clearly in the wrong. Despite repeated warnings, not only from the Bishop but also from the Intendant, that they could only expect the most severe treatment from both the secular and clerical authorities, they persisted in their defiance. When, after three months of repeated admonitions, they still refused to submit, the Bishop placed them, as well as their church, under the interdict.

Although the Bishop had legalistic grounds for his action he was so blinded by personal fury he sought to justify it on a moral issue and in doing so he made a nasty situation infinitely worse. He published letters of admonition asserting that the superior of the Récollets had tried to compromise his Bishop by inviting him to participate in a ceremony at which the local Governor had been given precedence, and that he had permitted gross irregularities in his friary when several women had been allowed to enter and there behave in a scandalous manner. These charges were bad enough, but when he stated in thinly veiled language that Callières was guilty of an illicit relationship with the sister of the superior of the Récollets, he overstepped the bounds of reason.

Callières was, of course, highly incensed when these admonitions were read out in the parish church at Montreal. While the town was still buzzing with this juicy scandal, the urgent beating of a drum reverberated through the narrow streets. Rushing out of their houses the citizens saw the Town-Major, with an escort, march to the parish church, nail a document to the door, and post an armed sentinel to make sure no one tore it down. This was Callières's reply to St Vallier. In it he declared that the Bishop's accusations were completely false; that the Bishop sought to use these false charges to excuse his unwarranted procedure against the Récollets, and that the interdict against them was not only without just cause but contrary to the order's ecclesiastical privileges. He then went down to Quebec and requested the Sovereign Council to order the Bishop to make reparation for the gross insults that he had offered. There was, of course, nothing that the Sovereign Council could do in this matter, except to refer it to the King. When St Vallier informed the Council that he intended to take ship for France to inform the King of all that had transpired and offered to convey any documents the Sovereign Council wished given to the Minister, the members hastily declined. When one of their number, the Sieur de la Martinière, informed the Council that he was going to France on business they gladly accepted his offer to take the documents pertaining to all these cases to the Court.

Then, as though to remind everyone that the entire fracas had originally revolved about him, the Sieur de Mareuil escaped from custody. Assisted by some of his disreputable friends he broke into the seminary gardens, smashed some of the windows in the Bishop's Palace and committed further mischief on the steps. He was quickly recaptured and hauled before the Provost Court, along with one of his accomplices, and fined 300 *livres* and costs. When the ships sailed for France he was still in custody awaiting trial before the Sovereign Council on the original charges laid by the Bishop. He challenged the competence of the court to hear his case on the grounds that certain of its members had shown bias against him, and on November

29, seeing that the case would be long drawn out, Frontenac intervened. He sent the captain of his guards to the Intendant's Palace, where prisoners were held, with an order that Mareuil be released. He later read a statement before the Sovereign Council declaring that he was not asserting Mareuil's innocence of the charges against him and that he would cause the accused to be placed at the disposal of the Council of State in France when this high court had had the opportunity to investigate the charges, the evidence, and Mareuil's challenge of the Soverign Council's competence. Champigny and the Attorney General protested this arbitrary action, but that was all they could do. And there things had to rest until the return of the ships from France the following summer. For all concerned, it had been a hectic year, the events of which the people of the colony were likely to discuss with infinite relish and embroidering for years to come.

When St Vallier and the Sieur de la Martinière arrived at Versailles with the mass of documents and their verbal accounts of these strange conflicts, the King ordered that all the evidence in the different cases, six in all, be studied by the *Conseil des Parties*, or Privy Council, the highest court in the land for civil cases. After a very careful study of the evidence, the Court found that the pastoral letter issued by Bishop St Vallier, publicly accusing Mareuil of blasphemies and impieties, was completely irregular and highly dangerous, in both form and substance. Were a Bishop allowed to proceed in this fashion, the Court concluded, there would be no one in his diocese whose reputation he could not destroy. Opinion was divided whether or not the Sovereign Council should have entertained the charges brought against Mareuil; usually such cases were either dismissed or heard in a lower court of first instance, but since this particular case was a very serious one it was felt that the Sovereign Council could adjudicate. Eventually, the King ordered that Mareuil be brought to France on the first ship and its captain was instructed to hand the prisoner over to the Intendant at Rochefort who would be told what to do with him. With that Mareuil disappeared from sight and it is doubtful if anyone regretted his passing.

As to the Bishop's pastoral letter denouncing the theatre and all its works, the Court declared this to be innocuous enough. It did not contravene any secular laws or require the secular authorities to uphold it. The Bishop was entitled to air his opinions, and the people to disregard them. It was regretted, however, that Frontenac had not chosen to ignore this issue instead of raising it in the Sovereign Council. The Court concluded that the best thing to do would be for the King to instruct Frontenac to let the matter drop and also tell the Bishop that for the public weal he should cease to fulminate against the theatre since no one would pay any attention to his attacks anyway.

The Bishop's letters of admonition in which he had levelled scandalous charges against Callières were condemned out of hand, and held deserving of public apology but for the fact that the dignity of a Bishop's office had to be protected. For Callières's riposte there was sympathy since a man had a right to defend his character and reputation, but in publicly declaring the Bishop's interdict illegal he had gone too far since he was not competent to judge in such matters. The interdict on the Récollets and their church was studied in detail but no decision was submitted, probably because this was not a civil matter.[9]

All in all, the judgements and recommendations of the Privy Council were marked by clearheadedness and commonsense. A great welter of letters and memoirs on the various disputes were studied and most of them dismissed as unworthy of credence, being merely expressions of opinion by interested parties. The King and the Minister, after studying the Council's findings, found that all concerned had behaved badly. Frontenac was reprimanded for his highhanded actions in the Sovereign Council and the Minister tartly informed him that the matter of the hundred *pistoles* "does not show you in any too favourable a light." The King had been particularly incensed by Frontenac's claim, at one point, to the title of chief and president of the Sovereign Council. Pontchartrain stated, with some bitterness, that he had had to assure the King that this could only have been a slip of the tongue. "I beg of you," he wrote, "be very careful never to do anything like this again."

The Attorney General was warned that he had come close to being dismissed from office, told never to behave with such disrespect for the Governor's rank and person again, and ordered to apologize to Frontenac in front of witnesses. Champigny was informed that neither the King nor the Minister saw any reason to commend him for the role he had played and he was severely criticized for not having supported Frontenac with greater vigour and aided him to keep the Bishop within bounds. Callières was tersely informed that it would have been far better had he behaved with moderation instead of carrying things to such extremes.

Although the King and the Minister of Marine voiced their displeasure with all concerned, there was no doubt in their minds, or in anyone else's, that the originator of all the trouble had been Bishop St Vallier. In France he very quickly alienated everyone at the Court, including the clergy. The members of the Missions Etrangères, the parent order of the Quebec seminary, refused to have him under their roof and he was obliged to stay with the Sulpicians who, although they tried, failed to find a satisfactory excuse to avoid extending him their hospitality. François de Callières, one of the King's four private secretaries and brother of the Governor of Montreal, tried to achieve a face-saving settlement with him, but when he broke their verbal agreement Callières used his considerable influence against him. St Vallier made one attempt to heal the breach with Frontenac through the Comtesse de Frontenac, but she would have none of it and they quarrelled violently.

By this time the King, the Minister, the Archbishop of Paris, the King's confessor Père la Chaise, and the *quondam* Bishop of Quebec Monseigneur Laval were convinced that St Vallier was completely unfitted for the see at Quebec. While St Vallier was in France, Laval wrote to the Archbishop of Paris declaring that his successor was quite incapable of taking advice from anyone since he believed the episcopal office somehow imbued him with insights and wisdom that precluded his ever being in error. Rumours quickly began to circulate in Paris and at the Court that the King would forbid St Vallier to return to Quebec; they were even reported in Netherlands' news sheets. This merely made St Vallier all the more determined to return. When some of his friends advised him not to, he declared he must; not to do so would be a victory for Frontenac and for the secular authority over the church, and the position of future bishops would be gravely weakened. Although Louis XIV would have liked to forbid St Vallier to return to New France, such a move was made difficult because the senior clergy refused to entertain the suggestion that he be given a post of equivalent status in France. On one pretext and another, however, St Vallier was kept in France until the summer of 1697. During his three years' absence from Quebec, tempers in the colony cooled; the Grand Vicar and the Intendant were able to smooth over the trouble with the Récollets and to restore peace among the clergy. Thus it was mainly the authority of the State, judicially exercised, that finally resolved this violent conflict among the clergy, and the authority and influence of the State over the Church was, as a result, considerably enhanced.

Throughout this time of troubles Frontenac had behaved with, for him, quite exemplarly restraint. He had suffered considerable abuse from the Bishop and also, indirectly, from some other of the clergy, without responding in kind. It was perhaps relatively easy for him to so conduct himself, since the Bishop had put himself so clearly in the wrong. When St Vallier first returned to Quebec in 1697 everyone was on edge, fearful lest something should cause the sparks to fly, but to everyone's relief nothing happened. During the Bishop's three years of exile much had occurred in the colony to divert people's attention. The Iroquois country had been successfully invaded and their attacks on the colony had now ceased. The crisis in the beaver trade and the new restrictive regulations on the western posts had caused considerable alarm. Early in 1698 came the news that the war with England and her colonies was over. The people in the colony had plenty to occupy their minds without concerning themselves too much with past clerical squabbles.

Then, toward the close of 1698, Frontenac and St Vallier were finally reconciled. For some little while Frontenac had suffered from asthma, which made it necessary for him to sleep propped up in an armchair. His condition gradually worsened, and on November 16 his physician had to inform him that he was nearing his end. A few days later he requested that he be given the eucharist. Bishop St Vallier himself went to the Château to administer it and gave instructions that the church bells were to toll. Frontenac then made his will, a very unrevealing document, bequeathing the bulk of his estate to his wife, and made his peace with Champigny with whom he had recently been disputing vigorously. On November 28, after receiving extreme unction from the Bishop, he quietly departed this world.

Possessed of great personal charm and highly skilled in the wiles of the courtier, Frontenac was always very adroit at making events redound to his credit, and throwing the blame on others when things went wrong. He was really a product an earlier, more turbulent age in the history of France and he was never able to accommodate himself to the age of Louis XIV when the ministers, intendants, and *commis* were creating a tidy bureaucratic administrative system. As a consequence of his conflicts with the colonial officials, the King and the Minister of Marine had been obliged to place limits on the powers of a governor and devise means to protect the humbler subjects from oppression. Although his subordinates, Callières, Vaudreuil, Champigny, and Iberville were mainly responsible for the successful defence of French territory, and his encouragement of western expansion created problems that were never to be satisfactorily solved, yet the fact remains that under him the English assaults had been beaten off, the Iroquois finally subdued, and French power extended far into the west. It was, however, not so much Frontenac who made this period in Canada's history so significant and colourful, but the clash of forces struggling for control of a continent that imparted to him his particular panache.

Although Frontenac's relations with the clergy had been uneasy at best, stormy at worst, yet they did not so much reflect his personal views as they did the attitudes of the Crown toward the Church. During his first administration his conflicts with the Jesuits had reflected the Gallican-ultramontane controversy at the Court. Similarly, his more accommodating attitude toward the clergy, his lack of combativeness, during his second administration reflected the changes that had taken place in France. When the Crown took over the colony in 1663 the clergy had still been quite militant, ready to fight over such issues as the brandy trade. By the end of the century they were anxious to avoid trouble, even if that meant subservience to royal authority. Religious zeal and fervour had subsided, Erastianism had begun to creep in.

CHAPTER 15

End of an Era

During the last quarter of the seventeenth century French policy in North America veered steadily away from the compact colony policy originally laid down by Colbert toward one of real, if unavowed, imperialism. In 1696 Louis XIV and the Minister of Marine had made a determined effort to return to Colbert's policy by ordering the abandonment of all but one post in the west, and this post in the Illinois country was to be retained merely to aid in quelling the Iroquois. This attempt to give the west back to the Indians had failed. The opposition of the fur-trading fraternity and the royal officials in New France made such a policy untenable. Whether the government at Versailles liked it or not, the French were committed in the interior of the continent. Colbert's policy had clearly been moribund for some time, since 1675 in fact, but it still had to wait on events in Europe to allow of its being officially interred.

Meanwhile, in New France more immediate problems had to be solved, and upon the death of Frontenac the most urgent was to discover who would succeed as Governor General. Within the colony itself there were two contenders for the post: Callières and Vaudreuil. Champigny sent word to Callières at Montreal informing him of Frontenac's demise and delayed writing to the Court, expecting a reply from Callières, either in person or by letter, but none came. Callières, without informing Champigny, on December 9 secretly sent the Sieur de Courtemanche to France by way of Albany and New England with letters to the Minister and to his own brother, the King's first secretary, soliciting the appointment.

By December 26 Vaudreuil, who was at Quebec, and Champigny either learned what Callières had done or surmised that he had done it. They therefore sent the Sieur de Vincelotte post-haste to New England with funds to hire a ship for France in the hopes of their dispatches reaching the Court before Callières's did. In his dispatch, dated December 22, Champigny informed the Minister of the circumstances of Frontenac's death and paid the old Governor a rather grudging, yet still touching, tribute:

> . . . the Comte de Frontenac died on the 28th of November last with the senti-
> ments of a true Christian. You may perhaps find it hard to believe, my lord,
> that I was deeply moved by his death in spite of the strained relations that
> had existed between us. The truth of the matter is that our misunderstand-
> ings sprang solely from a divergence of opinion as to what was best for the
> King's service. As private persons, we never quarrelled. Also I must state
> that during his last illness he used me most civilly; it would be ungrateful
> of me not to acknowledge the fact.

But he then went on to say:

> . . . the foremost favour that I could ask of you, my lord, is that you send
> us a Governor who has no other aim but to carry out the King's orders and
> enable me to act in concert with him with the deference that is his due, and
> always to abide by my instructions. In truth, my lord, it is hard on a man
> who wishes to serve the King well to see the contrary.

The man whom Champigny wished to see appointed was Vaudreuil, and in his dispatch he laid emphasis on Callières's infirmities. Vaudreuil, in his letter to the Minister couched in the rough, semi-literate French of a man more accustomed to holding a sword than a quill, bluntly asked for the appointment. He mentioned his thirty years of service, twelve of them in Canada, gave the Maréchales de Nouailles and de Choiseul, and a M. de Mopertuy (sic) as references, and then pointed out that unlike Callières he was not disabled by ill health.

Callières's envoy reached the Court only a short time ahead of Vince-lotte. He delivered his dispatches to François de Callières, who was able to gain immediate access to the King and press his brother's suit. Vincelotte, upon his arrival at Versailles, unaware that Courtemanche had preceded him, delivered Vaudreuil's and Champigny's dispatches to the Minister. When Pontchartrain went to the King to inform him of Frontenac's death he was told that Louis had been informed and had been pleased to appoint Callières Governor General of New France. The race across the Atlantic had indeed been close.

It is sometimes asserted that Champigny was himself a contender for the governor's post. There is no evidence to support such an assertion and much to refute it. There was, however, a third contender – Captain de Beaujeu, the naval officer who had commanded the ships in La Salle's ill-fated expedition to found a colony at the mouth of the Mississippi.[1] But his bid for the appointment arrived much too late.

Vaudreuil was given the now vacant post of Governor of Montreal and at the same time he was granted a commission to act as Governor General in the colony whenever Callières might be absent. This automatically strengthened his claims to succeed upon the latter's death or retirement, and it may have been felt that were the state of Callières's health as bad as Vaudreuil had claimed, then he should not mind waiting just a little while longer. He had, in fact, to wait four years. During those years relations between them were cool and there were occasional disputes, but no serious trouble. Between Champigny and Callières there was also some friction. Callières, from youth, had been an officer accustomed to command and be obeyed without question. He had commanded the troops throughout the Iroquois war and had been allowed a free hand by Frontenac in its tactical direction. In recognition of his services, in 1694, he had been made a Chevalier of the Order of St Louis, a much-coveted honour and one that Frontenac did not receive until 1697, much to his annoyance. As Governor General of Quebec, however, Callières had, on occasion, to defer to the views of the civilian intendant and this did not come easily to him. Samuel York, an English prisoner who spent ten years in the colony, summed up the general opinion of Callières very succinctly: "The present Governor of Canada is very severe, and not at all beloved by the French or Indians." He was definitely not the type of officer who courted popularity, but he did gain the grudging respect of his subordinates, and on policy matters Champigny and Vaudreuil were in complete agreement with him.

The most pressing problem that Callières had to face upon assuming the Governor General's powers was to negotiate a peace settlement with the Iroquois, one that could be expected to endure. What made this task such a difficult one was the need to include all the Indian tribes allied to the French, some of whom had warred with the Iroquois for longer than anyone could remember; had, in fact, been enemies before the first Frenchmen set foot in North America. To complicate matters the Earl of Bellomont, recently appointed Governor of New York, maintained that the Five Nations were under the suzerainty of His Britannic Majesty and hence no treaty could be negotiated with them without his sanction and participation. Callières refused to accept this claim and he astutely turned it against Bellomont. When an Iroquois embassy came to Montreal to discuss terms, he demanded to know if they could speak for the Five Nations since the English Governor at Albany declared them to be his subjects and unable to speak for themselves. Thus taunted, the Iroquois chiefs haughtily declared that they were no one's subjects; never having been conquered by either the French or the English, they were their own masters, and to prove it they began negotiating in earnest.

At the request of the Iroquois, Callières sent the Jesuit Father Bruyas, the Sieur le Moyne de Maricourt, and the Sieur Joncaire to Onondaga to settle the details of the treaty. All three were men highly respected by the Iroquois. Joncaire, who had been taken prisoner during the war, had impressed them so much by his courage in the face of torture that they had spared his life and adopted him into their nation. Bellomont had no men of their stature whom he could employ in his dealings with the Five Nations. Thus, when they spoke in the council meeting at Onondaga and an Albany official forbade the Iroquois to hear them, Father Bruyas quickly asked if the warriors of the Five Nations had become the dogs of the English, or their prisoners, or did the English wish to have war again? That was enough to silence the Albany delegate.

The really thorny question, the one which caused the negotiations to drag on for over two years, concerned prisoners of war. All the nations involved, Iroquois, French, and their allies alike, demanded the return of prisoners, but those captives who had had their lives spared by the Iroquois had been adopted into the families of their captors. Had this not been the case they would not have survived as prisoners. In fact, the Iroquois strength would have been far less than it actually was had they not incorporated many of their prisoners into their own ranks. Thus they were loath to give them up. Moreover, many of these prisoners refused to return to their own people when given the opportunity. Even some of the French, particularly the younger ones, refused to return to Canada, preferring the free, irresponsible life of the forest hunter to the restraints of civilization. Some fifty to sixty French captives did, however, return to New France, and Callières had finally to admit that the Iroquois appeared to be sincere. Although this question was not yet completely resolved, the treaty was agreed to and in July 1701 some thirteen hundred Indians from over thirty nations, from as far afield as the shores of the Atlantic to beyond the Mississippi and northwest to Lake of the Woods, gathered at Montreal.

Callières, Champigny, and Vaudreuil imposed a very strict ban on liquor while the Indians were there. Had they not done so, the narrow streets within the town walls, and the common stretching down to the river where the Indians encamped, would more likely have been a scene of horrible carnage than one of peaceful negotiations. These must have been nervous times for the people of Montreal as the speeches went on and on, day after day, with the interminable parables and allegories so dear to the Indian orator, with charges and counter-charges being flung back and forth and nerves becoming visibly frayed. Inevitably, the question of prisoners proved the chief stumbling-block, but a compromise solution was finally reached. All the nations agreed to leave this question to Callières to resolve as best he could. After a great feast that must have taxed the culinary resources of Montreal to the limit, the treaty was finally drawn up and signed by the leading officials of New France. The chiefs of all the Indian nations then drew on the document the symbol of their clan or tribe until it was covered with crude sketches of forest animals. Louis XIV and his ministers may well have been slightly nonplussed upon receiving this document and noting that some of the Indian signatories had indulged their earthy penchant for boasting of their virility in symbolical fashion.

The successful outcome of these extremely difficult negotiations was a very great achievement indeed. Not only had all the conflicting claims, counter-claims, charges, and counter-charges of these ancient foes been reconciled, but the Iroquois had finally accepted defeat in their near-century-long struggle to seize control of the western fur trade from the French. Yet they still remained strong enough to serve as a barrier between the western nations and Albany. This ensured that the fur trade of the west would continue to pass through Montreal to France rather than through Albany to London.

An even more significant aspect of the treaty was incorporated in one vital clause that Callières had managed to have included, a clause that altered the balance of power in North America in favour of the French. Callières had persuaded the Iroquois to agree that in any future war between England and France, the Five Nations would remain neutral. This, at one stroke, destroyed the English claims to suzerainty over the Iroquois and their lands. It also stripped New York of its main source of military strength. Without the Iroquois to protect their northern settlements and harass Canada in time of war the English of New York were extremely vulnerable. Thus, not only had Callières inflicted a stinging diplomatic defeat on the English, he had also stripped them of their first line of both defence and offence. With England and France at this time once again teetering on the brink of war, this was indeed a notable feat.

The long-drawn-out Indian peace negotiations were by no means the only, or even the most difficult, problem that Callières and Champigny had to grapple with during these years. Some of the problems they faced were old ones, others were new, the product of peace in Europe and North America. To bedevil matters, the North American problems were profoundly affected by events and policies then taking shape in Europe; thus were one policy to be pursued by the government at Quebec to solve an immediate problem, it might well prove to be the wrong policy to pursue to achieve new aims even then being entertained by Louis XIV and his ministers. All that Callières and Champigny could do was act on existing policy directives, advise the Minister, and wait on events.

In 1696 Louis XIV had given orders that all the *coureurs de bois* had to return to the colony and that the trade in furs must henceforth take place at Montreal, not at the few western posts allowed to be maintained for military or political reasons. Unlike Frontenac, Callières did make a determined effort to enforce the ban on trade in the west. In 1699 he confiscated several canoe loads of trade goods that two Montreal merchants had endeavoured to smuggle out of the colony to their *coureurs de bois* at Michilimackinac and had the merchants heavily fined to boot. The following year two officers at Fort Frontenac were summarily arrested for trading in furs, tried and convicted by the Sovereign Council, and then sent to France to be dealt with as the Minister saw fit.

These events had quite a salutary effect, and in September 1699 Champigny reported that the *coureurs de bois* were at last returning to Montreal in small parties as they exhausted their supplies of trade goods. Thus it appeared that the edict might be enforced and Colbert's old policy of concentrating French energies and activities in the compact colony of the St Lawrence valley made relatively effective. This hope, however, quickly proved to be illusory, and ironically enough it was the French government, so anxious for so long to have it realized, that destroyed any chance of eventual achievement it might have had. The decision of Louis XIV to establish a French base, and later a colony, at the mouth of the Mississippi finally wrote *finis* to the belated attempt to reimpose Colbert's policy. Once this step was taken the *coureurs de bois* were no longer dependent solely on New France for trade goods and an outlet for their furs; the new colony of Louisiana was quite prepared to provide both. Thus in 1700 only twenty *coureurs de bois* at Michilimackinac obeyed the orders to return to Montreal; another eighty-four refused. Callières and Champigny declared that their disobedience stemmed from the fact that the renegades could now flout edicts and orders with impunity by decamping to the Louisiana settlement. To make matters worse, some *coureurs de bois* had taken the furs, which properly belonged to merchants in New France, with them, sold them in Louisiana, and there obtained fresh supplies of trade goods.

Callières sent an officer, the Sieur de Boishébert, to Michilimackinac to report on conditions and to order, once again, the *coureurs de bois* to return to Montreal. In 1702 Boishébert reported that the old disorders were worse than ever. The entire west was now flooded with brandy and other merchandise brought up the Mississippi. He stated that when he tried to enforce the Governor's orders he was greeted with sardonic laughter and threats. "It is very fine and honourable for me, Monsieur," he wrote Callières, "to be charged with your orders but it is also very vexatious to have only ink and paper as my sole force to carry them out."

Callières, Champigny, and the merchants of New France now began to voice the fear that if something were not done to curb the flow of furs from the northwest to Louisiana then Canada would be completely ruined. Callières requested that the new colony be placed under his jurisdiction, but the King refused on the grounds that it would be much easier to send orders to Louisiana directly by sea rather than by way of Quebec. This meant that to the old conflicts between entry points into the interior of the continent, between the Hudson River, the St Lawrence River, and Hudson Bay had been added that of the Mississippi entrance. New France and the St Lawrence entry did, however, have one advantage over the new colony; the climate of the latter, being hot and humid, was unsuitable for storing furs; moreover, there were no beaver on the lower Mississippi; the alligators saw to that.

Nor was Louisiana the only threat to the Canadian fur trade. Some *coureurs de bois*, rather than submit to the edicts and return to New France, were voyaging over the Alleghanies to Carolina and trading their furs to the English who gave them a warm welcome and supplied them with trade goods. The danger was great that other renegades would follow their example. Another group of malcontents sent two of their number to New York where they offered to enter English service, aid in the establishing of an English post at Detroit, and divert the Ottawa trade to New York. Other reports told of English traders crossing the Alleghanies and carrying on a brisk trade with tribes in the Mississippi valley, tribes that had previously traded with the French. Callières informed the Minister that this situation in the west could not be ignored. The western tribes would all eventually come under the sway of either the French or the English. Until recently the French had dominated in the Illinois and Ohio country, and it would, Callières declared, be poor statesmanship to abandon a vast area that had been a French possession; for, once lost, it would never be recovered. He advised that the western posts should be garrisoned anew and the *congé* system restored. By these means the *coureurs de bois* could be deterred from defecting to the English. They were, he pointed out, men who would follow no other way of life than that of the semi-savage western trader and would never return permanently to the colony. The point that Callières was trying to make was that the edict of 1696, ordering a French disengagement in the west for economic reasons, had created a political vacuum south of the Great Lakes and the English were preparing to move in.

In France, meanwhile, Louis XIV was sidling, crabwise, toward a radical new policy for North America. Although this policy was intended to achieve the ends of France in Europe rather than France in North America, it did, almost inadvertently, serve to resolve some of the problems that Callières and Champigny had been struggling with. In Europe, following the peace treaty signed at Ryswick, the war-weary powers had sought a solution to the Spanish succession problem that would obviate the need for another war. The moribund King of Spain, Charles II, had no son to succeed him; the children of both Louis XIV and the Hapsburg Emperor had claims to succeed. The problem was to arrange a succession that would not upset the balance of power in Europe. A division of the vast Spanish Empire was at one point arranged, but the Spanish people rejected this solution. And while these involved diplomatic negotiations were taking place Louis XIV was making his dispositions so that, no matter what happened with the Spanish Empire, France would be in a strong position to counter any moves likely to be made by the other powers. North America figured prominently in these dispositions.

As early as 1698 Iberville was given command of an expedition to establish a French base at the mouth of the Mississippi. The following year he received secret instructions from the Minister of Marine to destroy by covert means any forts or trading-posts that the English might have founded between the Alleghanies and the Mississippi.[2] The aim here was to prevent the English expanding southwest to the Mississippi, then beyond to Mexico. It was feared that were they not forfended they would, before long, seize the mines of Mexico. But were the French to establish a secure base at the mouth of the Misissippi and a chain of forts to the north, on the rivers flowing from the Alleghanies westward, then the Indian tribes from the Great Lakes to the Gulf of Mexico could be maintained in an alliance with France. Then, were the throne of Spain to go to a French prince, the French could protect the Spanish colonies from English aggression; were it to go to the Hapsburgs, the new establishment at the mouth of the Mississippi would serve as a base for the French to seize Mexico.

No sooner had a base at the mouth of the Mississippi been established than the Canadian *coureurs de bois* had taken advantage of it, to the great dissatisfaction of Callières, Champigny, and the Canadian merchants. In February 1700 Iberville reported that the Sieur de Tonti, commandant at the Illinois post, had arrived at the mouth of the Mississippi with twenty-one *coureurs de bois* in six canoes, loaded with beaver pelts to exchange for trade goods.[3] It was by now quite clear that there was little or no hope of forcing the hard core of the *coureurs de bois*, numbering nearly a hundred, to return to take up sedentary occupations in Canada. In 1700, Callières wrote to the Minister asking that the officers commanding the new posts in Louisiana be instructed to arrest any Canadians who arrived there and ship them back to Canada. An official in the Ministry of Marine, in the margin of the abstract of this dispatch, suggested that these men, tough, brave, and capable of anything, should be encouraged to trade out of Louisiana with the Mississippi valley tribes and to drive out any English traders who might venture into the area. The Minister pencilled beneath the minute the one word "Bon" and initialled it.[4] The following year, when the same suggestion was made, he laconically ordered "Essayer."⁵ With these two pencilled words a new policy was inaugurated. The old policy of the Canadians, which for nearly forty years the French government had sought by all means in its power to suppress, had finally won acceptance; but only because it was in accord with the imperial policy of France in Europe. No longer were the *coureurs de bois* regarded as renegades and outlaws; whether they realized it or not they had suddenly been transmuted into agents of French imperialism; and so, too, had the missionaries now being sent from Quebec to the tribes in the lower Mississippi country.

This new policy received ratification and the endorsement of Louis XIV in the spring of 1701. The previous October Charles II of Spain, during a brief period of rationality, signed a will in which Philip, Duc d'Anjou, a grandson of Louis XIV, was named his successor as King of Spain and the Empire. On November 1 Charles died, and on the ninth the Spanish ambassador was at Versailles, pressing Louis for an immediate decision whether or not he would allow Philip to accept the throne. The decision was made more urgent by the fact that were Louis to decline, then the offer would be made to a son of the Hapsburg Emperor who was sure to accept. After conferring with the members of his council all that day and for four hours the next Louis accepted the Spanish offer.

To accept was easy, but to maintain the French prince on the throne of Spain would certainly prove more difficult. The decision meant war with the Empire and likely with the English and Dutch as well. Moreover, a strong faction in Spain was bitterly opposed to a French king on the throne. Louis had to demonstrate to the Spanish people that France was strong enough to maintain the succession and defend not only French interests but those of Spain as well. Among those interests was North America.

It was for this reason, then, that Louis now decided to continue and consolidate the work begun by Iberville at the mouth of the Mississippi. In a dispatch to Callières and Champigny dated May 31, 1701, Louis enunciated the new policy: "His Majesty has resolved to found a settlement at the mouth of the Mississippi . . . this has become an indispensable necessity to halt the advance which the English from the colony of New York have begun to make in the lands which lie between them and this river. . . ."⁶ Now the French were committed to hold all of North America from Hudson Bay to the Gulf of Mexico, and to confine the English to the coastal strip between the Alleghanies and the Atlantic. This was imperialism with a vengeance. What made it more starkly so, made it in fact essentially a dog-in-the-manger policy, was the fact that this vast new territory, to be controlled from the new colony of Louisiana, produced only a poorer grade of fur which was at this particular time a glut on the market and a source of acute economic embarrassment. M. Tremblay, a cleric in Paris who was well informed on developments in government circles, wrote in May 1701 to a friend in Quebec explaining the real reasons for the change in policy.

> It is not at the moment seen how the Mississippi area can be of much value to France, therefore it is not intended to found anything very considerable there, but to let it develop slowly. But as Spain has now fallen to a son of France, it is believed necessary, by means of the colony of the Mississippi and by drawing all the Indian tribes along this river into the French alliance, to create a barrier against the English from Boston as far as Florida, or Carolina as they call it; this to prevent them expanding farther into these lands and extending from one of these nations to another as far as the Spanish colonies, which they would lay waste were they to reach so far. It is therefore desired to block them, and in order to succeed in this aim, it is intended to place as many missionaries as possible among all the Indian nations between the Mississippi and the English.[7]

In 1666 Colbert had clearly foreseen where such a policy as that now inaugurated would likely lead and he had warned Jean Talon, "it would be far more worthwhile to restrict one's self to an expanse of country that the colony itself could maintain, rather than to grasp too vast an area and perhaps one day be obliged to abandon part of it with some tarnishing of the repute of His Majesty and of this crown."[8] But Colbert had been dead these fifteen years; his policy of moderation had finally been interred and the history of North America now began to flow in new channels.

CHAPTER 16

Conclusion

The thirty-eight-year period from 1663, when the Crown took over Canada and made it a royal province, to 1701 when Louis XIV made his decision to seize and hold the whole interior of North America, has a certain unity. This unity was given it by Colbert's policy of attempting to concentrate French energies on the establishment of a compact, self-sustaining colony in the St Lawrence valley. The main obstacles to the implementation of this policy were men's fashions in hats and the geography of North America. As long as beaver pelts could be sold at a profit, all attempts to prevent the French voyaging up the rivers far into the interior were doomed to failure. Although Colbert's policy never enjoyed the success he had hoped for, yet much had been achieved by the end of the century. Ironically, the greatest achievement of all, French dominance over the interior of North America, ran counter to Colbert's policy and undermined all that he had sought to achieve.

In 1663 French possessions in North America had consisted only of the thinly held settlements in the St Lawrence valley, from Quebec to Montreal. The constant harassing attacks of the Iroquois had so weakened the colony's military and economic sinews that drastic measures were required to save it from eventual extinction. Acadia had then been in the hands of the English, who showed a marked disinclination to relinquish their grip. As for the west, it was the Iroquois and not the French who dominated there.

By the end of the century Acadia had been regained, and retained, in the face of assaults by New England. The French had gained the upper hand in the struggle for control of Hudson Bay, and the English had been all but driven out of Newfoundland. Whereas in 1663 French authority had not extended west of the Ottawa River, by 1701 it extended through the Great Lakes to the great plains beyond and down the Mississippi valley to the Gulf. The Iroquois's fangs had finally been drawn and the Canadians were brim full of confidence that they could more than hold their own in any military contest with the English colonies.[1] In 1663 the very survival of New France had been in doubt; by 1701, the French held half the continent in fee.

During this period, too, the administrative framework, the legal system, and the institutions had been hammered into the shape they were to retain until the Conquest. These had become well-enough established by 1698 that the Intendant Champigny decided it was high time the colony had its own central registry to preserve the records of the Sovereign Council and all official dispatches in the colony, rather than having the senior officials, who remained in Canada only a few years, retain them in their possession when they returned to France. The following year he informed the Minister that the Canadian archives had been established.

At the close of the war with England and the Iroquois, the Canadian economy began to thrive as never before. During the ensuing four years the population increased by nearly twenty-five per cent. The children born to the great wave of immigrants sent out by Colbert between 1663 and 1672 were now married, had taken up land, and were producing large families. Despite terrible epidemics, such as that of 1685 and the smallpox epidemic of 1701 that carried off over a thousand persons,[2] the infant mortality rate remained astonishingly low and from 1672 on the population doubled every twenty-five years by natural increase. Thus by the turn of the century most of the population were Canadian-born. Canada was all they knew; they had no desire to remove to France. They regarded themselves, and were now regarded by the French, as a distinct people, and both were quick to point out the shortcomings of the other, a sure sign of incipient nationalism.

While it is true that what had been accomplished by the French in North America at the turn of the century was in no small measure due to the hardihood and great energies of the Canadian colonists, yet they cannot be given all the credit. Without the military forces, the capital, the direction, talent, and administrative ability provided by the Crown little could have been achieved. It was the Crown that had devised the policies and provided the means to pursue them. The colony could not have provided itself with trained administrators of the calibre of a Talon or a Champigny, or military commanders with the experience and abilities of Courcelles, Denonville, Frontenac, Callières, and Vaudreuil.

It was Louis XIV, his ministers, and their appointed officials who had harnessed the latent energies of the Canadian people, given them direction and the necessary means to pursue the aims of the French Crown in North America. Had Canada, after 1663, had to rely solely on its own resources in capital, manpower, and administrative talent it might have survived a while longer; but then again, it might not. In short, Canada in 1701 was yet a colony, a royal province of France, albeit a unique one. Although its achievements, its aspiration, its very flaws were to a considerable degree the product of the Canadian people and their environment, Canada still bore the unmistakable impress of one man, Louis XIV.

ABBREVIATIONS

A.N. : Archives Nationales, Paris

B.N. : Bibliothèque Nationale, Paris.

B.R.H.: *Bulletin des Recherches Historiques.*

C.H.R.: *Canadian Historical Review.*

C.S.P.: *Calendar of State Papers Colonial, America and West Indies.*

Mass. Arch. : Massachusetts State Archives.

N.Y.C.D.: *Documents Relating to the Colonial History of New York.*

P.A.C. : Public Archives of Canada.

P.A.C., A.N. : Transcripts of documents from the Archives Nationales, Paris, in the Public Archives of Canada.

P.A.C., B.N. : Transcripts of documents from the Bibliothèque Nationale, Paris, in the Public Archives of Canada.

P.A.C. Ministère des Affaires Etrangères : Transcripts of documents from the Archives du Ministère des Affaires Etrangères.

R.A.P.Q.: *Rapport de l'Archiviste de la Province de Québec.*

Sem. Que. : Archives du Séminaire de Québec.

NOTES TO CHAPTER TWO

1. See B.N., Fonds Français, vol. 8036, p. 10, Histoire abregée des Compagnies de Commerce . . . ; A.N., C¹¹A, VII, 56, Denonville au Ministre, Que., 20 aoust 1685.

2. A.N., C¹¹A, II, 3-7, Lettres de Réunion à la Couronne de la propriété de la nouvelle france sur la cession des Interessés, du 24 fevrier et mars 1663.

3. A.N., B, I, 98-9, Instruction pour le Sr Gaudais s'en allant de la part du Roy en Canada sur certaines poincts dont Sa Maté desire qu'il informe en secret.

4. See A.N., B, II, 120; III, 95.

5. See André Vachon, "L'Eau-de-vie dans la société indienne," *The Canadian Historical Association Report*, 1960.

6. A.N., F³, Moreau de St Méry, III, 311, Mésy à Laval, Que., 25 aoust 1664. (A copy of the original made and signed by Laval.)

7. *Ibid.*, p. 310, Laval à Mésy, Que., 25 aoust 1664.

8. *Edits, Ordonnances Royaux, Declarations et Arrêts du Conseil d'Etat du Roi concernant le Canada*, pp. 40-48.

9. For a detailed account of Mésy's conflict with Bishop Laval and members of the Sovereign Council, see Raymond Du Bois Cahall, *The Sovereign Council of New France* (New York, 1915), pp. 23-34.

10. *Edits, Ordonnances Royaux*, pp. 37-39.

11. B.N., Mélanges Colbert, vol. 119, p. 273, Colbert de Terron à Colbert, La Rochelle, 12 Feb. 1664.

12. On the establishment of the *Compagnie de l'Occident*, see S. L. Mims, *Colbert's West India Policy* (New Haven, 1912).

13. Sem. Que. Lettres, Carton N, No. 14, Colbert à Mgr de Laval, St Germain-en-Laye, 18 mars 1664.

NOTES TO CHAPTER THREE

1. A.N., C¹¹A, II, 102 [Colbert à Tracy] du 15 nov. 1664.

2. P.A.C., A.N., D², vol. 47 part I, Liste contenant les vies, moeurs et ages des officiers de guerre qui servent en Canada.

3. P.A.C., Ministère de la Guerre, Archives Anciennes Correspondence, vol. 191, p. 41, Le Tellier à M. de la Gallissonnière, Paris, 27 Jan. 1665.

4. *Jesuit Relations*, vol. 49, p. 225, Relation de 1664-1665.

5. Sem. Que. Lettres, Carton N, No. 48-52, J. D. Dudouyt à Mgr Laval, Paris, 1677.

6. P.A.C., Documents St Sulpice, Registre 25, vol. I, part 1, Copie d'un Mémoire dressé par un Missionaire de St Sulpice établi à Montréal.

7. P.A.C., Lettres de l'Abbé Tronson, I, Tronson aux Messieurs du Séminaire de Montréal, mai 1675.

8. R.A.P.Q., 1930-1931, p. 32, Talon à Colbert, Que., 4 oct. 1665.

9. R.A.P.Q., 1926-1927, p. 59, Colbert à Frontenac, 17 mai 1674.

10. R.A.P.Q., 1930-1931, p. 9, Mémoire du Roy pour servir d'Instruction à Talon, Paris, 27 mars 1665.

11. *Edits, Ordonnances Royaux*, III, 50, Commission . . . pour M. de Champigny, 24 avril 1686.

12. For a more detailed study of the military responsibilities of an intendant in New France, see my unpublished M.A. thesis, "Jean Bochart de Champigny, Intendant of New France 1686-1702," pp. 104-137, McGill University, 1951.

13. In 1670 Villeray possessed a private library of 50 volumes, 41 titles, valued by the notary Becquet at 126 *livres*. See B.R.H., vol. 28 (1922), pp. 178-80.

14. Sem. Que. Lettres, Carton N, No. 48-2, J. D. Dudouyt à Mgr Laval, Paris, 1777; Lettres, Carton S, No. 93, M. Dudouyt à Mgr de Laval, Paris, 12 mai 1677.

15. A.N., C¹¹A, VI, 91-92, De Meulles au Ministre, Que., 12 nov. 1682.

16. *Ibid.*, XVII, 104-106, Champigny au Ministre, Que., 20 oct. 1699.

17. A.N., F³, Moreau de St Méry, V, 28-31, Reglement pour les salaires des officiers de Justice du pays de Canada 1ᵉʳ May 1678.

18. I am greatly indebted to Dr W. J. Jones of the University of Alberta for information on English criminal law during this period.

19. Christopher Hill, *The Century of Revolution: 1603-1714* (Edinburgh, 1961), pp. 225-27, 268.

20. André Morel, "La Justice criminelle en Nouvelle-France," *Cité Libre*, janvier 1963, pp. 26-30.

21. R.A.P.Q., 1926-1927, p. 25, Colbert à Frontenac, 13 juin 1673.

22. See W. B. Munro, "The Brandy Parliament of 1678," *C.H.R.*, vol. II, June 1921; W. J. Eccles, *Frontenac: The Courtier Governor* (Toronto, 1959), pp. 67-68.

23. A.N., C¹¹A, XIV, 127, Frontenac et Champigny au Ministre, Que., Oct. 26, 1696.

24. Allana G. Reid, "Representative Assemblies in New France," *C.H.R.*, March 1946, pp. 19-26.

25. P.A.C., A.N., C¹¹A, XX, 55-6, Callières, Champigny, et Beauharnois au Ministre, Que., 3 nov. 1702.

26. A.N., C¹¹A, XVIII, 80-1, Champigny au Ministre, Que., 15 oct. 1700.

27. Francis Parkman, *The Old Régime in Canada* (Century Edition, Boston, 1923), pp. 467-68.

NOTES TO CHAPTER FOUR

1. N.Y.C.D., III, 118-19, A Relation of the Governor of Canada his March with 600 volunteirs into ye territoryes of his Royall Highnes the Duke of Yorke in America.

2. P.A.C., Ministère des Affaires Etrangères, Angleterre, vol. 88, pp. 27-29, Du Roy à M. de Tracy, 24 mars 1666.

3. R.A.P.Q., 1930-1931, pp. 46-50, M. Talon à MM. de Tracy et de Courcelle, 1 sept. 1666.

4. N.Y.C.D., III, 120, Colonel Nicolls to the Council of Massachusetts, Fort James, July 6, '66; *ibid.*, pp. 120-21, Samuel Willis to Colonel Nicolls, Hartford, July 11, 1666.

5. P.A.C., Ministère des Affaires Etrangères, Amérique, vol. V, part 1, p. 351, Lettre du Colonel Temple au Sr Dubourg, Baston, 19/29 novembre 1668; *ibid.*, Angleterre, vol. 94, p. 146, Mémoire des Directeurs de la Compagnie des Indes occidentales . . . 16 janvier 1669; *ibid.*, p. 151, Colbert de Croisy au Roy, Londres, 24 jan. 1669; B.N., Fonds Français, vol. 8027, p. 34, Colbert à Colbert de Terron, St Germain-en-Laye, 22 juillet 1669. A.N., C¹¹D, I, 136, Charles R., 6 Aug. 1669, per Arlington.

6. A.N., C¹¹A, III, 276, Mémoire du Sr Patoulet demandé par monseigneur 1672.

7. A.N., B, II, 57-61, Instruction pour Mr. le Chevalier de grandfontaine . . . Colbert de Terron, la Rochelle, 5 mars 1670.

8 *Ibid.*, III, 41, Colbert à M. le Chevalier de Grandfontaine, Paris, 11 mars 1671.

9. Instruction pour Mr. le Chevalier de grandfontaine, *op. cit*; III, 39, Colbert à Courcelles, Paris, 11 mars 1671.

10. *Ibid.*, p. 19, Estat de la depense que le Roy veut et ordonne estre fait . . . en Canada; R.A.P.Q., 1930-1931, p. 163, Talon à Colbert, 11 nov. 1671.

11. A.N., C¹¹A, III, 278, Mémoire du Sr Patoulet . . . Paris, 25 jan. 1672.

12. *Ibid.*, II, 95, Pour le Secours qu'il plaist au Roy donner au Canada l'an 1664; A.N., B, I, 144-45, Colbert à M. l'Evesque de Petrée, 15 May 1669; II, 15, Colbert à M. l'Archevesque de Rouen, St Germain, le 27 feb. 1670.

13. *Jesuit Relations*, LI, 167, Relation de . . . 1667 et 1668.

14. A.N., C¹¹A, II, 321, Talon à Colbert, 1667.

15. This brief description of the seigneurial system is based on Professor Marcel Trudel's excellent study, *Le Régime Seigneurial*, Brochure Historique No. 6, Publication de la Société Historique du Canada, Ottawa, 1956.

16. A.N., C¹¹A, XI, 262, Mémoire Instructif sur le Canada, Champigny, 10 mai 1691.

17. R.A.P.Q., 1930-1931, p. 9, Mémoire du Roi pour servir d'Instruction à Talon. Louis, Lionne, Paris, 27 mars 1665.

18. A.N., F²A, carton 13, novembre 1666, Canada. Mémoire de plusieurs choses Touchant le Canada; A.N., B, III, 18-20. Estat de la depense que le Roy veut et ordonne estre fait . . . au Canada [1671].

19. A.N., C¹¹A, III, 276-77, Mémoire du Sr Patoulet demandé par Monseigneur, Paris, 25 jan. 1672.

20. B.N., Mélanges Colbert, vol. 152, pp. 186-87, Colbert de Terron à Colbert, La Rochelle, 16 mai 1669.

21. P.A.C., F²A, carton 13, novembre 1666, Canada. Mémoire de plusieurs choses Touchant le Canada; R.A.P.Q.,

1930-1931, p. 34, Talon à Colbert, Que., 4 oct. 1665; *Jugements du Conseil Souverain*, I, 524-27, 30 oct. 1668; B.N., Mélanges de Colbert, vol. 141 bis, p. 822, Bourdon à Colbert, Que., 30 oct. 1666; P.A.C., B.N., Fonds Français, vol. 8036, p. 2, Chronologie des Compagnies de Commerce Etablies en France depuis 1626.

22. R.A.P.Q., 1930-1931, p. 37, Talon à Colbert, Que., 4 oct. 1665; p. 46, Colbert à Talon, Versailles, 5 avril 1666.

23. B.N., Mélanges de Colbert, vol. 151 bis, p. 739, Colbert de Terron à Colbert, La Rochelle, 22 avril 1669.

24. A.N., F³ Moreau de St Méry, II, 5-6, Mémoire de Canada. M. de la Chesnaye à de Lagny, Que., 4 nov. 1695.

25. *Jesuit Relations*, L, 172.

26. Not until the mid eighteenth century does one find a comparison of the societies in the English and French colonies, made by a neutral observer. Then, the Finnish botanist Peter Kalm made it quite plain that he found the society of New France much more agreeable than that of the English colonies. See A. B. Benson (ed.), *Peter Kalm's Travels in North America* (New York, 1937).

NOTES TO CHAPTER FIVE

1. See E. E. Rich, *The History of the Hudson's Bay Company 1670-1870* (London: The Publications of the Hudson's Bay Record Society, 1958), I, 44 ff.

2. See R. Glover, "The Difficulties of the Hudson's Bay Company's Penetration of the West," C.H.R., XXIX, September 1948.

3. R.A.P.Q., 1930-1931, p. 43, Colbert à Talon, Versailles, 5 jan. 1666.

4. Ministère des Affaires Etrangères, Series Amérique, V, 288-89, Au Roy, Mémoire sur le Canada, Talon, Quebec, Nov. 3, 1671.

5. Jean Delanglez, S.J., *Some La Salle Journeys* (Chicago, 1938), pp. 1-39.

6 Ministère des Affaires Etrangères, Series Amérique, V, 288-89, Au Roy, Mémoire sur le Canada, Talon, Quebec, Nov. 2, 1671.

7. In a lengthy memoir on the fur trade written in 1695, de Lagny, the *intendant de commerce*, wrote: "Ce fut a l'arrivée de M. Talon en Canada que sous pretexte des découvertes, les voyages dans la profondeur des terres furent autorisés et qu'il permit ce commerce et pour son compte. A.N., C¹¹A, XIII, 400, Colonies fevr. 1695. Commerce du Castor de Canada.

8. Baron de Lahontan, *New Voyages to North America*, ed. R. G. Thwaites (Chicago, 1905), I, 54.

9. A.N., C¹¹A, III, 274. Mémoire du Sr Patoulet demandé par Mgr A Paris, le 25 janvier 1672.

10. P.A.C., Documents de St Sulpice, I, 202, 204, R. P. Gabriel Souart à M. le Gouverneur, Mtl., 15 avril 1663.

11. P.A.C., A.N., M, vol. 204, part 1, p. 203, P. Carheil, S.J., à Champigny, Michilimackinac, 30 aoust 1702.

12. A.N., B, I, 134, Lettre du Roy à M. l'Evesque de Petrée, Paris, 17 mai 1669.

13. P.A.C., B.N., Cinq Cens de Colbert, vol. 204, p. 288, Colbert à l'Archevesque de Rouen, 1 nov. 1669.

14. Ibid., p. 300, Colbert à M. l'Abbé de Bourlemont, 8 nov. 1669; Fonds Français, vol. 8028, p. 17, Mémoire pour M. l'Abbé de Bourlemont. . . .

15. Ernest Lavisse, Histoire de France (Paris, 1905), vol. VII, part 1, p. 172.

16. A.N., M, carton 242, folio 44, Copie de la requeste presentée à M. l'Intendant par le R. P. Mercier, Superieur, 25 jan. 1666.

17. A.N., C¹¹A, III, 52, Mémoire de Talon sur le Canada, 1669.

18. A.N., C¹¹A, III, 51-53, Mémoire de M. Talon sur le Canada, 1669.

19. Loc. cit.

20. A.N., C¹¹A, III, 279, Mémoire du Sr Patoulet demandé par Mgr Paris, 25 jan. 1672.

21. See Sem. Que. Carton N, No. 52, M. Dudouyt à Mgr de Laval, Paris, 9 mars 1681; ibid., No. 54, id à id, Paris, 11 avril 1681; ibid., No. 61, id à id, Paris, 9 mars 1682; ibid., No. 62, id à id, 26 mai 1682; ibid., No. 64, id à id, 10 juin 1682; A.N., F³, Moreau de St Méry, II, 93, 1682. Le Sr Talon Represente. . . .

22. C.S.P., 1669-1674, pp. 110-11, Governor Francis Lovelace to Williamson, secretary to Lord Arlington, Fort James, Manhatans, Oct. 3, 1670.

23. B.N., Mélanges Colbert, vol. 176 bis, p. 581, Mémoire au Roy sur les affaires du department de Rochefort . . . 14 Dec. 1671; R.A.P.Q., 1930-1931, p. 169, Colbert à Talon, 4 juin 1672.

NOTES TO CHAPTER SIX

1. On Frontenac's early career see my Frontenac: The Courtier Governor, Chap. 2.

2. Jugements du Conseil Souverain, I, 845-47.

3. A.N., C¹¹A, IV, 104-5, Déclaration du Roy qui Confirment et regle l'Etablissement du Conseil Souverain de Canada, du 5 juin 1675.

4. Edits, Ordonnances Royaux, p. 233, de par le Roi, 7 mai 1679.

5. R.A.P.Q., 1926-1927, p. 100, Colbert à Fontenac, St Germain-en-Laye, 8 mai 1679.

6. On the "Frenchification" policy and the controversies it provoked, see Jean Delanglez, Frontenac and the Jesuits (Chicago, 1939), pp. 36 ff.

7. See my Frontenac: The Courtier Governor, pp. 63-68.

8. A.N., C¹¹A, II, 103, Colbert à de Tracy, 15 nov. 1664.

9. P.A.C., Documents St Sulpice, III, Extrait de la lettre de M. de la Chesnaye escrite à Québec, 6 nov. 1678.

10. See W. B. Munro, "The Brandy Parliament of 1678," C.H.R., June 1921.

11. A.N., C¹¹A, V, 198-204, Lettre du Roi à M. le Comte de Frontenac, St Germain-en-Laye, 29 avril 1680.

12. A.N., B, VIII, 53-55, Lettre à la main de Mgr Colbert à M. le Comte de Frontenac, St Germain-en-Laye, 20 avril 1680.

13. B.N., Fonds Français, vol. 22799, p. 46, De Villermont à M. Denys, Paris, 10 avril 1680.

14. A.N., C¹¹A, V, 238-39, Le Roi à M. Duchesneau, 2 juin 1680; A.N., B, VIII, 59, Lettre à la main de Mgr Colbert au Sr Duchesneau, Fontainebleau, 2 juin 1680.

15. R.A.P.Q., 1926-1927, p. 118, Frontenac au maréchal de Bellefonds, Que., 14 nov. 1680.

16. A.N., C¹¹A, V, 299, Duchesneau à Seignelay, Que., 13 nov. 1681.

17. Jugements et Délibérations du Conseil Souverain, II, 634.

18. Sem. Que. Lettres, Carton N, No. 67, M. Dudouyt à Mgr de Laval, Paris, 3 juillet 1682.

19. A.N., C¹¹A, V, 357-58, Lettre du Roi à Frontenac, Versailles, 30 avril 1681.

20. A.N., C¹¹A, V, 271, Frontenac au Ministre, Que., 2 nov. 1681.

21. Ibid., p. 281.

22. Jugements et Délibérations du Conseil Souverain, II, 635-51.

23. P.A.C., Lettres de l'Abbé Tronson, vol. II. Tronson à de Casson [Paris], 29 mars 1682.

NOTES TO CHAPTER SEVEN

1. B.N., Collection Clairambault, vol. 1016, p. 20, Relation des Voyages et des découvertes du Sr de La Salle.

2. A.N., B, VII, 31, Le Roy à Frontenac, St Germain, 16 avril 1676.

3. On the intrigues of La Salle and his supporters at the Court see Jean Delanglez, S.J., Some La Salle Journeys, passim. See also A.N., C¹¹A, XIII, 401-2, Commerce du Castor de Canada. Colonies, fevr. 1695.

4. Relation des Voyages et des découvertes du Sr de La Salle, op. cit. pp. 157-63.

5 Pierre Margry, Découverts et établissements des Français . . ., II, 246-62.

6. On the history of the Hudson's Bay Company during this period, see E. E. Rich, The History of the Hudson's Bay Company, 1670-1870, vol. 1, 1670-1763.

7. P.A.C., B.N., Fonds Français, vol. 8028, p. 28, Colbert à Colbert de Croisy, Paris, 5 aoust 1670.

8. For a more detailed account of Iroquois policy and French reaction to it, see my Frontenac: The Courtier Governor, pp. 99-126.

9. A.N., C¹¹A, VI, 47-48, Père de Lamberville à Frontenac, d'Onnontagué, 20 sept. 1682.

NOTES TO CHAPTER EIGHT

1. Pierre Clément (ed.), Lettres, instructions et mémoires de Colbert (Paris, 1861-1873), vol. III, part 2, pp. 9-10, 12-13.

2. A.N., C¹¹A, VI, 68-70, Mémoire de l'Assemblée tenu le 10 octobre 1682, Quebec, Le Febvre de la Barre.

3. Ibid., pp. 85-6, De Meulles au Ministre, Que., 12 nov. 1682.

4. A.N., C¹¹A, VI, 64-67, La Barre au Roy, 1682.

5. N.Y.C.D., III, 341, Sir John Werden to Governor Dongan, St James, 10 March 1684.

6. Arthur T. Adams, The Explorations of Pierre Esprit Radisson (Minneapolis, 1961), p. 164.

7. Sem. Que. Lettres, Carton N, No. 52, M. Dudouyt à Mgr de Laval, Paris, 9 mars 1681.

8. A.N., C¹¹A, VI, 153-56, La Barre à Colbert, Que., 4 nov. 1683; ibid., pp. 357-58, La Barre au Ministre, Que., 14 nov. 1684.

9. A.N., B, XI, 14, Ministre à La Barre, Versailles, 10 avril 1684.

10. La Barre au Ministre, Que., 14 nov. 1684, loc. cit.

11. On this Company and its conflicts with New England fishermen see Bruce T. McCully, "The New England-Acadia Fishery Dispute and the Nicholson Mission of August 1687," in Essex Institute Historical Collections, 1960, pp. 277-90.

12. Sem. Que. Lettres, Carton N, No. 62, M. Dudouyt à Mgr de Laval, 26 mai 1682.

13. A.N., C¹¹D, I, 193, Mémoire de la Compagnie de la pesche sedentaire de l'Accadie, 18 dec. 1685.

14. A.N., B, XI, 8, Le Roy à La Barre, Versailles, 10 avril 1684.

15. A.N., C¹¹A, VII, 96, Denonville au Ministre, Que., 13 nov. 1685.

16. Sem. Que. Lettres, Carton N, No. 72, M. Dudouyt à Mgr de Laval, Paris, 10 et 12 juin 1683; A.N., C¹¹A, VI, 138, La Barre au Ministre, Que., 4 nov. 1683.

17. A.N., C¹¹A, VI, 526-27, Julien Garnier, S.J., à La Barre, Sonnontouan, 23 avril

1684; pp. 534-38, R. P. Lamberville à La Barre, Onnontagué, 10, 11, 18 juillet 1684.

18. Loc. cit.

19. P.A.C., B.N., Fonds Français, vol. 22799, p. 179, De Machault Rougemont à M. de Villeray, Rochefort, 27 aoust 1684.

20. A.N., B, VII, 77-78, Colbert à Duchesneau, Paris, 28 avril 1677.

21. A.N., C¹¹A, VI, 388-93, De Meulles au Ministre, Que., 10 oct. 1684; pp. 400-401, id à id, Que., 12 nov. 1684.

22. A.N., C¹¹A, VI, 309-13, La Barre au Ministre, Que., 1 oct. 1684; pp. 343-44, La Barre au Ministre, Que., 13 nov. 1684.

NOTES TO CHAPTER NINE

1. Quoted in Maude E. Abbott, History of Medicine in the Province of Quebec (Toronto, 1931), p. 26.

2. A. D. Kelly, "Health Insurance in New France," Bulletin of the History of Medicine, XXVIII, Nov.-Dec. 1954.

3. Sem. Que. Polygraphie 6, No. 31, Metode (sic) Pour faire les Ecoles.

4. Sem. Que. Lettres, Carton O, No. 1, M. Dudouyt à M. Maizerets, Paris, 17 avril 1687.

5. Ibid., No. 2, M. de Brisacier à M. de Bernière, Paris, 13 juin 1687.

6. See Canadian Art, vol. XVIII, No. 4, July-August 1961.

7. P.A.C., Ministère des Affaires Etrangères, Angleterre, vol. 159, p. 103, Barillon au Roy, Windsor, 11 juillet 1686; p. 104, id à id, Windsor, 15 juillet 1686; p. 105, Le Roy à Barillon, Versailles, 23 juillet 1686; p. 110, Barillon au Roy, Londres, 9 déc 1686.

8. This episode of the Iroquois prisoners, the "treacherous" means used to take some of them, and the supposed betrayal of Father Lamberville, has generated more heat than light among historians. For detailed studies of the question see Jean Leclerc, S.J., "Denonville et ses captifs iroquois," Revue d'Histoire de l'Amérique Francaise, vol. XIV, No. 4, mars 1961, vol. XV, No. 1, juin 1961; W. J. Eccles, "Denonville et les galériens iroquois," ibid., vol. XIV, No. 3, Décembre 1960.

NOTES TO CHAPTER TEN

1. P.A.C., B.N., Fonds Français, vol. 22800, p. 181, Bégon à de Villermont, La Rochelle, 10 déc. 1688; Chronological List of Canadian Censuses, Bureau of Statistics, Demography Branch, Ottawa.

2. Jugements et Délibérations du Conseil Souverain, III, 219-23.

3. For a detailed account of the suffering endured by these garrisons see Jean

Leclerc, S.J., "Un aumônier militaire: le P. Pierre Millet (1685-1689)," Lettres du Bas-Canada, vol XVI, No. 2, juin 1962.

4. A.N., C¹¹A, VIII, 133-34, Denonville au Ministre, Que., 10 nov. 1686.

5. Jugements et Délibérations du Conseil Souverain, III, 194, 232-33, 237-38, 242, 258.

6. E. E. Rich, *The History of the Hudson's Bay Company 1670-1870*, vol. 1, *1670-1763*, pp. 207-64, *passim*.

7. A.N., B, vol. XV, Ministre à Denonville, Versailles, 1 mai 1689; Mémoire du Roy aux Srs Denonville et Champigny, Versailles, 1 mai 1689; see also Ministre à Denonville, Versailles, 8 mars 1688.

8. This was Champigny's opinion. See A.N., C¹¹A, X, 246, Champigny au Ministre, Que., 16 nov. 1689.

9. N.Y.C.D., III, 608, Messrs Philips & Van Cortland to Secretary Blathwayt, 5 Aug. 1689.

10. Désiré Girouard, *Lake St Louis, Old and New* (Montreal, 1895), pp. 124-35.

NOTES TO CHAPTER ELEVEN

1. *Livingston Indian Records 1660-1723*, p. 160; A.N., C¹¹A, XI, 10-13, Relation de ce qui s'est passé de plus remarquable en Canada depuis . . . novembre 1689 jusqu'au . . . novembre 1690, Monseignat.

2. A.N., C¹¹D, II, 98-99, Mémoire du Sr de Meneval à Mgr de Seignelay. Port Royal, 10 Sept. 1688; 130, Mémoire . . . du Sr de Meneval, Port Royal, 7 sept. 1689.

3. See my *Frontenac: The Courtier Governor*, pp. 313-23.

4. A.N., C¹¹D, II, 126-27, Mémoire Instructif de la Conduitte des Srs de Soulegre et Desgoutins au Port Royal de l'Acadie par le Sr de Meneval, gouverneur, Au Port Royal, le 7 Septembre 1689.

5. *Ibid.*, pp. 115-18, De Meneval à M. de Chevry, Port Royal, 8 Sept. 1689.

6. A.N., F³, Moreau de St Méry, II, 243-47, Mémoire de ce qui s'est passé. . . .

7. *Collections of the Massachusetts Historical Society*, vol. I, ser. 3, pp. 114-17,

8. Mass. Arch. Inter-charter, XXXVI, 233, 262, 264-68.

9. Mass. Arch. Court Records, 1689-1698, VI, 138, Wednesday, 28 May 1690.

10. See Lieut.-Col. G. W. C. Nicholson, *Marlborough and the War of the Spanish Succession*, Directorate of Military Training, Army Headquarters (Ottawa: Queen's Printer, 1955).

11. I am greatly indebted to Mr C. M. Cross, Chief of the Tidal and Current Survey, Canadian Hydrographic Service, Department of Mines and Technical Surveys, Ottawa, for detailed information on the times, heights, and rate of rise and fall of the tides at Quebec in October 1690.

12. N.Y.C.D., III, 761, Governor Sloughter to Lord Nottingham, Fort William Henry, May 6, 1691. (The original documents dealing with this assault on Quebec are printed in Ernest Myrand, *1690 Sir William Phips devant Québec* [Québec, 1895].)

NOTES TO CHAPTER TWELVE

1. New York State Archives, Colonial MS., XXXVIII, 85, By the Commander in Cheife & Council. A Proclamation. Fort Wm. Henry, 19 March 1691/92.

2. P.A.C., A.N., C¹¹A, vol. XII, part 2, Champigny au Ministre, Que., 4 nov. 1693.

3. See George T. Hunt, *The Wars of the Iroquois* (Madison, Wisc., 1940), Chap. 5.

4. C.S.P., 1689-1692, p. 212, Petition and

address of the inhabitants of Maine and the County of Cornwall in New England; pp. 563-64, Samuel Ravenscroft to Francis Nicholson, Boston, 5 Nov. 1691; p. 571, Extracts of a letter from David Jeffreys to John Usher, 19 Nov. 1691, Boston; A.N., C¹¹A, XIII, p. 81, Champigny au Ministre, Que., 24 oct. 1694; B.R.H., XXXVIII, 500-505, Lettre du Chevalier de Villebon, 1 oct. 1695.

5. Thomas Hutchinson, *The History of Massachusetts, from the first settlement thereof in 1628, until the year 1750* (Boston, 1795), II, 91-95.

6. A.N., F³, Moreau de St Méry, vol. 7, Relation de ce qui s'est passé au Canada . . . 1695-1696, Champigny; 383-84, Relation de ce qui s'est passé . . . 1695-1696 [Frontenac]; A.N., C¹¹A, XIV, 240-41, Iberville au Ministre, Plaisance, 24 sept. 1690.

7. Hutchinson, *op. cit.*, pp. 95-98.

8. A.N., C¹¹D, III, 54, Extrait, Baye d'Hudson, 1697.

9. The struggle in Hudson Bay is discussed in detail in E. E. Rich, *The History of the Hudson's Bay Company 1670-1870*, vol. I, and in Guy Frégault, *Iberville le conquérant* (Montreal, 1944).

10. For a more detailed discussion of the fur trade and related political problems see my *Frontenac: The Courtier Governor*, Chap. 16.

11. For an excellent, detailed study of this tangled problem see Guy Frégault, "La Compagnie de la Colonie," *Revue de l'Université d'Ottawa*, janvier-mars, avril-juin 1960.

12. A.N., F¹, X, 80, Estat des Fonds (1697).

NOTES TO CHAPTER THIRTEEN

1. For a more detailed discussion of the colony's economic development during this period, see my M.A. thesis, "Jean Bochart de Champigny, Intendant of New France 1686-1702," McGill, 1951.

2. F. W. Burton, "The Wheat Supply of New France," *Proceedings and Transactions of the Royal Society of Canada*, Ser. 3, 1936, XXX, 137-50.

3. In the transcripts of the Lettres de l'Abbé Tronson, vol. V, in the Public Archives at Ottawa are several references to this canal. See also the article by R. Bonin, P.S.S., "Le Canal Lachine sous le régime français," *B.R.H.*, vol. 42, mai 1936.

4. B.N., Nouvelles Acquisitions, Collection Arnoul, vol. 21334, p. 299, Croiset à M. Arnoul, Plaisance, 22 aoust 1687.

5. Sem. Que. Lettres, Carton N, No. 123, M. Tremblay à Mgr de Laval, Paris, 19 juin 1705.

6. A.N., C¹¹A, VI, 367, La Barre au Ministre, Que., 14 nov. 1684; pp. 402-3, de Meulles au Ministre, Que., 12 nov. 1684.

7. On losses from shipwreck and war, see Allana G. Reid, "General Trade between Quebec and France during the French Régime," *C.H.R.*, 1953, p. 18.

8. On the timber and mast industry see R G. Albion, *Forests and Sea Power*

(Cambridge, Mass., 1926); P. W. Bamford, *Forests and French Sea Power: 1660-1789* (Toronto, 1956); W. J. Eccles "Jean Bochart de Champigny," pp. 266-80.

9. C.S.P., 1693-1696, pp. 263-64, John Taylor to John Povey, 20 March 1694; *ibid.*, 1700, p. 66, 12 Feb., Admiralty Office.

10. *Ibid.*, pp. 591-92, Samuell York, Carpenter to Lord Bellomont, Albany, 2 Sept. 1700; p. 276, Examination of Abraham and David Schuyler by Rob't Livingston, Albany, 9 May 1700.

11. N.Y.C.D., IV, 347, Report of Messrs Schuyler and Dellius' Negotiations in Canada, New York, 2 July 1698; C.S.P., 1699, Bellomont to Council of Trade & Plantations, Boston, 24 Aug. 1699; *ibid.*, 1700, p. 679, *id to id*, New York, 28 Nov. 1700.

12. B.N., Fonds Français, vol. 22810, p. 418, Bégon à de Villermont, Rochefort, 29 nov. 1701; *ibid.*, vol. 22811, p. 358, *id à id*, Rochefort, 24 déc. 1702; A.N., C¹¹A, XIX, 237-38, Projets sur la Nouvelle Angleterre, Canada 1701.

13. *Loc. cit.*

NOTES TO CHAPTER FOURTEEN

1. Sem. Que. Lettres, Carton N, No. 93, M. de Brisacier à Mgr de Laval, Senlis, 20 mai 1689.

2. A.N., C^{11}A, XVII, 25-26, Callières et Champigny au Ministre, Que., 20 oct. 1699; Sem. Que. Lettres R, No. 42, P. Bergièr à Mgr de St Vallier, aux Tamarois, 29 fev. 1700.

3. See Ernest Lavisse, *Histoire de France*, vol. 7-2, pp. 56, 76.

4. P.A.C., Documents St Sulpice, IV, 165, Statuts publiés dans le premier Synode tenu ce neuvièsme Novembre 1690.

5. E. Z. Massicotte, "Comment on disposait des enfants du Roi," *B.R.H.*, jan. 1931, p. 49.

6. Fernand Lefebvre, "La Repression Satanique en la Nouvelle-France," *B.R.H.*, vol. 61, janvier, février, mars, 1955; E. Z. Massicotte, "Sacrilège, magic et Sorcellerie," *ibid.*, aoust 1933.

7. *Ibid.*, mai 1920, E. Z. Massicotte, "A propos des lutins."

8. Bib. Nat. Collection Clairambault, vol. 874, p. 35, St Vallier à de Lagny, Que., oct. 1693.

9. A.N., F^3, Moreau de St Méry, VII, 198-270, Extraits des procedures faites au Conseil Royal de Québec depuis le premier Février 1694 jusques an 20ième octobre suivant.

NOTES TO CHAPTER FIFTEEN

1. B.N., Fonds Français, vol. 22807, p. 145, De Beaujeu à de Villermont, Havre, 2 mai 1699.

2. A.N., C^{13}C, II, 47, Mémoire sur l'établissement de la mobile et du Misisipy.

3. A.N., C^{13}A, I, 231, Iberville au Ministre, Des Bayogoula, 26 féb. 1700.

4. A.N., C^{11}A, XVIII, 27, Extrait des depesches de Canada de l'année 1700.

5. *Ibid.*, XVIX, 47, Extrait des lettres du Canada 1701.

6. A.N., B, XXII, 278-9, Mémoire du Roy au Sr Chev. de Callières . . . et de Champigny, Versailles, le 31 May 1701.

7. Sem. Que. Lettres, Carton O, No. 34, M. Tremblay à M. Glandelet [Paris], 28 mai 1701.

8. A.N., C^{11}A, IX, 260, Colbert à Talon, 30 mars 1666.

NOTES TO CHAPTER SIXTEEN

1. A.N., C^{11}A, XIX, 232, Projets sur la Nouvelle Angleterre, Canada 1701.

2. B.N., Manuscrits Français, vol. 9097, p.

23, Extrait d'une lettre de La Rochelle du 19 décembre 1701.

SELECT BIBLIOGRAPHY

GUIDES TO MATERIALS

The Public Archives of Canada, Manuscript Division, has published several Preliminary Inventories of the documents in the various French archives, transcripts or microfilm copies of which it has obtained. Between 1891 and 1940 the Annual Reports of the Public Archives of Canada contained calendars of the transcripts of the documents copied in France.

The Public Archives of Canada also has copies of such aids as *Inventaire dressé par le bureau historique de la division des Archives*, Paris, 1898. In the manuscript section of the Bibliothèque Nationale in Paris are some very useful indexes of the documents on deposit there.

MANUSCRIPTS

It was not until 1671 that the French government took steps to conserve official documents. Many documents pertaining to Canada prior to that date were, however, preserved – the correspondence of Talon and Colbert, for example – but many other important documents were lost. Of Tracy's and Courcelle's correspondence, very little has survived. When, in 1760, the French officials in Canada returned to France, all but documents of purely local interest, those concerning property and the like, went with them. Since then, successive governments in Canada have had copies made of selected documents, and more recently the important series have been microfilmed in their entirety. Most of the correspondence written by persons in Canada is contained in the $C^{11}A$ series and not a little in the F^3 Moreau de St Méry series, both located in the Archives Nationales in Paris. The registers of dispatches from the Ministers of Marine to Canadian officials are in the B series, also located in the Archives Nationales. Other documents pertaining to Canada are to be found in the Bibliothèque Nationale, the Archives du Ministère des Affaires Etrangères, the Ministère de la Guerre, and the Bibliothèque Mazarine. The archives in some of the French *départements* also contain documents pertaining to Canada or to persons who served in the colony.

The Quebec Provincial Archives also has transcripts of many of the French series, and some original documents. The archives of the Quebec Seminary contain a great deal of very important documentary material as also do the Judicial Archives of Montreal. The state archives of New York and Massachusetts have important documents concerning New France and Acadia, many of which have never appeared in printed form.

PRINTED SOURCES

In the annual *Rapport de l'Archiviste de la Province de Québec*, much original source material has been printed over the years; Talon's and Frontenac's correspondence, for example. Some documents are printed in the *Annual Report of the Public Archives of Canada*, which also contains calendars of much of the documentary material, but these last, unlike the British *Calendars of State Papers Colonial, America and West Indies*, are little more than an indication of what the documents are about. Some of the French documents have been translated and printed in the fifteen-volume *Documents Relating to the Colonial History of New York* (ed. E. B. O'Callaghan and J. R. Brodhead, Albany, 1856-1883), but the translation leaves much to be desired. This series contains some, but by no means all, of the New York colonial documents pertaining to New France. The *Jugements et Délibérations du Conseil Souverain de la Nouvelle France* (6 vols., Quebec, 1885) is of great value. P. Margry (ed.) published six volumes of documents on early western exploration in 1876, *Mémoires et documents pour servir à l'histoire des origines françaises des pays d'outre mer: Découvertes et établissements des Français dans l'ouest et dans le sud de l'Amérique septentrionale.*

This series has to be used with care, since the editor took liberties with the documents. The R. G. Thwaites edition of the *Jesuit Relations and Allied Documents* (73 vols., Cleveland, 1896-1901) is invaluable.

Other useful primary source material appears in the following published works:

Annales de l'Hôtel-Dieu de Montréal, by Sister Morin, ed. A. E. Fauteux, E. Z. Massicotte, and C. Bertrand, Montreal, 1921.

Annales de l'Hôtel-Dieu de Québec, by Mère de St Ignace Juchereau, ed. A. Jamet, Quebec, 1939.

BAUGY, LE CHEVALIER DE, *Journal d'une expédition contre les Iroquois en 1687*. Paris, 1883.

BELMONT, ABBÉ DE. "Histoire du Canada," *Manuscripts Relating to the Early History of Canada*. The Literary and Historical Society of Quebec, Quebec, 1868.

BOUCHER, PIERRE, SIEUR DE BOUCHERVILLE. *Histoire véritable et naturelle des moeurs et productions du pays de la Nouvelle France*. First published 1664. Ed. G. Coffin, Montreal, 1882.

CASSON, DOLLIER DE. *A History of Montreal 1640-1672*. Translated and edited by Ralph Flenley. London and Toronto, 1928.

CHARLEVOIX, PÈRE P. F. X. DE. *Histoire et description générale de la Nouvelle France, avec le journal historique d'une voyage fait par ordre du roi dans l'Amérique Septentrionale*. 3 vols. Paris, 1744.

CLÉMENT, PIERRE, ed. *Lettres, instructions et mémoires de Colbert*. 7 vols. Paris, 1861-1873.

Collection des manuscrits contenant lettres, mémoires et autres documents historiques relatifs à la Nouvelle France. 4 vols. Published by order of the Quebec legislature. Quebec, 1883-1885.

Edits, ordonnances royaux, déclarations d'état du Roi concernant le Canada. Ed. W. B. Lindsay. 3 vols. Quebec, 1854.

LAHONTAN, LOUIS ARMAND DE LOM D'ARCE, BARON DE. *Nouveaux voyages de Mr le baron de Lahontan dans l'Amérique Septentrionale*. 2 vols. La Haye, 1703.

—— *New Voyages to North America*. Ed. R. G. Thwaites. 2 vols. Chicago, 1905.

LECLERCQ, P. CHRÉTIEN. *Premier Etablissement de la Foy dans la Nouvelle France*. Paris, 1691.

The Livingston Indian Records, 1666-1723. Ed. Lawrence H. Leder. The Pennsylvania Historical Association, Gettysburg, 1956.

Mandements des évêques de Québec. Ed. Mgr H. Tetu and Mgr C. O. Gagnon. 7 vols. Quebec, 1887.

MUNRO, W. B., ed. *Documents Relating to the Seigneurial Tenure in Canada, 1698-1854*. Toronto, Champlain Society Publications, 1908.

NEW YORK. *Documentary History of the State of New York*. Ed. E. B. O'Callaghan. 4 vols. Albany, 1850.

PEASE, E. C., AND R. C. WERNER, eds. *The French Foundations: 1680-1693*. Collection of the Illinois State Historical Library. Vol I. Springfield, 1934.

PERROT, NICHOLAS. *Mémoire sur les moeurs, coustumes et relligion des sauvages de l'Amérique septentrionale*. Tailhan edition. Leipzig and Paris, 1864.

POTHERIE, M. DE BACQUEVILLE DE LA. *Histoire de l'Amérique septentrionale*. Paris, 1753.

QUEBEC. *Literary and Historical Society of Quebec, Historical Documents* (Ser. 1-9). Quebec, 1868-1915.

ROY, P. G., ed. *Ordonnances, Commissions etc., etc., des Gouverneurs et Intendants de la Nouvelle France: 1639-1760*. 2 vols. Beauceville, 1924.

SAVAGE, THOMAS. *An Account of the Late Action of the New Englanders, under the Command of Sir William Phips, against the French at Canada*. London, 1691.

ST SIMON, LE DUC DE. *Mémoires de St Simon*, ed. A. de Boislisle. 41 vols. Paris, 1879.

ST VALLIER, BISHOP JEAN DE LA CROIX. *Etat présent de l'Eglise et de la Colonie française dans la Nouvelle France*. Paris, 1686.

TAC, PÈRE SIXTE LE. *Histoire chronologique de la Nouvelle France*, ed. E. Réveillaud. Paris, 1888.

WRAXALL, PETER. *An Abridgement of the New York Indian Records*, ed. C. H. McIlwain. Cambridge, Mass., 1915.

SECONDARY WORKS

The first history of New France, *Histoire et Description générale de la Nouvelle-France*, 3 vols., Paris, 1744, was written by the Jesuit, Charlevoix, who spent some years in the colony in the early eighteenth century and on his return to France consulted the documents in the French archives. His approach to the evidence was decidedly uncritical, and much that was dubious, if not erroneous, was accepted at face value. The nineteenth-century historians, such as François-Xavier Garneau and Abbé Ferland, based their histories of New France largely on Charlevoix, repeated his errors, and added some of their own. The Abbé Faillon's three-volume history of New France unfortunately stops at 1672. Although written with a marked clerical bias it is based on original source material and is a very useful work. In English, the epic series by Francis Parkman, *France and England in North America*, published in the second half of the nineteenth century, for many years was regarded as the definitive history of Canada under the French régime. Only in recent years have historians, after studying the original source material, begun to make plain that Parkman's interpretation was marked by strong anti-clerical prejudice and an inability to see in New France much more than the reverse of the vices and virtues of New England in his own day. William Kingsford's *The History of Canada*, in ten volumes, merely lends substance to the cynic's comment that "all Canadian historians are either dull or inaccurate, and some contrive to be both." The works of Abbé Lionel Groulx, on the other hand, although marked by intense nationalism, are useful.

Other secondary works of value are given below:

The European Background

ALBION, R. G. *Forests and Sea Power*. Cambridge, Mass., 1926.

BAMFORD, P. W. *Forests and French Sea Power*. Toronto, 1956.

BLOCH, MARC. *Les caractères originaux de l'histoire rurale française*, Paris, 1952.

BOISSONADE, P. *Colbert: Le triomphe de l'étatisme, la fondation de la suprématie industrielle de la france: La dictature du travail, 1661-1683*. Paris, 1932.

CLARK, G. H. *The Seventeenth Century*. Oxford, 1929.

C. W. COLE. *Colbert and a Century of French Mercantilism*. 2 vols. New York, 1939.

—— *French Mercantilism 1683-1700*. New York, 1943.

DOUCET, R. *Les institutions de la France au XVIᵉ siècle*. 2 vols. Paris, 1948.

DUCHENE, A. *La politique coloniale de la France*. Paris, 1928.

HILL, CHRISTOPHER. *The Century of Revolution: 1603-1714*. Edinburgh, 1961.

DE LA RONCIÈRE, CH. *Histoire de la Marine française*. 4 vols. Paris, 1910.

LAVISSE, ERNEST. *Histoire de France*, vols. VII and VIII. Paris, 1905.

LEWIS, W. H. *Louis XIV: An Informal Portrait*. London, 1959.

—— *The Splendid Century*, London, 1953.

MARION, MARCEL. *Dictionnaire des Institutions de la France aux 17ᵉ et 18ᵉ siècles*. Paris, 1923.

MIMS, S. L. *Colbert's West India Policy*. New Haven, 1912.

MOUSNIER, ROLAND. *Les XVIᵉ et XVIIᵉ Siècles (Histoire Générale des Civilizations*, vol. IV). Paris, 1954.

SAGNAC, PHILIPPE. *La formation de la société française moderne*. 2 vols. Paris, 1945.

SAGNAC, PHILIPPE, ET A. DE SAINT-LÉGER. *Louis XIV (1661-1715)* ("Peuples et Civilizations Series," vol. X). Paris, 1949.

STANKIEWICZ, W. J. *Politics and Religion in Seventeenth-Century France*. Toronto, 1960.

The French in North America

ADAMS, ARTHUR T. *The Explorations of Pierre Esprit Radisson*. Minneapolis, 1961.

ALVORD, CLARENCE W. *The Illinois Country, 1673-1818*. Springfield, Ill., 1920.

CAHALL, RAYMOND DU BOIS. *The Sovereign Council of New France.* New York, 1915.

CHAPAIS, SIR THOMAS. *Jean Talon, Intendant de la Nouvelle France.* Quebec, 1904.

DALANGLEZ, JEAN, S.J. *Some La Salle Journeys.* Chicago, 1938.

—— *Frontenac and the Jesuits.* Chicago, 1939.

—— *Louis Jolliet, vie et voyages: 1645-1700.* Montreal, 1950.

EASTMAN, MACK. *Church and State in Early Canada.* Edinburgh, 1915.

ECCLES, W. J. *Frontenac: The Courtier Governor.* Toronto, 1959.

FAILLON, ABBÉ. *Histoire de la colonie française en Canada.* Villemarie, 1865-1866.

FAUTEUX, J. N. *Essai sur l'industrie au Canada sous le régime français.* 2 vols. Quebec, 1861-1865.

FRÉGAULT, GUY. *Iberville le conquérant.* Montreal, 1944.

GIRAUD, MARCEL. *Le Règne de Louis XIV, 1698-1715 (Histoire de la Louisiane française, vol I).* Paris, 1953.

GIROUARD, DÉSIRÉ. *Lake St Louis, Old and New.* Montreal, 1895.

—— *Les anciens Postes de Lac St Louis.* Montreal, 1895.

GOSSELIN, ABBÉ AUGUSTE. *L'Eglise du Canada.* 3 vols. Quebec, 1911.

—— *Le Vénérable François de Montmorency-Laval.* Quebec, 1906.

HAMMANG, F. H. *The Marquis de Vaudreuil.* Bruges, 1938.

INNIS, H. A. *The Fur Trade in Canada.* London, 1930.

GÉRIN, LÉON. *Aux sources de notre Histoire.* Montreal, 1946.

KELLOG, LOUISE PHELPS. *The French Régime in Wisconsin and the Northwest.* Madison, Wisc., 1925.

HAMELIN, JEAN. *Economie et Société en Nouvelle France.* Quebec, 1960.

KENNEDY, J. H. *Jesuit and Savage in New France.* New Haven, 1950.

LANCTOT, GUSTAVE. *L'administration de la Nouvelle France.* Paris, 1929.

—— *Réalisations françaises de Cartier à Montcalm.* Montreal, 1951.

—— *Filles de Joie ou Filles du Roi.* Montreal, 1952.

MURPHY, E. R. M. *Henry de Tonty: Fur Trader of the Mississippi.* Baltimore, 1941.

MYRAND, ERNEST. *Sir William Phips devant Québec.* Quebec, 1895.

NUTE, GRACE LEE. *Cæsars of the Wilderness.* New York, 1943.

PALARDY, JEAN. *The Early Furniture of French Canada.* Toronto, 1963.

ROCHEMONTEIX, R. P. CAMILLE DE. *Les Jesuites de la Nouvelle France au XVII siècle.* 3 vols. Paris, 1896.

SÉGUIN, ROBERT-LIONEL. *La sorcellerie au Canada français du XVIIe au XIXe siècles.* Montreal, 1961.

TRAQUAIR, RAMSAY. *The Old Architecture of Quebec.* Toronto, 1947.

TRUDEL, MARCEL. *L'esclavage au Canada français: histoire et conditions de l'esclavage.* Quebec, 1960.

WEBSTER, J. C. *Acadia at the End of the Seventeenth Century.* Saint John, 1934.

The Iroquois

BEAUCHAMP, W. M. *History of the New York Iroquois.* New York, 1904.

COLDEN, CADWALLADER. *History of the Five Nations of Canada.* London, 1747.

DESROSIERS, L. P. *Iroquoisie.* Montreal, 1947.

HUNT, GEORGE T. *The Wars of the Iroquois.* Madison, Wisc., 1940.

MORGAN, LEWIS H. *League of the Iroquois.* Rochester, N.Y., 1851.

TRELEASE, ALLEN W. *Indian Affairs in Colonial New York.* Ithaca, N.Y., 1960.

The English Colonies and the Hudson's Bay Company

CRANE, VERNER W. *The Southern Frontier: 1670-1732.* Ann Arbor, Mich., 1929. (Reprinted, 1956.)

FLICK, A. C., ed. *History of the State of New York.* 10 vols. New York, 1933.

GIPSON, L. H. *The British Empire before the American Revolution,* vols. IV and V. New York, 1942.

HUTCHINSON, THOMAS. *The History of Massachusetts, from the first settlement thereof in 1628, until the year 1750.* 2 vols. Boston, 1795.

RICH, E. E. *The History of the Hudson's Bay Company 1670-1870,* vol I, 1670-1763. ("The Publications of the Hudson's Bay Record Society.") London, 1958.

Articles in Learned Journals

ADAIR, E. R. "Anglo-French Rivalry in the Fur Trade during the 18th Century," *Culture*, vol. VIII, 1947.

—— "France and the Beginnings of New France," *C.H.R.*, vol. XXV, 1944.

BUFFINTON, ARTHUR H. "The Policy of Albany and English Eastward Expansion," *Mississippi Valley Historical Review*, vol. VIII, March 1922.

BURTON, F. W. "The Wheat Supply of New France," *Proceedings and Transactions of the Royal Society of Canada*, ser. 3, vol. XXX.

Canadian Art, Issue No. 74 on Quebec, July-August, 1961.

ECCLES, W. J. "Denonville et les galériens iroquois," *Revue d'Histoire de l'Amérique Française*, vol. XIV, Décembre 1960.

FRÉGAULT, GUY. "La Compagnie de la Colonie," *Revue de l'Université d'Ottawa*, janvier-mars, avril-juin, 1960.

KELLY, A. D. "Health Insurance in New France," *Bulletin of the History of Medicine*, vol XXVIII, Nov.-Dec. 1954.

LECLERC, JEAN, S.J., "Denonville et ses captifs iroquois," *Revue d'Histoire de l'Amérique Française*, vol. XIV, mars 1961, vol. XV, juin 1961.

MUNRO, L. B. "The Office of Intendant in New France," *American Historical Review*, vol. XII, 1906.

REID, ALLANA G. "General Trade between Quebec and France during the French Regime," *C.H.R.*, vol. XXXIV, 1953.

—— "Representative Assemblies in New France," *C.H.R.*, vol. XXVII, March 1946.

—— "Intercolonial Trade during the French Regime," *C.H.R.*, vol. XXXII, 1951.

—— "The Nature of Quebec Society during the French Regime," *Canadian Historical Association Report*, 1951.

RICH, E. E. "Russia and the Colonial Fur Trade," *Economic History Review*, vol. VII, April 1955.

INDEX

ACKNOWLEDGEMENTS

We wish to thank the following sources for permission to use their material in the illustration sections.

ARCHIVES DES COLONIES, *Paris*: for "Page of an abstract of a dispatch from Canada," taken from microfilm copy at Ottawa.

ARCHIVES PHOTOGRAPHIQUES CAISSE NATIONALE DES MONUMENTS HISTORIQUES, *Paris*: for "Bust of Louis XIV, by Giovanni Lorenzo Bernini."

OFFICE DU FILM DU QUÉBEC: for the portrait of Monseigneur Jean-Baptiste de la Croix de Chevrières de Saint-Vallier.

PROVINCE DE QUÉBEC, INVENTAIRE DES OEUVRES D'ART: for the portraits of Jean Talon and Monseigneur François de Montmorency-Laval.

PUBLIC ARCHIVES OF CANADA: for the portraits of Jean-Baptiste Colbert; Alexandre de Prouville, Sieur de Tracy; Daniel de Rémy, Sieur de Courcelle; Pierre Boucher; Jacques Réné de Brisay, Marquis de Denonville.

PUBLIC ARCHIVES OF CANADA, MAP DIVISION: for "New France, 1678"; "Quebec, circa 1670"; Fort St Louis residence of the governors of New France"; "Jesuit map of the West, 1682"; "Jolliet map of North America, 1678"; "Quebec under attack by the New England forces, 1690"; "Section from Map of New France by Jean-Baptiste Louis Franquelin"; "Acadia, 1702"; "North America, 1701"; "Quebec, 1699."

THE CANADIAN CENTENARY SERIES

A HISTORY OF CANADA IN SEVENTEEN VOLUMES

The Canadian Centenary Series is a comprehensive history of the peoples and lands which form the Dominion of Canada.

Although the series is designed as a unified whole so that no part of the story is left untold, each volume is complete in itself. Written for the general reader as well as for the scholar, each of the seventeen volumes of *The Canadian Centenary Series* is the work of a leading Canadian historian who is an authority on the period covered in his volume. Their combined efforts have made a new and significant contribution to the understanding of the history of Canada and of Canada today.

W. L. Morton, Master of Champlain College, Trent University, is the Executive Editor of *The Canadian Centenary Series*. A graduate of the Universities of Manitoba and Oxford, he is the author of *The Kingdom of Canada; Manitoba: A History; The Progressive Party in Canada; One University: A History of the University of Manitoba;* and other writings. He has also edited *The Journal of Alexander Begg and Other Documents Relevant to the Red River Resistance*. He holds the honorary degree of Doctor of Laws from the University of Toronto and honorary Doctorates of Letters from the Universities of New Brunswick, McGill and Manitoba, and has been awarded the Tyrrell Medal of the Royal Society of Canada and the Governor General's Award for Non-Fiction.

D. G. Creighton, Professor of History, University of Toronto, is the Advisory Editor of *The Canadian Centenary Series*. A graduate of the Universities of Toronto and Oxford, he is the author of *John A. Macdonald: The Young Politician; John A. Macdonald: The Old Chieftain; Dominion of the North; The Empire of the St Lawrence*, and many other works. He has received honorary Doctorates from the Universities of Manitoba, McGill, Queen's, New Brunswick, Saskatchewan, and British Columbia. Twice winner of the Governor General's Award for Non-Fiction, he has also been awarded the Tyrrell Medal of the Royal Society of Canada, the University of Alberta National Award in Letters, and the University of British Columbia Medal for Popular Biography.

220

PRINTED AND BOUND IN CANADA BY
THE HUNTER ROSE COMPANY